ARCHAEOLOGY
AND THE
BIBLE

ARCHAE

AND THE

ΛΛΛΛΛΛΛΛΛΛΛΛΛΛΛΛΛΛΛΛΛΛΛΛΛΛ

G. Frederick Owen

OLOGY

ΛΛΛΛΛΛΛΛΛΛΛΛΛΛΛΛΛΛΛΛΛΛ

BIBLE

FLEMING H. REVELL COMPANY

Special acknowledgment is made to the following for permission to use previously printed material:

THE AMERICAN BAPTIST PUBLICATION SOCIETY for material from *The Monuments and the Old Testament* by Ira M. Price, Ovid R. Sellers, and E. Leslie Carlson, copyright 1958 by The Judson Press, used by permission.

BARNES & NOBLE, INC., AND ERNEST BENN LIMITED, for material from *Excavations at Ur* by Leonard Woolley.

ERNEST BENN LIMITED for material from *Ur of the Chaldees* by Leonard Woolley.

DODD, MEAD & COMPANY for material from *In the Steps of the Master* by H. V. Morton, copyright 1934 by Dodd, Mead & Company, Inc., reprinted by permission of Dodd, Mead & Company.

JAMES B. PRITCHARD AND FRANK J. TAYLOR for material from "We Found the Lost City" published in *The Saturday Evening Post*.

THE RICHARD R. SMITH COMPANY, INC., for material from *Against the Tide: An Autobiography* by A. Clayton Powell, Sr., copyright 1938 by Richard R. Smith. Also to Mrs. A. Clayton Powell, Sr.

THE VIKING PRESS, INC., for material from *The Dead Sea Scrolls* by Millar Burrows, copyright © 1955 by Millar Burrows, reprinted by permission of The Viking Press, Inc.

Dedicated to

DR. WILLIAM FOXWELL ALBRIGHT

World-renowned scholar, faithful teacher, never failing friend, wise counselor, and perpetual inspiration to all who study archaeology of the Middle East,

and to

FOUR HUNDRED AND FIFTY STUDENTS

who have studied archaeology with me, aided in research, and thrilled me with their unflagging interest.

PREFACE

ARCHAEOLOGY's intensely interesting task is that of laying open to view layer after layer of the mound-covered cities of the Middle East, and tracing back through the centuries ancient man's absorbing past. That task is only well under way, yet it has gone a long way. So far that the ancient world of the Bible has arisen from the grave of centuries to intrigue the minds, enliven the emotions, and contribute to the education of modern man.

Herein lies the purpose of this book—to reveal archaeology as an indestructible bond between the lands of the Bible and the people of our day by allowing the remains and inscriptions of civilization after civilization, city after city, and individual after individual rise and tell their story so that the past will be as much with us as the present and that a knowledge of the past will make for a better understanding of the present and serve as a guide for the future. In this endeavor we realize with Aristotle that "The search for truth is in one way hard and in another easy. For it is evident that no one can master it fully nor miss it wholly, but each adds a little to our knowledge of nature and from the facts assembled there arises a certain grandeur."

G. FREDERICK OWEN

ACKNOWLEDGMENTS

For thirty-three years it has been our happy privilege to enter into the company of learned men, able scholars, and faithful students in the field of archaeological study and research. The high intellectual and moral plane on which they have moved, and the cheerful spirit of helpfulness which they have always shown on excavations, in field work and classrooms, at libraries and museums make this book possible.

Special and distributive gratitude goes to the following who have read portions of the manuscript and offered helpful suggestions: Dr. Robert J. Braidwood, Professor, University of Chicago, checked our statement and evaluation of the radiocarbon method of dating. Lt.-Col. Harry M. Smith, sometime U. S. advisor to the Iranian Government, read the chapter on Persia; Dr. Nelson Glueck, President of Hebrew Union College and Jewish Institute of Religion, went over the chapter on archaeological discoveries in Transjordan; Dr. Harry M. Orlinsky, Professor, Jewish Institute of Religion of New York, corrected the entire section of the book dealing with discoveries in Palestine.

Dr. John C. Trever, Professor, Baldwin-Wallace College, read the chapter on the Dead Sea Scrolls; Dr. G. Ernest Wright, Professor, Harvard University, and co-editor of the *Biblical Archaeologist* permitted quotations from his writings and from the *Biblical Archaeologist;* and last, but not least, is Dr. William F. Albright, Professor Emeritus, Johns Hopkins University, and sometime director of the American School of Oriental Research of Jerusalem, who not only read and suggested improvements for the latter part of the chapter on discoveries in Babylonia, but has by his writings, teachings, and private correspondence exerted a steady influence on the preparation of the volume throughout.

To writers and publishers, whose names appear in reference notes and bibliography, thankful acknowledgment is given, and assurance expressed that there has been a conscientious and continuous effort made to give due credit where the writer has quoted from or been influenced by the works of others.

G. F. O.

CONTENTS

11

LIST OF ILLUSTRATIONS

The following illustrations are grouped between pages 192 and 193, in the order given below:

13

ARCHAEOLOGY
AND THE
BIBLE

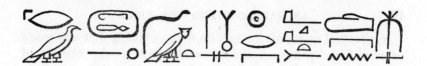

CHAPTER I

The Meaning and Scope of Archaeology

ARCHAEOLOGY IS THAT BRANCH of historical science which patiently searches out and interprets the records and material remains of man's past. It is concerned with a systematic investigation, classification, restoration, interpretation, publication, and preservation of all materials from which a knowledge of a particular country or people may be derived.

Archaeology is constantly contributing invaluable materials that substantiate, supplement, and enrich historical facts; therefore it is often spoken of as the "handmaid of history." Yet archaeology has long since reached the stature of a full-fledged science in its own right. It is distinguished from other historical sciences only by the kind of materials with which it is concerned. These materials are usually divided into the following categories: monumental, artifactual, written, and traditional.[1]

The *monumental* remains include such objects as city walls, streets, fountains, forums, fortresses, amphitheaters, temples, statues, obelisks, tombs, catacombs, palaces, churches, and synagogues. It is concerned with the altars at which men worshiped, the shops in which merchants sold their wares, the bath houses in which people cleansed their bodies, and the homes in which lived the rich and the poor. In most cases only remnants of these will be found—the lost, the broken, and the discarded. With these archaeology endeavors to reconstruct the whole and interpret the meaning in terms of human activity. It also reads facial features, styles of clothing, and occupational pursuits as recorded on imperishable materials such as stone and pottery.

Artifactual materials have to do with anything that was made or modified by human art or workmanship—the objects of handicraft made by the artists and the artisans. They include products of the arts and crafts such as amulets, beads, jewelry, stone calendars, shovels, pickaxes, liquid and dry measures. They have to do with the tools with which the people tilled the soil, the sickles with which they cut the grain, the instruments with which they threshed and the mills with which they ground their grain; the looms with which they wove their cloth, the pottery in which they stored their victuals and in which they cooked their food; the lamps with which they lighted their homes, the musical instruments on which they played, the coins with which they bought and sold, and the signets or seals with which they signed their signatures, the instruments with which they wrote, the chariots in which they rode, the ships in which they carried their cargoes, and the weapons of war with which they defended themselves or carried on conquest. All these artifactual remains go a very long way in revealing the cultural life of a given people or civilization.

The *written* materials involve inscriptions on painted wood, copper plates, upright stone slabs, marble and alabaster walls; on clay tablets, cones, coins, seals, cylinders, potsherds, papyrus, and parchment scrolls. The scripts and systems of writing employed are those used by the people whose remains we study. In Bible Lands these are usually the Old Persian, Median, and Babylonian cuneiform, the hieroglyphic and demotic Egyptian, the Hebrew, the Aramaic, the Syriac, the Arabic, the Greek and the Latin. When this writing is found it may be complete, or it may be fragmentary. In some cases it may be archaic in style, whereas in others the story may be recorded in more highly developed characters. The portion of writing found may be a receipt for money paid, a listing of oil and wine in storage, a vow, a blessing, a curse, a contract, an epitaph, a bit of family history, a diplomatic correspondence, or even a manuscript for a book, or a completed scroll. The sources on which they throw added light are: the Bible, the Apocrypha and Pseudepigrapha, Herodotus, Manetho, Philo, Josephus, Eusebius and other ancient and medieval literary works; and on the manners and customs of the people.

Traditional materials have to do with the fact that in all ages men have said things which were never reduced to writing, but which were considered worthy of being passed on to succeeding generations. Or, in certain instances, they may have been written at one time, but when lost, only the verbal account remained. The archaeologist carefully lists every vestige of evidence bearing on these stories, and endeavors to decide if they are substantially true, if they contain a kernel of distorted truth, or if they were fabricated merely to achieve certain effects.

Archaeology involves a careful study of the ground surface of sites and localities, as well as of antiquities found either by accident or by design. It involves the excavation of sites, the discovery and study of ancient monuments, the discovery and decipherment of inscriptions, the reading of manuscripts, the classification of human and animal skeletons, skulls, and mummies, and the gathering of all kinds of objects and information that will add to the sum of human knowledge.

The work of the archaeologist is in small measure like detective work. To the trained eye the grave may tell its story by a word or two engraved on stone, by a picture painted or carved on the wall, or by the very position in which the corpse is found buried. In other cases the nature of the information sought is such that highly scientific techniques are employed, the cooperative efforts of many scholars pooled, and all possible evidence gleaned from all known researchers taken into consideration before a conclusion can be reached.

In viewing the field broadly, however, it is generally understood that by all that is found, and especially *where* it is found, archaeology must piece out the story and make its contribution in corroborating, correcting or supplementing written history, and in adding to the ever accumulating store of cultural knowledge that goes far in assisting humanity in ordering their daily lives.

Archaeology is definitely on the material side of life, yet its fruitage in contributions is exceedingly valuable in that its scientific approach satisfies the mind, and goes far toward strengthening Jewish and Christian faith in God and the Bible.

Archaeology has its basis of interest and glamor in the fact that men and women have always been deeply interested in exploring and in making discoveries, as well as in the common wish of every people to know the past. This interest has been further deepened by the introduction of scientific methods into our modern educational procedure, and by a vigorous demand for the evidence that would confirm, supplement, or condemn the reliability of the narratives of the Bible, Herodotus, Josephus and other notable works of ancient literature.

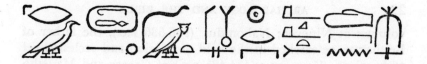

CHAPTER II

The Rise of the Laboratory Method of Research

EUROPE AND THE Western world, through the many centuries, regarded Palestine and adjacent countries as "The Holy Land," and the Bible as the inspired Word of God—the Book of books —and the final authority on any subject of which it spoke. These lands, which served as a background for the Bible, and which were so consistently revered by millions, offered a potential field of research that was unparalleled, yet few concerned themselves with anything more than a brief visit to Palestine. The few who carried on any semblance of study were interested only in topographical observations, which at best were somewhat superficial. More exact researches, by scientific method, were not possible at the time, nor did Jews and Christians feel the need of such. They merely *believed* the Bible to be true, and left it at that.

Developments during the seventeenth, eighteenth, and nineteenth centuries, however, went far toward changing the minds of many adversely toward the Bible and other ancient literature, and therefore encouraged sincere men to do something about more careful researches in Bible lands. One of these developments was the improvement of educational procedure by the expeditional and laboratory methods of research, and the other was the incoming of a tide of rationalism, in its varying forms.

Scholarly inquiry, known as "research," has ever involved "gathering the facts" concerning any given subject. And men have long concerned themselves with certain aspects of this work. Ashurbanipal of Assyria (669-633 B.C.) gathered sufficient materials to make up a vast library of some thirty thousand

21

volumes at Nineveh; Nabonidus (556-536 B.C.), the father of Belshazzar, researched in the field of religion and ecclesiastical archaeology; Herodotus (484-425 B.C.) of Greece and Manetho (285-246 B.C.) of Egypt gathered facts and wrote histories of their respective countries; Eusebius (A.D. 265-340), Jerome (A.D. 340-420), and the "Bordeaux Pilgrim" (A.D. 333) were untiring in their efforts toward a better knowledge of Palestine. The monks and many others of medieval times did fair work at "gathering the facts" on various subjects.

However, new procedures were made possible and a deeper interest in research came during the seventeenth century when Hans Lippenshey, Galileo Galilei, Johannes Hevelius, and Sir Isaac Newton invented and developed the telescope with which they viewed the immensity of the universe, and when Zacharias Jenssen, Anton Van Leeuwenhoek and others invented and perfected the microscope, with which they viewed myriads of minute living creatures teeming in a drop of pond water— animals and plant forms that the eye of man had never seen before. Between 1831 and 1836 Charles R. Darwin sailed around the globe on the H. M. S. *Beagle*, postulated many of his theories, and become engrossed in experimentation and speculation. In due time biological, chemical, physical, and psychological laboratories were set up for speculation and scientific experimentation.

It soon became fashionable to speculate and to investigate almost everything. The Bible, along with the works of such men as Herodotus, Manetho, Josephus, and Jerome could not go unnoticed. Men of a philosophic turn of mind took up the Bible, read portions of it, interpreted it by subjective methods, then flung their doubtful opinions to the four winds and permitted them to float where they would over the tides of men.

Contributions toward doubt and skepticism began to be made as early as the middle of the 17th century, and during the next two centuries, every day and in almost every way skepticism concerning the Bible was spreading over the earth, leaving myriads of wrecks of faith in the wake of "advancing reason."

During those trying times many good people were tempted to ask, "Where is God, that He does not come to the rescue of His Word?" But God was at work, goading well-meaning men into actions that would eventually result in controlled researches in Bible Lands. In the making was a science called Archaeology that would remove the chariot wheels of the pseudo-scientists and force them to heavy driving in the years to follow. Assyria, Babylonia, Persia, Egypt, Syria, Trans-Jordan, and Palestine were to become vast research laboratories wherein brilliant, well-trained men and women from various nations would, with adequate measuring rods, test the validity and trustworthiness of the Bible and other ancient literatures.

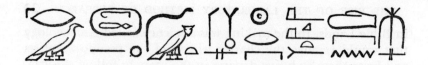

CHAPTER III

Early Researches in Bible Lands

MANY SINCERE MEN and women from every generation during the past seventeen centuries have gone to Palestine, Egypt, Assyria, and Babylonia. Interest, intellect, and background of training with a few have been sufficient to stimulate interest in gathering factual information to impart to those who have not gone.

In A.D. 325, some few years after Constantine had become emperor of Rome, he sent Helena, his royal mother, to Palestine to seek out the sites made sacred by Christ and other Biblical characters. On arriving in Palestine Helena secured the services of Eusebius, bishop of Caesarea, who had grown up in the country and was familiar with many places of interest.

Backed by funds and encouragement from the imperial capital, Eusebius, Helena, and their associates not only located sites for the Church of the Nativity at Bethlehem, the Church of the Holy Sepulchre at Jerusalem, and the Church of the Ascension on the Mount of Olives, but traveled extensively in Palestine. Eusebius continued the search for sacred sites until he had developed an extensive dictionary of Biblical place-names he called the *Onomasticon*.

In 333, while Eusebius was yet in the midst of his work, an unidentified Christian traveler, known as "The Bordeaux Pilgrim," visited Palestine. He carefully recorded the route he took while in the Holy Land, and wrote a *Pilgrim's Guide Book* in which he listed many place-names whose identity he probably learned from Eusebius and others.

Eusebius died in 340; but his valuable book, the *Onomasticon*, was later translated from Greek into Latin by Jerome, a devout and brilliant scholar who spent the better portion of his life at Bethlehem. It was there that Jerome completed his translation known as the Vulgate. After traveling extensively throughout the Holy Land he translated, revised, and enlarged Eusebius' *Onomasticon*. It included more than a thousand place-names, three hundred of which were definitely designated as to location. That treatise, which was the fruit of Eusebius' and Jerome's labors, was valuable but was frequently inaccurate because it was too often based on poorly founded traditions rather than adequate researches.

Paula, a devout, wealthy, and famous matron of Rome, in 382 set out to see for herself the sacred places of Palestine. Going by way of Cyprus and Antioch, she arrived in Palestine in 383; then spent two full years viewing the sacred spots of the land. Paula wrote private letters to friends, telling of the places she visited; and Jerome wrote a graphic account of her travels down the seacoast to Joppa, up to Jerusalem, then through Syria and northern Phoenicia. Some sixty sacred sites were noted, including such places as Upper and Lower Bethhoron, Nob, Ajalon, Engedi, and Tekoa.

During the latter part of the fourth century, an unidentified woman, thought by some to be St. Silvia of Aquitaine, left a record of more extensive travels than those of Paula. She traveled to Mount Sinai, across the Jordan to Mount Nebo, and eastward in search of the Land of Uz. The whole of her manuscript indicates an exceptional knowledge of the land, its people, and its legends.

During the fifteenth century Felix Fabri, a devout and intelligent Dominican monk, spent some time in Palestine. On his return to Italy he endeavored to tell of what he had seen, but discovered that his knowledge of exact recorded fact was embarrassingly meager. It seemed impossible for him adequately to answer questions of interested people. As a result, his embarrassment goaded him into a determination to make a second trip.

For one year Fabri studied all literature available on the Holy Land; then in 1483 he returned to Palestine as chaplain and director of a party of four nobles. Beginning at Jerusalem with the Church of the Holy Sepulchre, he made careful critical notes of a historical nature. All along the way from Jerusalem to Gaza he sought to identify places, study the manners and customs of the people, and record what he saw. On a thirteen-day trip to Sinai he recorded many details about the mountain and the places near it. In a free and comparatively untrammeled style he arranged, classified, and wrote in such a manner as to earn for himself a small but important place as a pioneer in the field of research.

Early in the Turkish period when travel was extremely perilous, Rev. Henry Maundrell, an English chaplain, traversed certain sections of Palestine. His journey was made exceedingly difficult by tyrannical chiefs who robbed and annoyed him. Among them was Sheikh Shibleh, whose tomb is now a sacred shrine near Kefr Kud.

In 1714 Hadrian Reland produced a book that was later pronounced "next to the Bible the most important book for travelers in Palestine." Although his work was not based upon actual personal observation, it made a great contribution to the field of Palestinian research.

Then, in 1798 archaeological research as we now know it, began when Napoleon Bonaparte organized a research group of nearly one hundred distinguished scholars and artists to accompany him on his expedition to Egypt. They were commissioned to investigate and report on ancient civilizations and monuments of the country. Under his supervision they made diligent search in both Upper and Lower Egypt, wrote out systematic descriptions, copied texts, produced water-color drawings, and collected vast stores of movable monuments and inscriptions.

When their invaluable archaeological collection had been loaded on ships, they began their homeward voyage. But the British attacked the French fleet and seized all their ships with the exception of two. In 1802 all those archaeological finds were ceded to the British as prizes of war.

The British made a slight concession in that they granted the French government the privilege of publishing the results of the researches by Napoleon and his men. Those appeared between 1809 and 1822 in the form of seven magnificent and elaborate volumes, but they received little publicity, for France was a defeated nation. Today Napoleon's archaeological collection makes up a large share of the vast and almost unparalleled Egyptian collection in the British Museum.

The 1803 journeys of Seetzen and the 1809-16 travels of the

celebrated Burckhardt are regarded as of special value. Those explorers studied out-of-the-way places and the area across the Jordan river. Of necessity both Seetzen and Burckhardt often disguised themselves as physicians in quest of herbs. However, they both died in the East before their self-allotted tasks were complete. In 1816 the explorer Buckingham also visited Palestine; and in 1817, despite the hazards of travel, Irby and Mangles made an adventurous journey in the country east of the Jordan.

Then, as the nineteenth century advanced, Edward Robinson entered the field of Palestinian research. Born April 10, 1794, of sturdy New England stock and the son of a Congregational minister, Robinson grew up in an environment that was almost ideal for furnishing the background for the work he was to accomplish. In college he specialized in Biblical studies, then entered a law office for a time after graduation. Later he became tutor in Greek and mathematics at Hamilton. In 1821 he moved to Andover, Mass., where he studied Hebrew and tutored at the Andover Theological Seminary until he sailed to Europe for graduate study. While in Europe he came in contact with such men as Gesenius, Tholuck, and Neander. On his return to America he was appointed professor extraordinary of Sacred Literature at Andover, but because of ill health he soon gave up his teaching duties and again resumed intensive study and writing for a four-year period. During that time he completed a translation of *Gesenius's Hebrew Lexicon* and wrote his own *Greek and English Lexicon of the New Testament.*

In 1837 Robinson received a call to become professor of Biblical Literature in Union Theological Seminary of New York. He accepted on the condition that, before entering on his duties, he be allowed to carry out his intentions of exploring the Holy Land.

Embarking at New York, July 17, 1837, he landed at Liverpool eighteen days later, spent a few days "amid the calm dignity of Oxford," and a few weeks in London. After a short stay in Berlin, where he left his family and conferred with certain scholarly men, he proceeded on through Italy and Greece to Egypt. After traveling up and down the Nile and studying the monuments for some time, he was joined by

Rev. Eli Smith, a former student and friend with whom he had long planned the trip. Together they purchased tents and equipment, employed natives for camp and caravan duties, and, with a thirty-day supply of food, took up their journey on March 12 through Goshen, and on toward Mount Sinai.

Never before had there been such extensive researches undertaken by one so well qualified. Robinson was reverent, devout, scholarly, and painstaking. His "scientific motive," and the firm belief that ecclesiastical tradition was to be regarded of value only when authenticated by the testimony of the Holy Scriptures, served to protect him from the fallacies of poorly founded traditions.

His companion had long lived at Beirut and knew the Arabic language. Smith possessed a thorough knowledge of the conditions of travel and understood the psychology and customs of the people. For years, and from every available source, he had industriously gathered proper names so that when the opportunity came on his journeys he might test them on the spot. The two had a common interest, and were strengthened and qualified by nearly two decades of careful study and preparation for the work they were beginning. They had their Bibles in Hebrew, Greek, and English, and the works of Reland and other travelers. Their equipment in the way of instruments consisted of "an ordinary surveyor's and two pocket compasses, a thermometer, telescopes, and measuring tapes."

At Suez, and all along the way, they studied the journey of the children of Israel, carefully weighing the evidence to ascertain where and how the events in the journey took place. Careful measurements were taken and estimates made of the "Plain of the Tribes" and observations made while on the summits of both Jebel Musa, or Mount Sinai, and of St. Catherine, as well as the lower peak often called Horeb.

From Sinai, Robinson and his research party went northward to Akaba, and continued toward Beersheba. They entered Palestine on April 12, 1838. Two months and a half later, on June 26, they finished their first expedition at Beirut, Syria. They had located many new sites, measured buildings, identified arches, explored tombs, copied inscriptions, checked elevations, and measured distances. Their work had been thorough and the territory covered had been greater than ever before; yet they realized that it was incomplete.[1]

Fourteen years later the Union Theological Seminary, of its own initiative, voted Robinson a second leave of absence for a second expedition to complete his exploration in Palestine. Accordingly, Robinson joined Smith at Beirut, and on April 5, 1852, they rode southward from Beirut on the very road they had traveled together toward the end of their first expedition. After writing of pitching their camp the first night at Nebi Yunis, Robinson continued:

Here we were once more in our own tent, not the same, indeed, as formerly, yet so like it as hardly to be distinguished; the furniture and all our traveling equipments were similar; several articles were as of old. It was as if we were continuing a journey of yesterday, and the intervening fourteen years seemed to vanish away. And when we reverted to the reality we could not but gratefully acknowledge the mercy of God in preserving our lives and permitting us once more after so long an interval to prosecute together the researches which we had together begun. We could not but regard it as a high and certainly an unusual privilege thus . . . again to take up the thread of our investigations at the very point where they had been broken off.

Smith accompanied him on the second journey as far as Jerusalem and thence northward to the foot of Mount Hermon. But with Smith's departure Robinson was joined by W. M. Thompson, a man who had traversed Syria most extensively and who accompanied Robinson to Banias and back to Hasbeya, and thence to within a day's journey of Damascus. There Robinson was joined by Dr. Robson of the Damascus Mission, who traveled with him to Baalbek, then around the northern end of Lebanon to the Cedars, and so to Beirut, which was reached on June 19th.

During the two expeditions Robinson had spent about seven months in Egypt, Sinai, Palestine, and Syria, locating many lost sites, gathering an astounding wealth of information, and thereby setting the precedent for a superior type of real scientific exploration in Palestine. At Berlin, where he had unrestricted use of the royal library and the valuable private collection of Ritter, Neander, and Hengstenberg, the fruit of his work was converted into three large volumes under the title,

Biblical Researches in Palestine, Mount Sinai, and Arabia Petrea. This work has long continued to be the standard authority on the physical and historical geography of the Holy Land.

Titus Tobler of Germany made four trips to Palestine and in the end accomplished almost as much as Robinson. The first was a pleasure trip in 1835 that fired him with the ambition to become a scientific explorer. During a period of twenty weeks, in 1845-46, he carried out a much more thorough study of Jerusalem than had Robinson. That study involved the topographical features of the city, its walls and gates, its ancient and modern buildings, and the immediate surroundings of the city. In a third journey, taken in 1857, he focused his attention entirely on Judea. Returning again in 1865, Tobler planned to explore Nazareth and its environs as he had Jerusalem, but his work was cut short by a cholera epidemic in that area. His carefully detailed and thus valuable literary works were a contribution that could have been made only by one of long experience in Palestine.

W. F. Lynch of the United States Navy, led an expedition in 1848 that determined the size, the depth below sea level, the water depth, and the mineral deposits of the Dead Sea.

Pisgah was identified in 1870 by Rev. John A. Paine, who worked under the auspices of the American Exploration Society. The same organization sent R. Myer, an engineer, to prepare a map of Palestine; but his surveys and researches were inadequate for satisfactory results.

Charles W. Wilson's surveys of Jerusalem and travels in Palestine in 1864-66, together with the accumulated researches of others, aroused British interest and on June 22, 1865, a large distinguished body of men met in Willis' Rooms, London, under the chairmanship of the archbishop of York and the patronage of the throne, and formally organized the Palestine Exploration Fund. Eight thousand pounds, or $40,000, were raised and Charles Warren was sent to Jerusalem, where he made a careful survey of the city, sank shafts at several places about the Temple that furnished satisfactory answers to questions raised by Robinson about the Tyropoeon Valley.

But the most monumental work done by that Fund was a complete survey of western Palestine during 1871-78 under

C. R. Conder and Kitchener. From those careful surveys a great map was made embracing about 6000 square miles from Tyre southward to the desert of Sinai, and from the Mediterranean eastward to the Jordan valley.

The Fund employed Clermont-Ganneau, a French scholar, who made a study of antiquities between Jaffa and Jerusalem, and sent Edward Hull and Kitchener, who made a complete geological survey of the valley of the Dead Sea and of Wadi Arabah, south of the sea. Then in 1890 under the same organization, W. M. Flinders Petrie began excavations on a city mound 120 feet high known by the Arabs as Tell el-Hesy. Frederick J. Bliss continued the excavation and, when taken together, their work revealed a variation of pottery which marked the horizontal strata of eight successively occupied cities. By painstaking care those men began to lay the foundation for the scientific excavation of the many buried cities of the Bible lands.

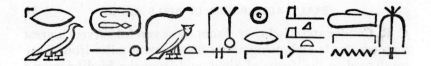

CHAPTER IV

The Discovery of the Archaeological Keys

FOR SOME CENTURIES travelers to the Near Eastern countries had brought reports of various monuments, inscriptions, and writings which to them were "curious." None of these could be read and seemed destined to remain a mystery. Then with the close of the eighteenth century, there were developments of great interest to everyone concerned about the Bible Lands. A number of inscriptions were found that proved to be keys wherewith learned men would unlock the archaeological storehouse. The Rosetta Stone and Behistun Inscription were noteworthy.

In 1798 Napoleon Bonaparte wrote a brilliant chapter in French history when he organized an Egyptian expeditionary force for the purpose of invading and exploring Egypt. Aside from the personnel of his regular military force, he took with him nearly one hundred distinguished scholars and artists, who were commissioned to investigate, record, and report on ancient civilizations and monuments of the country.

The most notable of the discoveries made on that expedition was the Rosetta Stone, which was uncovered in 1799 while Boussard, one of Napoleon's engineers, and his men were digging the foundation for a new fort at Rosetta, near the mouth of the western branch of the Nile. The stone was of black granite and measured three feet, nine inches high, by two feet, four and a half inches wide, and eleven inches thick. The upper portion and lower right corners were broken off. The inscription on it was written in three different languages, only one of which was understood.

The stone was taken to Cairo, where Napoleon's scholars read the lower register in Greek. It merely disclosed the story of how the stone was set up about 195 B.C. by the priests of Memphis in honor of their ruler Ptolemy V for having canceled certain priestly taxes and having restored the priests to their places in the temple.

Napoleon gave orders for copies of the trilingual inscription to be prepared and sent to Paris. Soon the scholarly world saw the copies, as well as the original, and came to realize that the characters engraved in the upper register must constitute a language. They corresponded with the strange hieroglyphics found on temple walls, palaces, obelisks, and tombs throughout Egypt.

Scholars almost all over the world accepted the challenge to read the two unknown languages. Sylvester de Sacy of France and J. D. Akerblad of Sweden came to believe that the middle register of the writing was the "native" script the Greeks called "demotic," or the "common" language spoken by the Egyptians.[1] This demotic text they supposed to be a mere repetition of the Greek on the lower portion of the stone.

Thomas Young of England was enabled to identify the name of Ptolemy in the upper portion where groups of signs enclosed in oval forms, called "cartouches," corresponded with Ptolemy's name in the Greek register.

News concerning the Rosetta Stone was sounded throughout the scholarly world. In 1802, in France, the story found eager reception among an intellectually industrious family. Jean François Champollion caught the challenge to read the whole of the Rosetta Stone. So intense was the interest and determination of young Champollion that he took up a study of the classical languages, thoroughly reviewed the history of Egypt, and applied his conquering diligence to the Rosetta text. His brother Jacques financed Jean's study and encouraged him in the belief that he could attain his purpose. For years Champollion studied so intensely that from prolonged reading by candlelight he contracted a permanent defect of his left eye.

By the age of eighteen his accomplishments were so remarkable he was appointed as professor of history at Grenoble. He had succeeded in mastering the modern Coptic, then the language of the Christians in Egypt, and was able to decipher the middle register of the Rosetta Stone, which, as he had surmised earlier, was written in an ancient form of the Coptic language. The language in that register was called "demotic," or the vernacular used by the common people. Thrilled by his new accomplishment and spurred on by the mystery before him, Jean set to work on the upper section. By painstaking and skilled comparisons he eventually fitted the unknown picture-language into the identical accounts he had found in the Greek and the demotic.

When in 1822 all the writing on the Rosetta Stone had become clear in Champollion's mind, he published a complete translation of the entire inscription, coupling the demotic and the hieroglyphic with the Greek, thus proving that the Rosetta Stone was written in three languages: (1) the upper register of fourteen lines being written in the picture-writing of the ancient Egyptians known as "hieroglyphic," or "sacred writings"; (2) the middle register of thirty-two lines being the more highly developed cursive form of the same picture-writing known as "demotic," or the vernacular used by the common people; (3) the third and lowest register of fifty-four lines being in Greek capital letters.

As a result of Champollion's work the authorities were able to announce that the key to the ancient language of the pharaohs had been found, and that the door was unlocked to the hitherto unknown historical and literary treasures of the Nile valley. At first, some few questioned the accuracy of his research work, but soon it was accepted in every respect. Then, having already accomplished what most men could not in four lifetimes, Champollion set out to recapture more of ancient Egypt. Suddenly at the early age of forty-one, with yet a vast store of unpublished Egyptian lore locked in his mind, Jean François Champollion went to meet his Maker.

The Rosetta Stone proved to be Egypt's most important trophy and today is one of the most highly valued possessions of the British Museum. The man who gave it worth is hailed as the founder of Egyptology and one of the most proficient scholars ever to have worked in that field.

Since the tenth century travelers had noticed a very large bas-relief high on a rocky cliff of the Zagros mountains near Hamadan. The huge rock towered high above a famous old watering place beside the highway running from Babylonia to Persia. The relief was 350 feet above the base of the cliff, and bore on its smoothed surface a representation of a large figure with a number of smaller figures of men standing in an attitude of great respect. The Arabian geographical writer, Ibn Hawkal, who was born at Mosul in the tenth century, described it as "a schoolhouse, with the master and the boys; further, in the schoolmaster's hand is an instrument like a strap wherewith to beat." Another traveler saw it in the early nineteenth century and took it to be Christ and the twelve apostles.

In 1835 Henry C. Rawlinson, an English officer attached to a military mission with the Persian army, observed the large bas-relief high on the mountain side. Taking up his field glasses, he saw on the smoothed limestone cliff an inscription fifty by twenty-five feet in size. Towering above the inscription was the figure of a king in the act of receiving homage from rebellious rivals he had conquered.

Realizing the possible importance of the inscription, Rawlinson determined to copy it with a view to its translation. The undertaking was exceedingly hazardous at such a height. However, just below the inscription was a ledge of rock fourteen to eighteen inches wide. Men of lesser courage and determination would not have climbed onto it, but Rawlinson stood on the narrow shelf and copied as far as he could reach. He then placed a ladder on the ledge and continued with the task while native helpers held it in place. It was through the daring of a wild Kurdish boy, who volunteered for the dangerous venture, that first attempts were made to reach the higher inscriptions from a suspended cable. It was from that breath-taking position that the first papercast, or "squeeze" impression of the upper columns of the inscription was taken. Rawlinson himself took his turn at working in the swing. Finally, after four years of painstaking labor and hazardous undertakings, Rawlinson succeeded in securing an impression of the entire inscription.

However, those years of copying work represented only the beginning of his long and arduous task. From the paper impressions Rawlinson discovered that he had not one, but three different languages to translate. Having knowledge of the

modern Persian, he proceeded to unravel the mysteries of
the ancient Persian cuneiform. By first deciphering the proper
names, Rawlinson was able to distinguish certain letters which
he tested against the modern Persian. Through diligent study
and comparison, plus a good bit of common sense, he was able
after six more years to translate the 400 lines of old Persian.
Working from the supposition that the other two accounts
were of the same story, Rawlinson attempted to translate them
also. Before long the second language, the Median or Susian,
yielded its secrets. Finally, even the Babylonian cuneiform
gave up its hidden treasures.

Rawlinson worked meticulously and made minute examination of every inch of the rock-face. In addition to studying the
actual inscriptions he made several other very interesting observations. Noticing large flakes of lacquer on the ledge, his
attention was drawn to the extraordinary finish over the face
of the rock. The massive area of approximately twelve hundred
square feet had been very carefully prepared and portions of
rock embedded in lead had been used to replace soft and
unsound areas in the natural limestone before the inscription
had been made. The entire surface had then been smoothed
and polished to an extent possible only by mechanical means.
Over the face of the entire work had then been applied a thick
coating of hard, siliceous varnish.

The story, told in each of the three languages—(1) four and
a half panels of 400 lines written in the old Persian cuneiform
alphabet of thirty-nine letters; (2) three panels written in
Median or Susian, a kind of cuneiform script; and (3) one
large panel containing hundreds of wedge-shaped characters
that have since come to be known as Babylonian cuneiform—
was of the exploits of Darius the Great, who in 515 B.C. per-
sonally led his troops in putting down insurrections in Shushan
and Babylon. The entire bas-relief goes down in history as the
greatest outdoor sign ever erected; but neither its size nor the
story it told were as significant as the fact that after twenty-two
years Rawlinson had completely translated each of the languages
and thus provided the keys with which to unlock the treasured
secrets of the vanished nations of the Babylonian-Assyrian
civilizations. Thriving cities, bannered armies, and industrious
citizenry of forgotten centuries came into full view. Hence-

forth the three ancient languages of Mesopotamia and Persia were to be translated by the keys furnished in the deciphering of the Behistun Inscription.

Twenty-three years had been utilized in the translation of the Rosetta Stone and twenty-two in deciphering the Behistun Inscription; yet the scholarly work of the two men furnished keys for unraveling the mysteries of the Tigris-Euphrates and the Nile valleys. Those six systems of ancient writing—hieroglyphic and demotic Egyptian, Greek, and Old Persian, Median, and Babylonian cuneiform—have been invaluable in the field of archaeological research.

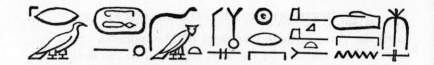

CHAPTER V

The Manner in Which Biblical Cities Were Buried

OF THE MANY SECRETS thus far revealed in Bible Lands, comparatively few have been derived from inscribed stones; fewer still from monuments raised high in the air like the Behistun Inscription. The finds that throw light on the past are, for the most part, dug from buried cities or gleaned from the surface of such city mounds.

The manner in which these cities became buried is the most frequent question one encounters when discussing the subject of archaeology with those untrained in this field of research. In general, the answer is that ancient cities became buried by dumped refuse, wars, fires, earthquakes, volcanic eruptions, floods, sandstorms, and the process of deterioration and covering over natural to all uncared-for objects of nature. But a more adequate understanding of the covering process may be gained only when due consideration is given to certain vital factors involved in the historical background of the city. Some of these are: (1) the original background of the city, (2) the manner in which the city was destroyed, (3) the refuse dumped about the city, and (4) the elements of nature that silently played their part in the after-centuries.

In ancient times men fought in hand-to-hand combat. Their principal instruments of war were the javelin, the bow and arrow, the battle-ax, the battering ram, and the slingshot. Their technique of battle was to surround a city and beat it into submission, or besiege it until its inhabitants were compelled to submit and yield the city.

This being the case, the people desiring to build a city usually sought for two things: a near-by water supply and a prominent hill on which to construct their homes. In the absence of a natural hill, the people often raised an artificial mound many feet above the level of the plain on which to locate their city. The entire place was then encircled by a massive stone wall with a gate or gates, as was deemed necessary for the convenience of the people. In the event of a siege the elevated position of the city gave the people being besieged the advantage over their besiegers.

As the city increased its population, other dwellings were constructed outside the walls. When the enemy came, these people left their homes and went inside the city walls. The enemy destroyed or took possession of everything of value outside the walls, and then laid siege to the city itself. Battering rams were put to work night and day, pounding the walls with the hope of making a breach. Towers were built from which missiles and fire were thrown over the walls. Finally the city fell by the disaster of war, or by fire, or both. The roofs fell in, walls were broken down, and everything combustible was burned, thus forming a layer of rubble made up of ashes and charcoal mingled with the refuse and debris of the streets. The buildings were, in some cases, razed, and in a few instances the ruined city was sown with salt, indicating that it should never be rebuilt.

After a greater or lesser interval, some of the inhabitants came back, or the conquerors rebuilt the city, or perhaps new people coming into the land chose the deserted site for a new habitation. Little or no attempt was made to clear away the rubbish of the former city; it was simply leveled off roughly, and new buildings were erected, partly on the old foundations, and largely without regard to them. Thus the ground level of the new city was several inches or even a foot or two higher than the old one, and everything in the ruins which had been covered over was simply left where it lay—below the floors and streets of the new city. In time this settlement, too, came to an end, and the process was repeated until a city-mound contained the ruins of anywhere from two to twelve or even twenty cities, one superimposed above the other. The plane or level on which each successive group of people lived was, thereafter, to be known as an "occupation level." Occasionally fire was the element of destruction, not only in time of war but also in time of peace. These destructive forces spoiled city after city, and left the ruins of each piled upon the other until the summit of the rising mound, in some instances, became too small to accommodate the town.[1]

With the final abandonment of the site, the mound of ruins was left to the chance misfortunes of fate. Earthquakes, in many cases, completed the shake-up. Sandstorms, as well as ordinary wind, blew additional dirt on the debris; grass seeds, weed seeds, and flower seeds were blown on, or carried by animals or birds. The winds and rains of many seasons leveled, smoothed, and widened the top of the mound, eroded its sides, and produced growths of vegetation as though nature were endeavoring to heal over an ugly scar on the face of the earth.

Where the hill was crowned by a city wall, the erosion process was limited, so that the shape of a steep-sided cone with its top cut off was preserved and accentuated. Almost all the important ancient sites in Bible Lands have this characteristic form and are commonly designated by the Arabic word "tell," meaning mound. Most of these ancient sites are known by the Arabs, and even today are called "Tells." Thus we have, Tell el Mutesellim (ancient Megiddo), Tell ed-Duweir (ancient Lachish), and Tell Beit Mirsim (ancient Kirjath-sepher). Ezekiel spoke of Tel-Abib, the "mound of ears of grain." [2]

The ruins of any given city that one desires to investigate are not found under the level of the plain, but usually above the plain on an eminence. Yet it is necessary to dig for them, seeing that they are far beneath the present level of the tell or mound, which may be anywhere from thirty to eighty feet above the plain. Where there is a wall, which is built higher each time the city is rebuilt, the "occupation level" one desires to investigate will be found deep within the piles of ruin. For example, the present city of Jerusalem lies some thirty-five feet above the level of the Jerusalem in which Jesus Christ and His apostles walked more than nineteen centuries ago. This depth of debris will vary with the several sections of the city, but thirty-five feet is the average depth.

Once in Jerusalem we went into a well-known building, and descended through the basement down to the level where the entire environmental remains were definitely Roman. There on the ancient pavement were plainly incised grooves which made up the complete markings of a well-known Roman game. Someone remarked that Roman guards could have been playing there while Jesus Christ was being examined before Pilate. Then a teaching sister of the Roman Church stepped forward and carefully explained the various details, and concluded with the remark, "The Lord Jesus once walked along this pavement. Probably stood on this very spot." As we turned to walk away the writer remarked, "And perhaps He will come again to Jerusalem and walk within the present city." The lady teacher replied, in low, firm tones, saying, "Yes, He will come again to our city, and walk our streets."

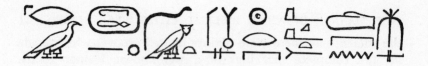

CHAPTER VI

Perfecting a Technique for Uncovering a Buried City

To THE UNTRAINED EYE the "tell" may appear as only a uniformly shaped mound, but to the trained observer it is a city-mound that holds literally thousands of secrets, if they can be laid bare.

From the time men first began to think of investigating these city-mounds, there was posed the problem of how one might best proceed. The manner in which these investigations were carried on went through various stages before archaeology reached the point where it could be classified as a real science. The word "method" can scarcely be employed with regard to the initial archaeological researches in Palestine. Those who dug into buried cities did so without any experience or schooling for the task. In fact there was no school to teach them; they dug only as their fancy directed without employing any particular technique. Their "finds," however, showed scholarly minds the weakness of possessing any given object without a definite knowledge of the exact place from whence it came, together with a careful record of every other object within that immediate area.

The methods or stages of investigation, as they were actually employed, are as follows:

First Stage. The first investigators dug into the side of the mound until they came to virgin soil and rock. But this method was slow, without order, and yielded very few satisfactory results. They went only a little way before striking virgin soil, while the great mounds with secrets unrevealed lay before them with tantalizing effects. This method, which might be styled

42

"the hit and miss" method, was soon abandoned because the "finds" were meager and unrelated.

Second Stage. The next procedure, which might be styled the "trench method," was then taken up. The workmen merely began at a given point and dug a trench five or six feet wide directly across the mound; thus a cross section of the mound was revealed. Walls, cisterns, bins, foundations, floors, implements, artifacts, coins, and a bit of almost everything that happened to be in the pathway were cleared. The objects found at various levels furnished some few clues as to dates, but it was found that the excavator could reach few worth-while conclusions, because the debris was so mixed and mingled that it presented little more than a jumbled mass of unrelated and unintelligible material from various occupation levels.

Third Stage. The stratigraphic or scientific method is the one which was finally developed, and is now in use. Credit for the development of the stratigraphic method belongs to a number of men, the principal ones being: Petrie, Bliss, Reisner, Fisher, Albright, and Pere Vincent.[1]

The story of how these methods came to be employed began with Botta at Khorsabad, and Layard at Nimrud, Ashur, and Nineveh. But it was Heinrich Schliemann at Troy (Troas) who first recognized he was dealing with the superimposed occupation levels of a city mound. During the eighties of the last century Petrie, an experienced excavator in the Egyptian field, suggested that the pottery found in such abundance in each city mound was an invaluable criterion for determining dates. He pointed out the fact that the pottery should be one of the most important considerations in every excavation. In 1890 the Palestine Exploration Fund prevailed upon him to leave his Egyptian field of research for sufficient time to make a preliminary examination of Tell el-Hesy, a splendid mound eighteen miles northeast of Gaza. Nature favored him in that a stream which ran past the tell had gradually cut away a portion of the artificial mound, thus leaving exposed the various "occupation levels."

With pocketknife in hand, Petrie climbed the mound's steep slope to the east and began an examination of the various strata or levels laid bare by the encroachment of the stream during the course of ages. Day by day, as he scraped and cleaned and sorted the potsherds and pottery from various levels, the story grew clearer. For six weeks he worked with the aid of thirty diggers, daring to rely for his chronological data chiefly on the pottery. When Petrie returned to his preferred sphere of Egyptian research, the work of Palestinian research had entered upon a new phase.

The Palestine Exploration Fund appointed Bliss to carry on the work at Tell el-Hesy, and made it easy for him to accept by sending him to Petrie in Egypt for a short apprenticeship in the art of practical digging. Petrie advised Bliss that there was nothing left for him to do at Tell el-Hesy but to cut down the mound itself, layer by layer, to ascertain the exact number of occupations and the character of each.

On returning to the mound in the spring of 1891 Bliss and his workmen confined their efforts to the northeast part of the hill, where almost one-third of each town or occupation level could be excavated and examined. When he rode away from the site two years later, 700,000 cubic feet of earth had been moved, the northeast corner of the mound had been shifted down sixty feet, and the levels on which had been built successively eight towns covering a period of approximately 1200 years had been laid bare. A large portion of every town—its ramparts, houses, granaries, etc.—had been removed piecemeal in baskets. Each town level had been carefully studied before the next level had been undertaken.

Two other names which stand high in the halls of fame with regard to the development of technique for field work are Reisner and Fisher.

George A. Reisner was born at Indianapolis, Ind., in 1867. He took his A.B. degree at Harvard University in 1891 and the Ph.D. degree in 1893. His graduate study was in the field of Semitic languages. On a traveling fellowship from Harvard he went to Germany to study cuneiform at Göttingen and Egyptian under Erman at Berlin.

In 1895 he was appointed an assistant in the Egyptian department of the Berlin Museum for a year; the following year he returned to Harvard as an instructor; then in 1897 he began his many years of work in Egypt. His first work there was as a member of the catalog staff of the Egyptian museum in Cairo. His contribution to the knowledge of *Amulets* (1907) and

Models of Ships and Boats (1913) was outstanding. He also studied the canopic jars at the Cairo museum.

In 1899 Reisner was able to interest Mrs. George Hearst, the widow of the former senator from California, in archaeological research; and in the same year he received from the University of California appointments as Hearst lecturer in Egyptology and director of the Hearst Expedition to Egypt.

Reisner did not serve an apprenticeship under some other field worker, but began on his own, having only the knowledge gleaned while studying Egyptology and while working in the Cairo museum and some gleanings from older field archaeologists. When he began there were certain field methods in use, of which Petrie's was the most advanced and scientific in the field of Egyptian archaeology. Reisner developed a system of his own for recording his finds, and his method became the most elaborate and meticulous ever to be used in Egypt.

Reisner's work for the first six years was at Naq ed Deir, near Girga in upper Egypt, and at the Gizeh pyramids after 1902. In 1905, he returned to the Harvard faculty as an assistant professor, but classroom work could not long hold him. Soon he had plans perfected for a joint expedition of the university and the Boston Museum of Fine Arts. For the rest of his life—more than thirty-five years—he directed expeditions in archaeological researches in the Sudan, in the royal and private cemeteries about the pyramids of Gizeh, and in a short campaign at Samaria, Palestine. The major portion of this time was spent at Gizeh in his home near the pyramids. He left the site only for short periods in summer and often remained throughout the year, taking no rest from his work.

After the First World War he published two volumes on his work in the Sudan, two on the excavation at Samaria, and recently there has appeared *A History of the Necropolis at Gizeh*. He also has written a treatise on *Development of the Egyptian Tomb* (1936) and *Mycerinus* (1931). Much important material is to be found in his many articles in the *Bulletin* of the Boston Museum of Fine Arts.

The collections of the Cairo museum and of the Boston Museum of Fine Arts have been greatly enriched by Reisner's work. The most spectacular of his finds was the famous gold-plated furniture of Queen Hetep-heres. His best and greatest contribution has been his careful observations recorded in his Gizeh work.

Clarence Stanley Fisher was born in Philadelphia on August 17, 1876. He was graduated from the University of Pennsylvania in 1897 as an architect, and devoted his entire subsequent career to archaeology. Part of this time was spent in resident activities in connection with the University museum in Philadelphia, but most of the time was spent in active field work in the Near East.

Fisher first engaged in archaeological research in Mesopotamia. Later he joined Reisner in Egypt, where he studied under him and assisted in the research which was to make Reisner famous as an Egyptologist.

In 1908 Harvard University began excavations at the mound of ancient Samaria with Reisner and Fisher in charge. Reisner was the director and Fisher the architect, but the two worked together. Aided by their combined experiences in the Mesopotamian and Egyptian fields, and by the work and suggestions of Petrie and Bliss, they worked out, or began to work out, a technique whereby each occupation level should be removed in its turn, all pottery given careful attention, and each find carefully recorded and preserved for immediate and future study. This excavation at Samaria resulted in brilliant discoveries which thrilled the scholarly world and placed these two men in the front rank as field archaeologists. The two, however, were not to continue their work together in Palestine, for Reisner returned to his former field of Egypt, where he continued his work at the pyramids.

Fisher was so fascinated with the Palestine field that he settled down there for his life's work. Profiting by the work and suggestions of Petrie and Bliss, and taking into account the techniques employed by Reisner and himself, Fisher worked out further details pertaining to field methods. Albright and Pere Vincent correlated pottery finds from various excavations and made invaluable suggestions for the use of pottery as a criterion for dating. By combining his rich background of experience with the experiences and suggestions of others, Fisher perfected pottery and recording techniques for field archaeology as no other man who has worked in the Palestinian field. His methods were so thorough and complete that for almost three decades the government of Palestine required that all excavations be conducted in harmony with Fisher's methods.

The techniques and methods worked out by Fisher and these other men soon became known as the "stratigraphic" method. It involves a careful study of the mound, and the complete removal of each occupation level before the next level is undertaken. Everything must be according to plan: all pottery must be considered, each object must be photographed, tagged, recorded, publicized, and preserved. Thus Palestinian archaeology was welded into a science with which the historian, the Biblical scholar, and the everyday Bible reader would reckon; and a science by which all mankind would be benefited.

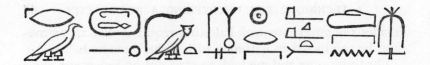

CHAPTER VII

Preparation for an Archaeological Expedition

ANY INDIVIDUAL who satisfies the department of antiquities of a government that he possesses sufficient skills and is acquainted with archaeological technique, is usually eligible as an excavator, or as the "director" of an archaeological expedition. The government requires, however, that he must have had previous experience in a similar field, or that he be trained by an excavator who has had such experience.

The director must have associates and assistants. If there are two men conducting an excavation, or a joint excavation sponsored by two institutions—as is sometimes the case—then one will be chosen as president, and the other as director of the excavation. These will almost invariably have an archaeological adviser, who will have become a veteran in the field, but will only be consulted from time to time.

When the site to be excavated is decided upon and the extent of the proposed excavation stated, then the government must be assured that the excavator has sufficient funds at his command to finance the expedition. When he has qualified as to skills and funds, and the permit is issued for him to dig at a given site, then he may make his own selection concerning members who will assist him and make up his organization. He may elect to call himself the president of the excavation, and select a more experienced archaeologist as his associate, and designate him the "excavator," or he may be the excavator and have complete oversight of everything connected with the expedition.

The staff of an archaeological expedition, when complete, will usually be composed of:

1. The president, who will have the general oversight of the expedition. He will hire, fire, and pay all employees.

2. The director, who will have the oversight of affairs pertaining to the technical aspects of the excavation.

3. The engineer, who makes surveys and draftings.

4. The architect, who helps in dating and identifying the buildings, and in designing plans showing the probable form of each structure as it was originally constructed.

5. Pottery specialist, who classifies all pottery as to form, texture, and ornamentation.

6. Senior recorder, who makes three specific records, and drawings of all finds.

7. Field recorder, who records and tabulates what and where and when and by whom everything is found.

8. Photographer, who photographs all important finds and keeps these photographic records classified.

9. Native overseer, who has charge of the native workmen— to keep them at work, and keep them supplied with whatever they may need.[1]

Each member of the staff has his own specific work, yet there usually is a general freedom of action, and in the end a pooling of efforts that will make for a greater degree of efficiency and understanding.

Nothing can be done, however, until rights to the "tell" or city mounds have been purchased. The department of antiquities may issue the permit, the expedition may be organized, but nothing may be done until lease terms are agreed upon and a contract drawn with the owner of the "tell." This is not always easy to secure, for the Arab may have the site planted in lentils or cauliflower, or he may be quite unsympathetic toward what he regards as "spying" or "snooping" into affairs pertaining to local interests.

In taking steps to secure contract for lease, the pattern of procedure will often run pretty much as follows: You call on the sheikh or chieftain, drink bitter coffee, visit with him a long time. He will finally ask you what brought you to his country. You will tell him you are interested in the history of his people. This interests him because he feels you regard him and his people as important. When you explain your intentions or desire to dig in the nearby tell he will seem both surprised and interested. The actual owner, or owners of the mound will be summoned, there will be further visiting, more coffee consumed, and gradually the bargaining will begin. No one will expect to conclude the business that day. There will be a visit another day, and compensation will be agreed upon for growing vegetables or anything which may encumber the ground. Finally, after long bargaining, a contract will be drawn. The terms will need to be as specific as is possible for them to be made, seeing many Arabs have the weakness of asking compensation in excess of the contract price when they see opportunity to feign some situation where they feel they might ask for more money. The terms of the contract usually bar the owner from the tell during the progress of the excavation. The contract will usually call for the replacing of the dirt after the mound has been excavated.

Following this, a native overseer will be employed. Then he, in harmony with the wishes of the president and director of the excavation, will take steps toward contacting the people of the nearby village and employing them to work on the excavation. Men, women, boys, and girls will be employed; one to cook, some to wield the pick, some to handle the hoe, two small boys to wash the pottery, but most of them will be called "basket men." The number employed for an excavation will vary from ten to 300—depending on the size, extent, and nature of the excavation. Heretofore these native workmen have been paid from four to eight piasters—twenty to forty cents— per day. This price constituted a very generous wage—so generous, in fact that they easily lived the entire year on the wages they received during a period of from three to five months. However, affairs have changed greatly during the past few years, and the native workmen are now paid considerably more.

The archaeological activity may, and usually will be conducted in the spring and early summer. It is called a "campaign" and is usually two to five months in duration. Some last the entire year, but this is quite unusual. Exposure, exertion, disease, and lack of conveniences in camp life usually dictate a fairly short duration for the campaign.

The equipment for an excavation will usually consist of living tents or huts, a cook and dining tent, a good camera, field glasses, compasses, angle protractors, measuring tapes, folding and sliding rules, square-traced drawing paper in blocks, squeeze paper and brushes and liquid latex rubber, pencils, pens, ink, adhesive tape, labels, specimen bags, small boxes, ammonia, chlorine, and caustic soda with which to clean coins and other objects.[2] Added to these will be a surveyor's transit level, and other up-to-date materials and equipment.

The tools with which the excavation will actually be made will consist of picks, shovels, short-handled triangular hoes, knives, trowels, and brushes. The spade is seldom used on excavations in any of the countries of Bible Lands. The term "spade" is more often a mere symbol for the entire set of tools used to unearth a Biblical city.

A careful study of the site must be made before the work of excavation actually begins. The preliminary study will usually begin with the photographer, who will go up in an airplane and photograph the mound from different angles and at different times of the day. The camera's lens will often detect things that would be unseen by the human eye. Short shadows in the carefully developed picture will often make it possible to trace a wall around the mound, or to detect a city gate or a tower by a break or slight rise in the mound. Graves in nearby areas are detected by heavier shadows cast by the greater growth of vegetation on the immediate spot.

The next step is to sink one or more trial shafts, in the midst of the mound, to examine and determine the various strata or occupation levels that make up the mound. The third step is for the architect or engineer to make a contour map of the entire mound showing its shape in every detail, and indicating every irregularity in walls, gateways, towers, and nearby areas.

The fourth and last preliminary step is to mark off the mound in squares of about ten meters each, and give to each individual square a letter and number symbol, so that all objects found in each square may be indicated on cards that will be used in the process of the excavation.

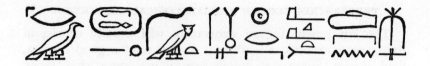

CHAPTER VIII

The Progress of an Archaeological Expedition

WHEN ALL PRELIMINARY preparations have been completed the workmen gather on the city-mound under the supervision of the director and a general foreman, who divides them into gangs consisting of pickmen, basket-fillers, and basket-carriers. The director gives a set of general rules to the foreman, who is held responsible for their strict observance and enforcement. They usually run about as follows:

1. No stone must be moved out of its find-location until it is certain that it does not form part of a wall, or in some other respect have architectural significance.
2. All objects found in a room, or tomb, must be cleared and photographed *in situ* before removal.
3. Every cover of an opening, whether of tomb, silo, or cistern, must be left untouched until photographed and inspected by the director, and no one may enter through such opening except at his request.
4. No basket of artifacts may be moved from its place, or brought down from the mound, until it has been provided with a provenience tag by the field recorder.[1]

Regulations for the control of workers on the mound will vary with directors, but those adopted by W. F. Badè for the Tell en-Nasbeh excavation are fairly representative:

1. Every worker must obey absolutely the directions of the foreman. Insubordination is punished with fines or dismissal. To guard against injustice, any case may be brought for review before the director.
2. Unless formally excused, employees must be in attendance promptly every day. Irregularity of attendance entails dismissal. But the offender may have a second chance by going on the waiting list for reemployment.

3. There must be no obscene songs or conversation. Offenders are subject to summary dismissal.

4. Brawling, fighting, and the carrying of weapons by workmen are strictly prohibited in the excavations.

5. Any person who finds an object of possible value or importance must at once show it to his foreman and indicate the exact find-location. The finder's name is then listed for appropriate reward or *baksheesh*.

6. Loafing villagers are not permitted to come as spectators into the excavations. Even the landowners may come only on business.[2]

The rules for both the work and the workmen being read, the order is then given for the pickmen to go over the surface of the mound and loosen the soil to a depth of three to four inches. The basket-fillers follow with short-handled, triangular hoes and pull the earth into fiber baskets; the basket women and girls hoist them to their heads, and boys hoist them to their hips, and all take their place in line and move away toward the dumping grounds with an order and precision that reminds one of the methodical march of ants.

The excavation is on, and with the hope of "pushing back the gates of the unknown" everyone is on the lookout for objects both large and small. The native foreman, under the supervision of the director, is in direct command of minor field activities, and must see that there is no lack of tools, implements, and baskets, and that the workmen are kept moving at the proper pace so that the work will move along smoothly. He usually stands on some high point from which he can observe the excavations, and as a symbol of authority carries a small stick or switch. Occasionally he strikes his skirt and admonishes the workmen to hurry along by the grace of Allah.

On an excavation of modest size there would probably be about ten or twelve pickmen, twenty or more basket-fillers, and fifty or sixty basket-carriers. On larger excavations there would be as many as two or three hundred workmen, with as many as eight or ten native overseers. These native workmen do practically all the manual labor in connection with the excavating. The staff members have their several duties and responsibilities connected with other aspects of the excavation.

The first few inches down have usually been disturbed by the plow, and reveal no objects of interest, other than potsherds, which the natives call "shikaf." These portions of pottery, which have shape, markings, or ornamentation in color, are important as criteria for determining dates, therefore they are placed in baskets which are then tagged with the level number, place on grid, and time found. This pottery is taken to a special place and washed by two native boys, and sorted and classified by one or more members of the staff who are pottery specialists. Sun-baked pottery is not washed lest it melt or disintegrate. Early Bronze pottery is first dry-cleaned, and examined for decorations. All pottery is spread out, examined, and recorded.

When a pottery vessel is found intact it is carefully preserved and set to one side. When a vessel is found crushed or broken to pieces, but with all or the major portion of the parts present, the workmen cautiously collect the several pieces which are taken to a pot mender, or restorer, who reconstructs the vessel and sets it away in its proper place for future reference. The more prominent rims, body fragments, bottoms and handles are often sorted and separated into series so that the professional pot mender may examine them, and when possible reassemble the parts of an unusual or important vessel and reconstruct it in its original form. Decorated, burnished, or otherwise unusual potsherds and vessels have first claim for attention. The texture, the color, and the shape, with peculiarities of base, neck, mouth, and handle usually tell the pottery expert the date of the vessel. Occasionally the imprint of a seal will tell where the vessel was made or to whom it belonged.

In excavating a tell the excavators begin at the top surface of the mound, or the level most recently inhabited, or occupied. Very little of importance may be found in this more modern occupation level. Everything down to the floor level of each occupation level is removed and considered before any work is started on the second or lower level. In the course of this procedure the lower portions of city gates, walls, fortifications, market places, shops, places of worship, and private homes will be laid bare, photographed, drawn and described so that in the future the originals could be reconstructed from these records if such seemed desirable.

"Intrusions" such as reservoirs, wells, silos, cisterns, cellars, storage bins, and graves usually extend below the floor level of the stratum being excavated. These frequently contain objects of material worth and social interest as well as scientific value, therefore they are given serial numbers and carefully cleared. One may find a figure of a god or goddess whom the people worshiped, gaming pieces with which they amused themselves, stone weights with which they weighed their merchandise, or art objects carved of wood, bone, stone, or ebony. When an inscription is discovered the usual tools are laid aside and by the use of a small knife and brush, a member of the staff cautiously brushes away all possible dust and dirt, that the writing may be laid bare and prepared for photographing and copying. In tombs the earth near the floor is sifted for coins, beads, and seals. When found these are provided with special smaller labels and are placed in bags or cardboard boxes adapted to their size.

The field recorder places a serial number on all rooms, silos, cisterns, and tombs the moment they come to light. He carries a package of paper tags for labeling baskets and all special objects. Each of these tags carry the date, level, grid location, and foreman's name under whom it was found. For every object found, the native workman who finds it is given a reward, the amount being graduated according to the value of the find. This bonus is given in addition to the daily wage, which means that even the basket boys and girls who carry excavated debris to the dumps search carefully for objects which might escape the eyes of the older diggers. Also, the rewards make it worthwhile for the workmen to hand over all objects found, rather than hide them in the voluminous folds of their garments and later endeavor to sell them to a private individual or an antique dealer.

In the recording room, located off the mound, the director and his staff maintain their headquarters, where each works at his or her given task. Movable objects with attached labels are taken into this recording room where in the hands of the chief recorder and the director all material takes two forms. First, all objects that can have any archaeological meaning are drawn accurately to scale and described on cards of uniform size. Second, all objects that are whole or by slight additions can be restored for exhibition in a museum must be registered in duplicate under serial numbers written on the objects. One copy of this list goes to the government museum, the other remains with the expedition. In this case a drawing and description sufficient to identify the object are entered along with the place and date of finding, the number of the photograph, and any other valuable information. These records, together with the photographs, maps, and plans of the excavation at its various stages are the basis of the final report.[3]

In the process of this campaign the workmen usually wield pick and carry baskets from sunrise to sunset, with a long break at midday and shorter pauses in the middle of the morning and afternoon. "At the end of each day," writes Andre Parrot, "an impressive volume of earth has been dug out and transported, basketful by basketful, to be heaped in giant cones outside the tell, so as not to cover up areas of archaeological interest that may be excavated in their own turn at some future date." There are times when the excavators make some important discovery almost every day; there are other times when they advance confidently anticipating finds, yet remove tons of earth without locating any object of interest.

An archaeological "campaign" in Palestine usually lasts from three to five months during the spring and early summer. In Egypt the search is usually conducted during the winter months. When the campaign is nearing completion, the accumulation of "finds" in the way of pottery, statuary, skulls, inscriptions, coins, seals, and other objects is sometimes so great as to seem almost unbelievable for value, volume, and variety. In others the finds are less numerous.

Usually everyone is obliged to work feverishly, because the maps, drawings, photographs, and records are to be completed and the entire collection displayed on tables and shelves for the inspection of the representative from the government museum.

When the representative arrives on the final day, the entire staff and the workmen wait in suspense for the outcome. The director and all who have been connected with the campaign see the unique pieces and the prize discoveries set aside for removal to the museum at Jerusalem, Cairo, Baghdad, or Beirut. The director and promoters of the expedition are permitted to keep only those objects that already have their counterpart in the museum, or for some reason are not desired by the government. Compensation for the staff members comes in the experience gained and in the consciousness of having contributed to the ever accumulating store of knowledge regarding the Bible and other ancient literature.

Then comes the task of packing the "finds," making the final feast for the workmen, breaking camp, going home, and complying with the antiquities law that requires publication of a complete report of the activities of the campaign.

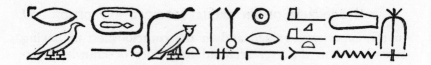

CHAPTER IX

Means and Methods by Which Dates Are Determined

DATES ASSIGNED to various archaeological discoveries may rightfully be said to be one of the chief factors contributing toward sustained and unflagging interest in the absorbing subject of archaeology. Without the dating factor we would have small romance and no true science in this important field of research and discovery. With a rudimentary knowledge of these processes one may more completely enter into a spirit of understanding with the archaeologists as they go forward with the work of unraveling the mysteries of the past. Therefore, a reasonably fair understanding of the means and methods employed in dating discoveries is exceedingly important for even the casual reader of archaeological reports, and much more for the student.

Various types of "measuring rods" and dating formulas have been devised for reckoning world chronology, and for assessing the amount of time which has elapsed since certain events took place in the distant past. Until very recent decades altogether too many dates for the archaeology of prehistoric civilizations were subjective estimates without sufficiently accurate basis for a reasonable degree of certainty.

Dating human remains according to the "record of the rocks," or the stratification of the earth's surface, has been used in various parts of the world, but cannot apply to the man-made mounds of Bible Lands. Conclusions drawn from cave remains are subject to the doubts that beset all calculations as to the rate of deposit of geological strata and to the rapidity of changes in climates and zoological characteristics.

In recent years a quite promising system for dating has been worked out by Willard F. Libby and his associates at the Institute of Nuclear Studies of the University of Chicago. This method, commonly called "radiocarbon dating," is based on the theory that during the lifetime of all plants and animals there is either a direct or an indirect absorption or intake of radiocarbon (C 14) into their tissues. At death this intake ceases, and the reservoir of radiocarbon not only begins to disintegrate with the tissues, but is thrown out at a given rate as negatively charged electrons and becomes nitrogen again. Thus by measuring the ever diminishing radioactive carbon (C 14) left in particles of plant and animal life—especially in wood, charcoal, cloth, peat and shell—many objects may be dated with a fair degree of accuracy. However, those directing the test must be furnished with enough suitable organic material for the test, which is made by burning the object to be tested so as to reduce it to gas, and then measuring the carbon in the gas.

The tests made by the radiocarbon system have proven very good in many cases, but not so good in a few others.[1] The entire method is based on the assumption that all the forces and processes of nature have always been as we now understand them to be in our modern world. Such factors as an appreciable climatic change, a possible change in the earth's atmospheric load of carbon dioxide, or the exposure and contamination of the object to be tested to certain acids and chemicals often found in earth and in surface water could lessen the reliability of the system to determine distant dates. Some consider the accuracy of the system to diminish as we go backward in time. Time need not be a deterrent factor, however, if the organic material tested has been well preserved and shielded from contamination, as were the linen wraps of the Dead Sea Scrolls.[2]

However useful this and other methods of dating may or may not prove for the future, it would seem that absolutely reliable methods of determining dates of historic settlements of the extremely distant past have not been easily devised, and certainly not so final as some have inferred. The condition and nature of existing materials, the variety and often conflicting claims made by reputable scholars and their endless shifting of positions reveal elements of uncertainty which would seem to give credence to the dictum that "we only begin to touch firm ground around 3000 B.C., and in many cases around 2000 to 1800 B.C." The great civilizations of Babylonia and Egypt, as we now know them, had their beginning about 3000 to 3200 B.C. All human remains and events grow increasingly "hazy" and uncertain beyond this date. For earlier periods more careful researches are being carried forward, but for the present we have only relative chronological data.

For research in the mounds of ancient cities of Bible Lands a quite reliable table for dating archaeological discoveries up to about 3000 to 3200 B.C. has been worked out by veteran authorities such as Petrie, Reisner, Fisher, Pere Vincent, Albright, Woolley, Kelso, Glueck, Wright and others. This method has involved more than a half century of minute and critical examination, comparison and correlation of the pottery and other objects found in successive occupation levels of the city mounds and nearby burial grounds of ancient inhabitants, and is the system of dating that has gone far toward making a true science of Middle Eastern archaeology. The designers of this most excellent system of dating frankly admit that archaeological dating cannot always be applied to specific events, but frequently applies to more or less extended periods, especially so when dating earlier events. The best authorities allow for a possible maximum error of fifty years or more back to about 2400 B.C. Beyond 2500 B.C. they "only reckon in centuries, with a maximum error of one to two hundred years at the beginning of the third millennium." [3]

There are, of necessity, variations in time tables and terminology for the historical periods of the various countries that go to make up what we call "Bible Lands." And, too, it is sometimes difficult to know what "time-lag," if any, there was between two given countries. Yet the interests and events of these countries have been so related that a definitely established date in one country often aids in establishing the respective chronologies of other nearby countries. And the results of research work in these countries may often be tied in with, or be corroborated or contradicted by written records for four or more millennia before the present.

A table for dating the major periods of history in terms of pottery and artifactual chronology cannot be given for all the countries, but the major archaeological periods for Palestinian history, as usually given, are about as follows.[4]

ARCHAEOLOGICAL PERIODS

I. Stone Age .... Indefinite time to 3000 B.C.
   [Usually divided into two eras: Neolithic (Old Stone Age),
   and Chalcolithic (New Stone Age).]

II. Bronze Age .... 3000 to 1200 B.C.
   1. Early Bronze .... 3000 to 2000 B.C.
   2. Middle Bronze (Abraham) .... 2000 to 1500 B.C.
      (a) First Phase .... 2000 to 1800 B.C.
      (b) Second Phase ...... 1800 to 1500 B.C.
   3. Late Bronze .... 1500 to 1200 B.C.

III. Iron Age .... 1200 to 333 B.C.
   1. Early Iron Age .... 1200 to 1000 B.C.
      (Ends with the expansion of the
      Phoenician seapower)
   2. Middle Iron Age .... 1000 to 586 B.C.
   3. Late Iron Age .... 586 to 333 B.C.

IV. Hellenistic .... 333 to   63 B.C.
V. Roman .... 63 B.C. to A.D. 323
VI. Byzantine .... A.D. 323 to 636
VII. Early Islamic .... A.D. 636 to 1096
   (Ends with the First Crusade)
VIII. Crusader .... A.D. 1096 to 1291
IX. Medieval Islamic .... A.D. 1291 to 1500
X. Turkish .... A.D. 1500 to 1900

In most cases these are but convenient terms. The Bronze Age, for example, does not mean that all the implements of this age were made of bronze. Stone implements were used all through the bronze age, and later. Some iron was used also during the latter part of this period, and it should be borne in mind that cultural changes do not always follow political changes.

The principal objects that aid materially in dating are masonry, inscriptions, signets, coins, and pottery, the latter being the more important.

MASONRY

Ancient and medieval builders of various periods usually cut and shaped their building stone after a pattern peculiar to their own times, therefore the types or styles of masonry found frequently aid materially in dating. There are six principal styles of masonry.[5]

Megalithic Masonry. The very early type of masonry is known as "Megalithic," and is composed of very large stones, wholly or partially rough on the face, but so exactly hewn that frequently a knife-blade cannot be inserted in the joints. These are usually laid in courses, and form a very substantial wall, although many of the stones are irregular in size. The following is an example:

Polygonal Masonry. In this type of masonry the stones are partially cut, but not squared. Some of these building stones may be two or three meters long, but usually they have smaller stones worked in with the larger ones. Also characteristic of this type are some stones which have "nobs" fitting into sockets, thus making a fairly strong wall. The following is an example:

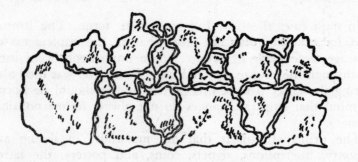

"Interlocked" Masonry. This is the more carefully "hewn" or "sawn-stone," an example of which follows:

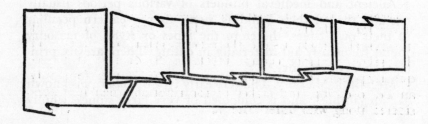

Solomonic Masonry. This type came into use during the reign of King Solomon, and was composed of long, slender slabs of well-hewn stone laid alternately. It looked like the following:

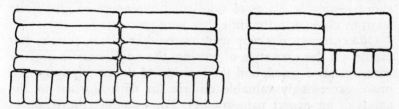

Herodian Masonry. This was used by Herod the Great in his extensive building operations between 37 B.C. and 4 B.C. It is characterized by marginal drafting all about the face of the building stone. It is the best type of masonry of which we have any traces today, with the exception of the pyramid masonry. It is as follows:

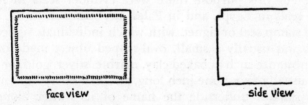

face view   side view

Crusading Masonry. This type of masonry was characterized by the diagonal or slanting stroke across the smooth face and may be pictured as follows:

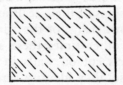

However, masonry techniques change too little and too slowly for walls themselves to be always exactly dated, except in unusual periods such as those described above. Gates lend themselves to more certain identification because they frequently possess architectural design. Masonry is, therefore, only an aid to dating, and makes its contribution when it is considered along with other criteria.

INSCRIPTIONS

The lands that cradled the alphabet and gave the world its richest and most extensive literature have yielded various inscriptions. Some of these have been inscribed either by or about people or places of sufficient prominence to give quite accurate clues as to the time they were written.

Other inscriptions may mention neither places, people, nor events, yet the very style of writing, the way letters in a given language are formed, and the location of the inscription often prove exceedingly valuable criteria for dating, when in the hands of an expert paleographer. For example, the ligatures or united characters used in the very ancient Hebrew script aided in dating the Dead Sea Scrolls.

SEALS OR SIGNETS

In ancient times the signet performed the important function of identification for all private and public letters and documents. For this purpose there were cylinder seals in Assyria, scarab seals in Egypt, and in Palestine, stamp seals.

The stamp seal or signet, with which individuals signed their names, was usually a small, oval-shaped object made of some hard substance such as baked clay, marble, silver, gold, or jasper. It was usually about one inch long, and had incised or engraved on its smooth underside the name of its owner along with some interesting design. At Megiddo, for example, a splendid seal was found bearing the imprint of a fierce lion in bold relief. Engraved in Hebrew characters located above and below the lion were the words "Shema, a servant of Jeroboam."

At times the impressions of these seals are found stamped on jar handles, showing ownership of the wine, oil, or grain contained in the jar. At other times these signets are found in graves, or their likeness cut on walls in connection with an inscription. In any case, they identify certain kings or prominent individuals, and prove exceedingly valuable dating criteria in that they supplement and give precision to the ceramic chronological scale.

COINS

The exact date when coins were first minted and used as a medium of exchange is uncertain. The oldest coins yet found were supposed to have been minted at Sardis, the capital of Lydia, sometime during the seventh century B.C. Inscribed records of loans and payments in Assyria dated in the years 676-671 B.C. seem to suggest coined shekels stamped with the head of Ishtar, yet no Assyrian coins of so early a date have been found.[6]

Cyrus the Great, who conquered Croesus, the fabulously rich king of Lydia in 546 B.C., soon made wide use of coins in Persia. Golden drams or darics of Persian mintage were brought to Palestine in 536 B.C. by the Jews returning from captivity. Since the third and second centuries B.C., coins have been found in almost all occupational levels in various cities throughout Bible Lands. Two hundred and seventy-nine different coins were found in the Beth-Zur excavation alone.

Coins often bore bits of historical information, and since the time of Alexander the Great (333 B.C.) they have frequently borne the likeness of the ruler under whose administration they were minted. Therefore, they often aid materially in computing dates.

POTTERY

The use of pottery has ever been intimately associated with the domestic and commercial life of all races. Fragments of sun-baked and burned dishes, jars, and receptacles in splendid state of preservation have been found in all parts of the inhabited world.

In every ancient city-mound the ground is well filled with broken pottery as far down as an occupational level extends. Even on the surface it lies strewn over the ground in large quantities, and usually in great variety. Tombs are often well stocked with unbroken pots which were in daily use, or had been made as funerary imitations. In each case they were placed there to contain votive offerings for the deceased, or deposited for the owner's comfort in the next world.

Archaeologists find that in pottery there have been *styles* which have changed from one period to another much like the "fashions" in other realms. The shape of a vessel, together with peculiarities of base, neck, mouth and handle, as well as the texture, color, and baking of the clay aid in identifying the vessel as to the period in which it was made. Therefore archaeologists look for distinguishing characteristics for each period. New shapes constantly replaced old ones, and often there was a difference in the composition of the ware and in its decoration. For these reasons the texture, color and baking of the clay is important. Some vessels were built by hand, others hand-turned, and still others "thrown" on the potter's wheel. In making the "hand-made" pottery, the vessel was built up of coils of wet clay, then with the fingers of one hand pressing against the inside of the jar and the fingers of the other hand working against the outside, the clay was rubbed into perfect union and molded into the desired shape. A poorer potter or a potter who was in a hurry often molded the clay over a basket or another vessel to achieve the desired form. Some of this hand-made pottery was of eggshell thinness, but in general it was inclined to be thick.

The "hand-turned" pottery was made by the clay being placed on a board or on any flat object and turned about as the potter desired, and the shape given it by the potter's hand, as the clay turned.

Pottery making came to be quite an art after the coming of the potter's wheel. However, the development of pottery cannot be taken as a sign of civilization, for the early Persians produced pieces of hand-turned pottery that have never been equaled by anyone in color or design. And the very best Greek pottery, far-famed for its form and artistically designed figure, was made during the fifth and fourth centuries before Christ.

Each of the above-mentioned archaeological periods has sufficiently diverse types of pottery—in *form, ware,* and *decoration*—to enable the pottery specialist to recognize the types and distinguishing features of pottery made and used during each period.

When, therefore, the archaeologist finds a group of characteristic types together, with the absence of other types, he can date the occupation level with reasonable accuracy. However, it is only the exhaustive comparison of all the forms found at each level in all the excavations that enables the specialists to reach reliable conclusions, and, even then the date is usually understood as being within a possible error of as much as fifty years or more.

Thus, the methods employed in computing dates in researches in Bible Lands involve a careful study and correlation of all facts with regard to masonry, inscriptions, signets, coins, and pottery found at a given occupational level of a city-mound and in nearby tomb groups. The pottery index, however, is by far the most important criterion for arriving at approximate dates, and therefore we furnish herewith illustrations of the forms of pottery found in the more important archaeological periods.

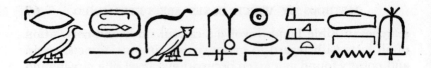

CHAPTER X

The Rise and Fall of the Signet

IN ANCIENT TIMES, when the art of writing was fairly well confined to a comparatively few learned people and to professional scribes, it was customary for the king and every other person of any importance to possess his own signet or seal, with which to "sign" his personal signature and thus to authenticate all letters and documents whether public or private. This seal, which in earlier times was known merely as a "ring," was usually a round or oval-shaped object about seven-eighths of an inch long and about five-eighths of an inch wide. Some were smaller, while many were larger. Some very important seals, especially those from Babylonia and Assyria, were shaped like a small cylinder from one to two inches in height. Such seals were rolled across soft moist clay when an impression was desired. Those from Egypt were made in the form of a sacred beetle, the underside being engraved with the owner's signature.

There were three classes of seals, each determined by its use: The *Hotham,* which denoted a seal for personal use, such as a private individual might carry about or wear on his finger as a seal ring; the *Tabaath,* a royal seal worn and used by the king; and the *Izka,* a royal seal given to the princes and high officials for their use in signing state documents and stamping government properties.[1]

The substance from which the signet was made may have been any hard-surfaced material from baked clay or shell-core to sapphire, known as lapis lazuli, but usually was made of rock crystal, basalt, chert, marble, agate, diorite, steatite, cornelian, blue chalcedony, jasper, ivory, silver or gold. A few were made of wood.

The work of incising or engraving these signets and seals

68

was known as "Glyptic Art." The artisan was known as a seal engraver, and was sometimes called a "gem cutter." When a signet was desired, the individual would go to the engraver who would shape the material, then incise or cut on its face certain designs and letters identifying the particular individual for whom it was made. The engraver not only entered the individual's name, but often was to carve exquisite designs and depict a wealth of detail, even though the area on which he worked was small. Much ancient art known today is in the form of seal impressions.[2]

To ensure privacy the engraver would often set the signet in a ring which would fit about the owner's finger, or in some instances, especially when it was a royal personage, he would attach it to a gold chain to be worn about the owner's neck, in which case it was what we now know as a "seal locket." Large cylinder seals were fitted into a small box or wrapped in something to keep them safe. Once an individual or an official was provided with a signet, he used it just as a person today uses his signature. To give a man your seal was to give him the use of any authority and power which your own signature possessed. Therefore privacy of use was always exceedingly important.

In Greece during the seventh century B.C., every freeman wore a signet ring, and to prevent counterfeits and forgeries the statesmen of Greece enacted a law forbidding seal engravers to keep in their possession the impression of any seal ring that had been cut for a customer. Some great kings had a "keeper of the king's seal" whose business it was to see that the royal seal was properly used.

When the professional scribe had finished writing a letter or a contract, the sender of the letter or the parties to the contract, along with the witnesses, would draw from around their necks or take from their fingers their small seals or signets and press them into, or roll them over the soft moist clay on which the letter or contract had been written, and thus affix their signatures. When a contract was paid, then there was "the breaking of the seal," which absolved the individual who had made the agreement. The part bearing the person's seal was usually then broken off, but the tablet proper was preserved in the archives as a record of the transaction.

Seals were also put on grain sacks and other containers to ensure the correctness of their contents. When an individual or a proprietor of an establishment wanted to show that a jar of oil or wine belonged to him, he would cover the stopper of the jar with clay and impress his seal while the clay was moist and pliable.

In Mesopotamia, both the oval signet and the cylinder seal were used. The oval seal was used very early, but in the third millennium B.C. the cylinder seal came into use, and dominated the field until around 300 B.C., when it was largely replaced by a cone-shaped seal with the design cut into the flat bottom of the cone.

The prevailing motifs on the Assyrian and Babylonian cylinder seals were processions of human and animal figures and fabulous monsters, together with the owner's identification. On some were pictured the god the owner worshiped. For example, the seal of Darius the Great shows the king in his two-wheeled chariot between two date palms. His charioteer is driving over a lion, and the king has a bow in his hand ready to shoot another lion standing on its hind legs. The winged disc is at the top center of the seal, together with the letters of the god Ahura Mazda. At the left is a trilingual cuneiform inscription stating in old Persian, Median, and Babylonian, "I am Darius the great king."

The Egyptians employed a type of seal called the "scarab." The obverse side of these scarabs was made in the form of a beetle's breast, and bore cartouches or stone-cut symbols enclosed by an oval line. The reverse side was made in the likeness of the scarab or dung beetle, which to the Egyptian mind signified immortality. Thus immortality, which was stamped deep on Egyptian consciousness, was embodied in their very signature, which to them was a very real part of the owner's very self.

The most valuable seals are those which carry cuneiform, Hebrew or hieroglyphic inscriptions as well as designs. The Egyptian "cartouche" is the equivalent of the royal signature in enclosed hieroglyphics, engraved on the walls of temples or tombs.

The Hebrew people usually avoided most forms of art, because the Mosaic Law forbade them to make "any likeness of any thing that is in heaven above, or that is in the earth beneath, or that is in the water under the earth" (Exodus 20:4). However, the one form of art in which native Israelite craftsmen attained a high degree of proficiency was that of gem-cutting or incising, as exemplified by the seals found in Palestine.[3] The Hebrew signet was either oval or conical in shape; sometimes the stone was set in a ring, at other times worn about the neck on a cord or chain, as is sometimes the case with modern Arabs.[4]

Some seals had a simple inscription of the owner's name, others were ornately decorated with carved emblems such as a lion, a bull, a ram, fighting cocks, a standing human being, a griffin with the crown of Upper and Lower Egypt, a four-winged cobra, and complex scenes of mythology, and miscellaneous symbols, such as palmettes, winged solar discs, and four-winged scarabs. On the inscribed face a line or a double line divided the surface; above it was placed the name of the owner, usually prefixed with the preposition "to," which meant belonging to, and below the line was the name of the owner's father, or his king or overlord, often prefixed with the word "Son" or "servant." For example, there is a well-known carnelian seal purchased in Jerusalem in 1885 that bears the beautifully engraved inscription "To Hananiah son of Azariah." [5]

Some of the ancients who were poor or unimportant did not own seals. As a simple substitute, the thumbnail was impressed in the soft clay, along side of which a scribe would write *supurshu,* which meant "his thumbnail mark."

There are many references to the signet or seal in the Bible. In Genesis we are told that Judah had a signet which he gave to Tamar as a pledge. The Book of Job was no doubt referring to the revolving of a cylinder seal when it said, "It is turned as clay to the seal. . . ." The lover in the Song of Solomon used the signet as a figure of speech, "Set me as a seal upon thine heart. . . ." [6]

Certain Old Testament Scriptures allude to the great importance attached to the signet by the Oriental. Thus Jeremiah says, "As I live, saith the Lord, though Coniah the son of Jehoiakim king of Judah were the signet upon my right hand, yet would I pluck thee thence." And Haggai says, "In that day

. . . will I take thee, O Zerubbabel . . . and will make thee as a signet. . . ." [7]

Egyptian rulers and court officials often used the scarab seal or signet mounted on a gold ring that encircled the finger, or on a chain about the neck. Thus with considerable ease they could delegate authority to those who were to assist them or to take over in their place. A graphic account of such a transfer is given in the Sacred Record when Joseph was invested with authority as the governor of Egypt:

And the thing was good in the eyes of Pharaoh, and in the eyes of all his servants. And Pharaoh said unto his servants, Can we find such a one as this is, a man in whom the Spirit of God is? And Pharaoh said unto Joseph, Forasmuch as God hath showed thee all this, there is none so discreet and wise as thou art: Thou shalt be over my house, and according unto thy word shall all my people be ruled: only in the throne will I be greater than thou. And Pharaoh said unto Joseph, See, I have set thee over all the land of Egypt. And Pharaoh took off his ring from his hand, and put it upon Joseph's hand, and arrayed him in vestures of fine linen, and put a gold chain about his neck; And he made him to ride in the second chariot which he had; and they cried before him, Bow the knee; and he made him ruler over all the land of Egypt. And Pharaoh said unto Joseph, I am Pharaoh, and without thee shall no man lift up his hand or foot in all the land of Egypt.[8]

When the Babylonian officials conspired against Daniel, and forced the king to cast him into the lion's den, a stone was rolled over the mouth of the den, soft moist clay was packed about the stone, and the king's signet was pressed into the clay to make the matter official. The seals of the other government officials, or "lords," were used also on this occasion. The record reads:

Then the king commanded, and they brought Daniel, and cast him into the den of lions. Now the king spake and said unto Daniel, Thy God whom thou servest continually, he will deliver thee. And a stone was brought, and laid upon the mouth of the den; and the king sealed it with his own signet, and with the signet of his lords; that the purpose might not be changed concerning Daniel. Then the king went to his palace, and passed the night fasting: neither were instruments of musick brought before him: and his sleep went from him.[9]

Haman bought from King Ahasuerus for ten thousand talents of silver (approximately $10,580,000) the privilege of using his seal on a decree calling for putting to death of the Jews. When Ahasuerus agreed to Haman's cruel scheme of killing all the Jews in the king's provinces, he took the ring off his hand and gave it to Haman. Afterward, when he commanded Mordecai to write letters annulling the former decree, he ordered them to be sealed with his ring.[10]

Jezebel, having access to Ahab's seal, made use of it in making good her word, "I will give thee the vineyard of Naboth the Jezreelite."

So she wrote letters in Ahab's name, and sealed them with his seal, and sent the letters unto the elders and to the nobles that were in his city, dwelling with Naboth.[11]

So this nefarious deed was accomplished quite smoothly because Jezebel had access to her husband's signet ring, and possessed enough power to put fear in the hearts of the elders of Naboth's city.

On returning home the penniless and repentant prodigal son was agreeably surprised when his gracious old father not only forgave him and welcomed him home, but placed a signet ring on his finger. This meant wealth and authority for the forgiven son, for he had the use of his father's signet.[12]

After the entombment of Jesus, the chief priests and Pharisees went to Pilate and said to him:

. . . Sir, we remember that that deceiver said, while he was yet alive, After three days I will rise again. Command therefore that the sepulchre be made sure until the third day, lest his disciples come by night, and steal him away, and say unto the people, He is risen from the dead: so the last error shall be worse than the first. Pilate said unto them, Ye have a watch: go your way, make it as sure as ye can. So they went, and made the sepulchre sure, sealing the stone, and setting a watch.[13]

Soft moist clay was placed about the stone and the entrance of the tomb, the official seal was pressed into this clay, thus sealing it officially. It would be a great crime to break this seal fixed by government authority, and would bring severe punishment.

Paul wrote to Timothy, ". . . The foundation of God standeth sure, having this seal, The Lord knoweth them that are his. . . ."[14] The stonemason often put his mark on his

work to denote the idea of workmanship, but more probably
here the reference is to the owner's mark or seal, denoting the
thought of ownership, security, and destination. For example,
the seal of Nebuchadnezzar was found imprinted in building
bricks of that period. A number of New Testament passages
refer to the sealing work of the Holy Spirit, emphasizing the
divine ownership of the believer.[15]

In Rome, and certain other parts of the empire, a property
qualification was necessary for the wearing of a ring. In the
light of this, we can better understand the words of James when
he says: "For if there come into your assembly a man with a
gold ring . . . And ye have respect to him . . . Are ye not
then partial in your selves. . . ." [16]

In almost every excavation numerous seals and seal impressions are uncovered. In fact, the seal or signet, aside from potsherds, is one of the most common objects to be found in
archaeological research. Thousands have come to light, and
among them are the signets of many notable people known in
the pages of the Old Testament and in other ancient literature.

Haggai Seal. In 1867, while digging under the pavement near
the so-called Wilson's arch, twenty-three feet below the present
surface in Jerusalem, Warren and Wilson found a signet of
"Haggai, the son of Shebaniah." It is an interesting fact that
the prophet Haggai is the only one of the minor prophets who
mentions the signet.[17]

Queen Shub-Ad Seal. There has been considerable interest
shown in the lapis lazuli seal of Queen Shub-ad, which was
found by Woolley at Ur of the Chaldees. It was tossed into
her grave after all her other treasures and her court had been
buried sacrificially with her. This tiny bit of art identified
this unusual find, which can be seen at the present time in the
University museum at Baghdad or in the University of Philadelphia (Pennsylvania) museum.

In this same excavation at Ur, Woolley found below the flood
level, numerous seals and clay jar stoppers stamped with the
impressions of the owners' seals. There were no inscriptions,
but the designs were sometimes of an elaborate geometrical
character, often with rows of animals walking in hilly country,
the figures drawn with astonishing loveliness and skill.[18]

Eliakim's Seal. At Kirjath-sepher (modern Tell Beit Mirsim), Albright and Kyle found, in the layer of ashes left by Nebuchadnezzar's fire, two jar handles stamped with a beautifully carved seal inscribed, "Eliakim steward of Jehoiachin." One of these is now in the Pittsburgh-Xenia Seminary. An identically inscribed handle was found by Elihu Grant at Beth-Shemesh in 1930, so that there were three different jars, all impressed by the very same seal, as shown by minute comparison. Evidently Eliakim was charged with the administration of Jehoiachin's crown property while the king was a captive prisoner in Babylon.[19]

Shema's Seal. At Megiddo a sensational find was that of a jasper royal seal showing a well-executed figure of a lion and carrying a Hebrew inscription which read, "Shema, a servant of Jeroboam." This is understood to refer to Jeroboam II, "the Napoleon of Israel."

Gedaliah's Seal. At Lachish in 1935, J. L. Starkey, of the Wellcome Archaeological Expedition, found near the "Persian" gateway, in the layer of ashes left by Nebuchadnezzar's fire, a seal impression made on a lump of pinkish-red clay bearing the inscription, "Gedaliah, who is over the house." The title *"over the house"* means *"Lord Chamberlain."* This Gedaliah is probably the one who was appointed governor of the cities of Judea by Nebuchadnezzar (Jeremiah 40:5) when, in 586 B.C., the Babylonian invader left the country in Gedaliah's care. His headquarters were at Mizpah. Jeremiah attached himself to Gedaliah, then later Gedaliah was treacherously slain by the Jewish "loyalist" leader, Ishmael.

Another seal found by Starkey bore the name "Shebna" in characters suitable to the age of Hezekiah, which recalls "Shebna the scribe" (i.e., Secretary of State) (Isaiah 36:3).

Jaazaniah's Seal. During the excavations at Tell en-Nasbeh (Mizpeh), Badè uncovered an ancient seal on which was engraved the likeness of a fighting cock and the words "Belonging to Jaazaniah, officer of the King." Jaazaniah was one of the army captains mentioned in II Kings 25:23 who went to Mizpeh in 586 B.C. to join the forces of Gedaliah, the governor appointed by the Babylonians over conquered Judah.

Amenhotep III's Seal. One of the most famous scarabs ever to be excavated is the huge pectoral scarab of Amenhotep III, which came to light during the Lachish excavations. It carries in eight parallel lines of hieroglyphics the record of a lion hunt in the tenth year (1403 B.C.) of the reign of Amenhotep III and Queen Tiy.[20]

Shallum's Seal. Another seal of the scarab type, bore the inscription "For Shallum the son of Mas." There is a Shallum mentioned in the Lachish Letters.

Hilkiah's Seal. Then a small clay seal, bearing the name of "Hilkiah the son of Mas" was found also in the upper burnt layers of the city of Lachish. Hilkiah was the name of Jeremiah the prophet's father, but we seem to have no knowledge of Mas.

Jotham's Seal. During the excavations at Ezion-Geber, Solomon's seaport near Elath, Glueck uncovered a beautifully designed seal in a copper casing which bore the inscription "Belonging to Jotham." It is now at our National Museum in Washington. Below the inscription was a saucy long-legged ram. Of this seal, G. Ernest Wright says:

While we cannot be sure, the seal's owner may well have been Uzziah's son of the same name, who became regent during his father's leprosy before his own reign began. In any event, it is a good Judean name, and the owner did not feel it necessary to give his father's name. Elath and Edom were lost to Judah early in the reign of Jotham's son, Ahaz, that is, about 734 B.C.[21]

Great importance was attached to the use of the seal or signet ring by eastern people, and particularly by those of the Old and New Testament world. It was so highly regarded in the Roman Empire, and was such a necessity in every day life, that a gentleman often gave his signet ring to his beloved either when they were betrothed or on their wedding day. Their general use in Europe declined after the fall of the Roman Empire in A.D. 476. They were revived during the Renaissance, but in time came to be little used.

The seal as such survives today in government, state and corporation seals. The private seal or signet ring now survives only in out-of-the-way places where civilization is more or less primitive.

There are exceptions, the most prominent of which is the signet of the Pope of Rome, which has long been known as "The Ring of the Fisherman." This is a steel signet ring the

Pope wears on state occasions and when receiving visitors. Otherwise it is kept at the Vatican by the Cardinal Chancellor for the use of the Pope when signing official documents. Lead has long been used by the Pope for making impressions. From the lead seal impression we get our expression "papal bull." The *bulla* was originally a circular plate or boss of metal, so called because it looked like a bubble of water (bullire, to boil). The term was applied to the leaden seals used on papal documents during the Middle Ages, and from that use the term "bull" came to be defined as "an apostolic letter with a leaden seal." However, a few times the metal used for making the impressions has been gold, therefore the few "golden bulls." [22]

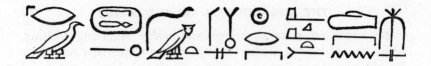

Archaeological Discoveries in Assyria

SOME 500 MILES east of Palestine lies Mesopotamia, "the Land of the Two Rivers." The Tigris and the Euphrates rivers rise 150 miles apart in the highlands of Armenia and after meandering down through the mountains they enter a vast plain and through this flow southeast for some 500 miles until the two rivers converge into a common channel, and as one river flow on 150 miles to the Persian Gulf.

Mesopotamia falls into three natural divisions of southern, middle, and northern. In their greatest known antiquity these were identified as Sumer, Akkad, and Aram, respectively. But for the most part the northern portion has usually been known as Assyria and the southern portion as Babylonia.

Assyrian and Babylonian archaeological research, in its earlier stages were almost synonymous with the names of Botta, Rich, Rawlinson and Layard. But in the century to follow, other illustrious names of men and institutions were to enter the arena of Assyrian and Babylonian research. Foremost among the city-mounds in Assyria that claimed their attention were: Khorsabad, Nimrud, Nineveh, Ashur, Nuzi, Tepe Gawra, Balawat, and Mari.

KHORSABAD

Paul Emile Botta, the amiable and brilliant French vice-consul at Mosul, became interested in the great mound of Nineveh across the Tigris to the east. He hired natives and began preliminary work in December 1842, and, though having little success, continued his work of superintending his work-

men and carefully examining every fragment that came out of
the ground until the middle of March 1843. Then, a native
from a neighboring village advised him in colorful language
that at Khorsabad, ten miles north, there were masses of inscribed brick, considerable alabaster, and some impressive
monuments.[1]

Botta sent two of his native workmen to investigate, and on
receiving a favorable report, he went with some of his workmen
and after "an all around examination" of the mound he started
operations at the top of the highest portion. Not far from
the surface he struck the top of a wall, which he found to be
built partly of gypsum. Digging a trench along the wall, Botta
soon found himself in a room of immense proportions. The
walls were wainscoted with sculptured alabaster slabs upon
which panorama after panorama unrolled as they were uncovered. These walls had scenes of battle sieges, triumphal
processions, hunting and like events, all in relief. Across the
face of many of these were lines of characters which only had
to be deciphered to tell many details of this ancient civilization.[2]

Believing that a great moment in his life had arrived, in
which he was witnessing the resurrection of a long forgotten
past, Botta sent a message to Paris, saying, "I believe that I
am the first to discover sculptures that can be truly identified
with the period when Nineveh was at its height." [3] He also
expressed the hope that some way might be found for financing
further excavations, and for the safe transport and final preservation of the treasures. The newspapers took up his message
and the world thrilled that someone was in the very doorway
of a great discovery. The Academy of Paris requested the minister to grant the necessary funds. The government not only
granted the request but they also sent E. Flandin, a skilled
architect and artist, to assist Botta in sketching all such monuments as could not be safely removed from Khorsabad.[4]

But many long months passed before the architect arrived
at the ruins, and in the meantime Botta had to fight his way as
best he could amid many hardships and almost insurmountable
difficulties and obstructions, of which some were intense summer heat, torrential winter rains, malarial illness to his own
person, and illness and death among his workmen; opposition
of natives, unskilled labor, and the lack of proper facilities for

packing and transporting the sculptures. The last, but by no means the least, was the interference of a despotic Turkish local governor who shared the general belief that the only explanation for Botta's tireless excavations was that he was looking for treasure. The governor ringed the mound of Khorsabad with guards to sieze any gold that might be found, threatened Botta's workmen with whippings, and often threw them into prison to extract a confession. He finally ordered the excavations closed on the pretext that Botta was evidently establishing a military station to take the country by force from the sultan. While Paris worked with the government at Constantinople, Botta tactfully and diplomatically triumphed over the obstacles and animosity of the native population, and improved his relationship with the local governor.[5]

Then with the beginning of May 1844, Flandin arrived from Paris via Constantinople bearing an official permit for the resumption of the work. With ample funds at their command, the two men employed 300 Christian refugees as workmen to assist them as they continued clearing the royal palace area in the northwest. The farther they went the more they were convinced that they were within the midst of a very unusual city, and that they were laying bare one of the most magnificent palaces ever known to man.

The entire city comprised 741 acres, was laid out in the form of a one-mile-wide fortified quadangle with seven gateways and an imposing palace area of twenty-five acres. The palace itself, along with its spacious domestic quarters, its luxurious harem, its three fine temples, and its towering ziggurat were all located on the twenty-five acre brick-terraced platform elevated forty-five feet above the surrounding area. A portion of this elevated area extended beyond the city walls, but it was well protected by unusually strong towers built at frequent intervals along its outer ramparts. The palace walls were constructed of large square stones and varied in thickness from nine and a half to sixteen feet. At one place they were twenty-five feet thick.

Within the palace there were almost inconceivable massive public reception halls profusely adorned with inscriptions, magnificent sculptures, and bas-reliefs representing gods, kings, battle sieges, and religious ceremonies. Elaborately decorated winged bulls, very beautifully cast or wrought in bronze, adorned many of the walls, and all principal doorways were flanked with human-headed winged bulls carved from gigantic monolithic slabs weighing many tons each. Gateways and reception rooms displayed all the splendor that Assyrian artists were able to give them, and the apartments in the harem were tastefully adorned with frescos, arabesques, and marble statues. All inner floors were either made of tile, or tamped clay, over which fine rugs were once laid. Outer courts and open spaces were paved with highly colored tile or marble blocks.[6]

Carved on the walls were a seemingly endless succession of sculptured pictures portraying in great detail the daily life, pleasures, appearance, customs, religion and history of the Assyrians. Wall slabs in three of the magnificent palace rooms gave in great detail the account of fifteen years of the mighty king's reign. Battles such as that of Raphia, and the second battle of Karkar were graphically portrayed. Various aspects of the active life of the powerful ruler were given, including his campaign to Palestine and the Mediterranean coast, where he crushed all resistance and brought about the collapse of all the countries except Judah.

Botta and Flandin found so many sculptures, statues, and so great a number of reliefs as to bewilder and even stagger them, yet they worked on with harmony, energy, and devotion during the hot and dusty summer months, and on until October when all traces of the palace walls disappeared. Careful observations convinced them that a part of the great building had been intentionally destroyed in ancient times, and although they supposed that another considerable part was yet preserved somewhere in the unexplored section of the mound, they temporarily suspended their excavation in which they had enjoyed such astonishing success and packed up the vast quantities of materials for shipment.[7] Botta had worked two years at Khorsabad, and much had been crowded into this period.

To convey the large museum pieces such as the gigantic winged and human-headed bulls from Khorsabad to the Tigris, Botta contrived a huge carriage with iron axles and wooden wheels "nearly a yard thick." But even with this and the pulling power of 600 natives he met with many discouragements and enjoyed only moderate success, because these huge and magnificent bulls weighed from ten to thirty tons each. One large bull had to be abandoned half way. On an enormous raft made up of native "keleks," or inflated sheep-skins, the prized antiques were floated down the Tigris to Basra, where after many months waiting, the "Cormorant," a French man-of-war, took them aboard and carried them safely to Le Havre, and from thence they went by rail to Paris.[8]

Flandin left Khorsabad in November of 1844 and went directly to Paris with his large collection of beautiful sketches and drawings made during the excavation. The people were deeply impressed with the drawings, but when the extraordinary monuments themselves arrived and found a worthy place in the spacious halls of the Louvre, the people came from far and near and were astounded when they looked upon the gigantic winged bulls, the reliefs showing the Assyrians at peace and war, and the strange cuneiform inscriptions which witnessed to the resurrection of an almost forgotten empire.

Enthusiasm among all classes of France knew no bounds. The government provided funds and appointed a commission under whose advice and through whose cooperation Botta and Flandin were able to publish the results of their combined labors in a magnificent work of five large volumes which contained 400 plates to illustrate the text.

The effect of these discoveries on the western world was refreshing indeed. Assyria, until then known only by a few Biblical references and vague accounts of classical historians, suddenly took the lead as "news." Illustrated articles appeared in magazines, lecturers declaimed on the conquests, religion, and daily life of the people, while Christians and Jews searched their Bibles for information on Assyria, and many a man quoted or read Lord Byron's famous lines about the defeat of Sennacherib:

> The Assyrian came down like a wolf on the fold,
> And his cohorts were gleaming in purple and gold;
> And the sheen of their spears was like stars on the sea,
> When the blue wave rolls nightly on deep Galilee.
>
> Like the leaves of the forest when Summer is green,
> That host with their banners at sunset were seen:
> Like the leaves of the forest when Autumn hath blown,
> That host on the morrow lay wither'd and strown. . . .

And the widows of Ashur are loud in their wail,
And the idols are broken in the temple of Baal;
And the might of the Gentile, unsmote by the sword,
Hath melted like snow in the glance of the Lord!

In 1851 the French Assembly voted a sum of money to make it possible for Victor Place, a skilled architect and Botta's successor as vice-consul, to continue the work at Khorsabad. He employed Botta's former foreman along with many other workmen and set about the work with the same kind of zeal that had marked his predecessor.

From 1851 to 1855 Place not only unearthed all the remaining rooms and sculptured halls connected with the palace, but continued in that section until he had reached the city walls. In nearby mounds, within the great city's walls, he unearthed seven gates, three of which were "flanked by large human-headed winged bulls and other sculptures, and their arches most beautifully decorated with friezes of blue and white enamelled tiles representing winged genii and animals, plants and rosettes, in excellent design and execution." All of which must have been welcome sights to home-coming Assyrian fighting men who had been long away in foreign wars.

At a very important place in the foundation of the palace, where two walls formed an angle, he made an especially valuable discovery in the form of an elaborately inscribed cornerstone box containing seven tablets of different size, in gold, silver, copper, lead, lapis lazuli, magnesite, and limestone. Each of these attractive tablets bore identical cuneiform records regarding the history of the palace buildings.

Victor Place discovered fourteen inscribed barrel cylinders with historical records. He found a regular storage room full of pottery, another full of tiles, and another containing iron implements of every description in such a fine state of preservation that several of them were used immediately on the excavation by his Arab workmen. He was especially successful in gathering small clay, stone, glass, and metal objects as would throw added light on the everyday life of the people. He unearthed "even the water-closets, the bakery and the 'wine cellar' of the King, the latter easily to be identified by a number of pointed jars resting in a double row of small holes in the paved floor, and discharging a strong smell of yeast after the first rain had dissolved their red sediments." [9] Place also discovered two magnificent human-headed bulls which are without doubt the most impressive products of Assyrian sculpture in existence. These he gave in exchange to Rawlinson, and they now stand at the entrance to the Assyrian transept in the British Museum.

Place had not made so many startling discoveries of large monuments as had Botta, yet the many smaller objects which he uncovered were exceedingly important. And beyond all this was the fact that his work had made it possible to get a clearer picture of the city of Khorsabad and its founder and mighty ruler, Sargon II, "the great king, the mighty king . . . the king of Assyria."

But who was this Sargon? Heretofore no secular historian had recorded the name and reign of an Assyrian monarch by this name. The only writer who had mentioned Sargon by name was Isaiah, the eloquent Hebrew prophet, who had parenthetically said:

In the year that Tartan came unto Ashdod (when Sargon the King of Assyria sent him,) and fought against Ashdod, and took it.[10]

But certain learned men, outside the realm of faith in the historicity of the Bible, had said there was no Assyrian king by this name. Yet there, in Sargon's annals, carved deep on the walls of his palace, was his own "authorized version" of the final siege and capture of Samaria, and the deportation of its people:

In the first year of my reign . . . the city of Samaria I besieged and captured. 27,290 people from its midst I carried captive. 50 chariots I took there as an addition to my royal force . . . I returned and made more than formerly to dwell. People from lands which my hands had captured I settled in their midst. My officers over them as governors I appointed. Tribute and taxes I imposed upon them after the Assyrian manner.[11]

And, further on in his annals, Sargon helps to explain a passage in Isaiah 20 when he described his capture of Ashdod:

Azuri, king of Ashdod, also planned in his heart not to pay tribute, and among the kings of his neighborhood disseminated hatred of Assyria. On account of the evil he had done I cut off his lordship over the people of his land. In the anger of my heart, the mass of my army I did not muster. I did not assemble my whole camp. With only my usual bodyguard I marched against Ashdod; I besieged it, and I conquered it. I took as spoil his gods, his wife, his sons, his daughters, his possessions, the treasures of his palace, together with the people of his land.[12]

From the records of Khorsabad and those subsequently found at Ashur, Nimrud, and Nineveh, it was seen that Sargon II (722-705 B.C.), an able general, had succeeded Shalmaneser V in 722 B.C. when the Assyrian capital was at Ashur, and had founded the last dynasty of the Assyrian empire. During the first year of his reign he had put down rebellion at home, completed the siege and capture of Samaria and settled nearly 30,000 of the ten tribes of Israel throughout the land of Assyria and Media. He had marched westward and dealt the Egyptians a staggering blow at Raphia in 719 B.C., fought the battle of Carchemish and captured immense booty from the Hittites in 717 B.C., invaded Arabia in 715 B.C., subdued Iran, Armenia and Kurdistan in 714 B.C., besieged and captured Ashdod in 711 B.C., drove from the Babylonian throne and defeated Merodach-Baladan, "that troublesome thorn in the side of Assyria," and completely annexed Babylonia to his domain in 709 B.C.[13]

While enjoying his successes at home and abroad, Sargon had moved his capital first from Ashur to Nimrud, then from Nimrud to Nineveh. Then while enjoying peace and receiving tribute from his "long-dreamed of realm," Sargon decided to satisfy his innate desire for fine new things and to perpetuate his fame by building a new city of 741 acres, and within it a beautiful and imposing palace for his royal capital at Khorsabad, ten miles north of Nineveh. On completing his new city he called it Dur Sharrukin, or Sargonsburg, and entered his magnificent palace in 706 B.C.; but Sargon was not to enjoy its luxuries very long, for he was mysteriously slain in eastern border wars during the very next summer. Sennacherib (705-681 B.C.), his third son, succeeded him on the throne, and moved the Assyrian capital back to Nineveh.[14] At a later date the city of Khorsabad was ruined, and for some twenty-five centuries had been hidden from the eye of man—until Botta, Flandin, and Place had uncovered its ruins and revealed its grandeur and its engravings.

In the spring of 1855 Place packed his finds in 120 crates, and conveyed them to Nineveh where they were loaded on two large rafts, together with sixty-eight cases of fine bas-reliefs from Ashurbanipal's palace at Nineveh (which Rawlinson had allowed him to select in return for the two magnificent winged bulls). These were floated down the Tigris. At Kurnah, near where the Shatt al 'Arab stream enters the Tigris, a large group of Arab brigands boarded the rafts in search of gold and treasures. On being disappointed at not finding what they had sought, they maliciously capsized the rafts, and the major portion of the valuable antiquities went to the bottom of the river. Fortunately, the Khorsabad material had already been meticulously drawn and recorded by Felix Thomas, and was subsequently published.[15]

In the century since Botta's far-reaching exploration of the mounds of Khorsabad there have been even greater discoveries, but none have had quite the influence or aroused again such a deep and general interest in archaeological research as did Sargon's luxurious palace which, after twenty-five centuries, arose almost suddenly from oblivion.

In the years 1932-33, the Oriental Institute of the University of Chicago re-explored the large palace of King Sargon originally discovered by Botta. There a complete list of Assyrian rulers was discovered which has been of value in setting dates for the reigns of these ancient monarchs.[16]

NIMRUD

Caught up by a youthful enthusiasm to travel and see the fascinating land of the Arabian Nights, Austen Henry Layard, a young English attorney prepared himself for the fulfilment of his urge by studying language, law, surveying, navigation, first aid, ways of combating tropical disease, and "everything that he conceived would be needed to travel freely in the land of his dreams."

Disdaining all prospects that might await him in jurisprudence, Layard at the age of twenty-two left his London law office on July 8, 1839, and accompanied by E. L. Mitford, of whom Layard says "he was no less curious" than himself, mixed with the people and wandered through Asia Minor, Syria, and Mesopotamia without a guide or servant. Careless of comfort and unmindful of danger, they traveled the antique land, "unconscious of distance and of the hour" and often found themselves, as the sun went down, "under some hoary ruin tenanted by wandering Arabs, or in some crumbling village still bearing a well known name." Always, as is their custom, the Arabs welcomed them, and as Layard says "Their scanty fare was placed before us. We ate and came and went in peace." [17]

On the tenth of April, 1840, Layard and Mitford rode into Mosul where they met Ainsworth and Hormuzd Rassam, and together they visited the ancient sites of Nineveh, Nimrud, and Ashur, and then returned to Mosul.

Layard wrote:

These huge mounds of Assyria made a deeper impression on me, gave rise to more serious thoughts and more earnest reflection, than the temples of Baalbec, and the theatres of Ionia.[18]

The mound that fascinated him was Nimrud, the "Calah" of Biblical fame, which lay on the east bank of the Tigris, twenty miles south of Mosul.

A few days later, he and Mitford embarked for Baghdad on a kelek, and as they floated down the Tigris, Layard again looked with awe on the great mound of Nimrud, and said of it:

The spring rains had clothed the mound with the richest verdure, and the fertile meadows, which stretched around it, were covered with flowers of every hue. Amidst the luxuriant vegetation were partly concealed a few fragments of bricks, pottery and alabaster, upon which might be traced the well defined wedges of the cuneiform character.[19]

His deep desire to excavate the mound prompted him to write a merchant friend in England suggesting that he furnish funds for excavating the site, and assured him that the antiquities discovered "would amply repay the expense." The merchant never replied, and thus failed to make a contribution to world scholarship.

Five years later, however, Sir Stratford Canning, British ambassador in Constantinople, did befriend Layard by providing funds to enable him to excavate the mound of Nimrud, which he thought might be as important as Khorsabad.

With money and authority, Layard lost no time, taking only twelve days to ride by horseback from Constantinople to Mosul, a distance of 350 miles. Through the agency of Rassam, the British vice-consul, he met Mohammed Pasha the Turkish governor of Mosul district. However, the governor was so slow in granting permission that on the eighth of November Layard boarded a native craft at Mosul and floated down the Tigris in company with Mr. Ross, a British resident merchant, a native stonemason and two servants. They had with them dogs, guns, spears, and other formidable weapons with which ostensibly, they would hunt wild boars, but they also had excavating tools which were not so plainly in sight.[20]

In the late evening of the same day they reached Nimrud, and became guests of a sheikh in a nearby village. On learning of their desire for workmen to assist them in digging into the mound, the sheikh, whose village was almost deserted because of recent trouble, went away to another village to secure the needed men. Anticipation of what the next few days held in store fired Layard's imagination and brought on a succession of half-waking dreams, of which he says:

Visions of palaces underground, of gigantic monsters, of sculptured figures, and endless inscriptions, floated before me. After forming plan after plan for removing the earth, and extricating these treasures, I fancied myself wandering in a maze of chambers from which I could find no outlet. Then again, all was re-buried, and I was standing on the grass-covered mound.[21]

At dawn the sheikh returned with six Arabs who were willing to work. Layard made a general survey of the mound and found that the city covered about a thousand acres, and had been laid out somewhat after the plan of Khorsabad, including a great platform upon which the palaces were built. He placed three of his workmen at a spot near the middle of the west side of the ruins, and the other three at the southwest corner. And although Layard and his men were without experience in excavating a city, yet before night interrupted their first day's labors, they had discovered and partly excavated two large rooms lined with alabaster slabs, all of which bore cuneiform inscriptions.

On the second morning he increased his force to eleven, and worked on with varying success. But his work was hindered, or stopped entirely at times, by credulous officials at Mosul. One morning Layard rode to the encampment of a neighboring sheikh, and was returning when he observed two Arab horsemen "urging their mares to the top of their speed." On approaching, one of them exclaimed, "Hasten, O Bey, hasten to the diggers for they have found Nimrod himself." On reaching the trenches he ascertained that the workmen had uncovered an enormous winged humanheaded lion, such as had been found by Botta at Khorsabad. Supposing it to be one of a pair, Layard measured the distance of what he supposed would be the width of a palace gateway, and by evening the workmen had cleared the rubbish from another lion of corresponding size. The two guarded the southern entrance to a gorgeous palace room. Unfortunately, "one of the workmen, on catching the first glimpse of the monster, had thrown down his basket and run off towards Mosul as fast as his legs could carry him. He had scarcely checked his speed before reaching the bridge. Entering breathless into the bazaars, he announced to every one he met that Nimrod had appeared." The news spread like wildfire. The Arab chief appeared with half his tribe and after cautious examination of the great man-headed lion, exclaimed,

This is not the work of man's hands but of those infidel giants of whom the Prophet (peace be with him) has said that they were higher than the tallest date tree. This is one of the idols which Noah (peace be with him) cursed before the flood.[22]

In a small temple nearby a statue of Ashurnasirpal II, about half life-size, was found, the only perfect statue of an Assyrian king now extant. By the end of March they had unearthed a second pair of winged human-headed lions, differing considerably in form from those previously found, but like the others covered with very fine cuneiform inscriptions. The winged lion was the emblem of Nergal, the deity which presided over the chase.

During the weeks that followed "scarcely a day passed without some new and important discovery" being made. In the south-west palace, which proved to be that of Esarhaddon, king of Assyria (680-669 B.C.), he found "a crouching lion in alabaster, a pair of winged lions in coarse limestone, the bodies of two lions carved out of one stone and forming a pedestal; the statues of two exquisite but crumbling sphinxes, and several interesting bas-reliefs" in which were united the head of an eagle or a lion with the body and arms of a man.

In the large royal reception hall of the northwest palace, he found a series of beautiful and most interesting sculptures glorifying King Ashurnasirpal (884-860 B.C.) in war and in peace. In realistic and well executed panels the king with his warriors is shown standing in a chariot and discharging death-dealing arrows while his enemies are tumbling from their horses or falling from the turrets of a besieged city; or in a boat crossing a river full of fish and lined with date palms and gardens; or, again, is shown receiving prisoners led by warriors and counted by scribes; and is then shown returning victoriously in procession, followed by his army and preceded by musicians and standard bearers.

Among the rubbish in nearby rooms Layard found large quantities of Assyrian armor and several copper helmets that gave essence to the sculptures on the wall. In other rooms he found glass and alabaster bottles, bearing the name and titles of Sargon II who had at one time resided here.

In all, Layard unearthed three palaces: Palace of Ashur-nasirpal, palace of Shalmaneser III and the palace of Esarhad-don. In the central building he found in an orderly record room over one hundred sculptured slabs "packed in rows, one against the other, and placed in a regular series, according to the subjects upon them." On these slabs were inscribed the annals of Tiglath Pileser III (744-727 B.C.), whom the Bible calls "Pul." The Biblical records in II Kings 15:19,20 says:

And Pul the King of Assyria came against the land; and Menahem gave Pul a thousand talents of silver, that his hand might be with him to confirm the Kingdom in his hand. And Menahem exacted the money of Israel, even of all the mighty men of wealth, of each man fifty shekels of silver, to give to the king of Assyria. So the king of Assyria turned back and stayed not there in the land.

In his annals, carved on the slabs, Tiglath Pileser III says:

I received tribute from . . . Rezin of Damascus, Menahem of Samaria, Hiram of Tyre, . . . Sibittibili of Byblos, and Zabibe, the queen of Arabia, (to wit) gold, silver, tin, iron, elephant-hides, ivory, linen garments with multi-colored trimmings, blue-dyed wool, purple-dyed wool, ebony wool, boxwood-wool, whatever was precious enough for a royal treasure; also lambs whose stretched hides were dyed purple, and wild birds whose spread out wings were dyed blue, furthermore, horses, mules, large and small cattle, male camels, female camels with their foals.[23]

Further on in his annals, he speaks of another trip to Palestine and says:

As for Menahem, I overwhelmed him like a snow-storm and he fled like a bird alone, and bowed to my feet. I returned him to his place and imposed tribute upon him.

In another portion of this central palace building Layard located a brick on which was inscribed the genealogy of the builder, Shalmaneser III. Pushing his trenches on, he found slabs with gigantic winged figures, and fragments of a large winged bull in yellow limestone, then the trench lengthened fifty feet without yielding anything of any value, and the excavator was making ready to abandon his researches in that part of the building, when his workmen encountered the corner of a black stone, and soon uncovered the now famous "Black Obelisk" of Shalmaneser III (858-824 B.C.), which he had erected within his palace. It was a four-sided pillar of black marble, six feet and six inches tall, and tapering at the top. It had twenty small bas-reliefs—five on each side—showing the officials from five different countries bringing tribute to the king. Above, below, and between the reliefs were 210 lines of cuneiform inscription which briefly tell the story of the monarch's achievements in war and peace during the first thirty-one years of his reign. Among other individuals it mentions Hazael of Damascus and Jehu of Israel. On the obelisk Shalmaneser says:

In the eighteenth year of my reign I crossed the Euphrates for the sixteenth time. Hazael of Damascus put his trust in his large army, and mustered his troops in great numbers, making Mount Senir (sa-ni-ru), facing the Lebanon, as his fortress. I fought with him and inflicted defeat upon him, killing with the sword 16,000 of his experienced soldiers. I took away from him 1,121 chariots, 470 riding horses as well as his camp. He disappeared to save his life, but I followed him in Damascus, his royal residence. There I cut down his gardens outside the city and took my departure. I marched as far as Mount Hauran destroying, tearing down and burning innumerable towns, carrying booty away from them which was beyond counting. I then marched as far as the mountains of Ba'lira'si, by the sea-side, and erected there a stela with my image as King. At that time I received the tribute of the inhabitants of Tyre, Sideon, and of Jehu, son of Omri.

Then, later, comes the section which is of even greater interest to the Bible student. It reads:

The tribute of Jehu, son of Omri: I received from him silver, gold, a golden bowl, a golden vase with pointed bottom, golden goblets, pictures of gold, bars of lead, staffs for the hand of the King, and javelins, I received.[24]

Jehu is shown kneeling with tribute, in front of Shalmaneser. The Assyrian monarch is accompanied by two attendants, one holding a sunshade above him, and stands proudly, with the symbols of Ashur and Ishtar in the area above. King Jehu of Israel wears a short, rounded beard, a soft leather cap, and a sleeveless jacket, which marks him as a prisoner. Following him come Israelites dressed in long garments, and carrying precious metals and other tribute. This relief is exceedingly important, seeing it is the only sculptured relief we have of any Israelite king.

Layard realized the value of the black obelisk, therefore carefully packed it, and guarded it by night until shortly thereafter on Christmas day 1846, with twenty-two other cases of antiquities, it was sent to Rawlinson who carefully copied all inscriptions, then sent it on to London, where it is now one of the choicest possessions of the British Museum.

In 1952 the British School of Archaeology and the New York Metropolitan Museum of Art sponsored an expedition to continue digging in the mound of Nimrud. Among the objects they discovered was a five-foot slab decorated with King Ashurnasirpal's portrait, and inscribed with the king's own narrative of his military campaigns, his building operations, and the fabulous feast he gave in the year 879 B.C. when he dedicated the city to his god Ashur. D. J. Wiseman of the British Museum translated the stone inscription, and M. E. L. Mallowan, the expedition's leader, transposed it into colloquial English.

NINEVEH

Nineveh, the famed capital of the ancient Assyrian empire and all that is implied in the glories of a mighty armed monarchy, was located 280 miles north of Babylon, on the eastern bank of the Tigris and on a fertile sloping plain just across from modern Mosul.

Biblical history has been so profoundly affected by Nineveh that mention is made of the city or its country from Genesis to Revelation. The entire Books of Jonah and Nahum have to do either directly or indirectly with the city. Its beginnings milleniums ago were very simple, but by the ninth century B.C. it had grown powerful, and thereafter served as the mighty stage on which was enacted a perennial play that time and again brought the principal players "from rags to riches," and then to the grave. The players were kings, priests, soldiers, and the people of Nineveh and its many suburbs and sister cities. The dramatic play arose and subsided in intensity for almost three hundred years, then its accumulated riches, its debaucheries, its revelings, its cruelty, and the curse of God took its final toll in 612 B.C. and Nineveh, "the Robber City," with all its host was defeated—killed by a coalition of forces led by the Medes and the Babylonians. With the ending of the tragic play, the city with all its grandeur lay buried beneath a covering of its own debris and the dust of the decades that slowly obliterated the plainer marks of its once vigorous life.

Only 200 years after its fall Xenophon and his 10,000 Greeks fought their way through the wilderness, passing the ruins of Nineveh without mentioning her name. One hundred years later, Alexander the Great fought a battle nearby and apparently did not realize that he was so near ancient Nineveh.

How truly had the words of the prophet **Nahum** been fulfilled:

And he . . . will make Nineveh a desolation and **dry like a wilderness,**
And flocks shall lie down in the midst of her . . . **both the cormorant**

and the bittern shall lodge in the upper lintels of it; their voice shall sing in the windows; desolation shall be in the thresholds. . . .[25]

In A.D. 1575 a German physician by the name of Leonhard Rauwolff spent several days in the vicinity and after noting that the mound covering the ancient site was honeycombed, portions of it being inhabited by poor people, he speculated that in this region Nineveh had been situated centuries before. In 1820 Claudius Rich carefully examined the mound, located a few inscribed bricks, and indentified the mound as that of Nineveh. In 1842 Botta carried forward his exploratory work on the mound for three months, but with meager results.

In the spring of 1845 Layard visited Mosul and acquired rights to excavate Nineveh. In his preliminary surveys of the mound he found that the east wall measured 16,000 feet in length, the north wall 7,000 feet, the west wall 13,600 feet, and the south wall 3,000 feet. The entire circuit of the ruined walls was 39,600 feet, or seven and one-half miles. Within this 1800-acre enclosure were many swells and mounds. There were two mounds, however, that lay close to the remains of the great west wall and stood out above all others. The southern mound was one hundred feet high, covered forty acres, and was known by the natives as "Nebi Yunis" (The Prophet Jonah). "For," said they, "the prophet Jonah preached repentance and was buried there." The north mound was ninety feet high, covered one hundred acres, and was called "Kuyunjik" (The Castle of Nineveh).[26]

With his workmen, Layard cut tentative trenches into the north mound of Kuyunjik, then halted the work and returned to the excavation at Nimrud. In July of the same year while on vacation he returned to Nineveh and brought to light a gateway flanked by two mutilated winged lions, and a wall on which was inscribed, in cuneiform characters, the name of Sennacherib. Again he returned to Nimrud.

A year later Layard returned to Nineveh with his expanded knowledge of the nature and position of Assyrian palaces, and with Rassam as his overseer and general agent, and with a large crew of workmen, extended his trenches in various directions. After four weeks' work he had laid bare many proofs of a large building partly destroyed at one time by fire. Many large and wonderful bas-reliefs, winged bulls, and inscriptions were unveiled, and at last, its writing disclosed to Layard that he had been privileged to discover the first Assyrian palace of the lost city of Nineveh. The palace had belonged to Sennacherib, one of the greatest of the monarchs of ancient times.

Sennacherib was the son of Sargon II who had reigned and lived so lavishly in his impressive palace at Khorsabad. When his father was killed, Sennacherib ascended the throne but chose to make the Khorsabad palace a place of secondary importance. Desiring to build for his own glory, Sennacherib chose Nineveh to be his capital and launched his career as a builder, a warrior, and a patron of letters. Under his supervision and lavish expenditure of money and manpower, Nineveh blossomed into beauty and greater splendor than she had ever known.

The walls surrounding his city were impressive bastions of security, thought by many to be impregnable. These were pierced by fifteen gates, which connected the main city with a considerable metropolitan area and led out to the nearby daughter cities that made up greater Nineveh. Fresh water was brought by aqueduct through hills and over plains from a clear stream thirty miles away.

Sennacherib's royal palace was extensive, commodious, and most profusely adorned with meaningful and impressive art work. It stood on an eight-acre brick-paved platform ninety feet above the level of the city. Lofty flights of marble steps led up to all four sides where each of the magnificent entrances were ornamented by five pairs of human-headed bulls, lions, and other colossal figures. The principal approach was on the eastern side, where the gigantic winged bulls bore on their bodies the cuneiform inscribed annals of King Sennacherib.

From the two chief entrances immense halls 40 feet wide and 180 feet long led to the interior of the palace, which contained many grand courts and no less than seventy or eighty spacious rooms, all of which were elegantly adorned with sculptures in relief.

In describing his experiences in uncovering this palace from its dusty grave, Layard wrote:

In this magnificent edifice I opened no less than seventy-one halls, chambers, and passages, whose walls, almost without exception, had been panelled with slabs of sculptured alabaster recording the wars, the triumphs, and the great deeds of the Assyrian king. By a rough calculation, about 9880 feet, or nearly two miles, of bas-reliefs, with twenty-seven portals, formed by colossal winged bulls and lion-sphinxes, were uncovered in that part alone of the buildings explored during my researches.[27]

On the northern wall of the great hall of the palace, Layard found very wonderful paneled relief pictures representing the actual construction of the city of Nineveh and the palace of the king. The platform upon which the palace was built was seen in the process of construction by skilled workmen, aided by war prisoners. In another picture a gang of workmen were seen dragging into position a human-headed winged bull colossus almost completely carved, while the royal guard, with their shields and spears and crested helmets stood watch. Another picture represented the workmen in the process of transporting a partly carved human-headed lion from the quarry to the palace.

These colossal winged bulls weighing from ten to thirty tons each and huge lion-sphinxes were used quite extensively. No less than twenty-seven portals formed by these bulls and sphinxes were found in one part of the palace alone.

In an inscription connected with these pictures the king tells of his construction activity:

Sennacherib, king of the universe, king of Assyria: white limestone, which at the command of the god was discovered in the land of Baladi, for the construction of my palace, the people of enemy towns and the men of remote mountain (districts), the conquest of my hand, with iron picks and pickaxes quarried, and I turned it into mighty protecting bull-colossi, for the gates of my palace.[28]

Great beams and framework, bronze, gold, silver, jewels, ivory boards, elephant skins, and other precious woods, stones, and metals were used by the monarch in his magnificent residence.

On seeing the remains of the palace Ferguson observed that,

. . . . The imperial palace of Sennacherib is, of all the buildings of antiquity, surpassed in magnitude only by the great palace-temple of Karnak;

and when we consider the vastness of the mount on which it was raised, and the richness of the ornaments with which it was adorned, it is by no means clear that it was not as great, or at least as expensive a work as the great palace-temple at Thebes.[29]

When in its glory, this royal palace was a veritable art gallery, on whose walls were faithfully portrayed in relief the national, religious, and domestic life of the people of Nineveh, as well as the natural history and topography of the country. The sculptors transferred to these alabaster walls scenes of lofty mountains covered with trees and broad flowing rivers filled with fish, extended plains, spreading palms, gardens wherein were fruitful trees and blooming flowers, and superb horses led by grooms. There were battle scenes and triumphal processions in which the king and his armies returned home bringing their captives of war and laden with riches taken in foreign lands. These sculptured panoramas revealed hunting scenes, religious ceremonies, modes of navigation, implements of agriculture, household furniture, musical instruments, festive scenes, along with a wide variety of foods, and many styles of cooking.

But Sennacherib's fame did not rest only on his architectural ability. As king of Assyria and a powerful ruler, his name is found in Hebrew, Assyrian, and Grecian annals. Much more is learned of him and his exploits, however, from the vivid pictures that lined the walls of his palace, and from three separate inscribed annals from his own royal archives found during the excavation.

The first of these annals consists of extensive records inscribed on the man-headed winged bulls that "protected" and ornamented the east entrance to the palace. These tell the story of Sennacherib's experiences over a period of six years. The second is inscribed on a large barrel-shaped terra-cotta cylinder, embracing two years. The third is a six-sided, baked clay cylinder, giving in cuneiform script an account of Sennacherib's eight campaigns, including the capture and destruction of the city of Babylon in 689 B.C., and his great drive down the east coast of the Mediterranean toward Egypt in 701 B.C. Special emphasis is laid on his treatment of the cities of the Philistines, his invasion of Judea, and the siege of Jerusalem, in which Hezekiah and Isaiah were involved.

In certain instances some allowance must be made for his boastings, but in the main the records of his exploits are well verified, and add much to our knowledge of Middle Eastern affairs.

The Biblical account of Sennacherib's invasion of Judah and siege of Jerusalem as given in II Kings 18:13-19 and Isaiah 36-37 can now be supplemented by the records of Sennacherib, in describing what he did in the land of Judah. Here is Sennacherib's own story as inscribed in his annals:

The officials, nobles and people of Ekron, who had thrown Padi, their king, bound by (treaty to) Assyria, into fetters of iron and had given him over to Hezekiah, the Jew—he kept him in confinement like an enemy—they became afraid and called upon the Egyptian kings, the bowmen, chariots and horses of the king of Meluhha (Ethiopia), a countless host, and these came to their aid. . . . As for Hezekiah, the Jew, who did not submit to my yoke, 46 of his strong, walled cities, as well as the small cities in their neighborhood, which were without number, by escalade and by bringing up siege engines, by attacking and storming on foot, by mines, tunnels and breaches, I besieged and took. 200,150 people great and small, male and female, horses, mules, asses, camels, cattle and sheep without number, I brought away from them and counted as spoil. *Himself, like a caged bird, I shut up in Jerusalem, his royal city.* Earthworks I threw up against him, and I took vengeance upon any man who came forth from his city.[30]

The account goes on to list the tribute King Hezekiah gave to Sennacherib. Among other things it mentions 30 talents of gold and 800 talents of silver (approximately $1,500,000). In II Kings 18:14 the amount of tribute is given as 30 talents of gold and 300 talents of silver. The difference between 800 and 300 talents of silver is accounted for by some authorities by the difference "in weight between the Babylonian *light,* and the Palestinian *heavy* talent." On the other hand it could be that, as some think, the exaggerated claims of the Assyrian "war bulletins" are corrected by the Biblical account.

The siege and storming of the city of Lachish during Sennacherib's campaign in Judah, is graphically pictured on the walls of the king's palace in Nineveh. From this picture we know pretty well how the battle proceeded. Seated upon his throne in the hilly districts of southern Palestine, and surrounded by his formidable army, is the Assyrian king, attired in his richly embroidered robes. All about the walls of the nearby city fighting is going on. From stone-paved embankments battering rams are operated. Expert spearmen, slingers and archers attack with vigor, while other soldiers are undermining the walls and arrows and torches are being rained upon the besiegers. A portion of the city has been taken. Beneath the walls are seen Assyrian warriors impaling their prisoners or flaying them alive, while from a gateway of a tower issues a long procession of captives, camels and carts laden with women and children and spoil, advancing toward the monarch. Above the head of the king are inscribed the words:

Sennacherib King of the Universe, King of Assyria, sat upon a throne and reviewed the spoil of the city of Lachish.[31]

When all of the account given by Sennacherib concerning his campaign against Judah is considered, together with the picture of the attack on Lachish, the agreements with the Scriptural story of what happened are striking.

Sennacherib gives the number of Palestinian cities he captures, and rather carefully lists the spoil, but merely says that he shut up Hezekiah "like a caged bird," and gives no reason for his not having captured Jerusalem, nor does he mention disaster having befallen his army which caused his hasty retreat without having gained decisive victory. The Biblical narrative admits the cities captured and the spoil taken, but explains in considerable detail how Sennacherib, while encamped at Lachish, sent a detachment of troops and messengers bearing a letter in which he discounted Judah's strength, ridiculed their confidence in Egypt, and scorned their trust in Jehovah. It tells how this letter was spread before Jehovah, and how King Hezekiah and the prophet Isaiah "prayed and cried to Heaven" and how that night,

. . . The angel of the Lord went forth, and smote in the camp of the Assyrians a hundred and fourscore and five thousand; and when they arose early in the morning, behold, they were all dead corpses. . . . So he returned with shame of face to his land.[32]

The great royal Assyrian warrior merely related those things which would make a good story and omitted that portion of the story which would not have been particularly to his credit. In further detail, the Biblical account says:

So Sennacherib king of Assyria departed, and went and returned, and dwelt at Nineveh. And it came to pass, as he was worshipping in the house of Nisroch his god, that Adrammelech and Sharezer his sons smote him with the sword: and they escaped into the land of Armenia. And Esarhaddon his son reigned in his stead.[33]

That portion of Nineveh known as Nebi Yunis, 900 yards south of the Kuyunjik site, interested Layard, but it was forbidden ground for excavation, seeing it was surmounted by the supposed sacred tomb of the prophet Jonah. However, through one of his native overseers, Layard contracted to dig some underground summer apartments for a Moslem who owned a home on the mound. As remuneration he was to retain all the antiquities discovered during the excavation. The few days he and Rassam dug proved profitable because they unearthed portions of Esarhaddon's palace, and obtained a large baked clay six-sided cylinder inscribed with the Annals of Esarhaddon, king of Assyria from 680-669 B.C.

This splendid cylinder, along with others found elsewhere, confirm and supplement the Biblical records. From them we learn that on December 20, 681 B.C. Sennacherib was murdered by his two elder sons, Adrammelech and Nergal-Sharezer, because of their jealousy of the favors shown Esarhaddon, their younger brother. Esarhaddon was at the time conducting a military campaign against Erimenas, king of Armenia. The two brothers fled to Armenia and joined forces with Erimenas. Some seven or eight weeks later a battle was fought near Malatiyeh, in Cappadocia, between the armies of Esarhaddon and the forces under his brothers and Erimenas. Esarhaddon won a complete and decisive victory, after which his army proclaimed him king of Assyria. At the head of his victorious armies he led a triumphal march into Nineveh where he was received with joy and great rejoicing. In part, the inscribed account reads:

In the month of Nisan. . . . I made my joyful entrance into the royal palace, the awesome place wherein abides the fate of kings. A firm determination fell upon my brothers. They forsook the gods and turned to their deeds of violence, plotting evil. . . . . They revolted. To gain the kingship they slew Sennacherib, their father. . . . The gods looked with disfavor upon the deed of the villains, which was committed in defiance of the will of the gods, and did not aid them.

I rent my garments, and raised a cry. I roared like a lion, my passion was aroused. . . . I made my way to Nineveh painfully but quickly . . . the people of Assyria . . . kissed my feet.

As for those villains who instigated revolt . . . they fled to parts unknown.[34]

After his triumphal entry, Esarhaddon remained in Nineveh only a few days, then marched southward to Babylon where he brought under control certain rebellious elements and then restored the city his father had destroyed. He rebuilt the walls, raised the temple of Bel, had the images of the gods returned, led back the people from captivity, and restored much of the wealth his father had carried away. Having thus conciliated the people, he proclaimed himself king of Babylon, as well as of Assyria. To aid in consolidating and establishing his kingdom, he constructed palaces for himself at Nineveh, Nimrud, and Babylon. He held court alternately at Nineveh and Babylon.

Esarhaddon was always shown wearing a curly beard. He was aggressive, industrious, politically alert, on occasions humane, yet, withall, a thorough-going warrior sufficiently versed in ruthlessness to permit him to destroy cities and lead vanquished kings back to his courts by cords through nose-rings.[35]

In his annals, he tells of successful military campaigns in Armenia, Media, Arabia, Syria, and Egypt, and of tribute collected from peoples of many nations. Esarhaddon is mentioned in Ezra 4:2 as having sent people to supplement the colony of Samaria. He rebuilt the temple of Ashur at Nineveh, and restored many temples in Babylonia. In Damascus, the capital of Syria, he established the worship of the heavenly bodies. And, it came about that Manasseh, king of Judah, whom Esarhaddon mentions as a vassal, copied the king of Assyria, and "built altars for the host of heaven in the two courts of the house of the Lord" at Jerusalem, and instituted the false worship there. Later, when Manasseh displeased Esarhaddon, he had him put in chains and brought to stand trial and be sentenced at his

winter court in Babylon. The chronicler, in writing of King
Manasseh, says:

. . . The captains of the host of the king of Assyria, which took Manasseh among the thorns, and bound him with fetters, and carried him to
Babylon.[36]

Subsequently when Manasseh bowed low in abject repentance
to God and was thoroughly converted, Esarhaddon restored him
to his kingdom in Judea.

On April 12, 669 B.C., while on his way to Egypt, Esarhaddon
died and Ashurbanipal, the eldest of his four sons, was elevated
to the Assyrian throne.

One day in the spring of 1851, while Layard and Rassam continued the excavations in the area of Sennacherib's great palace,
they made an unusually significant discovery. All during their
excavations, cuneiform tablets, or fragments of them had been
coming to light, but on this occasion the excavators came upon
two large rooms opening into each other. While removing the
rubbish from these rooms Layard noticed that "to the height
of a foot or more from the floor they were entirely filled with
cuneiform tablets of baked clay." Many of the tablets were
complete, but a far larger number of them had been broken
into fragments, probably by the falling in of the roof and
upper parts of the walls of the buildings when the city was
pillaged and set on fire by the Medes and Babylonians.

The two rooms in which these tablets were found proved
to be a part of the Temple of Nebo, adjoining Sennacherib's
palace. The inscribed tablets or clay-books formed a part of
the royal library collected by royalty and dedicated to Nebo,
the divine scribe who had "invented the arts and sciences"
and understood "all the mysteries connected with literature
and the art of writing." These thousands of volumes made a
valuable contribution to the British Museum. When they arrived many were still intact and others could be pieced together from scattered fragments.

In April 1851 Layard was obliged to close his excavations
at Nineveh for want of funds. Leaving the northern half of
the great mound of Kuyunjik unexcavated he packed and
shipped more than a hundred and twenty portable cases of

Assyrian finds, and "with a heavy heart" at leaving an unfinished task, he and Rassam turned their backs on the great mound of Nineveh, and returned to England. Layard soon resigned his position as director of the excavations at Nineveh and turned his attention to writing.

Within two years he was able to submit the total results of his researches in the form of two publications, *Discoveries in the Ruins of Nineveh,* and *The Monuments of Nineveh.* The public was thrilled, and he was acclaimed for his contribution in research and accorded the official recognition his work so well merited by being appointed ambassador to Constantinople.

During the summer of 1852 the trustees of the British Museum received a further grant of funds from Parliament for explorations in Assyria. They at once sent Hormuzd Rassam back to the Middle East to continue the excavations at Nineveh.

On arriving in Mosul, Rassam collected his men and organized his forces, only to discover that Rawlinson, who did not understand the nature of the lease held by Layard and Rassam, had given Victor Place permission to dig at Nineveh. Place's men were already at work on the northern half of the mound —the very portion of the mound that Rassam was most anxious to excavate for the British Museum. Rassam protested, but in vain. When he saw that Place intended to hold Rawlinson to his word, he and his men devoted their efforts to clearing out part of the southwest palace he and Layard had previously attacked but had not finished. Then, during the following year, when Victor Place became involved in excavations elsewhere, and Rassam's time for returning to England was drawing near, he grew desperate and decided to excavate the northern part of the mound secretly and by night. Therefore, on the night of December 20, 1853, when the moon was full and shone at its best, Rassam, with the help of a few trustworthy workmen, began to dig in what he considered the most promising spot of the whole mound.

On the first night they came upon indications of an ancient building, in the rubbish of which they found "painted bricks and pieces of marble on which there were signs of inscriptions and bas-reliefs." On the second night he located the bottom of a slab on which he recognized the feet of Assyrian soldiers and captives. On the third night he increased the number of his men and they dug for hours in an ascending passage leading into a great building. After entering the building they were digging a deep trench in a very great wall on which was carved a very large and beautiful bas-relief of King Ashurbanipal standing in a chariot, about to start on a hunting expedition, and his attendants handing him the necessary weapons for the chase. In another scene the excitement of the chase was shown as the king and his attendants were spearing the lions. In great astonishment the excavator and workmen stared at one of the most realistic and enchanting sculptured reliefs ever produced by Assyrian art.

On the following days Rassam and his men cleared the "lion-hunt" gallery and followed through its doorways into an adjoining high vaulted room. In wide areas of both the long gallery-like rooms they found the floors stacked high with thousands of priceless clay tablets. These proved to be a large portion of Ashurbanipal's royal library.

Two years before, in the nearby Temple of Nebo, Layard had found the vast library that must have been in existence from the time of Sargon, but the library found by Rassam was the creation of King Ashurbanipal. In his youth Ashurbanipal had access to the great royal library in the University Temple of Nebo, and by his teachers was taught to read and write in the various languages. As he stated it:

I, Ashur-bani-pal, within the palace, learned the wisdom of Nebo, the entire art of writing on clay tablets of every kind. I made myself master of the various kinds of writing. . . . I read the beautiful clay tablets from Sumer and the Akkadian writing, which is hard to master. I had the joy of reading inscriptions on stone from the time before the flood.[37]

So great was Ashurbanipal's interest in literature and scholarly pursuits, that on coming to the throne he quickly quelled an uprising in Egypt, conquered Lydia and Persia, then after consolidating his kingdom, gave himself to scholarly pursuits until he became the most powerful and enlightened monarch of his time, and one of the world's greatest patrons of literature. He sent learned scribes to Ashur, Babylon, Cuthah, Nippur, Akkad, Erech and other strategic centers throughout his vast empire where they collected and copied clay books of astrology, history, grammar, geography, literature, law, and medicine, together with letters, prayers, poems, hymns, incantations, oracles, dictionaries, chronicles, deeds of sales of land, business contracts and law records, and scores of other subjects of general and specific interest. All these were brought to Ashurbanipal's palace at Nineveh where he not only studied and collated them, but in many cases had fresh clay tablets made on which bilingual copies were inscribed in uniform script and filed away in methodical fashion "for the instruction of the people of Nineveh." When complete, his library contained something near 100,000 copies—one of the greatest and most valuable of all ancient times. The great gallery rooms in which the library was found proved to have been the king's private library and picture gallery. And they were only a part of the royal palace of the brilliant king.

Rassam should have had a full year, further financial support, and the aid of a European supervisor to make possible adequate exploration of the beautiful and famous palace, which was "a precious storehouse of historical documents and works of art." As it was, he had only three months time, a dwindling purse, and a flying visit from Rawlinson who viewed the new wonders, selected a number of slabs for the British Museum, and offered a few instructions regarding the manner in which the priceless tablets should be packed for shipping.

Rassam crated up the tablets, along with a tall terra-cotta prism inscribed with the annals of the king's reign—which he had found in a section of a nearby wall—and sent them to the British Museum, where they arrived in 1854. When reckoned with the tablets and documents from the Temple of Nebo, already sent from Nineveh by Layard, they numbered around 26,000, with other thousands of fragments. These tablets varied in size from less than an inch square for very short contracts to as much as fifteen by eight and a half inches for the longer documents.

A considerable number of these tablets were translated by Rawlinson while on his extended trips to London, but the main credit for their classification and translation belongs to George Smith (1840-76). As a boy, Smith was deeply interested in the study of the Bible, especially the historical books of the Old Testament. He read Layard's and Rawlinson's books, and spent considerable time studying in the British Museum. His zeal attracted the attention of S. Birch, assistant in the Department of Antiquities. At first he became a "repairer," but soon read the cuneiform script with such ease that he was made an assistant in Birch's department. Then, in 1866 the trustees of the British Museum employed Smith to assist Rawlinson in sorting, classifying and rejoining the tablets and fragments of the two libraries of Nebo and Ashurbanipal. The reduction of these tablets to some sort of order was mainly Smith's work, yet his personal interest in Assyriology was centered upon historical texts, especially those that threw any light on the Bible narratives. In the course of his search for stories of the campaigns of Sargon, Sennacherib, Esarhaddon and Ashurbanipal he found much that thrilled him as his understanding of the Bible was increased.

In 1872, while engaged in "sorting and joining" fragments of these broken tablets from the Nineveh libraries, he noticed pieces containing portions of mythical stories. Placing these to themselves, he continued his search until he had accumulated a fairly large pile which he labeled "Legends and Mythology." Then turning his attention to this pile, he says:

Commencing a steady search among these fragments, I soon found half a curious tablet which had evidently contained originally six columns. . . . On looking down the third column, my eye caught the statement that the ship rested on the mountains of Nizir, followed by the account of sending forth of the dove, and its finding no resting place and returning. I saw at once that I had here discovered a portion at least of the Chaldean account of the Deluge.[38]

The discovery made such a profound impression on him that he stepped up his researches; doubling his efforts, he gathered his materials, and reduced the results into a most excellent paper which he read before the Society of Biblical Archaeology on December 3, 1872. The distinguished audience included such noted men as Mr. Gladstone and Dean Stanley and the proprietor of the London Daily Telegraph. They were so thrilled by the discovery that the Daily Telegraph offered a sum of £1,000 ($5,000) to equip an expedition for the purpose of finding the missing fragments, providing that Smith himself would take charge of the investigation by going to Nineveh in person and searching for the fragments of the tablets that would fill up the gaps in his texts. He was to send accounts of his work to the Daily Telegraph.

Smith accepted the offer and the Museum gave him six months leave of absence. He left London in January of 1873, arrived in Mosul in March, and by May began his search in the ruins of Ashurbanipal's Palace at Nineveh. While digging a trench through the rubble thrown out by the previous excavations he found quite a few tablets and many tablet fragments. On the evening of the fifth day he had the good fortune to find the missing parts of the Deluge tablet for which he had come so far.

I sat down to examine the store of fragments of cuneiform inscriptions from the day's digging, taking out and brushing off the earth from the fragments to read their contents. On cleaning one of them I found to my surprise and gratification that it contained the greater portion of the seventeen lines of inscription belonging to the first column of the Chaldean account of the Deluge, and fitting into the only place where there was a serious blank in the story.[39]

Having completed his mission for the Daily Telegraph, Smith crated up the tablets he had discovered and soon returned to London. The following year he made a second trip to Nineveh under the auspices of the British Museum and secured more tablets. But he was not very successful as a field excavator because he understood neither Oriental ways nor the climate. On a third trip, in 1876, he found it impossible to resume excavations in the height of summer heat, and so set out to return with the tablets he had purchased from dealers. Being without adequate nourishment and subjected to the intense heat of the sun, he was seized by dysentery and died at Aleppo. Before his decease, however, he had recovered 384 fragments of clay tablets, arranged all the necessary fragments to complete both the Creation and the Deluge tablets, and in 1876 was able to publish his *Chaldean Account of Genesis*.

The story of the Flood, as found and translated by Smith was written on the eleventh tablet of the great Gilgamesh epic. This tablet contains 205 lines, and relates the supposed adventures of Gilgamesh, the ruler of Erech. He was afflicted with a dread disease, and had a great desire to consult his ancestor Ut-napishtim, who dwelt far away in an immortal state. His desire was so great and urgent that he sailed for one month and fifteen days on the waters of death until he reached the far-off land and met his revered ancestor, and prayed for aid and advice. He also asked Ut-napishtim "how he happened to be removed alive to the assembly of the gods." Ut-napishtim, who corresponds with Noah, then relates the story of the Deluge as it appears in the Assyrian account from the library of Ashurbanipal.[40] Just how old it was when Ashurbanipal's scribes copied it from the Babylonian records it is impossible to say. But there are so many resemblances to the Biblical story of Noah and the Flood and so many events are duplicated that to many scholars these Babylonian and Assyrian accounts merely constitute two more witnesses that such a disaster did overwhelm the earth.

As early as 1870, while searching through and sorting tablets from the Nebo and Ashurbanipal libraries in the British Museum, Smith found an allusion to the Creation on a fragment of a tablet. More of the missing tablets and fragments on this subject were located by him during his expeditions to Nineveh in 1873-74, and yet others came to light when he again searched in the British Museum. When assembled they formed the Babylonian Epic of Creation. The story, written in poetic form, was entitled *Enuma elish* (When Above), which was taken from the two opening words of the poem. It was written on seven clay tablets and consisted of one thousand lines. The tablets dated from about the seventh century B.C., but were based on a very ancient text which seems to have been written near 2000 B.C. or earlier.

The first of the seven tablets told of the primeval ocean mass when there were no heavens (firmament) and no earth, but only chaos, and of the coming of certain gods and of their conflict. The second and third tablets told of a conference of the gods and their choice of Marduk as their champion. Tablet four gave a graphic description of a terrific conflict of the major gods and how Marduk slew the goddess Tiamat and out of her body fashioned the heavens and the earth. The fifth tablet gave an account of the creation of the stars, the establishment of the year, which was divided into twelve months, and the appointment of the moon to rule the night. The sixth tablet told of the creation of man and represented this as the culminating act in the creation of the universe. The seventh tablet recorded the celebration of the gods as they sang the praises of Marduk.

Very little of the story coincided with our account of creation as it is given in Genesis, yet it was only the first of many such stories to be found over the world. Some would come nearer the Genesis account than did this Babylonian poem.

ASHUR

Some sixty miles south of Mosul, at a place now called Kalat Shergat, are the ruins of Ashur, an early metropolis and first of the four capitals of the mighty Assyrian empire. The city was named after the god Ashur, and was strategically located on a picturesque mound on the west bank of the Tigris, overlooking a great depression through which the river ran.

On the highest point of the hill is the lofty ziggurat or "great mountain house" shrine of Ashur, whom the Assyrians came to worship as their chief god. For over 2000 years this temple tower has kept its watch over the ruins of what was once a populous city and beautifully wooded countryside, but what is now a refuge for jackals and beasts of the field.

Ainsworth, Rassam, Layard and other famous research men visited the site and described it as being as large and extensive as Nimrud and Nineveh and to be "a place of rendezvous for all plundering parties." [41]

Layard's curiosity was excited by a current tradition among the Arabs that "strange figures carved in black stone" still existed among the ruins. He therefore sent a few Arab workmen down the river to begin excavations at certain promising points. Shortly afterward he spent two days directing the workmen as they dug on the western side of the mound where they brought to light a much damaged yet quite interesting life-size black basalt statue covered on three sides with a cuneiform inscription of Shalmaneser II. They also found inscribed bricks, portions of boundary stones, "fragments of slabs with cuneiform characters, and a few tombs with their usual contents belonging to a late period." Being obliged to return to Nimrud, Layard endeavored to have the researches continued under the supervision of a Nestorian Christian, but repeated attacks from the Bedouins soon forced his workmen to withdraw. The black-basalt sitting statue was later sent to London.

Place did some work on the site, and in 1853 Rassam was probing the mound when Rawlinson sent a message advising him to look for the "corner stone" contents at the base of the ziggurat of the shrine of the patron god Ashur. Rassam did so, and found two foundation tablets of Tiglath Pileser I (1110-1103 B.C.), which not only told of the erection of the temple in 1820 B.C. and of its being rebuilt by Tiglath Pileser, but gave an account of his campaigns, and definitely identified the site as that of Ashur.

However, nothing but casual and sporadic digging took place at Ashur until 1903 when the Germans were granted a concession to excavate the site. Robert Koldewey saw the expedition well under way, then went away to Babylon and the digging continued for many years in a very methodical manner under the direction of Walter Andrae. They found that the city site had been occupied continuously from the early part of the third millenium B.C. down to Parthian times, after which it declined into obscurity. One city after another had crumbled away and another built over it. The periods of greater prosperity had been "in the nineteenth century B.C. under Shamsiadad I, in the thirteenth under Adadnirari I, Shalmaneser I, and Tu-kulti-Ninurta I, in the twelfth and eleventh under Tiglath Pileser I, and in the ninth under Shalmaneser III." [42]

The tombs and sarcophagi of several of the later kings were uncovered, but were found to have been previously spoiled by tomb robbers. At various levels the Germans were fortunate in discovering tablet and wall inscriptions. They gathered quantities of pottery, traced the plans of ancient temples, shrines, palaces, streets and fortifications. In a triangular space, between the inner and outer southern wall of the city, they found a row of steles or sculptured and inscribed pillars of the kings of Assyria from Adadnirari I to Ashurbanipal, and a parallel row of many provincial governors. On one of these was a record of Sammuramat, daughter of Shalmaneser, wife of Shamsiadad V, and mother of Adadnirari IV, the original of the romantic legendary Semiramis.

Perhaps we shall never know all the Germans found in the

great mound of Ashur, for the fate of war decreed considerable irregularity both in handling the finds and in their publication. At the outbreak of the First World War in 1914 the Germans crated up large consignments of objects from the mound, and started with them to Germany by sea. They successfully passed through the Mediterranean, and were out on the Atlantic, when to avoid capture they put into Lisbon where the antiquities were impounded. After the war they were ceded to Germany. Andrae made many reports on the finds, but complete and adequate publications were never made.

NUZI

During the early twenties of this century peculiar cuneiform tablets that puzzled scholars because of their unusual contents kept coming into antique markets at Baghdad. Gertrude Bell, director of antiquities for Iraq, had the tablets traced and found that they came from a city mound known locally as Yarga Tepe, but more widely known as Nuzi or Nuzu, which lay in the mountainous region southeast of ancient Nineveh, near Kirkuk. At once she directed Edward Chiera's attention to the site, and suggested that he excavate with the hope of recovering more documents of the same kind.[43]

Preliminary arrangements were made and the excavation at Nuzi began in 1925 under the auspices of the American Schools of Oriental Research with Chiera as director. Soon after beginning they were probing in lower hillocks near the mound when they brought to light the magnificent villa of an eminent man of commercial worth and political importance. Room after room was cleared, and many objects of interest were found. Then during the very last days of the first campaign the workmen suddenly came upon a little room containing over 1000 tablets lying about in wild confusion, though evidence pointed to the fact that they had originally been placed in rectangular baskets and kept in perfect order. Disorder had come when the house had collapsed, damaging many of the tablets.

For three or four days the excavators and workmen were occupied in extracting and preparing the tablets for shipment to America. When the tablets reached Philadelphia a careful study revealed the fact that they constituted the complete archives of the "house of Tehiptilla" for four or five generations. From the tablets it was also learned that the name of the city during Old Testament times was Nuzi, and that the region about Nuzi was called Arrapkha, the Arphaxad of Genesis 10:22, 11:10-12.

All of this so heartened the excavators that they soon returned to Nuzi with added zeal, and with increased financial support from Harvard University and the University of Pennsylvania museum. With painstaking care Chiera, aided by Robert H. Pfeiffer, Richard Starr and a well organized staff, worked for four years and not only uncovered other villas, but also the palace of the local ruler, and the archives of the temple. When they concluded the excavations in 1931 they had uncovered about 3000 more tablets belonging to these other families and to the temple archives.

These clay tablets were written in Babylonian cuneiform, but they were written by the Hurrians, the long lost Horites of the Old Testament. This and other excavations showed the Horites to have been an important and influential Semitic people in the Middle East in patriarchal times, and to have ruled the great Mitanni empire during the fifteenth and fourteenth century B.C. It seems probable they were associated with the Hyksos invasion of Egypt. Nuzi was only one of their many provincial centers, yet to archaeology it has proven to be an important center, because it was the resident city of a local ruler and several wealthy and influential men whose scribes kept careful record of all that went on for four or five generations and faithfully filed them away in the family archives.

The majority of these tablets were written by Hurrian scribes in the Babylonian cuneiform language, with the occasional employment of Hurrian words. They are records of transactions of sale, loan, exchange; marriage, adoption, and divorce; legal documents and court proceedings. In each case, they are witnessed and sealed.

These 20,000 tablets give a very good picture of the lives and varying fortunes of these people and their city during the first half of the second millenium B.C., which means that the tablets reflect ways of living that are relatively close in time and place to the patriarchal age of the Old Testament: the period of Abraham, Isaac, Jacob, and Joseph. Therefore the Nuzi tablets have not only given confirmation to the patriarchal way of life but have also offered invaluable illumination of many incidents recorded in them.

Among the Nuzi tablets there are many that relate to adoption, and these throw light on Eliezer as Abraham's heir. These documents show that adoption was not only a common practice in Abraham's time, but that for practical, social, and religious reasons an heir had to be secured in one way or another to assist a person while he lived, to take care of the burial and mourning rights when he died, and to insure the continuity of the estate. If a person was unmarried, or married but childless, with no son to act in these important matters, then he could and should adopt a son who would be bound to show him filial respect, to take care of him as long as he lived, to bury and to mourn for him when he died. In return for these services, the adopted son became a member of the household and was designated as heir. If, however, the adopter should have a son born to him after the adoption, the adopted was obliged to yield to the real son the right of being the chief heir. These show why Abraham adopted Eliezer as his steward, and explain why Abraham mentioned him as his heir apparent until God announced Isaac's birth, and then added "This shall not be thine heir; but he that shall come forth out of thine own bowels shall be thine heir." [44]

The strange case of Esau selling his birthright to Jacob for a mess of pottage (lentils) has its parallel in the Nuzi records when Tupkitilla faced dire necessity, supposedly starvation, and sold his rights of inheritance of a fertile grove to his brother, Kurpazah, for three sheep.

Bible scholars have long been puzzled to understand the meaning back of the strange actions of Rachel in secretly carrying away her father's household gods, Laban's anxiousness to retrieve them, and Rachel's curious manner of keeping them concealed. However, we now know from the Nuzi documents that the principal inheritance fell to the one who possessed the household gods or idols. Rachel took them, "not so much for religious reasons but to secure the estate of her father for her husband and their children, rather than for her brothers, one of whom would normally have become the chief heir." [45]

TEPE GAWRA

While the expedition at Nuzi was in progress during 1926, Ephraim A. Speiser of the University of Pennsylvania, and at that time annual professor of the American School of Oriental Research at Baghdad, made an archaeological survey of several mounds in northern Iraq, and was especially impressed by a mound three miles northeast of Khorsabad which towered seventy feet above the surrounding plains. The natives of the neighboring villages called it Tepe Gawra, or "The Great Mound."

The size and shape of the mound, the tell-tale painted potsherds, and the archaic implements that covered the slope of the lofty mound were factors which influenced Speiser in choosing the site as the most promising in that area. The American Schools of Oriental Research and Dropsie College of Philadelphia furnished the equipment and $500 for the brief preliminary campaign of two weeks in 1927 that was staffed by Speiser as director, a European architect just out of school and a thirteen-year-old lad—a Philadelphia professor's son—as recorder. The results were considered sufficiently impressive to justify a systematic exploration which began in January 1931, with the Museum of the University of Pennsylvania as an added partner in the expedition. In all there were eight campaigns carried forward by Speiser and Charles Bache as directors.[46]

In the upper half of the mound of Tepe Gawra there was found a complete city, with municipal buildings, temples, and other important structures within the walls, and most of the private dwellings outside the walls. This indicated that the majority of the people lived outside the walls and took refuge inside only in time of siege or other danger.[47]

More than 2000 objects from the Tepe Gawra excavation reached the Museum of the University of Pennsylvania. About the middle of the eighth stratum was found an engraved stone seal about an inch in diameter, depicting a man and woman walking as if utterly downcast and broken-hearted, followed by a serpent. Almost instantly this became known as the "Adam and Eve" seal. This deduction was based on the general agreement that such seals usually record an important historical event. Thus this seal would seem to indicate that the story relating to Adam and Eve's temptation in Eden was known and graphically portrayed in that distant day.

Certain critical scholars had maintained that horses were unknown in the purported time of the patriarchs, and that mention of them in the patriarchal narratives was proof that the narratives were written at a late date. It was to the dismay of these scholars, therefore, that among the figurines found in the sixth stratum at Tepe Gawra were those of horses. They show that horses were well known in Mesopotamia almost a thousand years before the time of Abraham.[48]

BALAWAT

While on one of his trips back to London in 1877, Rassam received as a present from a friend in Mosul fragments of two bronze plates ornamented in relief with Assyrian figures and cuneiform signs in which Sayce recognized the name of Shalmaneser. On returning to assume the responsibility of the Nineveh excavations in the following year, Rassam inquired as to the origin of the bronze plates and learned that they had been found by a peasant while digging a grave at Tell Balawat fifteen miles east of Nineveh.[49]

When he visited the ancient site, Rassam found a mound about 300 yards in diameter, two-thirds of which was covered by a graveyard. His permit to excavate sites in Assyria was exceedingly generous, but like other permits it prohibited him from disturbing graves. Yet in this case he felt the prospect of an important find to be "well worth the risk of getting into hot water with the authorities, and even with the village."

In a very tactful manner, Rassam selected the foremost religious leaders of the village to supervise the proceedings, and went to work on a part of the mound free of graves. Within a few hours he discovered more copper plates like the ones he had received in London, and ascertained to his great delight that the enormous object of which they formed a part was for the most part located outside the limits of the cemetery.

Within three days, Rassam and his men cleared a sufficient portion of the area of its debris to reveal the "extraordinary character" of the find. He said:

The plates seemed to have belonged to the covering of a monument, which proved to be a huge gate with double leaves . . . each leaf had seven panels eight feet long; and according to the way they were lying, it appeared as if they were used to cover the wooden frame in the shape of belts . . . each leaf had a thick bronze pivot, which is shown by the bend at the end of the panels in the shape of a scroll. These revolved in hard stone sockets that were found still standing in their former position. . . . The plates which are embossed with a variety of subjects, such as battle scenes, triumphal processions, and religious performances, are divided into two panels surrounded by a border of rosettes.[50]

The ancient town buried under the mound of Balawat had been originally called Imgur-Bal. It had been chosen by Ashurnasirpal II as the site for one of his palaces. It had been restored and completed by his son and successor, Shalmaneser II. These great double-door bronze gates, some twenty-three feet high, had been erected by Shalmaneser as the gateway to some great Assyrian building, or perhaps merely as a memorial—a kind of precursor to the modern arch of triumph. The gateway was soon carefully packed and sent to London, where it is now one of the choicest exhibits in the British Museum.

Sixty feet to the northwest of this, a second set of bronze strips was uncovered, but the gates the strips ornamented were only half the size of the former, and differed in many characteristic features. And they were so much affected by the dampness of the soil in which they had been buried for more than 2500 years, that they fell to pieces immediately after the discovery.[51]

Rassam also discovered "a scientifically built Assyrian well" at Balawat, and probably would have found many more objects of interest but for the fact that he was obliged to abandon the excavation because of difficulties with regard to the graves on the mound.

MARI

Inscriptions found during excavations at the sites of numerous ancient cities of Mesopotamia bore reference to an important city by the name of Mari. From these inscriptions it was possible to determine the general region of the Euphrates valley in which Mari must have flourished and to sketch roughly the fortunes of the city in various periods of history, but no one had endeavored to pin-point the site until 1932 when Albright suggested with considerable confidence that Tell Hariri, near the Iraq-Syria boundary line, must have been ancient Mari.[52]

In August 1933 a group of Arabs were digging for stone in one of the mounds at Tell Hariri when they discovered a large statue weighing several hundred pounds. At once they went to Lt. Cabane, deputy-inspector of the French miltary district at Abu-Kemal, and inquired what they should do with the "man" they had dug up in the mound at Tell Hariri. Immediately Cabane went to the site and seeing that the statue bore cuneiform inscriptions, sent word of the discovery to Aleppo, whence the news was sent on to Paris. Five months later the distinguished French archaeologist, Andre Parrot, arrived at Abu-Kemal and began excavations on the mound, which covered about 300 acres. Continuing the excavations during the winter months for five years, he made some of "the most sensational discoveries in a generation of very important archaeological finds." [53]

All of these finds cannot be considered here, but three are of prime importance:

The inscribed statue that identified the mound. While uncovering the ruins of a temple in Mari, the picks of the laborers unearthed portrait statues and fragments in great number. One of these was the statue of King Lamgi-Mari, which bore an inscription to Ishtar, the goddess of fertility, of love, and of war. It read:

Lamgi-Mari, King of Mari, high-priest of Enlil, dedicated this statue to Ishtar.

Parrot wrote:

All at once we realized that Tell Hariri was in reality the dynastic city of Mari, and that the structure we were uncovering was the temple of the goddess Ishtar, in whose honor the faithful had brought their statuettes, jewels, weapons and precious vases. Gifts had been left there not only by the inhabitants of the city, but also by pilgrims who had perhaps crossed the desert to prostrate themselves at the feet of the deity, who among other attributes, was the goddess of fertility, of love and of war.[54]

The royal palace of the king. In January 1935, a new section of the mound was surveyed and laid out for excavation with the primary objective of determining more clearly the order and relative position of the strata of the mound. The first strokes of the pick revealed the thick brick walls of an important building, which proved to be the royal palace of Zimri-Lim, king of Mari during the first part of the eighteenth century B.C.

The palace was an imposing structure—one of the finest, and best preserved of any so far found in the Middle East. In extent it is well beyond our comprehension, for on its first floor it has over 250 rooms, halls, courts, and corridors, and covers more than seven acres: "A veritable town within a town." [55] In construction it is "truly amazing," for it was built of mud brick, the only material available in quantity in Babylonia, yet after the destruction of wars and "after the ravages of the elements for several thousand years, the walls are still standing here and there to a height of 15 to 20 feet." [56] The floors were covered with tile, flagstone, plaster, or of beaten earth. The walls were plastered and elaborately decorated. Here and there were mural paintings "whose discovery has revolutionized our idea of the development of Near Eastern art in the early secondary century B.C." [57] "With the Mari paintings we step back in time at least a thousand years." [58]

The palace of King Zimri-Lim was one of the show places of the then known world, and being so large and elaborate "it is only to be expected that it would include all sorts of accommodations and installations which would make it a small city in itself." And so it was, for "in addition to the royal apartments, protected by tremendously thick walls on the outside and well shut off from the rest of the palace, there were lodgings for visiting officials or couriers from other lands." And, as Parrot says, "The palace must certainly have housed, as well as the royal family, the civil and military households, and the offices which would correspond today to the various ministries of state." [59] There were large well-planned kitchens, with cooking vessels of varying shape and decoration, and a table service of almost fifty pieces. There were well arranged bathrooms, some of which still had two terra-cotta bath tubs in place—one for hot water and one for cold. The king's bathroom had an arm chair where he could relax while having his massage.

Two of the rooms were schoolrooms where scribes learned reading, arithmetic, and writing "in the difficult but colorful script of the day." At the center of the palace was the king's private chapel, consisting of three open courts, the innermost of which was seventy-five feet long and the walls were thirty feet high. In a nearby room the excavators found the statue of a goddess holding a hollow vase with a hole in the bottom connected with a channel leading through the middle of the statue to the base. Through this the water had bubbled up and flowed through the goddess and out of the vase which she held. Thus she was Ishtar, the goddess of fertility, the giver of the life-bestowing fresh water. The Hebrews called her Ashtaroth, "the goddess of the Sidonians." [60]

The royal archives. By far the most valuable discovery in the Mari excavation was the more than 20,000 tablets recovered from various rooms of the palace.

Some 5000 of these tablets were letters to the king from high officials and district officers from various sections of the state of Mari. Others were diplomatic letters from princes and rulers from all parts of Mesopotamia and Syria. A number of these diplomatic letters had been between King Zimri-Lim, the last king of Mari, and his ambassadors and agents. Still more interesting were the ones between Zimri-Lim and Hammurabi, king of Babylon and author of the famous code of laws that bears his name. Mari fell to Hammurabi in the 32nd year of Zimri-Lim's reign. In the correspondence bearing on military affairs of the eighteenth century there is related the demand for horses to draw their war chariots.[61]

More than half the tablets were business records. In these letters and business documents we have a wealth of data bearing on the patriarchal period. The Akkadian language used in the majority of these letters "must have been virtually identical with the ancestral Hebrew of the Patriarchs." Frequent reference is made to cities of patriarchal times, such as Harran, Serug, Peleg, and the "Mound of Terah." The city of "Nahor," mentioned as the home of Rebekah's parents in Genesis 24:10, appears often in these tablets. One letter from Nahor is sent by a lady of that town to King Zimri-Lim, and reads as follows:

To my lord say: Thus Inib-sharrim, thy maidservant. How long must I remain in Nahor? Peace is established, and the road is unobstructed. Let my lord write, and let me be brought that I may see the face of my lord from whom I am separated. Further, let my lord send me an answer to my tablet.[62]

Mention is made of the "Habiru" (Hebrews) and of the Benjamites. And the personal names of Reu, Terah, Nahor, Abraham, Isaac, Jacob, Joseph, Benjamin and David are common. Since so many of the Mari tablets have been translated and published, Dr. Albright says:

Abraham, Isaac, and Jacob no longer seem isolated figures, much less reflections of later Israelite history; they now appear as true children of their age, bearing the same names, moving about over the same territory, visiting the same towns (especially Harran and Nahor), practicing the same customs as their contemporaries.[63]

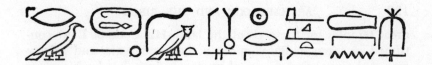

CHAPTER XII

Archaeological Discoveries in Babylonia

THE GREAT CITY OF BABYLON

THE ANCIENT CITY of Babylon was located on both sides of the Euphrates in the great plain of Shinar some fifty-five miles south of the present city of Baghdad. It was the greatest and most powerful city of the ancient world, and one of the oldest and most illustrious of all earthly cities. Nimrod, a distinguished hunter, a phenomenal builder, and a mighty ruler, founded the city and named it "Bab-il" or "Bab-el," which meant "The Gate of God." Later, actuated by illogical motives, its citizens busied themselves constructing a gigantic tower, when they were stricken by a strange confusion of tongues—so strange a phenomenon as to cause the very name of the city ever afterwards to become the synonym for "confusion."

The failure to extend the tower indefinitely, so that it would "reach to heaven," may have deterred the people for a time, yet they continued to build their city, and for long centuries it continued to grow great until it became the capital city for many kings, and its fame spread throughout the earth.

Babylon was extended and beautified from time to time by many succeeding sovereigns, but principally owes its greatness and fame to Hammurabi (1728-1686 B.C.) and Nebuchadnezzar II (604-562 B.C.).

Hammurabi, sixth king in the First Babylonian Dynasty, fortified Babylon and made it his capital. He engaged in extensive trade, unified the small states of Babylonia into one powerful kingdom, prosecuted successful military expeditions, gained vast wealth, embellished the city, and constructed many great temples for the gods of the land. His Code of Laws continued in force in Babylon for a thousand years, and is now one of the vital documents of human history, but his kingdom lasted only a few centuries, then fell under Assyrian domination. The old city was almost entirely destroyed in 683 B.C. by Sennacherib of Assyria, but was soon rebuilt by his more kindly-hearted son and successor, Esarhaddon.

On coming to the throne, in the closing years of the seventh century before Christ, Nebuchadnezzar II instituted one of the most far-reaching building programs ever known in history. For the most of forty-three years he labored with almost unheard-of power, energy, and determination to make the city of Babylon the romance and glory of an entire civilization, the grandest and mightiest metropolis in the world. Biblical writers of the time described it in such extravagant language as "Babylon the Golden City," "abundant in treasure," "the glory of Kingdoms," "the praise of the whole earth." A city that was great in all that men consider greatness. A city into which there flowed the wealth of the then known world. Herodotus, Cestius, Strabo, and Pliny concur in describing it as one of the wonders of the world, and the admiration of mankind.

According to these writers, the city was laid out in the form of a square, with each of the four outer walls some fourteen miles long, around which ran an enormous water-filled trench or moat. This great brick-faced outer wall surrounding the city was eighty-seven feet thick, and attained a height of 350 feet from the bottom of the moat to the top of the parapet. Around the top of the walls were 250 towers and a roadway on which four chariots could be driven abreast, leaving an ample margin on each side. One hundred gates of brass opened to fifty splendid avenues, twenty-five of which ran east and west, and twenty-five north and south, thus intersecting each other at right angles, and dividing the city into squares. Around these squares, and facing the streets, were buildings three and four stories high, while in the center of each square was a beautiful garden irrigated from the numberless canals conveying water from the Euphrates to the palace of the king and to the residences of the rich and poor of the entire city. Great walls lined both embankments of the river, while spanning the river and connecting the two parts of the city was a bridge 500 feet long and 30 feet wide. Broad steps led to the water's edge, and near the bridge there arose a beautiful obelisk 125 feet high to commemorate the completion of the work.

On the east side of the Euphrates, Nebuchadnezzar built for himself an impressive palace, surrounded it by a triple wall, and guarded it with gates of bronze. Its cedar of Lebanon roof was overlaid with gold, and its walls were adorned with pictures of the chase, military processions, and festive scenes. Its apartments were furnished with carpets of Persia, silks of Damascus, and jewels of Bokhara.

Near the king's palace were the Hanging Gardens, one of the Seven Wonders of the ancient world, which Nebuchadnezzar constructed to gratify Amyitis, his queen, that she might enjoy something even finer than the hills and woodlands that abounded in her native country of Media. These beautifully landscaped gardens occupied a square with a circuit of more than a quarter of a mile, and were made up of a great vaulted stone building with receding balconies which raised one above another in a series of receding terraces like a giant stairway to a height of 350 feet. The ascent from terrace to terrace was by means of steps ten feet wide and the whole structure was sustained by a vast system of arches, built arch upon arch, and strengthened on all four sides by a wall twenty-two feet in thickness.

To form a proper pavement for supporting the soil, and confining the moisture of the gardens, large flat stones, sixteen feet in length, and four in breadth, were first laid upon the top of the upper arches; over these was spread a layer of reeds, mixed with bitumen; upon this were two rows of brick, closely cemented, and the whole covered with sheets of lead, upon which the earth or mould was laid to a sufficient depth for the largest trees to take firm root. Under the mighty arched structure was a triple shafted well from which a hydraulic pump raised the water to a large reservoir on the upper terrace, from which it was sprayed over the gardens, or made to flow in fountains which sparkled in the sunlight, then ran away as baby brooks.

The entire city was laid out on such a grand scale, and its architecture so nobly executed, and the design of its ornamentation so far surpassing all other earthly cities that Nebuchadnezzar, untouched by the grace of God, strolled along the roof garden of his royal palace one evening and was so overcome with the splendor and grandeur of the crowning city that, in his pride he exclaimed, ". . . Is not this great Babylon, that *I* have built. . . ." [1]

But the renowned city was not to stand. Isaiah, the eloquent prophet, had said:

And Babylon, the glory of the kingdoms, the beauty of the Chaldees' excellency, shall be as when God overthrew Sodom and Gomorrah.[2]

And Jeremiah said:

And Babylon shall become heaps, a dwellingplace for dragons, an aston-ishment, and an hissing, without an inhabitant.[3]

The course of events verified the prophetic utterance. Nebu-chadnezzar was punished for his pride, and became convinced that Almighty God had to do in the affairs of men and gave the kingdoms to whom He would. After Nebuchadnezzar's passing, Babylon declined under his weaker successors.

Nabonidus and his son Belshazzar lived and ruled in the city until that fateful night of Belshazzar's feast when divine fingers wrote on the plastered walls of that grand and spacious re-ception hall,

. . . God hath numbered thy kingdom, and finished it. . . . Thou art weighed in the balances, and art found wanting. . . . Thy kingdom is divided, and given to the Medes and Persians.[4]

The principal Babylonian city of a Persian province, Babylon rapidly declined until in 331 B.C. its gates were opened to Alexander the Great. After marching on to take Susa and Persepolis, Alexander conquered portions of India, and then in 323 B.C. returned to Babylon where he met many envoys from nations near and far who had come to pay their homage to the young conqueror. Alexander laid extensive plans for the re-building of Babylon, for the reorganization of his army, and for the conquest of Arabia. Thinking to make this ancient city the capital of his mighty empire, he employed 10,000 of his men to repair the embankments of the Euphrates and to clear the debris from about the temple of Belus. But the premature death of Alexander caused the abandonment of the work.

In 130 B.C. Humeris, a Parthian conqueror, destroyed the fairest remaining part of Babylon. After the commencement of the Christian era, Babylon was in such a ruinous state that certain areas of the city were brought under cultivation while other sections were frequently overflowed by the swelling, swirling waters of the Euphrates. In the fourth century its remaining walls formed a sort of enclosure for the preservation of wild beasts, and it was chiefly used as a hunting-park for the kings and nobles of Persia. Centuries passed, and this once glorious city lay in ruins with no notice being taken of it. Then in medieval times, one Benjamin of Tudela, a Jew, visited the place, and wrote in his Itinerary,

Ancient Babylon is now laid waste; but some ruins are still to be seen of Nebuchadnezzar's palace, and men fear to enter there on account of the serpents and scorpions which are in the midst of it.[5]

Carsten Niebuhr visited the site in 1765 and is given credit for discovering the place now believed to be the site of the Hanging Gardens.

Claudius Rich visited Babylon in 1811, and on beginning to dig soon unearthed a portion of the palace of Nebuchadnezzar. Its walls and piers were so impressive as to strike one spellbound with awe and wonder. The walls were eight feet thick, built of burnt brick, laid in lime cement. In a vaulted crypt or cellar Rich found a number of contract tablets and a cylindrical tablet on which was Nebuchadnezzar's own account of his work in constructing one of the nearby canals.

Hormuzd Rassam, who had done so well at Nineveh and Balawat, excavated in Babylon during 1879-81 and found some inscribed bricks of considerable interest, two walls of red granite 140 feet high which were connected with the aqueduct that had supplied water from the Euphrates, and a quantity of contract tablets. He also found the now famous terra-cotta cylinder of King Cyrus on which was inscribed a complete account of his conquest of Babylon. In part it read:

He (the god Marduk) sought out a righteous prince, a man after his own heart, whom he might take by the hand; and he called his name Cyrus, King of Anshan, and he proclaimed his name for sovereignty over the whole world. . . . He commanded him to go to Babylon, and he caused him to set out on the road to that city, and like a friend and ally he marched by his side; and his troops, with their weapons girt about them, marched with him in countless numbers, like the waters of a flood. Without battle and without fighting Marduk made him enter into his city of Babylon; he spared Babylon tribulation, and Nabonidus, the king who feared him not, he delivered into his hand.[6]

Cyrus' account proves most interesting, especially so when read along with Isaiah's prophecy given almost a century and a half previous to the event.

Thus saith the Lord to his anointed, to Cyrus, whose right hand I have holden, to subdue nations before him; and I will loose the loins of kings, to open before him the two leaved gates; and the gates shall not be shut; I will go before thee, and make the crooked places straight: I will break in pieces the gates of brass, and cut in sunder the bars of iron: And I will give thee the treasures of darkness, and hidden riches of secret places, that thou mayest know that I, the Lord, which call thee by thy name, am the God of Israel.[7]

In January 1898, the German Oriental Society was organized in Berlin for the purpose of exploring the mounds of Babylonia. On Easter of 1899 Koldewey and his staff arrived and began excavation of the mound that covered ancient Babylon. For fourteen years they worked with 200 to 250 men, and had excavated only about half the city mound when the outbreak of the First World War forced them to cease excavating and return home.

Koldewey soon found that the city mound of Babylon had been a veritable brick and stone quarry for centuries, as the people of that area had plundered it for building materials and left the surface a confused mass of rubble. He dug into the mound from the east side and soon struck a wall that surpassed all expectations. Herodotus had said that the walls about Babylon were about 87 feet wide and some 350 feet high, and 56 miles in length. What was actually found was an outer or retaining wall 23½ feet thick built of baked brick and asphalt. Beyond this was a filling of sand and gravel 69 feet thick, and then another retaining wall 44 feet thick, making the entire wall 136½ feet thick. These walls were something less than fifteen miles around the entire city as thereby enclosed. This would look as though Herodotus underestimated the thickness of the wall, and overestimated the length of the wall. However, it could be that the bottom of the wall was wider than the top of the wall, and that an outer wall, only 87 feet thick extended on around and embraced the nearby suburbs of Kish, Birs, Nimrod, etc. In this case Babylon, with its gardens and large suburban extensions beyond the main walls, could well have been the size stated by Herodotus.

Also discovered was a clay tablet on which a map of Babylon was drawn. This map proved to be very useful in planning further excavations into the mound. It was a great aid to those who had the task of interpreting the finds.

The Famous Ishtar Gate

The city of Babylon was entered by a hundred gates, and of these the excavators found the Gate of Ishtar to be the finest and most famous. Its double portals, flanked by gigantic towers, formed a truly grand entrance through the double wall of the inner city's main fortification. Both the front of the gate and the pasageways were covered with shining glazed tile and ornamented with rows of enameled dragons and bulls and lions that glittered alternately from the walls where they were executed in brilliant colors. Some 575 of these animals and creatures were here depicted as advancing toward the travelers, who entered the gate. These tiles were so excellently made that many of them were just as bright and perfect the day they were found as when they glittered on the walls of Babylon twenty-five centuries before. The upper part of the gate was wrecked, but the preserved portions of the gateway and the ruins of the towers stood some forty feet high and retained intact 152 bulls and dragons in relief decorations. The Germans removed the surviving portions of the gate with its ornaments and reconstructed the famous Ishtar gate in full size in the Berlin museum.[8]

The Processional Street

The excavators found that through the city of Babylon, from north to south, there ran the Sacred Way, or what is usually called "The Processional Street." The main section of this elevated highway was made of white limestone blocks, while the sidewalks on either side were paved with blocks composed of red marble veined with white. Each slab had upon it an inscription of the king who built it: "Nebuchadnezzar, King of Babylon, son of Nabopolassar, King of Babylon am I. The Babel Street I paved with blocks of limestone, for the procession of the great Lord, Marduk. Marduk, Lord, grant eternal life." Along this mighty Sacred Way, on festal days, Nebuchadnezzar with his men of church and state, robed in gorgeous vestments, chanted to resounding strains of music as they marched in procession and bore the image of the great god Marduk through the Ishtar gate and southward past the north and south citadels, through the center of the city, and after skirting the eastern foundation of the "Tower of Babel" turned westward to the Temple of Marduk, where they performed ceremonies that climaxed the day.

Palace of Nebuchadnezzar

The excavators unearthed the remains of Nebuchadnezzar's great palace, but found it in such disorder that they reconstructed it, on a smaller scale, so that men of today might see what it was like. Among the ruins of the palace, Koldewey found a great ruined banqueting hall and throne room 56 feet wide and 168 feet long. This room was beautifully decorated with enameled brick in intricate designs and brilliant colors blended with esthetic perfection into the vivid blue background. Opposite the main entrance to the main reception room is a niche in the wall which would appear to be the place where the king himself sat upon a throne to rule Babylon and its vast possessions. In this great room Belshazzar held his impious feast at the height of which he drank wine from the sacred, golden temple vessels, and saw the strange fingers on the plastered wall trace the message of his doom. "Thou art weighed in the balances and found wanting." To this same hall they brought Daniel who interpreted his message of doom to him. "In that night was Belshazzar the king of the Chaldeans slain."

Palace of Nabopolassar

Just under and behind Nebuchadnezzar's great palace, was a portion of another palace, that of Nabopolassar (626-604 B.C.), father of Nebuchadnezzar, who had led in a revolt that had wrested Babylonia from the Assyrian Empire. Later he had joined forces with the Medes and Scythians to bring about the fall of Nineveh in 612 B.C. In his palace was discovered the burial place of a man, evidently of high rank, who had been laid to rest clothed in gold-spangled garments, and decked with golden ornaments. The explorers suggest that it may be that of Nabopolassar himself, interred with honor by his son Nebuchadnezzar.

Tower of Babel

In the Bible we are told of the building of a great tower called Babel. Researches and excavations have revealed that in various places in Babylonia great towers or ziggurats were used as focal points of worship during the earlier periods. These confirm that the people were interested in towers from whose tops they burned incense. However, at Birs Nimrud stands a mass of jagged masonry 150 feet above the plain. For long decades it was thought this was certainly the Biblical Tower of Babel, but none had proof. Again, it has been discovered that a great tower within the city mound of Hillah is called Babel by the Arabs. However, it is generally supposed that the Tower of Babel must have been within the walls of Babylon itself.

In the temple area, at the mound now called "Amran," is the ziggurat known as "E-Temen-an-ki," or "The House of the Foundation Platform of Heaven and Earth." This, the most conspicuous structure of Hammurabi's day, and one of the most imposing tower-ruins of modern times, is believed by many to have been the ill-fated "Tower of Babel." Nebuchadnezzar rebuilt this tower and made of it the most gigantic in all Mesopotamia. It consisted of eight towers, each 75 feet high, rising one upon another, with an outside winding staircase to its summit, which, with its chapel on the top rose to a height of 660 feet. The chapel of Belus on its summit was furnished with the most expensive furniture of any temple in the world.

Herodotus visited the temple in 458 B.C. and claims to have seen the golden image of Jupiter Belus, valued at $17,500,000. The golden tables, steps, sacred utensils of worship and other implements were reckoned to be worth another $200,000,000. Needless to say, these golden objects were not found during the recent excavations; the plundering of the ages had stripped it of all its valuable treasures. The influence and fame of this great temple was felt even during the time of Alexander the Great. It is said that Alexander intended to restore the tower, and that he expended 600,000 rations to have his soldiers clear away the debris. His untimely death brought an end to these plans.

It is today a mound of oblong form, the total circumference of which is 2286 feet. It rises in places to a height of 200 feet. The fire-burnt bricks of which it is built are still so well cemented together it is almost impossible to separate them or extract one whole.[9]

According to the records and references concerning it, this tower agrees in most every detail with the noble edifice whose "top almost reached to heaven." This particular tower, according to the records found, was so high that it was inclined to topple over and was often repaired. An inscription was found, in which Nebuchadnezzar says:

I raised the summit of the tower so that its top rivalled the heavens.

George Smith, in his account of Chaldean records, quotes a fragment regarding the collapse of such a tower. It says,

The building of this temple offended the gods. In a night they threw down what had been built. They scattered them abroad and made strange their speech. The progress they impeded.[10]

This passage is quite reminiscent of the Biblical story of the confusion of tongues and the scattering abroad of the people.

The Hanging Gardens

To the northeast of the great royal palace and near the beautiful Ishtar gate, the excavators uncovered a quadrangle area largely made up of high vaulted crypts or subterranean cellar rooms braced together with stone and brick arches and covered over with dirt, tumbled down stones, and debris of various kinds. Through this extensive vaulted quadrangle, which was enclosed by a thick supporting wall, there ran a central passageway with seven large arched subterranean rooms on either side of the central passage. In one of these large vaulted crypt-rooms was, according to Koldewey,

a well which differs from all other wells known in Babylon or elsewhere in the ancient world. It had three shafts placed close to each other, *a square one in the center,* and *oblong ones on each side;* an arrangement for which I can see no other explanation than that a mechanical hydraulic machine stood here, which worked on the same principle as our chain pump. . . . This contrivance . . . would provide a continuous flow of water.[11]

Taking all things in consideration the excavators considered this to be the remains of the foundation structure of the famous Hanging Gardens, one of the Seven Wonders of the ancient world.

At the bottom of a stair-shaft within this vaulted quadrangle the excavators discovered nearly 300 cuneiform tablets relating mostly to the distribution of sesame oil and barley to individual recipients. They supposed these tablets to have fallen here when the upper stories and balconies of the structure had collapsed.

The contents of these tablets have proven exceedingly interesting as well as enlightening "since they list payment of ration in oil and barley, etc., to captives and skilled workmen from many nations, all living in and around Babylon between the years 595 and 570 B.C." Among them are "Yaukin" or "Yow-Keen" (Joiachin) "king of the land of Yehud" (Judah) and his five young sons (royal princes) who were "in the hands of" Kenaiah, their attendant who was himself a Jew. Numerous other names of men of Judah appear in the tablets. Also "the sons of Aga king of Ascalon in the land of the Philistines, together with mariners and musicians from that seaport; mariners and craftsmen from Tyre, Byblos and Arvad in Phoenicia; Elamites, horse-trainers and monkey-trainers (among their names are Necho, Psammetichus, Haryotes and perhaps Apries);

Ionian carpenters and ship-builders, all with Carian or Lycian (localities in Asia Minor) names; and finally a number of Lydians." [12]

Today, if one visits ancient Babylon, he will find that its site has become an inexhaustible quarry where, through the long decades of the past, have come crews of men to obtain brick, and ready-cut stone for their structures in nearby villages and cities. Much of the site has sunk below the water level of the river, thus giving essence to the prophecy concerning the city whose earthly splendor surpassed all other cities of this world:

. . . Babylon is fallen, is fallen; . . . The sea (river) is come upon Babylon: she is covered with the multitude of the waves thereof.[13]

KISH

Kish, one of the world's oldest cities of which we have record, and the ancient seat of the earth-mother goddess cult, is located eight miles east of Babylon. Once it extended over an area of about ten square miles, and was considered one of the largest and most important cities of Sumer and Akkad. Today it is just an extensive series of mounds known as Tell Oheimir, covering an area two and a half by five miles.

Under a joint expedition sponsored by Oxford University and the Field Museum of Chicago and liberally financed by H. Weld Blundell, the excavation of the site was carried out by Stephen Langdon, professor of Assyriology at Oxford, and his colleagues, E. Mackay and M. E. Watelin. The excavation began in 1922 with 300 Arab workmen and was continued for twelve years. It has been regarded as one of the outstanding romances of archaeology—"laborious in detail but magnificent in planning and achievement." [14]

The extensive ruins of Kish consist of two parts lying on either side of an ancient river bed, which many regard as the old, old bed of the Euphrates before it began to shift westward. The eastern part of the city has a huge cemetery mound twenty-five feet high and three quarters of a mile long, a "harbor-mound" 60 feet high and 280 feet wide, an extensive temple area with two great towers, two ziggurats, and a great palace of the early Sumerian kings. There are also great temples to the earth and mother goddesses and to Ishtar, which were built and rebuilt by such leading monarchs as Sargon I (afterwards known as Sargon of Agade or Akkad), Hammurabi, Nebuchadnezzar, and others.

Western Kish has the remnants of two huge fortifications connected by massive walls and moats, and a great mound 90 feet high dominating the landscape for many miles around, and chains of mounds leading westward to the new bed of the Euphrates near Babylon. Many identify these with the outer defenses of Babylon which Nebuchadnezzar claims to have made. If this is true, it could well be that here is a substantial portion of the extensive Babylon which Herodotus and other ancient authorities say they saw or were told of in their day.

Langdon, Mackay, and Watelin carried their diggings down systematically to virgin soil, and in doing so revealed a sequence of life and cultures in ten or more stratifications or occupation levels, of which six were estimated as being more than 5000 years old. About 3000 to 2900 B.C. they found everywhere in the mound a layer of fine sand and clay, one and one-half feet thick containing no trace of sea shells or of marine life, laid down by a great flood. There were occupied levels both above and below the marine deposit.

This they regarded as visible proof of the great Deluge that bulks so large in the Bible and in Babylonian legend. Also a prism was discovered that gives the entire list of the Sumerian kings, before and after the Flood, down to 2000 B.C. The earlier reigns were of legendary length, but the later periods correspond fairly well with accumulative evidence found in many other excavations.[15]

At Kish the excavators found a well preserved Babylonian temple of about 550 B.C., begun by Nebuchadnezzar and continued by Nabonidus, but still unfinished. They also found a mother-of-pearl and lapis lazuli adorned palace, from the time of Sargon I (2400 B.C.), and various objects showing the art of the Sassanian period, and relics of the Sumerians, among which was a four-wheeled chariot made of wood and put together with copper nails. Before the chariot were the skeletal remains of the horses that had drawn it.[16]

They found a bone stylus, which for the first time showed how cuneiform characters were produced, along with hoards of cuneiform tablets and other objects of interest. One tablet seems to bear on its face the earliest form of pictographic script yet discovered in Babylonia. Three hundred tablets of a slightly later date disclosed the fact that their pantheon of gods included only a sky god, earth god and a sun god. The sky god was represented as being the original god from whom all other gods had descended—eventually about 5000 gods in all. After reading these tablets and considering other evidence found at Kish, Erech, and Shuruppak, Langdon wrote:

In my opinion, the history of the oldest religion of man is a rapid decline from monotheism to extreme polytheism and wide-spread belief in evil spirits. It is in a very true sense the history of the fall of man.[17]

NIPPUR

Fifty miles southeast of Babylon lie the twin mounds of the ancient and important city of Nippur where was located the great central sanctuary of the earth-god Enlil or Bel, to which pilgrimages were made from all parts of Babylonia. The two sections of the ancient city were divided by Shatt-en-Nil (River Chebar), and the ruined mound of each covered an area of about 90 acres of land. The site had often been noticed by travelers, but it especially impressed an American exploration party sent out in 1884.

In the summer of 1888 the University of Pennsylvania and the Babylonian Exploration Fund of Philadelphia fully equipped and sent out an expedition under the direction of John P. Peters, Herman Hilprecht, and John H. Haynes to excavate Nippur.[18]

On arriving in the vicinity of Nippur, they pitched their camps, employed a crew of over 200 Arab workmen and began the excavation. At first the expedition experienced many difficulties and one serious disaster, due in large measure to inexperience and a lack of acquaintance with the manners and customs of the Arabs. In time, however, the proper adjustments were made and fruitful results accrued from the splendid work of the expedition (1888-1900).[19]

On the eastern side of the river the excavators found the great temple area, where during the 1888-89 campaign they discovered a Parthian fortress that had been superimposed upon the remains of the ziggurat of the temple. Excavating further, they located over 2000 tablets, mostly identified as having come from the much-sought temple library. In the second campaign (1889-90) hundreds of graves, clay coffins, and urns were opened, and in the upper strata of the temple Haynes found an additional 8000 tablets.

After a two-year absence, Haynes returned in 1893 for the third campaign, during which he uncovered evidence indicating that the ziggurat had been the work of King Ur-Engur, king of Ur, who had built upon an artificial platform measuring 192 by 127 feet. In the occupation level just below this Haynes found the remains of the Sargonic period—numerous bricks bearing the name of Sargon I, who in 2400 B.C. had extended his powerful empire to the shores of the Mediterranean. Haynes also uncovered more than 20,000 additional tablets.

Finally, during the fourth campaign (1898-1900), the temple library itself was located, and from it were taken another 23,000 tablets, making a total of over 50,000 tablets discovered in the temple area. Among these was a complete set of multiplication tables from 1 to at least 1350, which apparently had been used in connection with astronomical calculations.[20]

The religious tablets included many incantations, hymns to the gods, a laudatory hymn to Ishtar, and a didactic work concerning a righteous man who had suffered persecution and who has been called the "Babylonian Job." [21]

Of particular interest to Biblical scholars was the discovery of a fragment of a tablet that has been called the "Sumerian Epic of Paradise," in which is related a traditional account of creation, a portion of which reads:

> After Anu, Enlil, Enki and Ninhursag
> Had created the dark-headed peoples
> Creatures with the breath of life on earth he made plentiful.
> The cattle of the field, them that are four-legged,
> On the plains he called them into being as was fitting.

Closely following the creation account is the story of a great deluge, before which the king and high priest Ziusudra sought guidance for a plan by which he could escape the destruction to be visited upon mankind, and was instructed as follows:

Ziusudra stand thou within and hear.
Beside the wall at my left hand, take thy stand. . . .
Beside the wall I will speak to thee. . . .
My instructions hear. . . .
By our hand a flood will be sent
To destroy the seed of mankind
This is the decision, the command of the assembly of the gods.

Here the mutilation of the tablet leaves us without whatever description there may have been of the building of an ark, but the next portion of the preserved passage tells of the flood:

All the mighty wind-storms together blew,
The flood . . . raged.
When for seven days and seven nights,
The flood had overwhelmed the land,
When the wind-storm had driven the great boat over the mighty waters,
The Sun-God came forth, shedding light over heaven and earth.
Ziusudra made an opening in the side of the great ship
The light of the hero, the Sun-God, he caused to enter into the interior
    of the great ship
Ziusudra the king,
Bowed himself down before the Sun-God;
The king sacrificed an ox and sheep in great number.[22]

This Sumerian story of the Deluge is earlier than the one found at Nineveh, and although it is polytheistic it is generally regarded as the closest and most striking parallel to the Biblical narrative yet discovered. There was the virtuous man, the warning from the gods, the flood, the great boat and the thanksgiving on the issue from the ark.

The half of the city that lay on the western banks of the river was found to have been the business center of ancient Nippur. Here they found the remains of large business houses, the shops of craftsmen, broken tablets, shattered weights, and an exceptionally large number of seal cylinders. And above all, they located over 30,000 inscribed tablets that proved to be largely business accounts and contracts dating from the early times down to the beginning of the Christian era. Seven hundred and thirty of these belonged to the business archives of a great Babylonian firm, "Marashu and Sons," bankers and brokers at Nippur, who lived in the time of Artaxerxes I

(465-425 B.C.) and Darius II (423-405 B.C.), and in whose reigns the documents were dated.[23]

The contents of these tablets have an unusual interest for Bible students, in that they not only graphically picture the active life as carried on in Nippur and the surrounding country at the very time when the descendants of the exiled Jews were returning to Palestine under the leadership of Ezra and Nehemiah, but they also contain an unusually large number of Jewish names found in the Old Testament, and especially in the books of Ezra and Nehemiah.

In the tablets mention is made of the nar-Kabari, obviously the Shatt-en-Nil, which flows through the center of the city and which by many is now regarded as "the river Chebar" spoken of by Ezekiel, by whose waters the children of Israel "sat down and wept." It is unknown how near Tel-Abib was to Nippur, but it seems to have been near the River Chebar, for Ezekiel mentions that after his vision by the banks of the Chebar he "came to them of the captivity" at Tel-Abib (Ezekiel 3:15). And within the radius of five to ten miles to the east and north of Nippur there are many traces of Jewish settlements with which the Marashu Sons conducted business. In that vicinity could well be the ruins of Tel-Abib, made famous by the prophet Ezekiel.

WARKA (ERECH)

Erech, the second of the four cities founded by Nimrod "the mighty hunter before the Lord" (Genesis 10:10), and the home of the mythical Sumerian hero Gilgamesh, lies less than twenty miles northwest of Ur, and is now known by the Arabs as "Warka." Its vast ruins, which cover an area of 1100 acres and measure almost six miles in circumference, have long interested travelers because they indicate a large city with a very long history.

In 1852 William K. Loftus, a geological member of the Turco-Persian frontier commission, undertook a three-week trial excavation at the site. He returned in 1854 in the employ of the Assyrian Fund and excavated at the site for three months, discovering and partly excavating a great Parthian temple, a section of whose walls was ornamented with colored mosaic work, and the Parthian cemetery, which proved to be an almost inexhaustible source of glazed "slipper" coffins. After "many fruitless trials and the demolition of perhaps a hundred specimens," he found a way of "strengthening them with paper and paste" so that a few of these coffins could be "removed intact to the river for dispatch to Europe." [24]

In his last campaign at Warka, accompanied by his friends, W. Boutcher and T. Kerr Lynch, Loftus began work in the southwest section of the city, where he partially excavated a 100-foot high pyramidal mound, which proved to be a ziggurat (one of three in the city) that had been part of the Parthian temple E-anna, built for the worship of the sun-goddess Ninna. It was constructed as a vast mass of clay, packed and hardened, then strengthened with layers of asphalt and bricks. Its corners were oriented with the four points of the compass. A baked brick taken from the center of one side of the ziggurat bore the name of King Ur-Gur (about 2700 B.C.) stamped upon it. To the south of the temple Loftus unearthed a thirty-foot portion of a wall composed of small, yellow terra-cotta cones, three and a half inches long, all arranged in half circles with their rounded bases facing outward. Other cones were variously colored and arranged in beautiful designs, such as diamonds, triangles, zigzags and stripes.[25]

Loftus found only a few portable items; among these were a number of cuneiform tablets, some of them in "envelopes," a few figurines, and some corroded copper objects.[26]

Extensive work of a scientific nature commenced at the site in 1912 under the direction of J. Jordan, C. Preusser, and W. Andrae, of the German Oriental Society, and continued through fifteen successful seasons of careful and methodical excavations.

The excavators were able to penetrate down to virgin soil, and by means of the stages and changes of the pottery discovered established a relative chronology dating back to 4000 B.C. or earlier.[27]

Two strata of flood deposits were apparent, their connection with the Deluge being uncertain. Also unearthed were remarkable remains of massive walls and wall decorations going back to about 3000 B.C., as well as thousands of clay tablets of the later Babylonian period. These tablets were mostly of a business nature, but also included a fragment of the Gilgamesh epic, and some mathematical texts that exhibited the rather complicated sexagesimal numerical system used, in which the unit was sixty, rather than the ten we use, and which was no doubt far superior to the decimal system. The sixty can be factored by 2, 3, 4, 5, 6, 10, 12, and 15, while the ten can be factored only by 2 and 5. The practicality of their system is seen in the division of the circle into 360 degrees, the hour into 60 minutes and minutes into 60 seconds.[28]

The excavators discovered some 575 primitive pictograph tablets, bearing the oldest type of writing found in the city's ruins, and from them learned much of the religious history of the inhabitants of Erech. It was the center of the worship of Ishtar, all other goddesses in Babylonia being reflections of and tending to merge into her.[29] The primitive pictographs indicated that in very early Erech the religion was near-monotheistic, having mentioned two deities, one of whom preceded the other, whereas the later Sumerian pantheon of some 750 deities was merely a reflection of the human tendency to depart from the belief in the One True God to a belief in many gods.[30]

Complete excavation of Warka was a task too great for the resources of the German Oriental Society which had to leave the task far from completed. According to Hilprecht, it would have required fifty years of digging and a fund of $500,000 to excavate thoroughly the ancient ruins.[31] The University of Pennsylvania and the Oriental Institute of Chicago carried forward the excavation there in 1952 and 1956.

TELL EL-OBEID

In 1919, while H. R. Hall of the British Museum excavated tentatively at Ur, his attention was drawn to Tell el-Obeid, a small mound four miles to the northwest. Here he traced the remains of three different temples that had succeeded one another on the site.

The original temple was a rectangular structure with its corners oriented to the cardinal points of the compass. It was constructed of sun-dried brick and faced with burnt brick, and was in a splendid state of preservation. A few feet away from the front of the building, where it had been thrown in the destruction of the wall in which it had once been embedded, was the foundation stone in the form of a slab of white marble on which was inscribed the following:

Nin-Khursag: A-an-ni-pad-da, King of Ur, son of Mes-an-ni-pad-da, King of Ur, has built a temple for Nin-Khursag.[32]

A-an-ni-pad-da was an unknown ruler, but his father Mes-an-ni-pad-da was known as the first king of the First Dynasty of Ur, a dynasty "which, up to the discovery of this tablet, seemed somewhat mythical." This, however, gave the earliest el-Obeid civilization a possible date of near 4000 B.C.[33]

This dainty little temple had been dedicated to the goddess Nin-Khursag, the Lady of the Mountain, the mother of fecundity, patroness of cattle and other living creatures. Appropriate to her sphere of interests, the whole temple had been adorned with a frieze of "amazingly realistic" sculptured bulls "wrought in copper, and with free-standing figures of bulls in the round, also of copper; while another feature of the decoration was a second frieze which ran above that of the copper bulls." It was composed of animals and men about a cow barn, with scenes of milking and storing the milk. A further element of decoration "was found in the shape of many artificial flowers composed of mosaics of small pieces of colored stone. These were apparently used in connection with the standing figures of bulls, and suggested that the animals were walking in a meadow spangled with flowers." [34]

This "dainty piece of architecture," along with these vigorous scenes of animal life wrought in copper, mosaic and mother of pearl show a wonderful achievement in old Sumerian art almost six thousand years ago.

UR OF THE CHALDEES

Ten miles west of the Euphrates and 140 miles south of the site of old Babylon, on a vast plain over which "the shimmering heat waves dance and the mirage spreads its mockery of placid waters," lie the remains of the ancient city known in Scripture as "Ur of the Chaldees." The ruins cover something more than 150 acres, are somewhat oblong in form, and are made especially conspicuous by the ruins of a gigantic brick and bitumen tower or ziggurat in the northern portion of the area. The natives call the place Tell Mugheir, which means "the Mound of Bitumen."

In 1854, under the supervision of the British Museum, J. E. Taylor, British consul at Basra, began the preliminary excavations at Tell Mugheir. In the course of Taylor's work he dug some trenches and cleared away the debris enough to get to the great tower or ziggurat, the ruins of which ascended in three stages to a height of seventy feet. Two stories in a fair state of preservation were found, as was a stairway leading to the ruined third story. In excavating at the south corner of the upper story, Taylor found a perfect inscribed cylinder within a niche formed by the omission of one brick in the layer. He then sank shafts at the other three corners, and found precisely similar inscribed cylinders. These four identical cylinders, when translated, proved to be foundation cylinders placed there just as we now place "cornerstone" records in edifices we construct.

These cylinders recorded the name of the city and that of King Ur-Dungi, the Sumerian founder of the temple in 2500 B.C. Taylor cleared lower chambers of the rubbish of past ages, and discovered a cache of cuneiform inscriptions prepared by King Nabonidus, in which he tells how he repaired the Temple of Nanna, the moon god, and records the prayer of Nabonidus to Nanna, lord of the gods of heaven and earth. The inscriptions read:

Nabonidus king of Babylon, the upholder of *Esagila* and *Ezida,* the reverent worshipper of the great gods am I . . . the Ziggurat in Ur, which *Ur-Nammu,* a king before me, had built but not completed, did Dungi his son finish. On the inscription of Ur-Nammu and his son Dungi saw I that Ur-Nammu had built but not completed that Ziggurat and Dungi his son had finished the work. Now was that Ziggurat old. Upon the foundations whereon Ur-Nammu and his son Dungi had built I made good the structure of that Ziggurat, as in old times, with mortar and burnt brick. . . .

After dedicating the restored building anew he then ends his prayer thus:

As for me, Nabonidus, King of Babylon,
From sin against thy divinity save me,
And grant me a long life.

And as for Belshazzar my eldest son,
The offspring of my heart,
Put into his heart fear of thy great divinity
So that he may commit no sin.
Let him be satisfied with the abundance of life.[35]

Before this discovery, Bible critics had said that there never
was a person by the name of Belshazzar, and if there were, he
could not have been the last king of Babylon, because
Nabonidus was the last king. But this inscription along with
other inscriptions found elsewhere about Nabonidus revealed
the fact that on his son's thirtieth birthday the king made him
regent, that the throne of Babylon was thencefore occupied
jointly by Nabonidus and Belshazzar; in the latter years Belshazzar actually did much of the ruling while his father Nabonidus followed his yen for archaeological research in locating
and restoring ancient temples. Despite his father's prayers,
Belshazzar did sin by taking to drunkenness, and was destroyed
one night while at a great banquet, his father Nabonidus
being away in another part of the kingdom. Therefore when
the Bible says that Daniel was made *third* ruler in the kingdom,
it was an accurate statement. Nabonidus was the first ruler,
Belshazzar the second, and Daniel was given the position of
the third ruler. Belshazzar was a grandson of Nebuchadnezzar,
and therefore called him his father "in harmony with Semitic
usage." [36]

Toward the end of the First World War when the British
were in control of Babylonia, the British Museum was instru-
mental in getting the government to appoint R. Campbell
Thompson as an adviser to the military authorities on the
preservation of ancient monuments of that land. In the early
part of 1918 he examined the site of Ur, and found it exceedingly interesting but hardly dug enough to call his work an
excavation.

In 1919 the British Museum sponsored H. R. Hall, who obtained the services of seventy Turkish war prisoners and cleared
the southeast face of Ur's mighty ziggurat, exposed a bit more
of the great temple of Nanna the moon god, and excavated
a part of a palace of the Third Dynasty of Ur. Then, when
Hall's attention was directed elsewhere, the mound was left
to lie unworked.

Seeing the necessity of following up these discoveries with large-scale excavations, the University of Pennsylvania Museum and the British Museum combined their funds and returned to Ur in 1922 under the directorship of Woolley, who carried out a series of campaigns between 1922 and 1934. His early investigations soon laid bare a well fortified port city covering about four square miles with shipping quays or wharfs extending far in among the commercial buildings in which merchants and bankers contracted business with distant peoples of both land and sea. Well defined streets led away from the business quarters to residential sections of substantial two-story brick and plastered homes with as many as twelve or fourteen rooms arranged about a paved court. There were fountains, fireplaces, sewer systems and many other comforts, and decidedly "modern" touches anticipating "almost exactly that of the richer houses of modern Baghdad." A look at one of them gives "a fair picture of the setting in which Terah might have passed his life at Ur four thousand years ago." [37] Some of these homes possessed private chapels containing brick altars on raised platforms above which were niches designed for a picture or clay figurine of the family god. Many small public chapels were located here and there throughout the city, and the towering ziggurat was at its heart.[38]

Woolley found school buildings; some for young children and others for more advanced students. In these schools were clay tablets written in the cuneiform script, conveying exact ideas of subjects taught. There were reading lessons, and writing and spelling exercises, together with dictation in vocabulary. Reading lessons were sometimes of hymns later to be chanted in temple ritual. There were multiplication tables; advanced students had their forms for extracting square and cube roots, and there were lessons in practical geometry. In grammar there were models for the declension and conjugation of Sumerian words. In the field of history they had treatises on the past, as we have today, only theirs were in abbreviated form and covered a more restricted area.[39]

Woolley excavated almost the entire temple area, of which the most conspicuous building was the ziggurat. The ziggurats were characteristic of Mesopotamia, as the pyramids were characteristic of Egypt. There was a difference in their use, however. The pyramids were tombs, whereas the ziggurat was the shrine of the chief god, a gigantic tower raised in grandeur above all other buildings and dominating the landscape of every city of any consequence. To the people of that day it was "the mountain of God." [40]

The architecture of the ziggurat shows it to have been built with carefully calculated curves. The walls not only slope inward, but the line from top to bottom is slightly convex. On the ground level, from corner to corner, the structure has a distinct outward bend; so that sighting along it one can only see to the center. This formed an optical illusion that was used many centuries later by the Greek builders of the Parthenon at Athens. These curves give to it an appearance of strength. The whole design of this structure is a masterpiece.

The ziggurat of Ur is the best preserved in all Babylonia. The Sacred Area connected with the temple and its worship activity stood on a walled platform or terrace which measured about 1200 feet long by 130 feet wide at its base. It ascended in three stages, the first being about 35 feet high. Its summit at 70 feet was crowned by a small shrine used on high days, especially at the great New Year's festival connected with the irrigation of the land and fertility of the crops. The sides, which were buttressed, were made to slope inwards, and thus the tower as a whole had the appearance of a stepped pyramid. It might well be called "a mountain of brickwork." There was not a single straight line in the entire building. The shrine at the top of the building had disappeared, but there remained many of the blue-glazed bricks with which it was coated. Woolley believes trees and shrubs were planted on its various stages.[41]

Crowded under the high terraces of the ziggurat and surrounding its base were numerous temples and shrines, the inner sanctuaries of which were rich with paneling and inlay. Directly in front of the ziggurat was a brick-paved open court 225 feet long. This was surrounded by an almost endless line of smaller buildings and rooms used as living quarters for the priests and as storehouses and magazines for the many offerings brought by the faithful worshipers or paid as rent by the tenants of the sacred estates. To the courtyard during the waking hours of nearly every day came an almost constant procession of people to pay tithes in kind from incoming cargos, from farm, from factory and every other pursuit at which men earned a living. Busy clerks took the tally, while scribes carefully recorded each item with three-pointed styluses on tablets of soft moist clay, which were carried by slaves to the nearby temple archives; here the tablets were registered and filed for future reference. White-tunicked priests, bearded and grave, attended the court to verify the correctness of the tithe laid aside as sacred in the service of the gods of the land.

This great temple-tower at Ur, was the work of Ur-Nammu (2112 B.C.), first king of the third dynasty. Later, Nabonidus (550 B.C.), the last king of Babylon, enclosed this ziggurat in a new building. Only a little of this building now remains, and archaeologists have been interested mainly in the earlier shrine because we know it was there in the time of Ur's greatest splendor and in the time when Abraham lived in the city. When Nebuchadnezzar was king of Babylon he restored the ziggurat and its worship after extensive remodeling. Also certain repairs and alterations were carried out in the days of King Cyrus. Nothing much was done to change the ziggurat after the days of Cyrus, and when the Euphrates changed its course and the city of Ur was deserted, the great temple-tower was buried with sand and was lost to men until archaeologists uncovered it.

Some of Woolley's most outstanding discoveries at Ur were made between the autumn of 1926 and the spring of 1929 when he dug just outside the walls of the inner city and located two cemeteries, superimposed one above the other. The lower was of course the older, and in it were two kinds of burials, the graves of the common people and the tombs of kings and queens. About 1850 of these graves were excavated; two-thirds had been rifled by tomb robbers but many yielded very important finds.

The ordinary tomb of the commoner was a rectangular shaft from four to twelve feet deep, in which the body was laid either wrapped in matting or enclosed in a coffin made of basketwork, wood, or of clay. Invariably the body lay on its side, the legs slightly bent at hip and knee in the attitude of one asleep. The hands were brought up before the face and usually held close to the mouth a cup which must once have contained water or some other liquid. With the bodies in the coffin the

excavators found such personal belongings as beads and earrings, a knife or dagger, a pin that fastened the dress or shroud,
and a cylinder seal with which to stamp the owner's signature.
Outside the coffin were food and drink in vessels of clay, stone
or copper, weapons, tools and toilet articles such as the individual might require for a journey to or for a sojourn in
another world. The bottom of the grave "was lined with matting and mats were spread over the offerings to keep them from
immediate contact with the earth" with which the grave was
filled.[42]

The "royal cemetery" was located in the southeast corner of
the temple enclosure, and was marked by larger and finer tombs
that distinguished the burials of kings and queens and honorary
personages. These royal tombs, which dated from the middle
third millennium B.C., were shafts or grave-pits approximately
thirty feet in depth, having a floor area of some twenty-four by
thirty to forty feet. A sloping approach or ramp was cut from
ground level to the bottom where was erected the stone or
brick burial chamber, which was frequently "elaborated into
a building containing several rooms and occupying the whole
area" of the floor. Usually there were two long outer rooms
which were vaulted and two smaller central rooms which were
covered with domes. The ramp led to an arched door in the
outer wall, and arched doors gave access from room to room.
One of these central rooms was the monarch's actual burial
chamber; the others were for the members of his court whose
lives were sacrificed so that they might accompany their beloved
ruler and faithfully serve him in the other world.

Out of the sixteen royal tombs excavated only a few had
escaped the attention of ancient tomb robbers. The first one
uncovered was, like many others, sadly despoiled of every thing
of value.

The first undisturbed tomb was of a queen whose name was
uncertain. It was reached through a square shaft from the
surface. About half way down in the filling the excavators found
two magnificent gold daggers and between them a white shell
cylinder seal of Prince Meskalam-dug, which apparently he
had affectionately flung into the death-pit during the final
"filling ceremonies." Digging deeper into the great pit through
layer after layer, the excavators found first a servant in his

coffin, then a guard with his weapons by his side, then the dome of the stone tomb-chamber. In front of the tomb door were the bodies of three sheep; inside, lay five bodies, four of which were men attendants and the fifth that of the queen. She wore a golden headdress; a long curved gold pin fastened her royal robe; in her hand was a fluted and engraved tumbler of pure gold, and by her side was a golden cylinder seal.

The excavators subsequently found the grave of her admirer —perhaps the prince consort—in which were copper and golden daggers, copper and silver bowls, copper jugs and plates, vessels of stone and clay, and, at both the head and foot of the grave, rows of spears with blades stuck downward, together with sets of arrows having chisel-edged points of chipped flint. The entombed body had about it a broad silver belt from which hung a gold dagger and a whetstone of lapis lazuli attached by a gold ring. Between its hands was a bowl of heavy gold, nearby was a larger oval gold bowl; near the elbow was a gold lamp in the form of a beautiful sea shell. Against each shoulder was a double axe-head of electrum.

Lying over the rotten fragments of his skull was a gorgeous wig-like helmet of beaten gold, with cheek pieces and golden hair hammered up in relief. "As an example of goldsmith's work" said Woolley, "this is the most beautiful thing found in the cemetery. . . . If there were nothing else by which the art of these ancient Sumerians could be judged we should, on the strength of it alone, accord them high rank in the role of civilized races." [43] On two of the golden bowls and on the shell-shaped lamp was repeated the inscription "Meskalam-dug, Hero of the Good Land."

The most impressive of all the sixteen royal tombs found in the cemetery, however, were those of King A-bar-gi and Queen Shub-ad, in which was shown so plainly the sinister practice of human sacrifice in connection with royal burials. It was during the season of 1927-8 that the excavators were digging along a sloping ramp leading down to an unusually large death-pit when they discovered the bodies of six soldiers, orderly in two ranks, with copper spears by their sides and copper helmets crushed flat on their broken skulls. Just inside the arched doorway were two four-wheeled wagon-like chariots, each drawn by three oxen lying in position with the grooms in front of the oxen and the drivers lying in the bodies of the chariots. The chariots were plain, but the silver and lapis ornamented rein-lines passed through stationary silver rings surmounted by two gold mascots in the form of bulls.

The king's fine vaulted tomb, at the far end of the great death pit, had been robbed of its more valuable contents, yet it contained the body of King A-bar-gi according to the inscription on his cylinder seal, and also the bodies of several of his attendants or close associates. On the floor were bits of gold, and over against the wall was a gaming board of shell plaques set in lapis lazuli, and two very fine model boats, one of copper and the other of silver. On the outside, along the passage in front of the tomb's arched doorway was a long line of soldiers carrying copper daggers. Along the end wall outside the king's tomb lay the elaborately dressed and richly adorned bodies of nine women singers who had with them two harps, one of which had the copper head of a bull and shell plaques adorning the sound box; the other harp was adorned with a bull's head in gold and a wonderfully fine set of shell plaques engraved with mythological scenes of animals playing the parts of men. The space between the women and the wagons was crowded with other dead women and men, and the passage leading from the wagons to the tomb was lined with soldiers armed with daggers and carrying sets of silver and golden spears. In all, there were more than sixty people who had been sacrificially buried with the king that they might accompany him on his last journey. Beside each body lay a copper cup from which they had drunk hashish, opium, or some potent drug which had swiftly sent them to their death without a struggle.

To the rear of the king's tomb, and on a somewhat higher level, the excavators found the queen's extensive burial quarters, "built either at the same time or, more probably at a later period." Her stone vault was arched over with burnt brick. These had fallen in, but no robbers had been there, and the tomb with all its rich furnishings had been left intact. Her name, Shub-ad, was carefully engraved on "a fine cylinder seal of lapis lazuli which was found in the filling of the shaft a little above the roof of the burial chamber and had probably been thrown into the pit at the moment when the earth was being put back into it." [44]

Of what he found in the queen's burial tomb, Woolley wrote:

At one end on the remains of a wooden bier, lay the body of the queen, a gold cup near her hand; the upper part of the body was entirely hidden by a mass of beads of gold, silver, lapis lazuli, carnelian, agate, and chalcedony, long strings of which, hanging from a collar, had formed a cloak reaching to the waist and bordered below with a broad band of tubular beads of lapis, carnelian, and gold: Against the right arm were three long gold pins with lapis heads and three amulets in the form of fish, two of gold and one of lapis, and fourth in the form of two seated gazelles, also of gold.

The headdress whose remains covered the crushed skull was a more elaborate edition of that worn by the court ladies: its basis was a broad gold ribbon festooned in loops round the hair—and the measurement of the curls showed that this was not the natural hair but a wig padded out to an almost grotesque size; over this came three wreaths, the lowest hanging down over the forehead, of plain gold ring pendants, the second of beech leaves, the third of long willow leaves in sets of three with gold flowers whose petals were of blue and white inlay; all these were strung on triple chains of lapis and carnelian beads. Fixed into the back of the hair was a golden "Spanish comb" with five points ending in lapis-centered gold flowers. Heavy spiral rings of gold wire were twisted into the side curls of the wig, hugh lunate earrings of gold hung down to the shoulders, and apparently from the hair also hung on each side a string of large square stone beads with, at the end of each, a lapis amulet, one shaped as a seated bull and the other as a calf. Complicated as the head-dress was, its different parts lay in such good order that it was possible to reconstruct the whole and exhibit the likness of the queen with all her original finery in place.[45]

For this exhibit a plaster cast was made from a well-preserved female skull of the same period (the queen's own skull being too fragmentary to be used) and over this Mrs. Woolley modeled the features in wax to approximate the features of a leading lady of the early Sumerians. On this head "a wig of the correct dimensions" was fitted, and over this were placed the three gold wreaths of beech and willow leaves, the broad gold hair ribbon, the golden side curls, the golden ear pendants, the golden "Spanish comb" and other adornments worn by Queen Shub-ad in her final earthly sleep. The reconstruction "presents us with the most accurate picture we are likely ever to possess of what she looked like in her lifetime." [46]

By the side of the queen's body lay a second headdress made of a diadem of soft white leather over which had been sewn thousands of minute lapis lazuli beads. Against this background of solid blue were set "a row of exquisitely fashioned gold animals—stags, gazelles, bulls and goats," between which were clusters of pomegranates and other tree branches of golden stems and pods. From the lower border of the diadem hung palmettes of twisted gold wires. The bodies of two women attendants were crouched against the queen's bier, one at its head and one at its foot.

All about the tomb room lay offerings of beautiful vessels of gold, silver, copper, stone and clay. In the room were two silver tables for offerings and on them, or nearby were seven silver lamps, the head of a cow in silver, and many large cockle shells containing a green paint-like substance which was presumably used as a cosmetic. There were two pairs of gold and silver shells and numerous other valuable objects evidently in everyday use at the time, but all placed there for the queen's use in her after-life.

Twenty-three attendants—five soldiers and eighteen musicians and court ladies—lay on the floor of the outer tomb. There were the remains of a chariot, beautifully decorated with three lion heads of gold on each side. It had been pulled by two royal donkeys. There were traces of their harness, and on the pole was a copper rein-ring surmounted by a charming little figure of a donkey in electrum, or gold alloy, which the excavators considered the forerunner of the present radiator cap mascots on the front of our automobiles.

The graves of King A-bar-gi and Queen Shub-ad were almost exactly alike. Apparently the king had died first, and it had been the queen's wish to lie as close to him as might be. When each died, in turn, the royal body, clothed and adorned in all possible splendor, was carried down the sloping passage and laid in a fine wooden coffin or upon a sumptuously covered wooden bier. The personal attendants of the dead took their places in the elegantly furnished vaulted tomb chamber. Then down into the open death-pit with its "mat-covered floor and mat-lined walls" came the members of the deceased ruler's court, the officers with the insignia of their rank, the ladies-in-waiting, with all their bright, colored garments and headdresses of carnelian and lapis lazuli, silver and gold; the musicians bearing harps or lyres, the drivers in the chariots drawn by oxen or donkeys, the grooms holding the heads of the draught animals. All took their appointed places in the extensive burial quarters and finally a guard of soldiers formed at the entrance.[47]

The inner-tomb rites were said, the musicians played softly, and at a given signal each of those present lifted his copper or silver cup and drank from it the potion each had brought or found prepared. They then composed themselves for insensibility and death. Someone came down and killed the animals and perhaps saw to it that all were arranged in order; the shaft was then filled in, loose dirt fell upon the white matting, the colored drapery, the treasures of Sumerian art, and upon the sleeping court. When the great grave-pit was completely filled, the ground was trodden down, the final religious rites were performed, and royalty had been sent away to live their future lives much as they had lived in Ur.

In another large royal tomb Woolley and his associates found the skeletal remains of seventy-four singers, musicians, and attendants who had marched down the ramp into the death-pit, performed his or her part, and at a given signal had drunk the potion that induced the slumber of death. Six of these were male guards, four were women harpists (one with her hands still on the strings of her instrument), and sixty-four were singers and ladies of the court. All the ladies were richly robed in ceremonial dresses, twenty-eight wore golden hair ribbons on their headdresses, and the rest silver. One of the maidens had apparently been late for the funeral rites, and having insufficient time to put on her silver hair-ribbon like the rest had pushed it still rolled up into her pocket, where Woolley found it almost 5000 years later.[48]

The four harps or lyres were among the most magnificent ever found. Two were all of silver, and another was edged in mosaic, encrusted with shell and lapis lazuli plaques engraved with animal scenes, above which there was projected a splendid head of a bearded bull wrought in heavy gold. And in the corner of this tomb on an oblong base of silver plate and mosaic, stood an upright ram whose front legs were bound with silver chains to the branches of a tree or bush. The tree and its leaves and flowers were of pure gold; the ram, with its mane, beard, and horns of lapis lazuli, and its head and legs of gold, looked out from between the leaves. Of this Woolley said, "Irresistibly we are reminded of the Biblical story of the 'ram caught in the thicket,' but the statues were made before Abraham was born, and the parallel is therefore difficult to explain." [49]

As a result of the excavation of the royal tombs, Woolley dug deeper and discovered what he considered undeniable evidence of the great Flood. He writes:

In the early spring of 1929, in the hopes of getting some chronological evidence, we began sinking shafts below the level of the deepest graves. . . . The shafts went deeper, and suddenly the character of the soil changed. Instead of the stratified pottery and rubbish we were in perfectly clean clay, uniform throughout, the texture of which showed that it had been laid there by water. The workmen declared that we had come to the bottom of everything . . . but after working out the measurements I sent the men back to deepen the hole.

The clean clay continued without change until it had attained a thickness of a little over 8 feet. Then as suddenly as it had begun, it stopped, and we were once more in layers of rubbish full of stone implements and pottery. Here was a remarkable change. The great bed of clay marked, if it did not cause, a break in the continuity of history. Above it we had the pure Sumerian civilization slowly developing on its own lines; below it there was a mixed culture which seems to have nothing to do with the Sumerians but to belong to a race which inhabited the valley before the Sumerians came to it. . . . The bed of water-laid clay could only have been the result of a flood; no other agency could possibly account for it.

Taking into consideration all the facts, there could be no doubt that the flood of which we had thus found the only possible evidence was the Flood of Sumerian history and legend, the Flood on which is based the story of Noah. A pit sunk 300 yards away to the north-west gave us the same bed of water-laid clay, with beneath it the same flints and colored pottery of the non-Sumerian folk. . . .[50]

Speaking of a test hole at another point in the ruins of Ur, Woolley says "About sixteen feet below a brick pavement which we could with tolerable certainty date as being not later than 3200 B.C. we were down in the ruins of that Ur which existed before the Flood."

In the ruins of the houses we found numerous lumps of hard clay which had been the stoppers of bottles or jars, and stamped on these were the impressions of the owners' seals; there were no inscriptions, but designs sometimes of an elaborate geometrical character, sometimes with rows of animals shown walking in hilly country, the figures drawn with an astonishing liveliness and skill. It is probable that where seals were employed the art of writing was already known, so that we may not unreasonably hope to unearth written documents actually older than the Flood. But in any case the carving of these seals with their combination of naturalism with formed style bespeaks a state of society well advanced on the road to civilization properly so called. . . .

In the house ruins under the Flood silt at Ur, we found two beads made of Amazonite, a stone of which the nearest known source is the Nilghiri hills of central India; it was a fairly sophisticated community that could import its luxuries from lands so far away. Even the terra-cotta figurines cannot be classed as primitive. The slender bodies, conventional as they are, are skillfully modelled and the queer reptilian faces with the high bitumen-covered head-dress are due not to lack of art but to intention; these are goddesses who must not be represented otherwise. What the religion of the people was we cannot tell, but religion of a sort they certainly had. . . .

And amongst the things which they handed down to their successors was the story of the flood. . . . Here there is no picturesque legend, only what the old historians meant to be a plain statement of fact. The statement is indeed so plain that it implies the legend, for otherwise it would have no meaning. "The Flood" was for the Sumerian reader the only flood that really mattered, what we call Noah's Flood.[51]

Far and wide the Associated Press carried Woolley's news release, that within the ruins of Ur he had found an eight-foot thick water-laid deposit that gave evidence of "The Flood . . . what we call Noah's Flood."

Professor M. E. L. Mallowan, who for six years served as Dr. Woolley's assistant at Ur, went to Nineveh in 1932-33 as assistant director of the British Museum Excavations. There, under the direction of R. Campbell Thompson, he sank a shaft or pit ninety feet deep. Between the fifty-eighth- and sixty-third-foot level he found an alternating stratum of mud and sand deposit about five to six feet thick. Its composition and date corresponded somewhat with the flood deposit which he and Dr. Woolley had found previously at Ur.[52]

Other flood deposits discovered in the Tigris-Euphrates valleys and announced as possible material traces of the Flood, were made at Kish, Warka (Erech), and Shuruppak (Fara). The dates for these deposits, as announced by the excavators of the sites, ranged all the way from 3300 to 2800 B.C.[53]

Some were satisfied to go along with the excavators in the belief they had discovered deposits left by Noah's flood. Quite a number of archaeologists were reticent, while others were entirely unwilling to accept the discoveries as material traces of the great Flood. They suggested that the dates of the various flood deposits did not agree, that there was little or no change of culture above the deposits, and that these deposits probably represented local floods.[54]

Two or more of the excavators were not easily changed or influenced away from the interpretations of their finds as announced. With regard to the eight-foot marine deposit Woolley found at Ur in 1929, William F. Albright said (April, 1957) that Sir Leonard "still adheres to his exaggerated chronology, and he still insists that the extensive three meter bed of clean alluvium which interrupts the stratigraphical development of the Ubaid (Obeidian) Period reflects the Flood of Utnapishtim and Noah. Since it brought no change of culture, most archaeologists consider it as a deposit laid down by a river flood which was higher than ordinary, somewhere about the 35th century B.C. or even later." [55]

The simple yet sublime Genesis narrative and the wide diffusion of Flood tradition—far removed from one another as China and America—leave very many earnest scholars with the feeling that the Biblical account and the wide-spread traditions had their basis on a common original catastrophe, and that the Flood must have been of more than local significance—far more than an exceptionally violent flooding of the Tigris and the Euphrates. Yet reckoning of the time of its occurrence presents difficulties.

The chronological data in the genealogical tables in the fifth and eleventh chapters of Genesis, recorded in our Authorized Version, influenced Archbishop Ussher (1581-1656) in arriving at 2348 B.C. as the date for the Flood. Others, in making use of these same tables, have arrived at the date of 2501 B.C. The Septuagint Version (translated from the Hebrew to the Greek during the third century B.C.) gives varying genealogical data from which some claim to have arrived at a date of about 3212 B.C. for the Flood. Dr. John Bright, after a very able discussion of the subject from an archaeological point of view, says, "It would seem, however, that we must regard it as a catastrophe taking place far back in the Stone Age." [56]

Archaeological researches have revealed no material traces

of a catastrophe such as the Flood having taken place either around 2348 B.C. or at 2501 B.C. The Septuagint date of uncertain reliability would fall nearer the time of the flood deposits as discovered and dated by Sir Leonard Woolley and Professor Mallowan at Ur and Nineveh.

Many dependable scholars, whose attitude toward the Bible is deeply reverent, consider it as virtually impossible to comprehend clearly the chronological data as preserved in the fifth and eleventh chapters of Genesis. Some regard these as "abbreviated" genealogies, while others consider them as "lines of descent" in which there may well be "gaps" caused by omissions —just as there are known omissions of names in genealogical lists in other places in the Bible.[57] It would require only a few narrow gaps in the Genesis tables to make possible the uncertain Septuagint date of 3212 B.C. for the Flood, while it would require more and wider gaps to make possible Dr. Bright's general reckoning.

In any event, it is quite probable we will be required to await other discoveries, and possibly a further extending and refining of our measuring rods before we can be altogether sure that archaeological researches have located material traces of the great Flood.

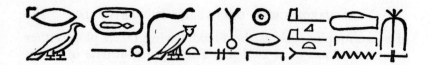

CHAPTER XIII

Archaeological Discoveries in Persia

PERSIA, ONE OF THE most interesting and colorful countries of the Middle East, consists mainly of a high, arid, mountain-rimmed plateau of 628,000 square miles, lying east of Assyria and Babylonia. North of this plateau beyond the jagged Alborz range of mountains is a fertile and productive expanse that slopes gently to the shore of the shallow, gray, brackish Caspian Sea. To the south of the plateau lies the torrid Persian Gulf, from whose waters are gathered costly pearls and upon whose shores grow the stately date palms.

The Persians call their country Iran, and themselves Irani, all of which stems from the word "Aryan." In about 1500 B.C. they came to the country as tribal invaders, speaking dialects of Indo-Iranian languages, and calling themselves "the Madai" or Medes.

After overcoming the aboriginal Caspians, who had long lived on the plateau, the Medes settled about Ecbatana, with Deioces as their first known king. Later, when they had filled the country with their increase, one large colony removed themselves from Media and settled in Elam, making use of the then ancient city of Shushan (Susa) as their capital. Another vigorous group of Medes went still further south and east, founding the small but powerful state of Anshan, or "Persian Land" with their capital at Pasargadae. Both colonial countries were more or less subject to Media.

The Median Empire reached its zenith about 600 B.C. under King Cyaxares, who was succeeded by Astyages in 585 B.C. Twenty-seven years later Cyrus the Great (600-529 B.C.) began his career as king of Anshan, the small province of Persia, some 400 miles southeast over the mountains from Babylon. At the time the Persians were subject to the Medes, but in 553 B.C. Cyrus organized the Persians for revolt against his own grandfather, Astyages, king of Media. Three years later, with the aid of Medians who were sympathetic to his cause, he emerged victorious as king of the new Medo-Persian Empire, and founder of the Acheamenid Dynasty. Soon Elam was absorbed, followed by Sardis, capital of Lydia, in 546 B.C., Babylon seven years later, and Egypt in 529 B.C.

Cyrus rebuilt and enlarged the capital at Pasargadae, and from this and the two capitals Ecbatana and Shushan, ruled over a territory which extended from the Indus in the east to the shores of the Mediterranean in the west, and from the cataracts of the Nile to the Caspian Sea. In this vast empire there was instituted a system of justice, and a network of roads over which relays of riders raced along night and day carrying government dispatches and royal mails in "pony express" style.

Cyrus was a wise and capable ruler, both Jews and Greeks acclaiming him for his generosity. On conquering the Babylonians, he so respected the sacred beliefs and customs of the people, and treated them with such consideration, that they themselves celebrated his victory. He spared the life of Croesus, king of Lydia and made him one of his advisers. The Jewish exiles in Babylonia and Persia were an object of his special favor. He read Isaiah's eloquent prophecy concerning him and in turn he treated them with the care a shepherd show his flock.[1] He made a written proclamation concerning the Jews, and the rebuilding of their temple, and sent about 49,000 of them back to Jerusalem with the treasures and vessels of their temple, ordering the local governors in Palestine to furnish them material and to give them practical assistance in the rebuilding of their temple.[2]

After his death in 529 B.C. Cyrus was buried in a colonnaded tomb at Pasargadae, and was succeeded by his son Cambyses II, who died violently in 522 B.C., after which the kingdom was rent by civil war. In a brilliant two-year campaign, order was restored and the country was reunited by Darius I (521-485 B.C.), who recorded his exploits on the famous Behistun rock carving, described in Chapter IV.

The empire built by Cyrus and Darius not only survived through periods of prosperity and adversity until the coming of Alexander the Great in 333 B.C., but in the courts of its capital cities of Ecbatana, Pasargadae, Persepolis, and Shushan there was enacted a series of colorful dramas, including such Biblical characters as Daniel, Ahasuerus, Esther, Mordecai, Haman, Ezra, and Nehemiah. Under the names of these four capital cities we now consider that empire's role as one of the most important of what the western world knows as Bible Lands.

ECBATANA

Ecbatana, the capital of the newly arrived Medes, and later one of the four capitals of the Persian Empire, stood at the foot of Mount Orontes (Alvand) approximately 160 miles southwest of the present site of modern Tehran. According to Polybius, Herodotus, and other ancient writers it was a city of astonishing strength and beauty. Its citadel, they said, was surrounded by seven walls, five being of ordinary construction and painted, one white, one black, another scarlet, a fourth blue, and the fifth orange, while the sixth was of silver, and the seventh and innermost being covered with gold.

Semiramis, an Assyrian queen of considerable fame, is said to have built a gorgeous palace there in 800 B.C., and it was to Ecbatana that Cyrus brought Croesus, along with his wealth and that of Lydia, which he conquered in 546 B.C. It was the city to which Antiochus came according to Maccabees 9:3.

In Ezra 6:2 we are told that the scroll on which Cyrus wrote his decree for the release of the Jews and the rebuilding of Jerusalem could not be found in Babylon, but was discovered in the palace archives at Achmetha (Ecbatana), the city of the Medes. Evidence points to the decree having been carried there by "Darius the Mede" (Gobryas), who, as Cyrus' elderly military leader, had been "made King" of Babylon for a short time, but in retiring to his own city of Ecbatana had carried the decree with him and placed it there in the palace archives just before his death.[3]

The city was visited twice by Alexander the Great, his favorite aide dying there on the occasion of the second visit, when the great warrior gave vent to his grief in so violent a manner that he destroyed many of the city's famous landmarks.[4]

Today, the modern city of Hamadan, a commercial center noted for its pottery and for the manufacture and sale of rugs, stands on the site of ancient Ecbatana, making it nearly impossible to excavate the city mound in which lie the ruins of the ancient capital of Ecbatana. The traditional tomb of Mordecai and Esther may be visited there today, and 80 miles to the west of Ecbatana and 40 miles to the east of Kermanshah, poised high on a mountainside, is the far-famed Behistun Inscription, picturing Darius the Great in the act of receiving homage from ten conquered kings.

PASARGADAE

Pasargadae was chosen by Cyrus as his first capital of Persia, and it continued in use as one of the three co-capitals of the Medo-Persian Empire after he conquered Elam and Media. Then it was destroyed and little was known of the ancient grandeur of the city during the long centuries in which it lay buried beneath the dust and debris of its own disintegrated sun-dried brick. In 1949, however, the Archaeological Institute of Persepolis began excavations there and found that it had once been a vast city of parks, gardens, temples and palaces.

In the midst of these royal parks and gardens, Cyrus built three palaces for himself. The first being his "Palace of Audience," with its great central hall, its four roofed colonnades, its 116 lofty columns, thirteen of which were found to be still standing when excavated. The same year (1950) the excavators uncovered the "private palace" of Cyrus, constructed much on the same order as was the Palace of Audience, and in 1951, they finished excavating the third palace, evidently the oldest of the three, for it was in a far worse state of damage than were the other two. This third palace seems to have been reserved for special occasions, such as receptions, religious ceremonies, and national celebrations.

All three palaces were decorated with beautifully sculptured reliefs, and paved with beautiful blocks of white stone, many of which had long since been removed for later construction and for tombstones.[5]

On the ruined buildings was found the repeated inscription

which read: "I am Cyrus, the King, the Achaemenian." Here and there throughout the ruins were found gold and silver vessels beautifully engraved in color, as well as masterpieces of fine masonry, enameling, gilding and other fine arts, and winged statues of human and animal figures.

To the northwest of the private palace was what has been regarded as a Fire Temple in the form of a square tower, with its two fire altars at which had been performed religious ceremonies reflecting the rites of the Zoroastrian religion.[6]

There were found remains of a vast underground stone water supply system which had interlaced the city, carrying running water from the River Pulvar, where in 1917 there was discovered the remains of a water dam.[7]

In one of the royal gardens near the private palace of Cyrus, was found his tomb. It rested on a platform reached by a flight of six steps, was of the single-room private mausoleum type, rather imposing, and was reached through a single doorway, above which was this inscription:

"Stranger, I am Cyrus, the founder of the Persian Empire and Sovereign of Asia; envy me not, therefore, this sepulchre." [8]

Upon a hill at the northern end of the plain, near the palaces and gardens, were the remains of great stone walls called "the Throne of Solomon," which appeared to have been a temple site. Here was discovered a plain piece of pottery inscribed in Syriac, along with several pieces of black pottery, a fragment of stone carved in the shape of a human head, a white stone upon which were carved flowers, and several small pieces of gold.[9]

The excavators found indications that after Cyrus had completed his successful conquest of Media, he returned to Pasargadae and enlarged many of its buildings in commemoration of his accomplishments.[10]

PERSEPOLIS

In 520 B.C. Darius the Great took his architects, artisans and workmen and went forty miles south of Pasargadae, where on a low rocky spur at the base of the Mountain of Mercy overlooking the lovely plain of Marv Dasht (Plain of the Waterfowl), he terraced a vast rectangular area and laid down enduring foundations for his enchanted palace-city of Persepolis. Gigantic and picturesque stairways led from one mighty terraced platform to another. On these platforms visionary architects raised a series of palaces and scores of buildings, which when encircled by graceful walls, formed the heart of one of the most famous cities of antiquity. Here Persian culture and civilization attained its highest level as the monarchs of the Achaemenian Dynasty passed the late spring and autumn months, while going to Ecbatana for the summer and to Shushan for winter. It was here that the great annual feasts of the vernal equinox were held celebrating the Persian new year. Because Esther was Xerxes' queen for thirteen years, she must have lived at Persepolis with him at brief intervals.

However, this mighty city, a veritable memorial to Persian culture, was short-lived, for in 331 B.C. when Persepolis was less than 200 years old it was looted and destroyed by burning at the hands of Alexander the Great, apparently a deplorable accident of war, or, as some think a deliberate act of revenge on Persia for the invasion of Greece. In handling the loot from the Persepolis treasury, Alexander is represented in legend as having made use of 20,000 mules and 5,000 camels to transport the booty to Ecbatana.[11]

Then the ruined city was abandoned, and lay crumbled and buried to blend with the sands and soil of the plain until near the middle of the nineteenth century when orientalists and archaeologists began investigations of the mound. It was not until 1931, however, that serious excavation began when Prof. Herzfeld of the Oriental Institute of Chicago began work, followed by Erich Schmidt, who worked from 1935 till the outbreak of the Second World War.[12]

The entire terrace was found to have been occupied by the royal buildings of Darius, Xerxes (485-465 B.C.), and Artaxerxes (465-425 B.C.). Access to these was afforded by means of a shallow ramp-like staircase of 116 steps located at the northwest corner of the terrace, beyond which stood the Gate of Xerxes, whose portal was guarded by two colossal stone bulls.

To the south, and upon a still higher platform, was the ruined "Apadana," or audience hall, built by Darius and Xerxes. This was reached, on the north and east, by the "grand staircase," one of the most elaborately sculptured and inscribed stairways yet discovered in Middle Eastern countries. This great audience hall, over one half acre in extent, was of hypostyle construction, its roof supported by enormous cedar beams from Lebanon and 36 richly ornamented columns sixty-five feet high. At the east entrance of this great hall, there is now, in fine sculptured relief, the likeness of Darius I on the throne with Xerxes (Ahasuerus) as crown prince standing behind him. Above them is the winged figure of Ahura Mazda, the one great god of Zoroastrian religion and the author of all good. Darius and his immediate successors were followers of Zoroaster, which is believed to be "a partial explanation for the enlightened policies of the Persian government." [13]

The audience hall provided access to the Tachara, or Palace of Darius, with its relief adorned walls and its numerous inscriptions, one of which reads:

Saith Darius the King: This country of Persia Ahura Mazda bestowed upon me . . . and Darius the King does not feel fear of any other.

Saith Darius the King: May Ahura Mazda bear me aid . . . and protect this country from foe, from famine, and from falsehood, this I pray as a boon from Ahura Mazda.

I am Darius, Great King, King of Kings, King of many countries, son of Hystaspes, an Achaemenian . . . who constructed this palace." [14]

The magnificent palace was supplied with running water by means of stone piping which carried water from the Apadana roof and from the nearby mountains. Drainage was facilitated by a vast system of sewers, similar to the later sewage system of Paris.

Further south beyond the palace were the queen's apartments, with their central hall and court. East of the Apadana was the "Hall of a Hundred Columns," so called because its magnificent cedar of Lebanon roof was supported by a hundred carved and fluted columns. It was second in area and magnificence to no other ancient building except the Temple at Karnak in Egypt. Beyond were numerous other rooms, including the royal treasury and a watchman's fort. About all these fine buildings were gardens in which flowers clustered thickly about pools and playing fountains.[15]

In 1951 the Archaeological Institute of Persepolis began

excavations below the platform of the terrace and found the ruins of another palace, a massive stone hall with a porch and additional rooms, together with a great stone reservoir.

Other finds of interest in the mound were thousands of fragments of hard stone vases, and an inscription of Xerxes, or Ahasuerus, husband of Queen Esther, in which he listed the many nations over which he reigned, including Media, Elam, Armenia, Parthia, Babylon, Assyria, Sardis, and Egypt.[16]

On the slope of the Mount of Mercy southeast of Persepolis are tombs of two of the last Achaemenian kings, and at Naqsh-i-Rustam, four miles from Persepolis, are the imposing tombs of Darius the Great, Xerxes (Ahasuerus), Artaxerxes I, and Darius II carved in the stony mountainside. Only the tomb of Darius the Great has a full inscription.[17]

SHUSHAN

Susa, the far-famed Shushan of the Scriptures, was located on a wide and fertile plain between the Ulai and Dizful rivers some two hundred miles east of Babylon. Its strategic position from earliest times made it exceedingly important for war, for commerce, and for communication. Its climate was milder than that of Ecbatana and Persepolis, and less sultry than that of Babylon, therefore it not only served as the capital of ancient Elam, but was the royal winter residence and capital of the powerful kings of the Medo-Persian Empire. Among its beautiful homes and stately buildings were beautiful gardens, groves of date, pomegranate and lemon trees. Shushan was so colorful a city throughout Biblical times that it has long carried "a halo of interest" for all Bible students.[18]

About 2200 B.C. the king of Elam, who had his winter capital here, invaded Babylonia and returned with many treasures. About 645 B.C. Ashurbanipal crushed and plundered Susa. In his account of this event he says:

I conquered Susa, a great city, the abode of their gods, the seat of their oracles. By the command of Ashur and Ishtar, I entered his palaces, and sat down with joy. I opened their treasures, wherein was stored up silver, gold, and possessions which the former kings of Elam, and the recent kings had collected and stored away, on which no other enemy besides me had laid his hand, and I brought it out and counted it as spoil. Silver, gold, property, and possession of Sumer, Akkad, and Karduniash (Baby-

Ionia), everything which the earlier kings of Elam had carried away as spoil in seven campaigns and had brought into Elam . . . precious stones, a costly ornament fit for kings, which former kings of Akkad and Shamash-shum-ukin had sent to Elam to effect an alliance; garments, fitting decorations for kings, weapons of war, trophies, everything used in battle fit for his hand; portable furniture of his palaces, upon which he had sat and slept, out of which he had eaten and drunk, poured libations, and anointed himself; chariots, state-carriages . . . horses and large mules with trappings of gold and silver, I took away as booty to Assyria. The temple-tower of Susa, built of alabaster, I destroyed . . . their gods and goddesses with their ornaments, their possessions, their furnishings, together with their priests and temple servants, I carried away to Assyria. Thirty-two statues of kings, of silver, gold, bronze, and alabaster . . . I took with me to Assyria. I turned over the bull colossi, and the guardian gods and all other watchers of the temple entrance, and tore down the fierce wild oxen, that decorated the doors. The temple of Elam I laid in total ruins . . . their hidden forests, into which no stranger had ever pressed, neither trodden its bounds, my soldiers forcibly entered, saw their places of concealment, and burned them with fire. The mausoleums of their kings, the earlier and the later ones, who had not feared Ashur and Ishtar, my lords, but had rebelled against the kings, my fathers, I destroyed, laid waste, and exposed them to the sun. . . .[19]

One hundred years later, Cyrus made it one of the strongest fortresses and richest storehouses in the then known world. Darius the Great completed the royal palace and made it the center of his vast empire which stretched from the Indus to the Danube and the Nile.

It was to this city that Daniel was transported in a vision, or was actually present at Shushan, when he saw symbolized the successive powers that should triumph and rule this area:

And I saw in a vision; and it came to pass, when I saw, that I was at Shushan in the palace, which is in the province of Elam; and I saw in a vision, and I was by the river of Ulai.[20]

Daniel and many of the most important Jewish people were transported to Shushan after the fall of Babylon. Here, as many think, he endured the trial of his faith as he prayed to God three times daily in defiance of the king's decree, and here he was cast into and miraculously delivered from the lion's den. It was here in Shushan that Daniel served as first "president" and wielded great influence for good during the riper, more mature years of his life, and tradition suggests that it was here that he died and was buried. Today one may visit the traditional tomb of Daniel, over which a mosque has been erected.

Here Xerxes (Ahasuerus), who "reigned from India even unto Ethiopia, over an hundred and twenty provinces," remodeled and redecorated the magnificent two and one half acre palace, and hung it with "tapestries of blue, yellow and green." Here, in the third year of his reign (482 B.C.), Xerxes gathered the "Persian Parliament," with whom he planned the Grecian campaign, and indulged in a prolonged drinking festival that culminated in the divorcing of Queen Vashti. Here, in "the seventh year" of Xerxes' reign, just after he had returned from the disastrous Grecian campaign, Esther was made queen, and there followed the fast-moving drama in which Haman was hanged high on his own scaffold, Mordecai was promoted to prime minister, and a decree favorable to the Jews was written in King Ahasuerus' name and sealed with the king's signet ring and sent throughout the kingdom by "riders on horseback, on mules, on camels, and young dromedaries." [21]

Here "in Shushan the palace" in the twentieth year of King Artaxerxes (444 B.C.), Nehemiah the king's cup-bearer, who was endowed with unusual energy and mighty moral worth, learned of the dilapidated condition of the walls of Jerusalem and gained permission from the king to go to Jerusalem and rebuild the walls of the city. Later, he left Shushan and made a second visit to Palestine where he carried out some very beneficial reforms among the more liberal-minded Jews.[22]

Here in the colorful capital of Shushan in 324 B.C., Alexander the Great "made a triumphal entry and found immense treasure; married the daughter of Darius, Statira, gave her sister in marriage to Hesphaestion, and united twenty-four of his generals and 10,000 Greek soldiers to Iranian girls at festivities lasting five days." [23]

Shushan's prosperity declined under Alexander's successors, became a part of the Parthian empire in A.D. 226, passed into the hands of the Mohammedans in 640, and was deserted about A.D. 690. Thereafter it was covered over and lay in ruins.

In 1852 when Williams and Loftus began digging at Shushan, they found the larger and more prominent ruins covered an area of three and a half miles in circumference, and was made up of four spacious artificial mounds, each distinctly separated from the other. Then beyond these great mounds were "numerous small mounds" which were "spread over the whole visible plain" west of the river.

Williams and Loftus were greatly hindered by misguided Moslems. Yet they succeeded in carrying forward the initial work of uncovering the ruins located on the lofty western mound, and those on the north mound. On the latter mound Loftus began to lay bare a portion of the great palace hall and throne room, which had been in part the residence of Darius the Great, who permitted the Temple in Jerusalem to be rebuilt; of Xerxes or Ahasuerus, who was Queen Esther's husband; and of Artaxerxes I, who authorized Nehemiah to restore the walls of Jerusalem.[24]

On the pedestals of four of the columns there was inscribed in three languages the following:

Says Artaxerxes, the great King, the King of Kings, the King of all the countries upon the earth, the son of King Darius, the son of King Artaxerxes, the son of King Xerxes, the son of King Darius, the son of King Darius Hystaspes. My ancestor Darius built this Apadana (throne room of the palace) in former times. In the time of Artaxerxes, my grandfather, it was burnt by fire. I have restored it.[25]

During 1884-86 the excavations were continued under the direction of Marcel Dieulafoy, a French architect and engineer, who with the aid of his wife revealed that the ruined city covered about 4900 acres and was divided into four sections: (1) the citadel-mound, (2) the royal city, known as "Shushan the Palace," (3) the business and residential area known as "the city Shushan," and (4) the district on the plain west of the river.

The Dieulafoys' attention was more particularly centered on the royal city, which the writer of the book of Esther calls "Shushan the Palace." This formidable palace fortress covered 123 acres, was raised high above the surrounding city, and was made up of the Apadana or throne room, the "House of the King," and "the house of the women," along with the inner and outer courts, the palace garden, the pylons, the great stairways, a vast terrace, and a few arched gateways.[26]

The Apadana was the king's throne room, or great Hypostyle Hall which covered nearly an acre of ground. It was

supported by thirty-six noble columns—six rows of six each—
with capitals carved in the form of bulls kneeling back to back,
and by long cedar of Lebanon beams spanning the great distance between the massive columns. Here came the king when
he "sat on the throne of his kingdom," and here were held his
banquets and state social events such as the prolonged banquet
described in the first chapter of the Book of Esther. The floor
of the throne room was "a pavement of red, and blue and white
and black marble," just as it had been described in the Book
of Esther. Across this marble floor had walked the beautiful
Queen Esther at the risk of her life, as she approached the crim-
son canopied throne, stopping before the carpet which only
the feet of the king were to tread, there to intercede for the
lives of her people.[27]

In front of the great pillared throne room were the palace
gardens where walked the king as he pondered the evil deeds
of Haman. Nearby were the ruined "House of the King" and
the "house of the women." These were separate yet adjacent to
each other. Then there was "the King's gate" where sat
Mordecai the Jew. And, in among the debris, Dieulafoy even
found a quadrangular prism or dice, on which were engraved
the numbers one, two, five and six. With this "die" or *pur*
they cast lots—"They cast Pur, that is, the lot" is an explanation for the Jew as to how Haman "cast lots" for fixing a date
for the destruction of the Jews.[28]

It all made so profound an impression upon Dieulafoy that
he made a scale model of the great palace in which had been
enacted so many of the events in the Book of Esther, and placed
it in the Museum of the Louvre in Paris. With these restora-
tions, one can readily locate "the King's gate," where sat
Mordecai, the "inner court of the King's house over against
the King's house" where Esther appeared without being bid-
den by the king; "the outward court of the King's house,"
where Haman came to ask the king to have Mordecai hanged;
and "the palace garden" where the king went to think and cool
off his anger against Haman. Thus we are aided in restoring the
structural surroundings of the palace and in gaining a more
exact acquaintance with the many events that took place there,
and of seeing the marvelous accuracy of the Book of Esther.[29]

On December 18, 1897, a brilliant French mining engineer

and geologist by the name of Jacques de Morgan assumed the leadership of the archaeological expedition at Shushan. He led the expedition for several years, in the course of which he made many important discoveries.

Of particular significance were the vast number of broken pieces of pottery found in the lowest occupational level of the mound and in the nearby cemetery. It is largely from these pieces of pottery (whole pottery being rarely found) that the story of the early Madai immigrants who came to this land, has been slowly pieced together. This pottery is wonderfully hard and thin—about the thickness of two postcards—and makes a beautiful ringing sound when struck. Its marvelously delicate geometric and floral designs, along with its quality of ware make it some of the finest pottery ever made by the hand of man.[30]

Other finds uncovered in the tombs were mirrors of 99 per cent pure copper, beads of black and white limestone, obsidian tools, copper axes, fragments of fine linen cloth, needles, and beautiful ointment bottles. So extensive were the finds that the Louvre has devoted two large rooms to the exclusive exhibition of treasures from the period of Xerxes.[31]

The discovery of an inscription of Darius I indicates that he had summoned Ionian, Carian and Lydian craftsmen and artists to Shushan to help in decorating his royal palace with stone from Ogia, cedar wood from Lebanon, silver from Egypt, gold from Bactria, and ivory from India. The bits of beauty found by the excavators among the ruins of the palace indicate that these decorations have not been surpassed in beauty by any civilization in subsequent history.[32]

The Laws of Hammurabi

The greatest discovery made in Shushan by de Morgan came in December 1901 when his workmen uncovered three fragments of black diorite, which when fitted together formed an impressive round-topped stele monument seven feet five inches high and proved to be the Laws of Hammurabi. At the top of the monument is a bas-relief showing Shamash the sun god in the act of giving the laws to King Hammurabi. Beneath the carving appears the lengthy code, inscribed in cuneiform script, and comprising some 282 statutes written in 3000 lines. Two hundred forty-eight of the statutes remain in a fairly good state of preservation, whereas from five to seven columns of the text at the bottom of the front side had been erased at some time previous to its discovery. Pere Jean Vincent Scheil, a brilliant French Assyriologist, translated and published the Code within three months. It soon came to be recognized as one of the most important legal documents that has come down to us from antiquity.

The laws were preceded by a lengthy prologue in which Hammurabi honored the gods of the land and represented himself as a shepherd and "a devout god-fearing prince" who caused the stele to be engraved and set up in a public place "that the strong might not oppress the weak," and that justice might "prevail in the land." Hammurabi's laws were for all the people of his realm—for the common man as well as for judges in deciding cases of law. Notice his reassuring appeal in his prologue:

Let any oppressed man who has a cause come into the presence of the statue of me, the King of justice, and then read carefully my inscribed stele, and give heed to my precious words, and may my stele make the case clear to him; may he understand his cause; may he set his mind at ease.[33]

In the code that follows there is legislation governing such subjects as:

Banking, bankruptcy, real estate, minimum wage, witchcraft, witnesses, judges; concerning offenses involving the purity of justice, as tampering with witnesses, jury, or judge; crimes of various sorts, as theft, receiving stolen goods, kidnaping, fugitive slaves, burglary; duties of public officers in their administrations; laws relating to landlords, tenants, creditors, debtors; canal and water rights, licenses, messengers, herdsmen, gardeners, slander, family relationship, marriage, divorce, desertion, breach of promise, adultery, unchastity, concubinage, rights of women, purchase money of brides, inheritance, adoption, responsibility for all kinds of assaults; fees of surgeons, failure in an operation, branding of slaves, fees and responsibilities of builders and boatmen, hiring of boats; agricultural life, etc.[34]

The code listed three classes of citizens as having lived in Hammurabi's realm: the *Amelu,* or gentlemen, the *Mushkenu,* or freemen, and the *Ardu,* or slaves; as well as three classes of officials: the *Judges*, the *Naqirum*, or coroner, and the minor officials who held land on feudal tenure and who were subject to military service. The rights and responsibilities of each were fixed in the laws.[35]

Hammurabi, in his epilogue to the code, recounts the accomplishments of his reign and reassures the oppressed of his kingdom that they will receive justice; then he *pronounces an anathema upon anyone who should intentionally change any of his laws or deface the monument.*[36]

Many have wondered how the stele came to be in Shushan in view of the fact that Hammurabi's main capital was the city of Babylon. Apparently the answer lies in one of two explanations: That it was carried from Babylon as a trophy of war and set up in Shushan, or as the writer believes, along with others, that at the height of Hammurabi's reign, Susa was a strategic city in his empire, and that he had the stone placed there for the enlightenment and well-being of his subjects in Elam.

The discovery of the cylinder was of singular importance to men everywhere, but especially to Bible scholars. First, it was evidence supporting the authenticity of Mosaic law. Critics had held that the art of writing and the science of law were unknown in that early period of history, but here was unquestionable evidence that both were well known many centuries before the time of Moses. Second, there are resemblances, even striking parallels, between some of Hammurabi's statutes and those of Moses in the Book of the Covenant. For example, in citing the law for personal injury, Hammurabi's statute 206 says:

If a man wound another accidently in a quarrel with a stone or his fist, and oblige him to take his bed, he shall pay for the loss of his time and for the doctor.

Moses' law for the same offense reads:

If men strive together, and one smite another with a stone, or with his fist, and he die not, but keepeth his bed . . . he shall pay for the loss of his time, and shall cause him to be thoroughly healed.[37]

The similarity between these and a few other statutes left the way open for certain critical scholars to advance the theory that Moses' laws of the Bible were largely derived from the Code of Hammurabi. After more careful examination, however, scholars in general have abandoned the theory, and are learning from other researches that in ancient times there were codes of law in various countries. Some of these were even older than Hammurabi's stele. The universal conscience within the breast of mankind has long declared to him that there is a right and a wrong, and that justice is the proper standard for humane treatment.[38]

Mosaic law is far superior to the Code of Hammurabi, or to any of the ancient codes of law, because of its high ethical standards, its stress upon the motive of love, both to God and to man, its demand for more humane treatment of slaves, the greater value placed upon human life, and the higher regard for womanhood. But basically, it is superior because it moves on a high moral and spiritual plane infinitely superior to all other codes. Moses taught the fact of sin within the human life and man's responsibility to God in respect to that sin; a fact that Hammurabi and other law givers failed entirely to comprehend. Hammurabi's code was exclusively civil and criminal, while Moses' law was ceremonial, religious, and deeply spiritual—being unique in this respect among law codes of all time.

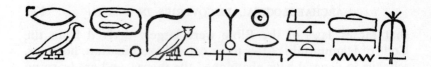

CHAPTER XIV

Egypt and Discoveries in Abydos

No more the lotus waves its head,
But grows the papyrus instead,
And still the Palms do bend and bow,
And tell strange stories to us now.
Pyramids high, Tombs buried deep,
Are seen in dreams by those who sleep.
—Source unknown

EGYPT, "the gift of the Nile," comprises all the land between the Gulf of Akaba and the Libyan desert, including the Sinai Peninsula. It extends from the Mediterranean in the north to the Sudan border at Wadi Halfa in the south. Its total area measures 363,000 square miles, all of which is desert except an area of about fifteen thousand five hundred square miles of tillable land along the Nile, in the Delta, and in its five or more oases.

In olden times Egypt was called Mizraim, which meant "The Two Egypts." This dual designation arose from the fact that the country was made up of Upper and Lower Egypt. Upper Egypt included all the peoples who lived along the Nile in the central and southern portions of the country. The symbol of their kingdom was the lotus. Their more important places were: Abydos, Thebes, and el-Amarna. Lower Egypt comprised all the great Delta near the Mediterranean, and all civilization southward to and including Fayum district. The symbol of their kingdom was the papyrus plant. Their more important places were Memphis (Noph), Heliopolis (On), and Zoan (Tanis).

Usually the two sections of Egypt were united under one king called "Pharaoh," who wore a double crown, had a palace in both Memphis and Thebes, and divided his time equally between Upper and Lower Egypt. Beside the double crown and the double residence, there were also two treasuries, and two federal granaries, so that the original independence of the two lands was never forgotten.

Ancient Egypt has long been known as a land immensely rich in climate and soil, and exceedingly colorful in history —a strangely pleasant stage on which illustrious civilizations have enacted impressive dramas. However, it is exceedingly difficult to trace any definitely dated history beyond 2800 to 3000 B.C., and yet Egyptian traditions suggest an older civilization that disappeared in some cataclysm of nature. Scattered traces of this older civilization seem to appear in a few places, but it is all too hazy for certainty.

Egypt's known history dates from about 2850 B.C. when Menes is credited with welding the people into the first of what we now call Empires. With Memphis as capital, Menes ruled as the first king of many during the six dynasties of the Old Empire. It was during the Third to the Sixth Dynasty that the pyramids were built, which caused this period to be designated as "The Pyramid Age" (2700 to 2200 B.C.).[1]

The Middle Empire, which began about 2100 B.C., was a period of aggressive expansion, including the conquering of Ethiopa and Arabia. But Egypt also suffered invasion in the North, and for a period of four centuries Lower Egypt was ruled by the Hyksos, or foreign "Shepherd Princes," who maintained Memphis as their main distribution center and Zoan or Tanis as their political capital. It was under these kings that Joseph rose to power and the children of Israel were made welcome in the Land of Goshen, a section of the eastern Delta country. Thus Joseph's official duties often required him to work in Memphis and Zoan, as well as to take trips to Abydos and Thebes.

The Hyksos were driven from the throne by Amosis, a Theban prince, about 1580 B.C. He restored the Egyptian rule and established the Eighteenth Dynasty. With Amosis began the reigns of those eminent Theban kings who built the magnificent temples and palaces at Thebes. With the New Empire came a new policy toward the Hebrews. Oppression of the children of Israel reached its peak, as is graphically pictured in the first chapters of Exodus, under Thutmose III, and culminated in their Exodus from the land about 1446 B.C. under the leadership of Moses.[2]

The New Empire came to an end after a succession of military forays to the East. Egypt then went into decline, and found itself unable to cope with the rising power of the Assyrian nation and later the Babylonians. It suffered decisive defeat at the hand of Nebuchadnezzar at Carchemish in 606-605 B.C. After a six-month campaign at Pelusium and the capture of both Memphis and Thebes, Cambyses annexed the country to Persia. It was that country's vassal until the conquest by Alexander the Great in 332 B.C. At Alexander's death in 323 B.C. a Macedonian general named Ptolemy was appointed governor of Egypt and for nearly three hundred years the country was ruled by his descendents, the Ptolemies. Then came the tragic death of Antony and Cleopatra and the end of the ancient glory of Egypt.

In 36 B.C. Egypt passed into Roman hands, and after 500 years into Mohammedan hands. Too frequently since then it has been the pawn of one nation after another. It was only in very recent years, under British control, that Egypt regained any considerable degree of strength. It now enjoys self-government, and is earnestly striving to recapture its ancient power and importance.[3]

The dominant factor in ancient Egyptian life was that of religion. The Egyptians loved life but recognized its brevity and therefore sought to procure for themselves endless life in a land which they envisioned as even better than their native Egypt, the Elysian Fields as they were sometimes called. They had many gods, many priests, many temples, and almost endless ceremonies and processions; and whatever they did, or wherever they went, their actions were definitely affected by their religious beliefs, and those beliefs were invariably influenced by their deep yearning for immortality. Immortality was the heart and center of all their religion, immortality for the body as well as for the soul.

Man, according to their system of religion, was composed of four different entities, each in itself complete but joined together in the body during life. These elements were: The body; the "Ka" (or double); the "Ba" (or the soul); and the "Khu" (or divine spark). The Ka was a sort of spiritual body corresponding to the material body, and being bound to it in life, then after death occupying the tomb along with the mummy. The Ba, represented as a human-headed bird, along with the Khu departed at death to the regions of the gods, but paid frequent return visits to the mummy and the Ka. Eventually the four different entities or elements would be reunited eternally in Osiris' land, situated below the western horizon and presided over by Osiris. No one, however, seemed to know just when this most happy reunion would take place.[4]

In the meantime immortality was contingent upon the preservation of the body, observance of the proper ritual, and a continued supply of food for sustenance. Therefore, the Egyptians developed an elaborate process of mummification by which they would insure the body against decay; they made fine coffins, and spent a major portion of their skills and ingenuity in constructing indestructible tombs whereby they hoped to safeguard the mummy and arrange for the welfare of the Ka remaining in the tomb, and for the Ba when at intervals it returned. The tomb was the "house of the Ka," and the priests responsible for its maintenance were the "servants of the Ka." [5]

Thus the tomb was made as comfortable, as attractive and as home-like as possible. Familiar scenes and pleasant sentences were inscribed on the walls, and some of the most intimate possessions of the deceased were placed in the tomb—fine clothing, gold, jewels, furniture, chariots, weapons of war, and everything else that could make the dead happy in the world to come. An audience room with an altar was arranged so loved ones and friends might visit the tomb and bring food and place it on the altar and commune with the dead. This is why an unmolested tomb, when opened, yields such a rich store of objects.[6] Of course, only kings, high officials, and the wealthy so arranged and enriched their tombs. The less fortunate did not hang their hope of immortal life on such a burial, but felt that in some way their fortunes were tied up with the royal, divine king whom they had served so loyally. Having served faithfully here, they apparently rested their faith in the need for their services in the world to come.

Egypt is a paradise for archaeologists, a land where the vestiges of by-gone civilizations stare at you and challenge you. And an overwhelmingly large percentage of Middle East archaeologists have accepted the challenge either by studying there or by excavating some of its sites.

The chief cities of Egypt that have been excavated are: Abydos, Memphis, Zoan, Heliopolis, Thebes, and Amarna; these reveal most of our knowledge of the Egyptians and their part in the drama which unrolled in Bible Lands.

Abydos or Thinis, in Upper Egypt, is one of the most ancient of the historical sites of the Nile valley. It is situated fifty miles north of Thebes on the west bank of the river, at the edge of the fertile land where one of the old traffic lines led westward to the oasis in the Libyan desert. The city had been founded by pre-Menite kings, and already had a cemetery and a center of worship when the kings of the First and Second Dynasties (2800 B.C.) built their elaborate tombs. The early rulers renewed and enlarged the town and temple built by their predecessors. Great forts were built on the desert behind the town by three kings of the Second Dynasty. The temple and town were rebuilt at intervals down to the time of the Thirtieth Dynasty.

At an early date Abydos became the holy city of the land, the place to which every Egyptian desired to make a pilgrimage either during his life or after his death. The reason for this extraordinary development of devotion lay in the strange, yet pathetic and powerful myth of Osiris.

According to the legend, Osiris the son of the sky goddess, and Isis his god-wife, had born to them a son Horus. This completed the triad at Abydos. Osiris had ruled wisely and judged justly, but Seth (or Setekh) the god of evil, coveted both his kingdom and his queen.

When Horus was only a few days old, Osiris was trapped and drowned by Seth. Isis, by enchantment, recovered the body of her divine husband, but in her sorrow and weakness she did not bury the body as well as she might, and Seth found it and tore it into fourteen pieces and scattered it over the land of Egypt.

Weeping, and in deep sorrow, Isis went throughout the land and by the use of her powers of enchantment, collected the fragments of the body of Osiris. While she searched she wept so profusely that the Nile overflowed, but she brought the body together again and with the aid of Nephthys, another goddess, she buried it at Abydos.

Osiris soon rose from the dead and made armor for Horus his son, and sent him out to do battle with Seth, who was vanquished but not slain outright. Osiris reigned with Isis for a time, but was too good and great and wise for this world alone; therefore he became not only the god of life, death, and the resurrection but also the ruler of the kingdom of bliss in the other world—the great and wise judge to whom the dead at the final judgment must answer for their deeds. He alone could grant admission to the land of eternal bliss, but would do so to those who were worthy.[7]

To every pious Egyptian the setting and reappearance of the sun, the rise and fall of the Nile, and many other events of everyday life figured in this legend of Osiris. The conflict between Osiris and Seth was made to symbolize the struggle between light and darkness, the fight between right and wrong, between life and death. The resurrection of Osiris became the type and symbol of the immortality of the soul, and this the Egyptian longed for more than all else.

Therefore most Egyptians desired in some way to be linked with Osiris, the great god of the resurrection and the judge of all mankind. To be buried near Osiris was to secure without fail all the blessings the god could bestow; if this was impossible, the channel of blessing could be kept open by erecting a stele or memorial stone near the tomb of the great god. If even this was beyond the means of the aspirant, he could send a votive offering in a beautifully designed pottery vessel that was placed as near as possible to the holy place.

Accordingly, wealthy men frequently left orders for their bodies to be transported in boats by the way of the river to Abydos where with suitable ceremonies they were to be interred near the tomb of the great god Osiris. If the nobleman had to be put to rest near his king in the capital, he erected a cenotaph at Abydos and furnished it with all that might be needed for his soul when it visited the abode of the great god. Others erected small commemorative steles, while the poor, who constituted a vast majority of the populace, sent pottery votive offerings. In time, therefore, there grew up a vast accumulation of tombs, a forest of steles, and a veritable wilderness of broken pottery, which gave meaning to the modern Arabic name for the site, "the Mother of Pots."

The principal excavators at Abydos were Auguste Mariette, Amelineau, Petrie, Edouard Henri Naville, H. R. Hall and T. E. Peet. Each had his turn and each had his assistants. They made enormous finds, of which the more important were in connection with the Temple of Rameses I (1319-1318 B.C.), the Temple of Seti I (1318-1301 B.C.), the Temple of Rameses II (1301-1234 B.C.), and the cemetery with its vast assemblage of tombs, especially the mastaba tombs of the royalty.

In the ruins of these magnificent columned temples, some large and some small, were found impressive sculptures and paintings depicting the exploits of the kings. In one was Seti I with his son Rameses II, offering incense to seventy-six of their princely ancestors seated on their royal thrones accompanied by their names and titles. Then there was the "Pool of Osiris" used in connection with a "passion play" at Abydos, and a small ivory statue of Pharaoh Cheops, which seems to be the only portrait of him ever to have been found.

The cemetery, together with the mastaba tombs of the kings of the First and Second Dynasties, lay southeast of Abydos on a low spur slightly raised above the plain. The largest of these mastabas was 54 by 223 feet. In it had been buried the monarchs with plenteous provision for use in the Otherworld, and nearby had been buried the pharaoh's court circle and leading officials. Represented among them were his chief butler, royal seal-bearer, royal architects, the keeper of the king's vineyards, and the provisions officer, all of whom aid in giving realism to the narratives in the Bible.

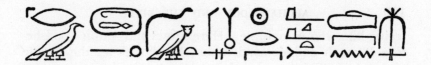

CHAPTER XV

Archaeological Discoveries in Lower Egypt

OUT ON THE WEST BANK of the Nile, some fourteen miles south-west of the present city of Cairo, on a slightly elevated plain facing the rising sun is the site of the ancient city of Memphis. It came into prominence about 2850 B.C. when Menes united the two lands of Upper and Lower Egypt into a single nation and constructed this city as his capital. Around the city Menes built a strong wall made of brick overlaid with fine white gesso plaster, which gave rise to the name "Menofer" or "White Walls," from which the Greeks derived the name "Memphis."

Memphis was Egypt's largest city and most important commercial center, the depository of vast treasure, and its principal seat of learning. It was also important for many peoples of the Middle East and southern Europe, as well as for Libya, Arabia, and other countries near and far. As a chief seat of government, of commerce, of learning, and religion for more than three thousand years, it attracted and fascinated a wide variety of peoples from many lands. Here came the Phoenician sailors with their cargos, the Greek with the arts, and the Hebrews with their religion and their search for refuge.

It was here that Abraham and Sarah his wife, and his nephew Lot, came some 4000 years ago to "sojourn in the land." Here Joseph was sold as a Hebrew slave, but later as prime minister and "federal food" administrator went out "over all the land of Egypt." It was here, or near here, that Moses was brought up and became learned in Egypt's wisdom. It was here he braved the wrath of the pharaoh, made his choice, and "endured as

179

seeing him who is invisible." Here Moses and Aaron stood before Pharaoh and demanded that he should let the people of Israel go. This was the place where ". . . Pharaoh rose up in the night, he, and all his servants, and all the Egyptians; and there was a great cry in Egypt; for there was not a house where there was not one dead" (Exodus 12:30).

As the chief seat of learning, Memphis majored in the worship of Ptah and the sacred Apis bull. Ptah, according to Egyptian belief, was "the Mind of the Universe," who created all gods and men by thinking them into existence. He was especially revered by artists, skilled craftsmen, and men of letters. Osiris was god of the living and the dead. Almost all phases of life here and hereafter were controlled in one way or another by Osiris. For Apis the Sacred Bull, a magnificent temple was constructed which was known as the "Cathedral" of Egypt. These two great temples—that of Ptah and Apis—were united by a long avenue of sphinxes.

At the height of its prosperity the main portion of the city measured some eight miles long by four miles wide, and sustained a population of near 500,000. It was the southern capital of Egypt through many dynasties, and was the "commercial" capital for most of its history. It shared supremacy with Thebes during the Eighteenth to Twenty-fifth Dynasties, and continued great until the founding of Alexandria by Alexander the Great in 332 B.C.

Its final fall was the result of the rise of the Arabic city of Fostat on the east bank of the Nile, and to the building of the newer and greater city of Cairo by the Mohammedan conquerors during the seventh century A.D. Many of its fine ruins above ground were used in the construction of the new city. And of Cairo it is well said that it grew out of the more ancient city's ruins. Many pillars in the Mosque of Cairo were taken from the temples of Memphis.

The only remains of Memphis were in the form of ruined structures, granite blocks, broken obelisks, statues, and its alabaster columned streets, which lay buried beneath ten to twenty feet of shifting sands until the latter part of the nineteenth century, when excavators were able to show its lay-out and to exhibit the many interesting objects discovered after having lain under the desert sands from 1200 to 2000 years.

The various excavators uncovered the remains of four temples, of Ptah, of Proteus, of Isis, and the Temple of Apis, founded by Psammetichus. They found the remains of two palaces, and a fortress that covered two acres and possessed a great court 110 feet square. Later they found the gigantic colossus of Rameses II, and the lesser colossus of the same, and a large and beautiful alabaster sphinx 26 feet long, 14 feet high and weighing 80 tons. In 1928 the writer, while a guest of Reisner, saw them uncover wide, stone-paved streets, bordered by long lines of extremely beautiful alabaster columns. But of all the finds in or near Memphis the great necropolis or cemetery west of the city was the most interesting and revealing.

Here, along the rim of the desert, well out of the reach of inundation by Nile waters and in keeping with the Egyptian's idea of immortality, is a vast cemetery two miles wide and some sixty miles long, beginning at the Pyramids of Abu Roash in the north and ending with the Lahun Pyramid southeast of the Fayum. Like a gigantic field of death, seventeen miles of this "silent city of the dead" is extremely crowded with the remains of some forty to fifty millions of animals, men, women, children and pharaohs. Some are merely covered in the sand, some are in carefully dug graves, some are in well built mastabas, and some are in over seventy pyramids—a fabulous necropolis in which ancient men laid away the bodies of their dead. Perhaps no cemetery in the world is so extensive, and certainly none so famous. How aptly did the prophet Hosea exclaim "Memphis shall bury them," for certainly they have buried on a scale that is unprecedented anywhere in the world.

THE APIS BULL

The animals buried here were only the exceptional ones selected by the priests and worshiped by the people. Because the Apis (Ah-fis) or Sacred Bull was the principal animal to whom the ancient Egyptians paid deep devotion on the grounds that both Osiris and Ptah were incarnate in the sacred Apis bull, he was continually present among men. The Apis bull was recognized by twenty-eight distinctive marks that identified him as the god incarnate whom they were to worship. According to Herodotus, he was black with a square or triangular spot on his forehead, a crescent on his flank, an eagle-shaped figure on his back, and double hairs on his tail, and on the underside of his tongue was a knot like unto a scarab or sacred beetle.

When this bull was found he was led in grand ceremony to the magnificent Apis Temple where he was secluded behind curtains, waited on by numerous priests, fed choice food, bathed and brushed, exercised, and bedded down on a soft bed. The cow so favored as to have been the mother of this deified animal was given honorable quarters near the vestibule of the temple. From time to time the Apis bull was shown briefly to those who came to worship him and to those who would obtain his oracular verdict. The sacred bull's birthday was an occasion of public rejoicing, a kind of Christmas for the Egyptians. On this day the people donned their richest apparel and lined the streets as worshipers while the bull was led by in a sacred procession.

At death, the Apis bull was embalmed by the intricate process of mummification, and accompanied by mourning and elaborate ceremonies the huge body was placed in a granite sarcophagus. At a cost of $50,000 to $100,000 it was buried in a private burial chamber within the Serapeum or mausoleum located under the great temple. Within the burial room of each mummified bull many costly gifts were placed, together with an engraved tablet stating the regnal year of the Pharaoh in whose reign the bull was born, the regnal year in which he died, and the length of his life.[1]

In time the magnificent Apis temple was destroyed, and the shifting sands passed over the Serapeum and it eventually became buried from view.

In the year 1856 Auguste Mariette observed the head of a sphinx protruding from the sand west of Memphis near the great stepped pyramid. On the sphinx he found an inscription referring to Apis the sacred bull. Remembering that Strabo had described the Serapeum of Memphis as approached through an avenue of sphinxes, he at once hired a gang of Arab workmen, equipped them with shovels and set them to digging. With immense exertions the sand drifts were cleared away and the excavators found themselves in an ancient avenue lined with 141 crouching sphinxes, in addition to many pedestals for others. Although the magnificent cathedral temple of the sacred Apis had been wrecked and most of the stones carried away, many ruins still remained. As Mariette patiently worked away during the late afternoon of November 13, 1856, he became conscious of being close to an important discovery. He requested his men to stay with him, and together they kept working into the night. Finally, when they had dug through a deep shaft-like stairway, they broke into an underground avenue 320 feet long. Later excavations increased the total length of the tunneled avenues to 1120 feet.

Guided by flickering torchlights, Mariette and a few of his workmen soon discovered sixty-four large burial chambers arranged along the avenue. Near the center of each burial room was a huge red or black granite sarcophagus approximately 12 feet long, 9 feet high, and 6 feet wide, each weighing nearly 60 tons. In each of these a sacred Apis bull had been buried, but long centuries ago tomb robbers had entered, pushed off the lids, and stolen the valuables. In going from chamber to chamber in this amazing city of dead bulls, Mariette found one vault that had escaped the violating hand of the treasure-seeker. There, in the mortar was the imprint of the fingers of the mason who had set the last stone during the reign of Rameses II, and there in the dust were the footprints of those who had last trod the floor more than 3000 years ago. There also were the votive offerings dedicated by visitors who had come and gone so many centuries ago, among them an inscribed tablet of Rameses' own son, high priest of Apis and one of the chief dignitaries of the time. It is little wonder that when the great explorer stood in this tomb and saw things as they had remained inviolate for thirty-one eventful centuries, he was overwhelmed and burst into tears.[2]

The pomp and splendor with which the worship of the bull Apis was celebrated at Memphis and at Thebes accounts for the apostasy of the Israelites in the wilderness, when, having made a molten calf, they said, "These be thy gods, O Israel, which brought thee up out of the land of Egypt." They had been so accustomed to see divine honors paid, even by the mightiest of their taskmasters, to this supposed incarnation of the Deity that at Sinai itself they yielded to the worship they had long observed and "corrupted themselves, turning aside quickly out of the way which the Lord commanded them."[3] Later in Palestine Jeroboam set up golden calves to be worshiped, the one at Dan, and the other at Bethel, and said unto the people: "Behold thy gods, O Israel . . ." (I Kings 12:28, II Kings 17:16).

THE MASTABA TOMBS

Hidden away in the womb of this gigantic old desert cemetery, on which the yellow shroud of sand has grown thicker and thicker as the centuries have passed, are millions of bodies of the poor buried in simple graves or merely dipped in a chemical wash to retard decay and hurriedly thrust into the desert sands. In contrast to these are the "mastaba" tombs, which in a very real sense were the "houses of the dead" and in which were laid away the lesser members of the royal families, nobles of the court, influential officials, and the well-to-do or famous of the kingdom. These mastabas were usually of stone or marble and constructed so as to form an oblong, flat-topped mass of masonry with steeply sloping sides. Some of the mastaba tombs were large; one measured 280 feet in length, 150 feet in breadth, and 33 feet in height. The average attained a length of 50 to 80 feet, and many were smaller.

There are many types of mastabas, but usually they appear as one-storied houses containing an entrance, some small rooms and a well ornamented mortuary chapel or reception room decorated with mural paintings and furnished with many conveniences placed there for the comfort of the dead. Here the relatives and friends of the deceased assembled at the time of burial, and on stated occasions thereafter, to commune quietly with their departed dead and present their offerings of food upon a low altar built before a false door in the west wall of the room. A connecting shaft or corridor led downward from the chapel room to the subterranean burial apartments in which the mummy and the Ka were supposed to pass their existence until such a time as they were again reunited with the Ba and the Khu, the deceased then taking his place of identity with the god Osiris.

Like the homes of the living, these "houses of the dead" were laid out in regular streets and formed extensive "towns" grouped about the pyramids of the kings.[4] The walls of many of these great mastaba tombs are richly adorned with paintings, reliefs and inscriptions depicting the daily round of life in

Egypt during the Pyramid Age through the Ptolemaic Age (300-30 B.C.). In these "houses of the dead" are frequently found the keys to the religious life of the occupants and their beliefs concerning life here and life hereafter.

The mastaba of Ti, for example, is the tomb of a man who in his youth rose up from the ranks, developed his architectural talents, married Neferhotep the pharaoh's daughter, and had as his sons Thi and Tamut who ranked as princes. Ti attained high office and was architect under two kings of the Fifth Dynasty and an owner of large estates which he operated with pleasure as well as profit. His tomb has its court-like chapel surrounded by fine columns, its long halls and many rooms, and is distinguished by elaborate and richly detailed wall paintings, reliefs, and hieroglyphic narratives showing not only the daily domestic and official life of the deceased but also that of all those who worked for him. All these are shown in action, together with the animals, fowl, and fish that were a part of this energetic man's earthly career.[5]

The pyramids of Egypt are the climax of royal tomb building in the vast necropolis at Memphis. They are the loftiest and most stupendous works of man and the world's mightiest national monuments to man's faith in life everlasting. High on the lofty rim of the Libyan desert, overlooking the "white walled" city of Memphis and the fertile valley of the Nile, they rest like the perpetual hills in solid tranquility on their rocky bases. They were constructed between 2700 and 2200 B.C. and are an architectural triumph unequaled by modern man. In stern and gloomy grandeur they have survived the prodigal waste of the ages. While cities have risen and flourished and fallen in the valley below, they have remained as solid and unshaken as when ancient Greek fathers brought their sons to see them. They bid fair to survive all the ravages of time in their mountain massiveness until the mountains themselves shall depart and the hills be removed.

THE PYRAMIDS

The pyramids of Lower Egypt begin with the Pyramids of Abu Roash in the north and extend to the Pyramids of Lahun in the south, a distance of some sixty miles. They number between seventy and eighty in all, with an additional ten smaller ones in Upper Egypt. Some are small and some exceedingly large. Some stand out in bold relief whereas only the tops of others peek above the desert sand. Some are well preserved whereas others are mere heaps of ruins. We take a hurried view of the Step Pyramid, the Meydum Pyramid, the Great Pyramid, the Second Pyramid, the Third Pyramid, and the Pyramids with Texts.

The Step Pyramid

The transition in royal tomb building from the flat-topped mastaba tomb to the pyramidal form occurred about 2700 B.C. when King Zoser (Djoser) of the Third Dynasty conferred with Imhotep, his gifted chief architect and counselor, and laid plans for and began the construction of a most unusual funeral monument and burial complex in the necropolis west of Memphis, now called "Sakkara."

It was unique in that at its core it included a square ground-plan mastaba, which to begin with was 26 feet high and about 207 feet wide. Each side was oriented to face one of the four cardinal points and was faced with an outer layer of dressed Tura limestone. The outer layer was extended and enlarged from time to time into a series of steps, each step being flat-topped and forming a platform on which to build the next. Finally it was completed as a six-stepped pyramid (hence the name, Step Pyramid), oblong in plan and resembling six superimposed mastabas. The base level measured approximately 411 feet from east to west and 358 feet from north to south. Each succeeding level was progressively smaller in area, making a succession of six unequal steps, each diminishing in size to the very apex, which was 204 feet above ground. The whole building was cased with a final layer of dressed Tura limestone.

This entire complex was built entirely of hewn stone, and was surrounded on all four sides by a wide platform and an immense stone wall enclosure approximately thirty-three feet high and more than a mile in perimeter length. This vast enclosure contained a fine mortuary temple, an elaborate group of shrines, altars, courts, storehouses and gateways. From within this enclosure a deep shaft led downward to a maze of corridors and rooms forming a network of underground buildings and crypts in which the king and certain members of his family were eventually buried. It all formed a veritable two-level city in itself, planned and executed to accomodate King Zoser with the setting necessary for repeating his jubilee and numerous other ceremonies connected with his after-life.

The king's tomb chamber at the bottom of the ninety-two foot shaft was built entirely of pink granite from Aswan. After the body was interred in the chamber the entrance was filled with a six-foot granite plug, weighing about three tons.

The walls of the subterranean rooms were decorated in places with carved designs of plants and bundles of stems. At numerous places on the buildings, as well as on the enclosure wall, artisans had carved imitation doors, which appeared to stand in open position.

Among King Zoser's tomb furniture was found an alabaster wine jug, a bowl, many alabaster vases and some 30,000 beautifully shaped stone dishes and vessels. Human remains were found in the tomb chamber, but they have not been proven to be Zoser's. The finding of his mummy awaits some future discovery.

Time has reduced everything except the pyramid itself to ruined heaps of masonry, but it still stands as one of the most remarkable architectural works ever produced by the ancient Egyptian craftsmen. No other pyramid was surrounded by so imposing an array of buildings to provide for the needs of the king in his after-life, and the chief credit for the structure goes to Imhotep, the architect, astronomer, physican, priest, writer and chief counselor to the king, who immortalized his own name and that of King Zoser by producing the world's first pyramid and the oldest building of hewn stone known in the world. Two long rows of elegant fluted columns have been unearthed near the pyramid, which shows that this kind of column was known to the ancient Egyptians long before the Doric art was known to the Greek architects.[6]

The Meydum Pyramid

The Meydum Pyramid, located forty miles south of the city of Cairo, was constructed about 2650 B.C., and is usually considered the connecting link between the Step Pyramid and the later smooth outline pyramids we regard as true pyramids. It is the tomb and monument of Pharaoh Snefru, founder of the Fourth Dynasty, whose architect, though not entirely free of conventional step construction, did master the problem of smooth sloping surface.

It was begun as a mastaba tomb, but went through successive enlargements and developed into an eight-stepped structure which was finally overlaid with expertly jointed and polished blocks of Tura limestone, thus making it a geometrically true pyramid measuring 474 feet square at the base and rising sharply at an angle of about 52 degrees.[7]

Surrounding the Meydum Pyramid is a plastered pavement enclosed by a stone wall. Within this courtyard are the ruins of a mortuary temple, two steles, small storehouses and a mastaba.

The marching centuries and the thoughtlessness of man have combined to destroy part of the superstructure of the Meydum Pyramid, so that it now has the appearance of three square towers with sloping sides placed in retreating stages one over the other, and nestled in a mound which is really a fourth tower covered with debris. Its tower-like appearance is the result of the breaking away of the lower steps. Yet it is thought by many to be the most magnificent of all the pyramids of Egypt. As Murray has said "In the rosy glow of the dawn it towers majestically against the sky, the vastest and most impressive building that the hand of man has ever raised." [8]

In 1882 Maspero located the pyramid entrance, which is in the northern face about 53 feet above the ground. It opens into a passage that slopes downward at a 28-degree angle for 60 feet and enters solid rock. The passage then continues for 130 feet, at which point it levels and extends for an additional 31 feet to a vertical shaft terminating at an opening in the limestone paved floor of the burial vault.

The burial vault was found to be empty, having been violated before the Ramesside Age. The despoilers had left behind a set of beams and ropes which were evidently used in removing the sarcophagus from its place. Opinion is divided as to whether Snefru was buried in this pyramid or in the other one he built at Dahshur. Most authorities, however, favor the Meydum Pyramid as the place of his burial.

Petrie excavated at this pyramid in 1891 and again in 1910,

when he discovered a tiny mortuary temple against the east face of the pyramid and about 80 feet from the enclosure wall. This temple, composed entirely of Tura limestone and covering an area of little more than 34 square feet and standing but 9 feet high, is probably the oldest complete Egyptian temple known and remains almost entirely intact. The building is extremely simple, having no reliefs or inscriptions on its walls. Within the little courtyard of the temple stand two 14-foot steles between which is a low, flat limestone altar used for the daily offerings of food and drink to the dead king.

Were it not for the discovery of this temple, the name of the builder of the Meydum Pyramid would have remained in doubt, but happily Petrie found written on the temple walls some scribblings left by ancient Egyptian visitors who came to see the tomb. These typical visitors yielded to the tourist instinct to write the purpose of their visit and their names on the walls, thus leaving no less than five testimonials to the fact that it was the pyramid of Snefru.

The largest and the best known pyramids of Egypt are those which make up the "Gizeh group." They are the tombs of the great kings of the Fourth Dynasty: Cheops (Khufu), Chephren (Khafra), and Mycerinus (Menkaura). East of the first and "great pyramid" are three smaller pyramids designed for members of Cheops' royal family. Then, south of the third pyramid lie three more, designed for the members of Mycerinus' family. The largest and most famous of these, and all other pyramids, is the Great Pyramid of Cheops.

The Great Pyramid of Cheops

Khufu, or Cheops as he was called by the Greeks, was the son and successor to the throne of Snefru, who had built the Meydum and Dahshur pyramids. Thus, from his youth he had breathed the air of pyramid construction and had often visited the resting place of his mother at Dahshur and that of his father at Meydum.

Soon after coming to the throne he summoned his priest, his architect, his engineer, and his chief counselor, and other ministers. Together they planned a larger, more beautiful and more enduring pyramid tomb than had yet been built. With wisdom befitting such august counsel, the site for the grand structure was chosen on the rim of the desert in the district now known as Gizeh.

Suitable quarters for the workmen were constructed and the making of proper tools and equipment was begun. The latter included large and small copper chisels, bronze saws set with diamonds, circular saws, tubular and gem-studded drills, stone hammers, wedges, sledges, cradles, try squares, and others practical to the times.[9]

The first ten years were consumed by the architects, engineers, artisans, masons and workmen in setting out the sides with great exactitude and in carving from the solid rock a thirteen-acre four-terraced pyramid base or foundation; in building a still larger and more extensive platform about the entire pyramid; and in constructing a great ramp-like causeway which led up from an especially prepared wharf or landing platform more than a quarter of a mile from the pyramid platform. Within the great solid rock foundation they tunneled a sloping passage almost 300 feet to a subterranean chamber, and on both the north and south sides of the extensive platform about the pyramid base, they carved a pit-like boat-room for the Pharaoh's two solar boats—one for travel by day, and one for travel by night.

In July, about 2700 B.C., when the Nile had begun to overflow and all work in the fields was consequently suspended and the greater part of the population idle, Cheops increased his force of workmen to 100,000 men, and one of the world's greatest federal works projects was under way. The men were given free food, clothing, and lodging, and were doled out scrip suitable to their barest needs. Water carriers served them on the job, and doctors were constantly on hand to treat wounds and fractures as well as illnesses.

In the great Tura limestone quarries in the Mokkotan hills just eastward across the Nile, large crews of men worked from one year's end to another under the supervision and direction of specially trained engineers, masons, and overseers. Other crews worked in Egypt's finest red and gray granite quarries near Aswan, 500 miles up the Nile. Still other stonemasons secured black and green diorite and white, peach and rose alabaster from other quarries. By the beginning of July of each year, these stonemasons and workmen would have vast quantities of stone blocks cut and ready, and the carpenters would have heavy barges prepared so that the great gangs of common laborers, coming on the job for the summer season, could load the huge blocks of stone and granite on the fleets of floating barges and craft. Then while the Nile waters rose to make the river big and wide in its annual inundation, the block-laden barges were floated by the swelling waters and were ferried down and across the Nile and the flooded delta to the great landing base or wharf near the pyramid. Here the blocks were placed on strong sleds or rollers and dragged by means of ropes and cables up the great ramp or pyramid causeway by more laborers. On reaching the site, the blocks received their final finish, and by the ingenious use of wedges, cradles, cables, and beams acting as levers they were lifted and moved to their final resting place, where they were adjusted and laid with an "extreme nicety" that would ever cause following generations to marvel.

For twenty years the mighty controlled phenomenon went on, until finally Cheops, together with his counselors and chief officers of state, watched while skilled hands set the highly polished granite cap or pyramidian on the massive structure, raising it to the prodigious height of 481 feet. Then, when all scaffolding and earthen rampways were removed and the mortuary temple and lesser buildings at its base were complete, the pharaoh, his hierarchy of officials and the masses—which probably numbered more than a million people—gathered for the colorful and solemn ceremony of dedication. Few days, if any, ever equalled this day in Egypt, because for almost a generation the major energies of the nation had been directed toward the construction of their pharaoh-god's great pyramid. To the people, this mighty pyramidal-tomb and temple would secure their deified monarch's eternal well-being, and he in turn would plan for them in eternity as a father cares for his children.[10]

After the death and funeral of Pharaoh Cheops, his mummy was sealed inside the burial chamber, the tunnels were blocked with sections of hard granite and granite trapdoors that slid into grooves, and the entrance was closed over.

For long centuries the Great Pyramid of Cheops inspired

the just pride of all who dwelt in Egypt and evoked the wonder and perpetual admiration of the long line of distinguished visitors who came from around the globe. The Greek historian Herodotus explored it about 445 B.C., and Pliny, Alexander, and Dionysius were among other early visitors. The Great Pyramid remained structurally intact until A.D. 818 when Caliph Ma'mun, son of Harun al-Rashid of Arabian Nights fame, expended considerable time, energy and money in entering the pyramid in the mistaken belief that it contained hidden treasure. It was found to have been robbed long centuries before, yet no one knows exactly when or by whom.

In modern times the exterior and interior of the Great Pyramid have been surveyed and measured with great care and with a high degree of accuracy by such distinguished authorities as François Jomard (a scientist of Napoleon's staff), Richard Howard Vyse and J. S. Perring (1837-38), Petrie (1880-82), Ludwig Borchardt, Alan Rowe, Reisner, J. H. Cole of the Survey Department of the Egyptian Government in 1925, and in more recent years by Ahmed Fakhry and Zakaria Ghoneim. The finds have gone far in verifying Herodotus and other ancient writers who wrote their impressions of the great structure. Men like David Davidson of London and others have supposed they saw in this pyramid "a miracle in stone," a veritable foretelling of events for the centuries.

The facts found by surveys, measurements, and study of the Great Pyramid may be summarized as follows. It was constructed for Pharaoh Cheops about 2700-2680 B.C. It took the architects, engineers, and their crews of assistants many years to survey the outline, carve the foundation from a solid stone base, and to construct the great causeway. In all, it took 100,000 men twenty years to build the pyramid itself. Originally each side of the pyramid base or foundation measured 767 feet, and each of the four sides faced one of the four cardinal points of the compass. It rose to the height of 481 feet above the rim of the sandy desert. Its slant height was 612 feet. It contained some 2,300,000 stone blocks, averaging 50 by 50 by 28 inches and weighing an average of two and one half tons, or 5,750,000 tons in all. Some of these stone blocks weigh as much as sixty tons, and were laid with a layer of cement or glue no thicker than a sheet of writing paper. The whole limestone mass covered

Upper: The tri-lingual Rosetta Stone became the key with which learned men unlocked the civilizations of the Nile Valley.
Lower: A portion of the Behistun Inscription which served as a key to unlock the secrets of the cuneiform scripts of Babylonia and Persia.

Upper: Basket girls carrying débris on Dr. Petrie's excavation at Tell el-Ajjul (ancient Gaza).
Lower: All objects must be recorded and photographed before being moved.

The Black Obelisk has twenty small bas-reliefs showing the officials from five different countries bringing tribute to King Shalmaneser III of Assyria. In the second register from the top, Jehu, king of Israel, is shown prostrating himself before the king.

Upper: An Assyrian winged bull from the palace gateway of Sargon II.
Lower: A reconstructed drawing of King Sargon's twenty-five-acre palace area at Khorsabad, with its spacious domestic quarters, luxurious harem, three temples and towering ziggurat.

Upper left: This hexagonal baked clay cylinder of Sennacherib, king of Assyria, is inscribed with the details of eight military campaigns, including the capture and sack of Babylon, and his invasion of Palestine, when he besieged King Hezekiah in Jerusalem. The cylinder was found among the ruins of the palace of Sennacherib under the mound of Neby Yunis (South Nineveh), and was bought by Colonel J. Taylor, Consul-General of Baghdad in 1830, and released to the British Museum in 1855.

Upper right: This is one of the Nuzi tablets which tells of the adoption of a son, and throws considerable light on Eliezer as Abraham's heir.

Lower: Some uncovered ruins of the ancient city of Babylon.

The ruined is the Grand Staircase leading to the Audience Hall

Upper: An air view of a portion of the mound of ancient Shushan (Susa), the city of Queen Esther and King Ahasuerus. Here de Morgan found the stele of Hammurabi in 1901.
Lower left: The tomb of Cyrus the Great at Pasargadae, erected about 529 B.C.
Center: A carved and painted tomb at Marissa.
Lower right: Through Ishtar Gate, on festal days, King Nebuchadnezzar with his men of church and state marched southward along the Sacred Way to the Temple of Marduk.

Upper: The "Ba" (or the soul), represented as a human-headed bird, departed at death to the regions of heaven, but paid frequent visits to the mummy in the tomb.
Lower: The earliest of the pyramids was King Zoser's Step Pyramid.

ft: An air view of the famous pyramids of Gizeh. The Great Pyramid is farthest, the cond Pyramid in the center, while the Third Pyramid is the nearest of the larger ones. The aller pyramids were tombs of the Pharaoh's family and of nobles belonging to his court. e shadows on the sand show the outlines of the walls about the platforms which surrounded : pyramids.

ght: The Grand Gallery within the heart of the Great Pyramid is 153 feet long and 28 feet h. Its floor is made up of a deep-grooved ascending passage, 3 feet 5 inches wide, bordered each side by a flat-topped ramp, 2 feet high and 20 inches wide.

Upper left: A Tell el-Amarna Tablet—a letter from Tushratta, king of Mitanni, to Amen-hotep III of Egypt.
Upper right: The upper portion of the Israel Stele on which King Merenptah tells of his raid in Palestine during the Period of the Judges.
Lower: Weighing the heart of a soul in the great Judgment Hall of Osiris.

Upper: These close-packed Mastaba Tombs of the Egyptian nobles and men of wealth are laid out in rows to form streets like those of a village. The view is from the top of the Great Pyramid.
Lower: The Sphinx, solemn sentinel which guards the Gizeh pyramids and Mastaba Tombs.

Left: Tut-ankh-amen's magnificent form-fitting coffin is wrought of solid gold, inlaid with lapis lazuli, and weighs about 1800 pounds. Its proportions are so correct, its symbols so suitable, and its craftsmanship so perfect that it has long remained Egypt's most exquisite piece of work—the most enchanting thing of its kind in the world today. (*Photograph by Harry Burton, The Metropolitan Museum of Art.*)

Upper: The Moabite Stone on which Mesha, king of Moab, tells of his conflict with Israel.

Lower: High on the rugged cliffs, south of the Dog River, have been carved a series of fascinating inscriptions—memorials of the conquerors of antiquity who passed this way and left a record of their achievements.

Upper: Over King Tut's face was his sculptured portrait of beaten gold. The vulture and cobra, symbols of upper and lower Egypt, are on his forehead. The whites of his eyes are crystalline limestone, the irises are obsidian. (*Photograph by Harry Burton, The Metropolitan Museum of Art.*)
Lower: The horse stables at Megiddo with hitching-posts and a few of the rock mangers in place.

Upper: Air view of the mound of Megiddo, in the process of being excavated.
Lower: Isaiah Scroll "A" opened to columns 32 and 33 (Isaiah 39-40).

Khirbet Qumran looking south from defense tower. Two large cisterns are at the right with conduit in between. Pantry (with two pillar bases) is at left.

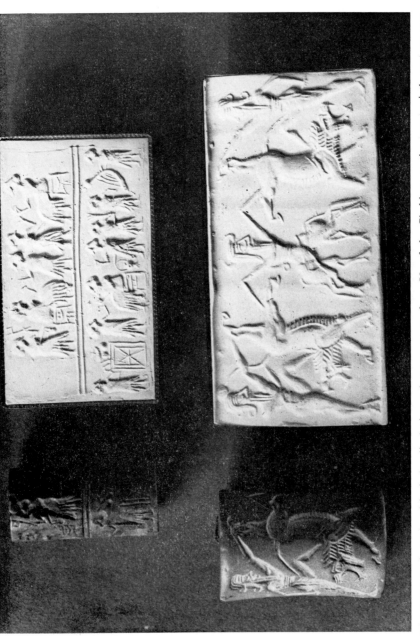

The upper seal, made of lapis lazuli, depicts a banquet scene from Ur of the Chaldees, c. the twenty-sixth century, B.C. The lower seal, made of jadeite, came from one of the tombs in the Royal Cemetery at Ur, and also dates from the same period.

thirteen acres and was a perfect mathematically correct pyramid, with the apex exactly above the center of its base.[11]

The Great Pyramid is large enough to contain St. Paul's Cathedral, Westminster Abbey, St. Peter's at Rome, and the cathedrals of Florence and Milan. It has been reckoned that if the stone of the pyramid were sawn into cubes of one foot each, and these cubes placed in a row at the equator, they would extend two-thirds of the way around the earth.[12]

When viewed from a distance, the Great Pyramid gives the impression of being preserved substantially intact, but closer observation reveals that its outer surface has been marred and sadly despoiled. The highly polished granite capstone and about a dozen courses of stone blocks have been removed from the apex, thereby lowering the top of the pyramid by about thirty feet. The whole of the smooth outer facing of fine Tura limestone, with the exception of a few pieces at the base, has been stripped from the sides, thus revealing it as an uneven stepped structure, and showing it to be a fraction smaller than when it was originally built.[13]

At the northeast corner countless thousands of tourists have climbed, with the aid of Arabs, to the top, which at the present is 451 feet high. Here from the 36-foot square limestone top they may view the city of Cairo, the green country irrigated by the Nile, the scattered palm trees with their oases of shade, the great cemetery with its graves, mastabas, and pyramids, and the vast desert with its reminders of Egypt's glory.

To gain entrance to the interior of the Great Pyramid, one climbs up on the north side some forty feet above the ground level, and enters a three- to four-foot wide, high tunnel-like passageway that descends partly through the masonry and partly through solid rock, for some 345 feet, then becomes level and continues horizontally for a further 29 feet, where it reaches an unfinished subterranean chamber 46 feet long, 27 feet wide and 11 feet 6 inches high.[14] The descending passage gives a clear and uninterrupted view of the northern sky, a fact which has given rise to the belief that the Great Pyramid was built for astronomical observations.

About 63 feet from the original entrance an ascending passage leads upward in the mass of the pyramid until it reaches the "Grand Gallery." Here a horizontal passage leads southward for 109 feet to the "Queen's Burial Chamber," which lies exactly midway between the north and south sides of the pyramid. It is 18 feet long, 17 feet wide, and 20 feet high. It is artistically roofed with blocks leaning against each other to resist the pressure of the mass above. Its walls are of the finest granite masonry, most carefully dressed and polished, whereas the floor is left rough. In the east wall there is a niche designed presumably to hold a statue of the king, or queen or perhaps of his or her favorite god.[15]

The Grand Gallery was built as an enlarged continuation of the ascending passage or corridor, and is one of the finest things of its kind known to man. It is 153 feet long and 28 feet high. Its floor is a deeply grooved ascending passage measuring 3 feet 5 inches in width, bordered on each side by a flat-topped ramp 2 feet in height and twenty inches in width extending the length of the gallery. The carefully tooled and highly polished granite masonry in this and other inner portions of the pyramid is considered the world's finest stone work. Much of it is so well done that a knife blade could not be thrust into the masonry joints.

As one leaves the Grand Gallery by a "high step" it is necessary to stoop to gain access to a low, narrow, short passage leading into a granite-lined vestibule or antechamber. Then proceeding in a stooped position through another low horizontal passage, one enters the King's Burial Chamber, which is 140 feet above the ground level.

The King's Burial Chamber is the very heart of the grand pyramid design, the royal room where the divine king, the "Great Shepherd" was buried. It is built entirely of fine highly polished red granite, and measures 34 feet in length by 17 feet in width, and is 19 feet high. In the north and south walls of this burial room, at a height of about three feet above the floor, are two shafts or tubes that slant upward at angles of approximately 30 degrees to the outer surface of the pyramid. "The object of these shafts is not known with certainty; they may have been designed for the ventilation of the chamber or for some religious purpose" or for both.[16]

Near the west wall of the royal burial chamber stands a lidless sarcophagus carved from a solid block of red granite. It measures 7 feet 6 inches long, 3 feet 3 inches wide, and 3 feet

4 inches high. It once enclosed an inner casket of fine wood, within which lay the king's mummy. Nearby, within the granite floor, is an empty niche which some regard as the treasure chest that once held the king's gems and jewels.

The ceiling of this far-famed tomb room is composed of nine enormous granite slabs extending from wall to wall and weighing in the aggregate about 400 tons. Above these slabs are

five separate compartments, the ceilings of the first four being flat and the fifth having a pointed roof. The purpose of this construction, it appears, was to eliminate any risk of the ceiling of the chamber collapsing under the weight of the superincumbent masonry. . . . Access to the lowest of the relieving compartments is gained by a passage leading from a hole at the top of the east wall of the Grand Gallery. When or by whom this passage was cut is unknown; the first European to mention it was a traveler named Davison who visited the Pyramid in 1765. The four upper compartments were not discovered until 1837-38, when Colonel Howard Vyse and J. S. Perring forced a way to them by hollowing out a shaft from below.[17]

In the two uppermost of the five compartments Vyse and Perring discovered the quarrymen's marks, drawn in red ochre. Among these markings were two oval rings in which was written, in hieroglyphic characters, the name Khufu (Cheops), whom Herodotus gives as the name of the king who built the largest pyramid. These are the only inscriptions found in or on the great pyramid, though Herodotus says that in his day there was an inscription on the outer casing.[18]

The Great Pyramid is the only one of the Seven Wonders of the World left standing today, and it is one of the architectural marvels of history that "still arouses the admiration of the ablest engineers." It is not only a magnificent monument to the Egyptian's supreme mastery of stone in architecture, but it is an enduring monument to the Egyptian people's faith in immortality, and especially "their faith in a glorious after-life for their Kings." [19]

To ascend the pyramid is an event to be remembered, but to go to the very heart of its interior and stand without light within the King's Burial Chamber is even more impressive.

The black impenetrable darkness; the utter stillness; the feeling that above and around and below are solid masses of stone reared by hands long dead; the knowledge that one of the mightiest of the mighty trod those floors and hoped to rest for ever within the structure; all combine to make the Great Pyramid one of the most mysterious and solemn of all the ancient buildings of the Valley of the Nile." [20]

The Second Pyramid

The Second Pyramid, or the pyramid of Chephren (Khafra) brother of and successor to Cheops, stands on a slightly elevated spot 500 feet southwest of the Great Pyramid. It is so situated that the diagonals of both pyramids are in a straight line.[21]

In completed form it covered an area of more than 11 acres, or double that of the Roman Colosseum. It measured 706 feet on each side at the base, and arose majestically upward at an angle of 52 degrees for a distance of 577 feet, its vertical height being 457 feet. It was encased with another coating of fine red granite below, and with Tura limestone above. It is thought that the capstone, which has now disappeared, may also have been of granite.

The cubic area of this, the second largest pyramid, has been estimated at about 60,000,000 cubic feet of rock, and its total weight is said to have been 5,309,000 tons. It has been said that the stone used in Chephren's pyramid would build a city of 18,000 homes accommodating 100,000 people.

A high wall surrounded the pyramid on every side, and between the pyramid and the wall there was a pavement about 34 feet in width on the north, east and west sides, and somewhat wider on the south side where a single subsidiary pyramid stood approximately opposite the middle of the king's pyramid.

In years gone by this pyramid also became a convenient quarry for builders who removed much of the facing stone, to be used in other construction. The pillaging resulted in a 17-foot reduction in the length of the sides, 14 feet in the slant height, and 10 feet in the vertical height. The casing has been retained for about 150 feet down from the top, making ascent of the pyramid very difficult.

This pyramid is inferior in the accuracy of workmanship to that of the Great Pyramid, its errors in measurements of length being almost double, and the errors of its angles being almost four times as great. In sharp contrast, however, the sarcophagus is much superior to that of Cheops.

The pyramid has two separate entrances, both in the north face, one about 50 feet above the base, and the other directly below in the pavement at ground level. The corridors leading from these entrances merge within the pyramid at floor level in a horizontal passage, which then leads to the tomb chamber, hewn entirely out of rock, and measuring 41 feet in length, 16 feet in width, and 22 feet in height. The chamber has a pitched roof of limestone blocks leaning one against the other, the inside being painted. The lid of the sarcophagus was broken and the sarcophagus was filled with rubbish when discovered.[22]

Across a paved alley to the east was built the mortuary temple, a low rectangular building 370 feet by 160 feet, composed of local stone and lined with red granite. Close to its north and south walls five boat pits were hewn in the solid rock to house the boats that were to furnish transportation for the king in his after-life. But no boats were found by the excavators.

West of the pyramid, outside the enclosure wall, may still be seen a series of 91 barracks, each measuring 88 feet long, 9½ feet in width, and 7 feet in height. These barracks provided lodging for the workmen employed in building the pyramid complex, and were capable of accommodating about four thousand men.[23] It is quite probable that they were constructed in Cheops' time.

The Third Pyramid

The Third Pyramid, sometimes called the "Red Pyramid" because of the red granite casing covering the lower sixteen courses of stone, was built by Mycerinus (Menkaura), the son and successor to Chephren.

It stands in the southwest corner of the plateau, occupying less than half the area covered by the Great Pyramid. Its sides measure 356 feet 6 inches, and its vertical height is now only 204 feet. When complete it was fourteen feet higher. For beauty and regularity of construction many regard it as the most magnificent of the three major pyramids of Gizeh.

Several attempts to enter it were made during the early nineteenth century. It was eventually opened by Vyse in 1837-38, and was further excavated and studied by Reisner for Harvard University and the Boston Museum of Fine Arts between the years 1905-27. These researches seem to indicate that the original plans called for a small, modest structure, but that for some reason the design was altered, and the pyramid was constructed eight times larger in size.

When completed it covered a suite of three subterranean apartments, which were reached by means of a sloping passage leading from the entrance in the south face. The first apartment was a white stuccoed room 12 feet long that gave access to the second, which measured 46 feet by 12 feet and was located almost directly under the apex of the pyramid. In this apartment a recess had been dug in the rock floor for a sarcophagus.

Beyond and at a lower level was the third apartment, somewhat smaller than the second, composed entirely of granite and having a barrel-vaulted roof. This apartment was reached by means of a narrow passage hidden behind the slabbing of the second apartment. Inside was an elegant sarcophagus cut from a single block of blue-black basalt, polished and carved into the form of a house. Its broken lid was found in the second apartment.

The empty mummy-case of cedar wood was carved in the form of a human body with a man's head. It was unpainted and ungilded, but was carved with a double-column inscription on its front, giving the name of the king and a prayer in his behalf.

Osiris, King of the two Egypts, Menkauri, living eternally, given birth to by heaven, conceived by Nuit, flesh of Sibu, thy mother Nuit has spread herself out over thee in her name of "Mystery of the Heavens," and she has granted that thou shouldest be a god, and that thou shouldest repulse thine enemies, O King of the two Egypts, Menkauri, living eternally.[24]

The beautiful sarcophagus was carefully packed for shipment to England, but the ship transporting it sank off the coast of Spain in 1838.

The foundations and core of Mycerinus' mortuary temple were of limestone, with floors and wall facings partially of granite. Reisner discovered fifteen unfinished statuettes of the king, and found many parts of the temple and valley buildings either hastily finished in materials of inferior quality or even left incomplete. All these were taken as evidence that Mycerinus met an untimely death, and that the buildings had been hastily completed by Shepeskab, his successor, as had been suggested by Herodotus.[26]

South of Mycerinus' pyramid and well within the walled enclosure are three subsidiary pyramids, each approximately 100 feet in height. These are believed to have been burial tombs for members of King Mycerinus' family. Each of these pyramids had its own mortuary temple adjoining its respective pyramid, and each temple was built of crude brick.

At the end of the causeway was the Valley Building, which in addition to its other purposes provided quarters for the priests charged with the care of the pyramid and the other buildings, and whose duty it was to perform temple services in honor of the departed king.

The Pyramids with Texts

The Pyramids with Texts are a part of the Sakkara group, and are located near the Step Pyramid of King Zoser. They are five in number and were built by King Unas, the last king of the Fifth Dynasty, and by Kings Tety, Pepy I, Mer-en-ra and Pepy II (Neferkere) of the Sixth Dynasty. Some writings are also found in the nearby pyramid of a king named Iba and in the pyramids of Pepy's three queens.

The period of time covered by these pyramids would be from about 2450 to 2250 b.c. They are all much smaller than the Step Pyramid, and are generally of poorer construction, yet they are exceedingly significant in that they contain writing.

Mariette, the French archaeologist, had devoted his efforts primarily to the larger pyramids, feeling certain that these smaller ones contained nothing of great value. However, in 1880 as one of his last official undertakings he opened those of Pepy I and Mer-en-ra, and on his deathbed received the news that they contained much writing. After Mariette's death, Maspero took over and continued the work until 1894.

Each of these five pyramids contained a long vestibule or passageway leading to the tomb room and to the other subsidiary rooms. In each case, the interior walls of these vestibules and rooms, and in some cases the ceilings, were completely covered with texts carefully carved and painted in vertical columns of hieroglyphics. A very few verses reflect the things that made for a good life in the Nile Valley, while men lived.

They tremble that behold the Nile in full flood. The fields laugh and the river-banks are overflowed. The god's offerings descend. The visage of men is bright, and the heart of the gods rejoiceth.

But for the most part the Pyramid Texts are concerned with the future life, with prayers, hymns, incantations, and magical spells to be used by the deceased king as he appeared at the gates of heaven or at the judgment. Heavy with thoughts of immortality, they had been written by the funerary priests, and were intended as aids for the dead, especially for the king in his search for a happy "after-life," and pictured him enjoying that life. Therefore, the standing theme, "repeated over and over with innumerable variations," is that the king is not dead but still lives, and that the "mortal part" of him "goest to the earth," whereas "the immortal part goest to the sky." They locate the future world as "above, in the eastern part of the sky." They describe it as a place where there are gardens, canals and lakes, and as the "field of life" where grows "the tree of life whereof they live." [26]

The pyramid itself was regarded as the means whereby the deified king could rise from the dead and begin his ascent to heaven. Thus the texts represent the king as leaving the pyramid and climbing to heaven by the celestial stairway, or as being ferried across the "Lily Lake" in a solar boat, or as flying to heaven as a falcon. [27]

On the king's arrival at the lofty gate of the Other World, the texts tell of heralds standing in readiness to spread the news of his arrival, and of the immediate gathering of the gods to greet him. He was then obliged to undergo the ordeal of the Judgment of the Dead, an "ethical test" which consisted essentially of the weighing of the heart. The ceremony took place in the Hall of Maat, goddess of Truth. In the middle of the hall of justice stood a large pair of scales, in one pan of which rested the heart of the dead man and in the other the feather of Maat. The heart, which was the seat of the intellect and the emotions, was weighed while its owner stood by. The scales were adjusted by Anubis and the result recorded by Thoth. Maat watched the procedure, while a fierce monster called the Devourer, with the head of a crocodile, the forepart of a lion and the hindquarters of a hippopotamus, waited eagerly to devour the dead man if the judgment went against him. If, however, the balance of the heart and the feather was equal, Thoth then turned to the great company of the gods who were present and declared the petitioner justified. After this he was conducted into the presence of Osiris, who was wrapped in his winding sheet and sat on his throne.

On being received the petitioner became a god who could then sit on the throne of Osiris and at the festive table with the gods, and feast on the food of the better world, which consisted chiefly of bread, milk, wine, cakes, sweetmeats, roasted geese, quail, various kinds of animal flesh, fresh fruits and "thousands of everything on which the gods live." It was a land in which the king would sit upon "a throne of precious metal" attended by thousands of his servants, would always have an abundance of royal wearing apparel, would never more hunger nor thirst, and would live forever.[28]

There were more than 4000 lines in the Pyramid Texts. Some of these were so archaic in style as to lead Egyptologists to regard them as having been composed during the beginning of the Old Empire, and some even in the prehistoric period.

During the Middle Empire many texts were written on the insides of private coffins, and this collection is known as the Coffin Texts. The Book of the Dead was written for the most part on papyrus rolls and belongs to the New Empire.[29]

The Great Sphinx

In Egyptian mythology the lion often figured as the guardian of sacred places, and from the Fourth Dynasty onward there were many sphinxes of many kinds located in many places in Egypt.[30] A few were alone, some were in pairs, and many lined long avenues of approach to temples and other sacred edifices. But the sphinx of all sphinxes is the Great Sphinx located almost one-third of a mile east of the Second Pyramid. It is not only Egypt's grandest sphinx, but the largest and oldest single sculptured figure on earth. It symbolizes the union of physical and intellectual strength.

From a gigantic spur of rock, left by the pyramid builders, the sculptors of Chephren's time carved the body of a huge crouching lion 240 feet long and 66 feet high. Its human face, raised above its extended paws, was fashioned in the likeness of King Chephren, combined with the features usually representing the sun god, Aton. "A possible reason for the identification of the Sun-god's features with those of the deceased King" says Edwards, "may be the Heliopolitan belief that the King, after his death, actually became the Sun-god. The Giant Sphinx would therefore represent Chephren as the Sun-god acting as guardian of the Giza necropolis." [31]

The head of this solemn sentinel guarding the vast cemetery is 30 feet long and 13 feet 8 inches wide at its greatest breadth. The nose is 5 feet, 7 inches wide, the ears 4½ feet long, the mouth 7 feet 7 inches wide, and the paws, which are made of blocks of stone, are 50 feet long, between which a tiny 5-foot temple was built by Thutmose IV. Standing against this temple is the "Dream-Stele" of Thutmose, which contains a poetical account of his clearing the sand from the lower body of the sphinx in loyal response to a request in a vision he beheld while resting in its shade in weariness from a hunt. He was promised the double-crown of Egypt if he would faithfuly perform this labor, and upon receiving the kingship he set up the stele to commemorate the event and his accomplishment.[32]

What a striking figure that splendid face must have been, with the lion's mane, the regal headdress, the royal cobra on the brow, and the kingly beard, all of which have since been mutilated by ten thousand sandstorms and by the exploding shells of the Mamelukes, who used it as a target for artillery practice. The nose and eyes were also disfigured, but in more recent years they have been partially restored.[33] Yet, though it has suffered the ravages of time and the abuse of thoughtless mortals, the hand of man cannot alter its superb dignity.

There it has been, in calm dignity—part lion, part man, part god—in the midst of the world's greatest necropolis, facing the east as though anticipating the break of day, and witnessing the vast parade of famous people as they have entered and left Egypt through the past centuries. Powell suggests that as he stood before the Great Sphinx and looked into its face, he seemed to hear its big stone lips say:

I was here when Abraham passed by with his wife Sarah and declared that she was his sister. I was here when the Ishmaelites brought Joseph and sold him to Potiphar. I was here when Joseph resisted temptation and went to prison. I was here the day Joseph came out of prison and stepped into the second chariot of the nation while all Egypt cried, 'Bow the knee!' I was here when Joseph's brethren came down with fear and trembling and fulfilled his dreams by bowing to him like sheaves of wheat. I was here when old Jacob and the seventy souls of his household came down to keep from starving to death. I was here when a Pharaoh rose up who knew not Joseph and bound the Israelites in slavery. I was here when the cruel Egyptian taskmasters beat the backs of God's chosen people, and when the midwives murdered the babies of the Hebrew children. I was here the day that Pharaoh's daughter pulled the babe Moses out of the bulrushes. I was here the day that Moses slew the Egyptian slave driver. I was here the night the death angel passed through the land and took away the first born from every Egyptian home. I was here the night that God divided the Red sea, and the Israelites walked over dry-shod. I was here the day that Mary walked by carrying the son of God in her arms, and I will be here when He comes again riding on the clouds of heaven to gather His loved ones home! [34]

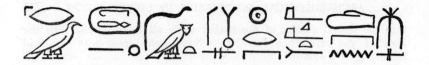

CHAPTER XVI

Archaeological Discoveries in Upper Egypt

THEBES, THE CAPITAL of Upper Egypt and the best known site in Egypt, with the exception of Memphis and the pyramids, was situated on a broad fertile plain stretching away for miles on both sides of the Nile, 418 miles south of the present city of Cairo. Its origin dates from the beginning of Egyptian history, yet our first record is from about 2100 B.C. when the pharaohs of the Eleventh Dynasty reigned there in magnificence. It reached the height of its power during the Eighteenth to Twenty-first Dynasties, or between 1550 B.C. and 950 B.C., at which time it possessed so many stately public buildings, magnificent temples and rich memorials and was adorned with so many monuments of gold, silver, and ivory and such a multitude of colossi and obelisks that it was considered "the great metropolis of the world, the center of art, of learning, of religion, of luxury, and of political power—the heart and brain of a mighty empire which extended from the headwaters of the Nile to the Euphrates." [1]

The name Thebes, which first appears in the *Iliad*, was given to the locality by the Greeks, who transformed the native name Ta-ape. The Egyptians often called the city Weset, but more often called it No-Amon, or the city of Amon, because it was the center of the worship of Amon, together with Mut the mother goddess, and Khonsu the god of the moon. These three gods formed the great Theban triad, and the power of Amon in particular increased as he came to be identified with the ancient sun god Ra under the name of Amon-Ra, the king of the gods.

To all the ancient world Thebes was a symbol of splendor,

might, and glory. Only at a later period did Babylon and Nineveh vie with it in grandeur and earthly importance. Thus the prophet Nahum used Thebes as an example in his message to Nineveh when he said "Art thou better than populous No (Thebes), that was situate among the rivers, that had the waters round about it, whose rampart was the sea, and her wall was from the sea?" [2]

Homer wrote:

> The world's great empress on th' Egyptian plain,
> That spreads her conquests o'er a thousand states,
> And pours her heroes through a hundred gates,
> Two hundred horsemen and two hundred cars,
> From each wide portal issuing to the wars. [3]

Thebes continued in its grandeur and importance as a religious and administrative center for more than a thousand years. Then with the death of the last great Egyptian soldier Rameses III in 1167 B.C., Thebes began a long decline climaxed with the crowning disaster that fell upon the city under Tan-ut-Amon in 667 B.C. His attempt to assert himself as pharaoh of all Egypt caused Ashurbanipal of Assyria to march upon Egypt and to deal the city of Thebes a blow from which it never fully recovered. The ordeal to which the city was subjected is recorded in Ashurbanipal's cylinder (now located in the Nineveh gallery, British Museum):

Tandomonu [Tan-ut-Amon] heard of the progress of my expedition, and that I had crossed the border of Egypt. He abandoned Memphis, and to save his life he fled to Thebes. I took the road after Tandomonu; I went to Thebes, the strong city; at the approach of my army he abandoned Thebes and fled to Kipkip. My army took the whole of Thebes; by the help of Ashur and Ishtar, my hands took silver, gold, precious stones, the furniture of the palace, costly and beautiful garments, great horses, men and women; two lofty obelisks covered with beautiful carving, which were set up before the gate of a temple, them I removed and brought to Assyria. Its spoils unnumbered I carried off.

The city was rebuilt after the disaster, but in 525 B.C. it suffered a second destruction at the hands of Cambyses. After this it gradually sank into comparative insignificance. The Ptolemies restored its temples and carried on considerable building activities, but Thebes never again regained its former importance. Then in 27 B.C. an earthquake wrought havoc with many of its ancient buildings, and the place was abandoned to time and the elements.

Thebes, like ancient Babylon, was divided by a great river, the Nile. Yet the division of the city was strangely different from that of Babylon. On the east side of the Nile lay the metropolis, the land of the living; on the west side lay the necropolis, the land of the dead. The city is often referred to as "hundred-gated Thebes," yet it seems never to have had a wall about it, other than the splendid walls that formed enclosures for its sacred areas wherein were twenty or more temples. The "pylons," or truncated pyramidal gateways surmounted by a heavy cornice, that pierced these walls were both numerous and impressive, and it is from these that Homer derived his description of the city as "hundred-gated Thebes." There were from fifty to one hundred thousand people living in Thebes— some say as many as three hundred thousand—yet no bridges spanned its waterway. For crossing back and forth on the one-half mile wide Nile the populace depended upon boats, barges, and ferries.

THE CITY OF THE LIVING

Eastern Thebes was designed for the living. There were miles of streets thronged with people, litters and chariots. These and other thoroughfares were lined with impressive residences of high officials, ornate homes of the rich, as well as many homes for the middle and lower classes, and the hovels of the very poor. There were ample quarters for the tradesmen and artisans, and suitable quays for the accommodation of ships from Phoenicia, Greece, Arabia, and many other foreign lands. Here the gorgeous finery of Eastern lands was yearly discharged.

But the most prominent of all its buildings were its temples, and the two most wonderful of all the temples of Thebes were the Temple of Amon and the Temple of Luxor, both on the eastern bank of the Nile. These were connected by a paved avenue seventy-six feet in width and a mile and a quarter in length, known as "The Avenue of the Sphinxes." On either side were palms, beautiful gardens, flowers, and shrubs, but the immediate border of the avenue was lined with almost one thousand human- and ram-headed sphinxes, about five hundred on each side.

The Temple of Amon

The Temple of Amon, popularly known as the Temple of Karnak, was the expression of the Egyptians' devotion to their god Amon, who was to them the maker of the universe and the creator of all things. He was the patron and senior partner in the gold mines of Nubia and the Sudan. Amon's image accompanied the armies on military expeditions, and received a generous portion of the spoils of war. Over a period of fifteen hundred to two thousand years the various pharaohs vied with each other in employing the best possible architects, masons, sculptors, and painters of their day to aid them in expressing their devotion and in making their contribution to their great god's temple, which they came to think of as "the throne of the world."

Founded by King Usertesen I during the early years of the Middle Empire, the temple was then but a small building, constructed of limestone and sandstone, with granite doorways. It was adorned by various princes, but was unaltered until the eighteenth century B.C. when outstanding contributions began to be made. The main work was accomplished by Amenhotep I, Thutmose I and Queen Hat-shep-sut. Thutmose III rebuilt certain pylons and the processional hall and made the lake whereon the sacred boats were launched on festal days. Amenhotep II carried on the construction and Rameses I began the great Hypostyle Hall, which was completed by Seti I and decorated by Rameses II.[4] Other pharaohs made their contributions; even the Ptolemies added the ornate entrance facing the Nile. When complete, the vast edifice was a composite structure 338 feet wide and more than 1200 feet long. The principal buildings were four main halls or courts, now known as "The Great Court," "The Great Hypostyle Hall," "The Central Court," and "The Great Sanctuary." About this mighty Temple of Amon there were subsidiary temples, chapels, obelisks, a sacred lake, and long sphinx-lined avenues that converged on the grand temple or led up to various pyloned gates forming triumphal approaches. The entire sacred precinct covered 200 acres, all enclosed by a stone wall eighty feet high.[5]

From the south the temple was approached by way of the Avenue of the Sphinxes, yet the great temple was oriented so that its main entrance or official gateway would face the Nile, to the northwest.

On approaching this front entrance by the impressive sphinx-lined avenue coming up directly from the Nile, one was struck with wonder and respect at the immense colossal statues of the pharaohs seated on each side of the gate, and the pair of granite obelisks pointing heavenward. The entrance was a huge pylon with an impressive gateway, flanked by two great rectangular towers 142 feet high and 370 feet wide. This was the part of the temple built by the Ptolemies. One of these towers yet retains a great part of its original height, but has lost its summit and cornice.[6]

The Great Court was reached through a gateway of beautiful bronze doors plated with electrum and studded with gold. The Great Court measured 338 by 276 feet and was traversed by a double line of colossal columns.

A second massive pylon led into the Hypostyle Hall, which was so large and so ornate that it has been regarded as "one of the wonders of the ancient world." The great lintel stone of its doorway is forty feet ten inches in length, and the grand hall of assembly measures 170 by 338 feet. Its roof is supported by 134 enormous columns in sixteen rows. The twelve columns of the two central rows are 78 feet high, each having a circumference of 33 feet.

Each of these is adorned with a most beautiful open papyrus capital. The additional 122 smaller columns have bud capitals, and are $41\frac{1}{2}$ feet in height and $27\frac{1}{2}$ feet in circumference. The vast array reminds one of a great forest of enormous columns. Both columns and interior walls are brilliantly sculptured and painted with inscriptions, scenes of nature, men, pharaohs, priests and gods. One views this vast architectural wonder amazed and bewildered by its size, its symmetry, and its indescribable beauty.

The Central or forecourt of the Sanctuary, sometimes called "The Processional Hall," was a long vestibule court that was the extreme limit any one might go, other than the officiating priests.

The beautiful hall of red and black granite, sandwiched

between the great Hypostyle Hall and the Sanctuary, was originally the work of Thutmose I and his daughter the great
Queen Hat-shep-sut. On the north and south within this enclosure she erected two large pylons decorated with painted
reliefs depicting herself participating in various religious ceremonies before Amon-Ra and other gods. Here she also erected
her two famous granite obelisks, one of which was 97½ feet
high, and the other rising to a height of 109 feet. She had part
of the roof of the colonnade removed to erect them in honor of
her jubilee. They were quarried at Aswan, ferried 130 miles
down the Nile, and erected, inscribed, and polished within
seven months' time. These two obelisks were coated with electrum, and when in position they made a tremendous impression,
a lasting tribute to the queen and her architect and to the
ingenuity and skill of the ancient Egyptians. On the base of
one of the monoliths she inscribed "a cry of triumphant womanhood" that has been echoed down the centuries.

Oh, ye people who shall see my monument—after years, beware of
saying, "I know not why this was made and a mountain fashioned entirely of gold." These two great obelisks my majesty hath wrought with
electrum that my name may abide, enduring in this temple for ever and
ever.[7]

Today one of the queen's obelisks lies in ruin in a heap
of sandstone blocks, the other is still there on its pedestal,
ninety-seven and a half feet high "perpendicular to the fraction
of an inch, clean cut, almost untouched by time,"—the tallest
obelisk still standing in Egypt.[8]

The Great Sanctuary and Festal Hall is the inmost sanctuary,
the "holy of holies" of this great temple complex. Its thirty-
two rectangular columns ranged on the sides and two rows
of ten columns running down the center have the peculiarity of
being inverted. It was here in this "holy of holies" that the
strange, mystic rites of the Egyptian religion were carried out,
and the emblem of the god Amon was kept in a monolithic
shrine. Around the sanctuary itself are the treasure chambers,
robing rooms, and laboratories for the creation of incense and
other necessities connected with the temple rites. Beneath in
crypts the most precious and sacred of treasures were concealed.

The exterior walls of this massive temple are covered with

"miles of painted reliefs" and with the histories of various monarchs. Here on the south wall, Thutmose III (1479-1447 B.C.), the veritable "Napoleon of Egypt" and in all probability the "great oppressor of Israel" who "knew not Joseph," recounts his deeds of valor and gives a long list of cities he conquered in western Asia. King Seti I is shown in a chariot riding down his enemies. Farther along on this south wall, Rameses II is shown fighting the Hittites. The accompanying inscription recounts his deeds and gives the text of the peace treaty.[9]

On the south wall of the second pylon is an historical relief commemorating the victory of King Sheshonk (spelled "Shishak" in the Bible) over Rehoboam the son of King Solomon when Sheshonk invaded Palestine during the fifth year of Rehoboam's reign (c. 926 B.C.) and ". . . took away the treasures of the house of the Lord, and the treasures of the King's house . . . and he took away all the shields of gold which Solomon had made" (I Kings 14:25,26). Not only is the expedition recorded, but Shishak and the god Amon are shown with more than 150 captives, each of whom represents a Palestinian town taken by Shishak. In each case the name of the town is enclosed in an oval marked out near the head and shoulders of the captive. Many of the cities are found in the Old Testament, including Taanach, Shunem, Beth-Shan, Gibeon, Beth-horon, Ajalon, Megiddo, Socoh, Arad, Edrei and Mahanaim. One of them is labeled "The Field of Abraham." In the inscription Shishak indicates that his purpose in capturing these cities was to bring all Palestine back into subjection to Egypt.[10]

At the height of its prosperity, under Rameses III, the Temple of Amon possessed ninety thousand slaves, half a million head of cattle, four hundred orchards, eighty ships and fifty warships. It commanded the revenues of sixty-five selected townships in Egypt and Asia, and was respected and revered as far as the power and sway of Egypt extended. Today it is regarded as the largest religious temple ever known to have been constructed.

The Temple of Luxor

The Temple of Luxor, located at the southern end of the "Avenue of the Sphinxes," was dedicated to Amon, Mut, and Khonsu. It was largely the work of two monarchs, Amenhotep

III (1413-1376 B.C.) and Rameses II, although Seti I, Harmhab, and Tut-ankh-amen contributed to its decoration and enlargement.

Before the temple entrance, which faces the temple of Karnak to the north, are two fine obelisks, two huge statues, and four flag-pole or streamer sockets grooved deep into the stone. The obelisks are 77 and 75½ feet high, respectively, and are covered with hieroglyphics executed in masterly style. The entrance to the temple is formed by a thick-based pylon wall 80 feet high and 200 feet wide, the face of which is covered with "animated battle scenes" depicting war as it was in ancient times. The pylon gateway leads into an impressive hypostyled outer court 234 by 174 feet, which is supported by a double row of pillars with bell-shaped capitals.[11]

South of the hypostyle hall is the long, narrow colonnade of Seti I with its seven pairs of columns 52 feet high and 22 feet in circumference. This colonnade leads upward to the entrance of the temple of Rameses II with its great pylon, the faces of which are covered with dispatches and scenes of the battle field on which may be studied almost day by day the campaign of Rameses II against the Kheta (Hittites), which took place in the fifth year of his reign. Passing through this huge pylon, one enters the inner court of the temple, which measures 160 by 140 feet, with two rows of pillars on each side.

Beyond a thick group of 32 enormous columns is the sanctuary or holy of holies, which is surrounded by spacious halls supported by columns and contains a mass of the most beautiful sculpture in the best style of execution. Here in this sanctuary was carried on the strange and often mystic ritual that characterized the worship of Amon, Mut, Khonsu, and other gods of the day.

The overall length of the Luxor temple was about 852 feet. So richly sculptured and painted are all the inner walls that it is considered second only to the temple of Amon at Karnak in beauty. Later pharaohs added to the temple, but without altering the fundamental design.

THE CITY OF THE DEAD

Eastern Thebes, with its two great temples of worship and its many smaller ones, was the "City of the Living." But western

Thebes, on the opposite bank of the river, was as definitely the "City of the Dead." As in life the majority of the people who pursued normal occupations dwelt in eastern Thebes, so in death they were ferried across the Nile where their bodies were prepared and laid away in graves, mastabas, pyramids, and hillside tombs on the other side of the river.

Western Thebes was the region of Osiris, who welcomed the dead to their tombs. Those who lived there were for the most part engaged in matters pertaining to the preparation, burial, veneration, and the after-life ritual of the dead. There were the outcasts who erected the many temporary booths in which they opened the bodies of the dead and prepared them for embalming, after which they destroyed the structure; coffin carpenters who produced finely carved and elaborately decorated mummy-cases; stone-workers who cut fine sarcophagi from quarried blocks of granite; portrait artists who painted the likeness of the dead to accompany the body in the tomb; weavers who manufactured the linen bandages for use in swathing the mummies; and shopkeepers who made available such items as oils, perfumes, flowers, food, and everything needed by mourners or for burial and ceremonies of the dead.[12]

Here the undertakers provided showrooms for the display of mummy models and mummy-cases. Here also were the homes of the embalmers, or "physicians" as the Bible calls them (Genesis 50:2). They belonged to the all-important Guild of Embalmers, received their charter by law and handed down the secrets and mysteries of the fraternity from father to son.[13]

In a secluded portion of the suburbs were located the shops of the coffin carpenters, a glass factory, a pottery, the embalmers' laboratories, and hundreds of ovens for heating the natron and other oils used in the preservation of the bodies. Also living in this metropolis of the dead were the specially designated priests responsible for the spiritual welfare of the deceased. These services were richly endowed and the charge was passed on from generation to generation.

Western Thebes was an open park-like district of rich bottom land that began at the water's edge and for from two to three miles unrolled like a great carpet up to the approaches of the abrupt Libyan cliffs, which rose to a height of several hundred feet, and were honeycombed for many miles with the tombs of many centuries.[14] In two places the city of the dead over-flowed through narrow mountain passes into valley cemeteries —one valley on the south for queens and one on the north for kings.

Here, in this park-like area were silent lines of innumerable tombs, crowding one another from Kurna on the north to Medinet-Habu and the western palace of Amenhotep III on the south. Its stately mortuary temples of departed pharaohs, its striking memorial statues, its long, graceful avenues of sphinxes, its secluded Valley of the Tombs of the Queens, and its lonely Valley of the Tombs of the Kings, certainly invested the term "going west" with deep meaning to the people of Thebes.

To the north and northwest of the village of Kurna and extending approximately one mile to the vicinity of Draga Abu Naga, are thousands of common graves of many nobles and private citizens of the ancient capital city. Immediately southwest of this area and to the west of Kurna, extending for more than a mile along the southern brow of the hill is the oldest section of the cemetery. Here were found the brick pyramid-tombs of the early Theban monarchs and the kings of the Eleventh Dynasty, surrounded by numerous tombs of the nobility as well as the unpretentious graves in which the dead of the common people found their last resting places.

Farther to the south and west, near the southern spur of the western mountains, is the hill Sheikh Abd el-Kurna, known also as the Theban Necropolis. The many tomb passages that have been burrowed into its sloping sides give it the appearance of a gigantic honeycomb. Here were found the tombs containing the remains of many dignitaries of the Eighteenth Dynasty, including Amenemhab, a military commander in the service of Thutmose III; the vizier Rekhmere, one of the outstanding ministers of his time; Harmhab, the general of Thutmose IV; and a host of other great and valiant men of that era.[15]

Farther on, at Deir el-Medina, is another burial ground, less crowded than that at Sheikh Abd el-Kurna. Just beyond is the Valley of the Tombs of the Queens nestled in the foothills of the western mountains. In this secluded valley many of Egypt's famous queens were buried, among whom was Tiy, the mother of Akhenaton. The workmanship of these tombs was of excellent quality. They were decorated with pleasant scenes depicting the gods and the life beyond, and executed in large, bold figures with fresh vivid coloring, much of which was found by the excavators to be in a good state of preservation.

VALLEY OF THE TOMBS OF THE KINGS

Actuated by motives of security and desiring ample space for their individual sepulchres, the pharaohs of the Eighteenth, Nineteenth, and Twentieth Dynasties, or from about 1500 B.C. onward for some 500 years, selected for themselves suitable grounds for burial in a secluded mountain valley north of the great plain of western Thebes. The valley was difficult to reach and therefore was relatively secure from tomb robbers.

The main entrance was a mile northwest of Kurna, where one suddenly leaves the plain of western Thebes and advances through a wild and waterless valley that quickly narrows to a winding gorge called el-Wadigen, the walls of which are of a "tawny desert rock, eroded into fantastic shapes of jutting buttress and towering pinnacle."

Turning sharply westward, the gorge continues its windings for nearly one mile, during which there are few if any of the usual signs of life; hardly a tree, a flower, or even a blade of grass grows to relieve the barrenness and burning heat. Suddenly the gorge terminates in a spacious, waterless amphitheater that is one of the most weird and desolate places of all the earth. The barren, rock-filled valley divides into two sections; one continues southwest, and the other bears westward for a short distance to divide into two wild, short valleys known as "Central" and "West" valleys.[16]

Here, in this lonely, remote and isolated valley the pharaohs from Thutmose I (1525-1495 B.C.) through the next 500 years secretly sought burial places, tunnelling underground passages into the rocky cliffs and constructing spacious apartment tombs, of which the shortest was fifty-three feet and the longest descended to a distance of 470 feet. Because secrecy was the watchword, when the burial was over the entrance was filled with rock and the natural slope of the mountain side was restored as skilfully as possible.

Rameses I was one of the earlier kings who chose this as his last earthly resting place. Then followed his son Seti I, then his grandson Rameses II, who was buried beside him. The Ramesside pharaohs and others followed one after another until more than thirty pharaohs and more than a score of other important people were laid away here, until the tomb-crowded valley came to be called "The Valley of the Tombs of the Kings," a name it retains to this day.

Into this valley in modern times went Napoleon, Champollion, Mariette, Belzoni, Maspero, Petrie, Quebel, and Carter, together with a great line of Egyptologists who searched the way of the dead. They found that most all the catacomb tombs ended with a cluster of rooms somewhat resembling an expensive suite of rooms in a great hotel.

On October 6, 1817, Belzoni began his excavations in the Valley of the Tombs of the Kings. By the third day he found "two tombs of considerable importance, one of them beautifully painted; the other undecorated, but containing some funerary furniture and two female mummies whose hair was long and well preserved." On the fifth day he found another tomb of still greater importance in which was a "sarcophagus of granite, two mummies . . . and in a corner a statue standing erect, six feet six inches high, and beautifully cut out of sycamore wood." On October 16th he began digging a few yards away and on the following day penetrated the tomb of Seti I, which extended back into the mountainside for 470 feet and possessed many rooms, the halls and walls of which were crowded with impressive painted and sculptured scenes, most of which were religious. In one long corridor the artist made use of a series of well executed scenes in which with great wealth of detail the whole journey of the Sun through the world of Night and Darkness was displayed with a vividness that makes Egyptian theology of the dead look almost real.

In his search in the rooms and corridors, Belzoni found no less than 182 life-size figures in relief and an estimated 800 more smaller ones varying from one to three feet in height, together with nearly 500 hieroglyphics of four different sizes, ranging from one to six inches in height, all done in exquisitely beautiful colors.

Far back in the deep recesses of this extensive burial complex Belzoni and his workmen found Seti's beautiful sarcophagus room measuring seventeen and one-half by forty-three and one-half feet. Its walls were richly adorned with illustrations and extracts from the best religious literature of the day. In the center of the ornate room sat a sarcophagus of the finest oriental alabaster, nine feet five inches long, and three feet seven inches wide. The alabaster was but two inches thick, and was translucent when a light was placed against it. Several hundred minutely sculptured figures, within and without the casket, gave a graphic account of the funeral procession and ceremonies. And, although the king's mummy was not in the sarcophagus (it was found later, as we will relate below), there were other compensations.[17]

Belzoni spent many months in the suffocating atmosphere of the tomb, faithfully reproducing the findings. The inscriptions he copied and the figures he molded in wax. The beautiful alabaster sarcophagus was removed from the tomb and placed in the Soane Museum in London. The great tomb of Seti I had yielded a vast store of valuable information which has contributed immeasurably to our knowledge of ancient Egyptian life and religion.[18]

In this lonely valley in 1898, Loret discovered the tomb of Amenhotep II (1447-1425 B.C.), whom many regard as the "Pharaoh of the Exodus." The discovery was unique in that the mummy of Amenhotep was found still resting in his coffin under the gold-starred and blue-painted ceiling of the sepulchre room—the first pharaoh up to that time found in the tomb in which he had been laid. The king was still wrapped in his shroud and adorned with garlands. In life he had been widely known for carrying and shooting an unusually large bow, and strange to say, this formidable weapon was found in the tomb along with its owner. In one of the side-rooms of the tomb the excavator found nine royal mummies, including those of Thutmose IV, Amenhotep III, Septah, Rameses IV, Rameses V, Rameses VI, and Merenptah.[19]

Of the royal women, only the great Queen Hat-shep-sut succeeded in locating her tomb in this valley, but strangely enough here in the valley was buried a woman who was a commoner, alongside her commoner husband, the parents of Queen Tiy, Yuaa, and Tuau, who were no doubt laid to rest there by their devoted daughter. This tomb was discovered by T. M. Davis, an American, and it was described as "the richest and most interesting which was ever discovered, up to that time." It contained carved and inlaid funeral furniture, blue enameled wooded coffins, figures in gilt gesso, gold and silver plated canopic jars, a Theban chariot, down-stuffed cushions, alabaster vases, a supply of mummified meats, and such other equipment that made of it a vast storehouse of all Egyptians deemed necessary or desirable in this life or the next.

MORTUARY TEMPLES

In the Valley of the Tombs of the Kings there were no mortuary temples. At first this seemed strange; then it was found that just as Kings Zoser and Cheops as well as other kings who built pyramids had elaborate mortuary temples as close to their pyramids as possible, so did almost all of those whose tombs were in the Valley of the Tombs of Kings. However, their temples were not built adjacent to their tombs, but were located out on the fertile plain of western Thebes between the shore of the Nile, and the sharp, rugged precipice of the Libyan cliffs.[20]

These temples were all dedicated to the god Amon, but were primarily intended by their royal builders as chapels for the presentation of offerings of food and drink, incense and flowers by relatives of the deceased kings, and for the performance of the rites for the dead by a "perpetually endowed" priesthood.

The first of these magnificent structures was the mortuary temple of Seti I at Kurna, one of the earliest and in many ways one of the best of the Theban mortuary temples. Its pyloned entrance, which faced eastward toward the Nile, was at the western end of a grand avenue of sphinxes reaching all the way from the temple to the Nile. This entrance opened into a grand court beyond which another pylon gave access to an additional court, at the west side of which was the hypostyle hall, and further on, the sanctuary.[21]

The entire wall surface of the temple, with the exception of one room, was covered with the most delicate limestone reliefs and mural decorations which are recognized as being among the finest in their class. The long corridors were covered with texts of fine hieroglyphics pertaining to death and burial, among them being an inscription by Rameses II telling of the death of Seti his father in these words: "Lo, he went to his retreat, he reached heaven, he joined Ra in heaven." [22]

The Ramesseum

Beyond the scant ruins of the temple of Thutmose III and a tiny chapel of Septah, is the gigantic mortuary temple of Rameses II, now known as "the Ramesseum." It is the largest and in certain respects the most impressive of the mortuary temples forming the line.

King Seti I started the extensive structure as a memorial to his father Rameses I, but died when the building was only well begun. Rameses II, the son and successor of Seti, was one of the most spectacular of all the pharaohs, one with a flare for the superlative. He reigned for sixty-seven years and lived past the age of ninety. He married many wives and was the father of more than one hundred sons and fifty daughters. His unbounded energy, coupled with a fair measure of ability, vanity, and personal courage, caused him to lead his armies into many foreign lands and to bestrew the Nile valley with numerous monuments, obelisks, pylons, temples, and colossal statues executed on a staggering scale. These he usually dedicated to Osiris and other prominent deities, but in his vainglory he always covered the walls of these buildings with sculptured inscriptions and pictures celebrating his own deeds of valor.

Here, in the very midst of the Theban necropolis, Rameses II took up his father's unfinished structure and during the first eight years of his reign completed it as his own mortuary temple.

The Ramesseum measured 220 feet across its great pyloned front, and was 520 feet deep. It had two lofty gateways, a many-columned open court, a great hypostyled hall of assembly surrounded by a beautiful columned cloister, and a heavy stone-covered sanctuary, which lent a religious atmosphere to the entire structure and aided in making the Ramesseum one among the more perfect monuments of Egypt. Its library, which Diodorus styled "the Medicine of the Mind," was attached to the rear of the building and was only one of many subsidiary buildings that made up the temple complex, which was enclosed within a high brick wall.[23]

Today the grand pylon and lofty gateways are badly damaged,

yet much of the building remains, and on its walls are many reliefs depicting the military triumphs of Rameses. The one on the front pylons shows as the supreme scene the battle of Kadesh, in which Rameses threw himself alone at the front of the battle, killed the chief of the Hittites, crushed many of the royal guard under his chariot wheels and put the foe to flight. Underneath, the proud inscription runs:

The princes and captains did not join hands with me in fight; by myself I have done battle; I have put to flight thousands of nations, and I was all alone.

In front of the temple, close beside the sculptured record of his courage, lie the shattered fragments of the colossal statue of Rameses himself, "the most gigantic figure that the Egyptians ever carved out of a single block of granite." Diodorus says that in his day (c. 10 B.C.) the work was wonderful, not only for its size but for the art, and also for the excellence of the stone in which, huge though it was, there was neither crack nor blemish. This huge seated statue once measured fifty-seven feet in height and weighed more than 1000 tons, but now the whole upper part of the statue has been broken and thrown down by some superhuman power, and nearby the twelve feet high severed head sprawls on the sand as a fitting symbol of ancient Egypt's shattered empire.

In 1817 it provided the inspiration for Shelley's poem, "Ozymandias," which referred to Rameses by a Greek version of his throne name.

> . . . Two vast and trunkless legs of stone
> Stand in the desert. . . . Near them on the sand,
> Half sunk, a shatter'd visage lies . . .
> And on the pedestal these words appear:
> "My name is Ozymandias, king of kings:
> Look on my works, ye Mighty, and despair!"
> Nothing beside remains. Round the decay
> Of that colossal wreck, boundless and bare
> The lone and level sands stretch far away.

Merenptah's Mortuary Temple

Merenptah (1234-1223 B.C.), the thirteenth son and successor of Rameses II, was not an overly strong character, yet on coming to the throne he inherited the perplexing problems of a growing Asian power and a reinforced Libya. He fought battles with both and seemed fairly successful, but like other monarchs he began in the early part of his reign to plan for his after-life. He selected a site one half mile southwest of the Ramesseum, "borrowed" considerable material from Amenhotep's nearby temple, brought in some new materials, and constructed a fairly ordinary mortuary temple for himself.

This temple was being excavated in 1896 by Petrie when, as he says,

The site of Merenptah's temple was disastrously dull; there were worn bits of sandstone, scraps looted from the temple of Amenhotep III, crumbling sandstone sphinxes, laid in pairs in holes to support columns. I was tempted to leave it as fruitless; then came the half-length figure of Merenptah, a fine portrait work, and in the last corner to be cleared there lay a black granite stele, over ten feet high and five feet wide. . . . I had the ground cut away blocking up the stele on stones, so that one could crawl in and lie on one's back, reading a few inches from one's nose. For inscriptions, Spiegelberg was at hand, looking over all new material. He lay there copying for an afternoon, and came out saying, "There are names of various Syrian towns, and one which I do not know, Isirar." "Why, that is Israel," said I. "So it is, and won't the reverends be pleased," was his reply. To the astonishment of the rest of our party I said at dinner that night, "This stele will be better known in the world than anything else I have found," and so it has proved.[24]

This massive stele measures ten feet three inches high, by five feet and four inches broad and fourteen inches thick. It had been inscribed on both sides, one being covered with the carvings of Amenhotep III, in whose tomb it was originally placed. But Merenptah had taken it for his own use, and on its highly polished reverse side, had engraved the story of his victories in battle with his enemies. This was in the fifth year of his reign—about 1229 B.C.

On the upper part of the stele is shown the double image of the god Amon-Ra presenting a curved sword to the king. Behind them on the right is the moon god Khonsu, son of Amon and Mut. At the left is Mut the mother goddess. Below are twenty-eight closely packed lines of about 3000 hieroglyphics with the pharaoh's cartouche repeated ten times. The following is a translation of a portion of the inscription.

The kings are prostrate saying, "salaam."
Not one holds up his head among the nine foreign nations.
Wasted is Libya,
The Hittite land is pacified,
Plundered is Canaan with every evil,
Ashkelon is carried captive,
Gezer is taken,
Yenoam is brought to naught.
Israel is devastated, their crops are not;
Palestine has become as a widow for Egypt.
All the lands together are at peace,
Everyone who was turbulent is punished by king
Merenptah, who gives life like the sun every day.[25]

Among Egyptian inscriptions it was the first and only one to mention Israel, therefore it became widely known as "The Israel Stele." As already noted it was written during the fifth year of King Merenptah's reign or about 1229 B.C., and tells us plainly that Israel was already settled and well established in Palestine and that he had raided or devastated the country, and had destroyed its crops. Therefore, it definitely discredits the theory that Rameses II was the Pharaoh of the Oppression and that the Exodus of Israel from Egypt took place under his son and successor Merenptah. For had Israel left Egypt at so late a date there would have been no time for the forty years of wilderness wandering nor for Joshua's campaign in Canaan. And, conversely, it tends to confirm the Biblical dating of approximately 1446 B.C. as the more logical date for the Exodus, and 1406 as the approximate date for their entry into Palestine. Thus, Merenptah's military raid could well have taken place during the later period of the Judges, when affairs in Palestine were so unsettled as to permit of just such a campaign as Merenptah describes.

Mortuary Temple of Amenhotep III

A short distance south of the Temple of Merenptah stood the once great Temple of Amenhotep III. The Great Pharaoh, as did those who had gone before and those who followed him, sought carefully to make every possible preparation for his eternal existence, and having built and equipped his temple he rested in the assurance that all was now well and that he would be impartially served throughout eternity.

Its workhouse is full of male and female slaves, of the children of the princes of all the countries which his Majesty captured. Its storehouses contain (all) good things, whose numbers cannot be known. It is surrounded with the settlements of Syrians, colonized with the children of the princes. Its cattle are like the sands of the shore; they make up millions.[26]

Rising in majestic splendor above the surrounding plain, the temple was a sight to stir the heart of its beholder, with its massive gateway, upon which hung gigantic bronze-covered cedar doors. Within these beautiful doors other wonders awaited the eyes of the visitor: Floors overlaid with silver and gold, a gigantic stele upon which had been inscribed many of the heroic exploits of Amenhotep, and the "Station of the King," where the priest performed his ceremonial functions.

Eastward, a short distance from the temple are seated two giant statues, commonly known as the "Colossi of Memnon." They are the figures of Amenhotep and his wife Queen Tiy, each carved from a single block of quartzose sandstone weighing seven hundred tons each. The blocks had been quarried some seventy miles up the Nile beyond Edfu and then transported down the river. These gigantic colossi, scarred and gaunt, are perhaps the most awe-inspiring sight on the entire western plain of the Nile, their crownless heads rising to a height of fifty-two feet.

The northernmost statue was long known as the "Vocal Memnon," because it was reputed by the ancients to emit a sweet, sad wail at the moment of the rising of the sun. It was believed by the superstitious to be either an oracle or a wailing protest on the part of the colossus for the sadistic treatment it had received at the hands of the invader, Cambyses. Quite a few persons attributed the sound to a clever hoax perpetuated by the priests upon a gullible citizenry. The priests were said to have secreted themselves inside the statue where they themselves produced the sounds. But men of a more scientific turn of mind have endeavored to unravel the mystery by explaining it as the result of natural causes. Some have thought that it was caused by grains of sand trickling through cracks of the fissure, whereas others have been of the opinion that it was the result of the evaporation of moisture from the stone as the heat of the sun fell upon it. Still a third theory was that it was caused by the expansion of the rock under the heat of the sun after it had contracted in the cool of the night, in the course of which minute particles would be thrown off its surface.[27]

On the legs of the "Vocal Memnon" there are numerous inscriptions in Greek and Latin left there by the Emperor Hadrian, the Empress of Sabina, several governors of Egypt, and many distinguished travelers from distant places, testifying that they had visited the Memnon and had heard his voice at sunrise. Today, the voice of the giant is no longer heard. The Emperor Septimius Severus sought to repair the damages caused by the ravages of time and the savagery of man, building up parts of the broken statue with blocks of limestone. The wailing voice was never heard again.

Amenhotep had these massive stone figures placed there as guardians to the gateway of his mortuary temple. But they would seem to have failed in their mission because the temple has all but disappeared, and now the giant sentinels sit in stately dignity, with hands on knees in idle loneliness, turned toward the East where once extended, from their feet to the very brink of the Nile, a long avenue of crouching jackals.

Medinet-Habu

The southernmost of the mortuary temples on the Theban plain is the magnificent memorial temple complex of Rameses III, known today as Medinet-Habu. The temple was dedicated to Amon, and is in an excellent state of preservation, including many of the very colors with which its reliefs were originally painted. It now rates as the best available example of an enclosed temple precinct of ancient Egypt and the best preserved of any Egyptian temple of the pre-Ptolemaic period. In addition to the principal temple structure itself, "the enormous walled enclosure contained numerous dwellings for the priests, officials, soldiers, administrative buildings, magazines, granaries, gardens, and pools. The temple proper stood at the very center of the great precinct." [28]

The main entrance to the vast temple was a unique structure at the east end known as the "high gate," which was modeled after Syrian fortified strongholds. Lofty windows afforded a magnificent view across the Theban plain, with its monumental buildings on both sides of the Nile. Sculptured on the outer walls of this great pyloned gateway are scenes of Rameses III leading a hunting expedition in which he and his associates bring down wild bulls, mountain goats, birds and other wild life. In other scenes the warrior king is pictured as a great conquering hero with the falcon sun god flying protectingly above him while he successfully wages war on the Libyans, fights a naval battle at sea, and leads before Amon and Mut long lines of Philistine prisoners taken in campaigns during the eighty years of his reign.

Within this exquisitely decorated temple are two spacious quadrangular courts and the great hypostyle hall, as well as colonnaded cloisters, robing rooms and the sanctuary. On these inner walls are religious scenes of the deepest significance to the worshipers. In one scene the harpists are shown playing their instruments. Rameses III is shown ritual plowing a field with a yoke of oxen, and later he is depicted reaping the grain.[29] There are two representations of the sun god, one in which he is shown rising in the east in his morning bark, and the other, on the opposite wall, in which he sails down the sky "to rest in life in the western horizon." [30]

"I, Rameses III, won victories in war and sacrificed richly to my gods" is in brief the context of the pictures and hieroglyphs that cover the walls and pillars of Medinet-Habu.

Queen Hat-shep-sut's Mortuary Temple

Queen Hat-shep-sut, who reigned from 1504 to 1497 B.C., was Egypt's first female pharaoh, and one of the first great women rulers of history. Young, brilliant, beautiful, and deeply religious, she was "worshiped by the multitudes and adored by the great." According to the reckoning of many conservative scholars—which fits fairly well into Biblical chronology as given in I Kings 6:1—she was that "daughter of Pharaoh" who rescued Moses from the bulrushes in the backwaters of the Nile, adopted him, and had him trained in "all the learning of Egypt" (Exodus 2:5-10).[31] Other scholars object to this identification, but we think on insufficient grounds.

In managing the affairs of Egypt, Queen Hat-shep-sut promoted general prosperity, raised impressive monuments, restored deteriorating temples, constructed ornate chapels, and carried on peaceful commercial enterprises. But her greatest memorial was the impressive mortuary temple she raised against an imposing cliff at Deir-el-Bahri, almost three miles west of the banks of the Nile.

In selecting the site, she and Sen-mut, her brilliant architect, chose this imposing bay-like cove forty feet above the green bottomlands of the plain, and so oriented that when complete the temple was immediately opposite the great Temple of Amon (Karnak). Certainly for Hat-shep-sut's temple it was "the most imposing spot in the whole amphitheater west of the river." [32]

Just above the level of the western plain the courts of this lovely temple of white limestone, 800 feet long, were built on gently rising ground in three successive colonnaded terraces, each higher than the other. First was the long ascending ramp leading through long lines of graceful colonnades to the great black bronze doors, beyond which was a large rectangular court bounded by a splendid portico of double and triple rows of columns.

On the second terrace was a long line of ornate colonnades before a spacious court, beautiful because of its richly colored reliefs and significant because of its historical inscriptions. To the left was a chapel to the goddess of Hathor, the roof of which was supported by pillars surmounted by attractive Hathor heads. To the right was a similar chapel of the jackal-headed Anubis, god of the dead. There was a vestibule with twelve sixteen-sided "proto-Doric" columns that gave access to three rock-hewn chambers, the walls of which were covered with bas-relief carvings of religious and historic scenes. Another ramp led to a third terrace where was located the actual temple court—the ornate, sacred sanctuary, the holy of holies—which was hewn back into the very heart of the mountainous cliff towering almost 600 feet above the plain. To the right and left were numerous halls and chambers, chiefly devoted to the cult of the queen and her parents. In the center, beyond the holy of holies, within the deep recesses of the red rock was the queen's own carved tomb room, which she was never to use.

With its salmon-pink tints in the foreground, its broken ranks of glittering white columns forming the temple vista, and the dark red cliffs towering beneath an oriental sky, one can well understand why the queen looked upon the lovely scene as her own "dream of beauty in stone," and why later generations looked upon it as a "rare architectural gem"—the "loveliest" of all Egyptian temples.[33]

Because she was deeply devoted to Amon-Ra, the queen not only erected her temple directly opposite the great Temple of Amon (Karnak) on the east bank of the Nile, but from the base of the lowest terrace of her temple had constructed an avenue straight across the three-mile expanse of the valley to the river's edge opposite the pylon-entrance to the Temple of Amon. Thus, she created a broad and beautiful mall or boulevard between the two buildings broken only by the waters of the sacred Nile.[34] To make the mall more picturesque and impressive, she bordered it with trees and lined it on both sides with enormous sphinxes facing each other, the head of each sphinx formed in the likeness of the Queen herself.[35]

The fabled home of the Egyptian gods was the mythical land of Punt, where the ground was terraced down to the sea. On these terraces were beautiful meadows shaded by myrrh and other incense-bearing trees from which the gods derived their greatest delight. The queen, who thought of herself as the creator on earth of a temple-home for Amon-Ra and other gods, endeavored to build her terraces like those of the fabled land of Punt. When the terraces were finished, however, the incense-bearing trees were lacking. She prayed to Amon-Ra and firmly believed that the god appeared to her and bade her go and bring back these fragrant incense trees for the terraces about the temple.

In the eighth year of her reign (1496 B.C.) Hat-shep-sut fitted out a fleet of five ships with high carved bows, bright colored sails, and beautifully canopied cabins, manned them with 210 men, and placed them under the command of Nehsi, her chief steward. At the queen's command the fleet sailed away down the Nile, through a canal to the Red Sea, and then southward on the long and seldom attempted voyage to Punt.[36]

The following year the fleet returned safely to Thebes bringing thirty-one fragrant myrrh trees whose roots were potted in great baskets or tubs. Three of these trees were very large. In addition to the trees the fleet brought back rich cargos of myrrh-resin, cinnamon, ebony, gold, electrum, ivory, "the green gold of Emu," incense of many kinds, cosmetics, apes, monkeys, wild dogs, and many panther skins. Finally, "they led ashore a live panther, spitting and snarling at its captors. This was an individual present to the Queen, and she was childishly delighted with it." [37]

The queen was especially delighted with the thirty-one incense-bearing trees, which she planted along the terraces about her temple. Then she held a royal court of triumph during which she delivered from her electrum throne a speech ending with the jubilant words:

It was done. . . . I have made for him [Amon-Ra] a Punt in his garden, just as he commanded me. It is large for him; he can walk abroad in it.[38]

The land and people of Punt and the entire progress of the expedition are graphically pictured and described in detail in a set of painted reliefs on the walls of the second spacious court of Queen Hat-shep-sut's mortuary temple. They constitute the most interesting sculptures to be found on the monuments of Egypt.

Finding the Pharaohs at Deir-el-Bahri

About the year 1880 many priceless tomb relics began to appear in and around Thebes offered for sale by certain Arabs, and purchased by tourists who visited the region. The nature of the valuable purchases led authorities to believe with certainty that someone had discovered a long-lost royal burial place of great magnitude and importance, and that the finder was growing wealthy from the loot he had found. Close investigation caused suspicion to fall upon the Egyptian family of Abd-el-Rasul, who were guides by profession but thought to be tomb robbers in practice. One of their number was arrested by Maspero and turned over to Egyptian authorities for interrogation.

The investigation, though apparently fruitless, struck fear to the heart of the suspect, who upon being released convinced his brothers of the wisdom of surrender. The older brother

came to the authorities with a full confession and an offer to
guide an official of the Cairo museum to the place of his
fabulous find.[39]

Emil Brugsch was appointed to undertake the intriguing
task and in July 1881 he set out, accompanied by two other
museum officials. The repentant thief led them up a long
mountain slope and along the foot of an escarpment to the
unfinished tomb of Princess Astemkheb, a short distance southwest of the mortuary temple of Queen Hat-shep-sut. Their
guide announced that the treasure they sought lay at the
bottom of the six-foot wide shaft. With many misgivings as
to his personal safety, but spurred on by the hope of a great
discovery and trusting in his loaded rifle for protection, Brugsch
allowed himself to be lowered into the forty-foot deep shaft,
the hands of his reluctant guide holding the rope. One after
another the Arabs and his museum assistant slid down the
rope.

At the bottom Brugsch found a passage proceeding northward for twenty-five feet, after which it turned west into the
heart of the mountain. As he groped his way along the rocky
passage he was hampered by a vast array of funerary furniture;
beyond the bend his gaze fell upon a cluster of mummy-cases,
which upon examination proved to contain the mummies of
pharaohs, queens and other royalty, among whom were Seti I,
High-Priest Nebseni, and Queen Hent-taui. All about the
chamber were strewn innumerable treasures of burial equipment, including canopic vases, porcelain funeral offerings, and
statuettes of exquisite beauty. It all seemed incredible, absolutely amazing. Yet the Arab led the way on through another
passage until they came upon a second room, measuring twenty-
three feet in width, thirteen feet in breadth, and six feet in
height. It contained an even greater number of gold-covered
coffins and mummy-cases of stupendous size, leaning against
the wall or scattered about the floor as if left by someone in
a great hurry. The great room seemed like an Aladdin's cave,
for all around there were royal mummy cases so exquisitely
carved and decorated, and so well preserved that many of them
seemed as though they had been placed there the day before. On
gaining his poise the archaeologist examined the royal names

and titles and read among many others the names of Queen
Nefert-iti, Amenhotep I, Thutmose II, Thutmose III, Rameses
II, and Rameses III. In all the two chambers contained forty or
more mummies, many of which were of the greatest rulers of
the Egyptian empire.[40]

What was the meaning of this mass burial? How did these
mummies come to be there? The answer was that long before
our Christian era began the Theban cemeteries suffered such
an unbroken series of robberies that the faithful funerary priests
of ancient Thebes came to realize that even the seclusion of
the Valley of the Tombs of the Kings was insufficient to provide the necessary safety for the royal mummies to repose unmolested. For even there the industrious clan of grave-robbers
invaded and plundered, forcing the long-suffering priests to
seek a new place in which their charges could await the resurrection in peace and safety.

Under the cover of night the faithful ones went stealthily
out into the Valley of the Tombs of the Kings and the Valley
of the Queens and brought the mummies and other treasures
to this new hiding place, where they rested undisturbed for
over 3000 years until again the silence was broken, this time by
the pillaging hands of the Abd-el-Rasul family.[41]

Brugsch realized that his significant find demanded prompt
action if wholesale looting was to be prevented. Hiring 300
Arabs, who worked for six days without let up, he had the
entire contents of the tomb removed and transported across
the western plain to the bank of the Nile, where three anxious
days were spent waiting for the steamer he had ordered from
the museum.

The natives became surly and threatening, being highly displeased that their pharaohs had been disturbed and that a
source of revenue had been cut off. However, the precious cargo
was loaded without incident, and the journey down the Nile
began, amid the frenzied protests of the inhabitants, the wailing
of the women, and the rifle shots of the men, all this being
re-enacted as the steamer passed each town and village on its
northward journey. At the end of the journey the mummified
pharaohs were placed in the museum at Cairo, where they
were once again safe from the desecration of tomb robbers and

could be viewed by the millions who would come from the ends of the earth to study the secrets and ponder the mysteries of the great land of Egypt.[42]

PALACE OF AMENHOTEP III

The most beautiful palace of antiquity of which we know was the palace of that "merry emperor," Amenhotep III, the husband of Queen Tiy and the father of Akhenaton.

The western plain in general had been given over to the burial, care, and worship of the dead. But the upper portion or the southwestern part of the plain was most beautiful, and, being unused for burial purposes, offered a background of natural surroundings that made for private living at its best.

Amenhotep loved nature and was a great hunter (he issued a special scarab to celebrate the killing of a hundred and ten lions). He was also a great builder, a great lover, husband and father, but most of all he was a lover of pleasure. Therefore he chose that high southwestern portion of the plain as a suitable site for his royal domain, and moved there with Tiy his wife to the magnificent palace built for them by his favorite friend and architect, Amenhotep.

On this extensive estate, just south of the royal palace, he constructed a magnificent park in honor of Queen Tiy, the "Great Royal Wife," and in the midst of the park of shade trees, shrubs, flowers and flowing fountains, he dug out a lake more than a mile long and twelve hundred feet wide on which the imperial couple might sail in the royal barge, "Aton Gleams." Pharaoh Amenhotep dedicated the lake with a dazzling festival, in which he led a procession of fantastically decorated boats out onto the lake where he met and boarded the pleasure barge of the Queen. Following the ceremony the populace of the city of Thebes abandoned itself to the pleasure and festivities characteristic of the reign of Amenhotep III.[43]

The palace was constructed largely of wood and stucco, and there are some indications that it was only fairly ostentatious on the exterior. Within there was a grandeur, a beauty, and a symmetry that in certain respects has seldom been equaled.

Beyond the gate of the great brick enclosure wall was a canopied entrance to a vestibule leading into a magnificent state reception and banqueting room two stories high. Around the inside of its walls was a row of columns that supported the roof in a position several feet above the wall, providing cross ventilation for the comfort of the people below. Beyond the state room were a series of elaborate courtyards, each with its tiled fish pool and its vine-covered walls, behind which were built all sorts of shops and workrooms, including kitchens and bakeries. Above were the living quarters, each with its own private bathroom and built-in wind scoops that wafted cool breezes over the occupants.

The white walls and the ceilings of the palace were lavishly adorned with frescoes of nature and open air scenes depicting white doves and golden butterflies flitting across a blue sky. The smooth, composition floors were decorated with beautiful scenes of pond and marsh life. The art was the best known to that period of Egyptian culture, and some ranks with the best of any culture.[44]

The palace was a fitting tribute to Egyptian taste and culture, and was a most suitable dwelling place for Amenhotep III, who as a prince had dreamed at the feet of the Sphinx, and for his son Amenhotep IV (Akhenaton), and later for the colorful King Tut-ankh-amen. It was excavated by the Metropolitan Museum of Art of New York.

AKHENATON AND EL-AMARNA

In the twenty-fourth year of the reign of Amenhotep III his beloved Queen Tiy bore him a son who though frail in body was destined as Amenhotep IV to become one of the most individualistic and fascinating rulers of the Egyptian Empire.

Amenhotep IV bore the stamp of a dreamer, an intellectual genius and an esthetic and religious reformer. As a lad he absorbed the teachings of his mother; as a young man he married the beautiful and brilliant princess Nefert-iti, and for three years he served as co-regent with his aging father. In 1376 B.C. the one-time "Merry Emperor" died and his son Amenhotep IV seemed set for a notable career. And notable it was, a career unique in the annals of Egyptian rulers.

Within his life there strove the influences of many monumental characters of the recent past, among whom was the great Queen Hat-shep-sut who as some suppose had adopted Moses and had steered such a wise course for her nation and people;

Moses with his brilliant career and mighty monotheistic teachings; his mother Queen Tiy, whose teaching had been a near-monotheism, and lastly his brilliant wife Queen Nefert-iti, who was an Asiatic and a firm believer in one god. Then, too, there were those among the priesthood who secretly believed that one god was better than many. Only one year after his royal father's death, therefore, he shook and shocked the world of the Nile by officially substituting the simplicity of one god, the sun disc Aton, who reigned over all men everywhere, for the complex edifice of Egypt's pantheon of some 2200 gods.

Amenhotep not only announced his firm belief in Aton as the one and only god, but constructed temples to him in Thebes and other strategic centers. When the entrenched priesthood and apostles of Amon objected and brought on a bitter fight Amenhotep IV changed his name to Akhenaton (The Light of Aton), and accompanied by Queen Nefert-iti and his devoted court and government, withdrew from Thebes with its age-long associations with Amon, and journeyed some two hundred miles down the Nile to the Plain of Amarna, where he caused to be built for himself and his god a new city named Akhet-Aten (Horizon of Aton).[45]

The city was built in the midst of a vast level plain eight miles from north to south and from twelve to seventeen miles from east to west. It included within its borders many towns and villages, the boundaries of the entire district having been marked out by fourteen giant steles carved in the limestone cliffs. When the city was completed Akhenaton issued a decree in which he dedicated the entire region to Aton:

Now as for the area within the . . . landmarks from the eastern mountains to the western mountains of Akhet-Aten opposite, it belongs to my father, Aton, who is given life forever and ever; whether mountains, or cliffs, or swamps . . . or uplands, or fields, or waters, or shores, or people, or cattle, or trees, or anything which Aton, my father has made . . . I have made it for Aton, my father, forever and ever.[46]

Within the city itself were built many wide and beautiful streets, lovely gardens, pools, and magnificent villas for the nobles of his realm. Akhenaton initially built three great temples to Aton in his new city, but during the course of his reign many others were erected throughout the empire. His religion was one of light, rather than darkness, one of openness rather than secrecy. He rejected, therefore, the traditional places of the temples of Amon with their vast dimly lighted halls and yet darker sanctuaries, and constructed in his new temples a series of open courts, where worship was carried on in the full light of the solar disc, whose rays flooded every corner of the temple. This gave reality to the worshiper's faith in the sun.[47]

In the midst of the new city there rose the king's magnificent palace. The walls and halls and columns and outer courts, as well as his "Balcony of Royal Appearance," were decorated with gold, bronze and precious stones. Some were sceltpured whereas others were adorned with statuary and paintings. Even the floors were frescoed with artistic designs of plants, animals, and fish, drawn with a perfection and truthfulness to nature seldom equaled in any age. In all things the sculptor and artist strove to create natural designs, to make the chisel and brush tell exactly what they saw.

Akhenaton had as his associates some of the finest architects and artisans ever to breathe the air of the Nile valley, yet he was the driving genius in back of all that helped to spread his religion throughout the length and breadth of the land. In the realm of music and worship and devotion he not only worked with the musicians and singers and priests, but he himself composed or helped compose a beautiful hymn of praise that not only ranks among the finest pieces of literature bequeathed by the Egyptian civilization, but plainly set forth the chief doctrines of the new faith, which regarded Aton "as creator, regulator, and governor" not of Egypt alone but of the whole world.[48]

The Aton religion appears to have been more than mere sun worship, the solar disc having been only the visible manifestation of the unseen power they worshiped, as indicated in a prayer made by Queen Nefert-iti:

Thou disc of the sun, thou living god, there is none other beside thee!
Thou givest health to the eyes through thy beams, creator of all things.

This is indicated in another prayer by an officer of Akhenaton:

Thou, O god, who in truth art the living one, standest before the two eyes. Thou art he which createst what never was, which formest every thing, which are in all things: we also have come into being through the word of thy mouth.[49]

King Akhenaton and his talented followers were offering to Egypt a religion that in many respects was superior and more enlightened than the religions to which they were accustomed, yet the tide of reaction and opposition was too strong. The priests at Heliopolis gave large place to many aspects of sun worship and therefore were not too strongly opposed, but the priests at Thebes were bitterly and unalterably opposed. They were for the most part filling endowed positions that bound them to Amon-Ra, to Osiris, and to other gods whom with little encouragement the bulk of the people were pleased to continue worshiping. As a result, the tides of civil strife and war rose higher and higher against Akhenaton and his regime until the adherents of Amon drove a wedge that divided the followers of Aton. Some accounts infer that even Akhenaton himself, after some fifteen years of opposition, was so weakened and humbled and unmanned that he attempted a reconciliation with the still powerful priesthood of Amon, and in so doing incurred the displeasure of Queen Nefert-iti, who removed herself to a palace in the extreme southern section of Akhet-Aten, and took with her their second daughter Ankhesenpa-aton and the latter's husband, Tut-ankh-aton.

THE RISE OF KING "TUT"

However, under rather mysterious circumstances Akhenaton died in the eighteenth year of his reign and was buried in his family tomb in a lonely valley east of Amarna, where his daughter Meket-aten had already been buried. He was succeeded by Smenkh-ka-re, his son-in-law by marriage to his oldest daughter Mer-aten. But the young king died within a short time, and the youthful Tut-ankh-aton took the throne and reigned in the capital at Amarna for six difficult years. Then through increasing pressure from the old established priesthood and on the advice of his prime minister Eye and his general Harmhab, he moved the capital back to Thebes and returned to the worship of Amon.

At Thebes he re-established the royal residence in the ornate palace of Amenhotep III, changed his name from Tut-ankh-aton to Tut-ankh-amen (Living Image of Amon), and for some nine years threw the weight of his influence toward reviving the religion and worship of the god Amon, which to the Egyptian was "the old-time religion." Then, while yet a young man, he died and was elegantly buried in a cliff tomb in the Valley of the Tombs of the Kings, where his body was to rest unmolested for 3300 years.

TELL EL-AMARNA

On the Plain of Amarna the destructive forces of nature and of man exacted their due and changed the face of the earth as the centuries slowly passed. Then one day in 1887 at Tell el-Amarna (the name by which Akhenaton's ruined city is now known) a Bedouin woman was digging in the mound of ruins in search of rich soil for her garden, when she accidentally unearthed a hoard of clay tablets inscribed for the most part in Babylonian cuneiform. She informed others of her find and sold her right in the discovery for ten piasters or about fifty cents.

Knowledge of the woman's "find" reached Rev. Chauncey Murch, an American missionary stationed at Luxor, and he, suspecting the value of the tablets, called them to the attention of Ernest Budge. On examination they proved to be the official diplomatic records of the Egyptian foreign office during the reigns of Amenhotep III, and his son and successor Amenhotep IV (Akhenaton). Museum authorities, native dealers, and individuals converged on the mound in a frantic effort to secure every tablet possible. These precious clay tablets sold at prices ranging from $5 to $750 each, and eventually about 370 of them were recovered. Eighty-two went to the British Museum, 194 to the Royal Museum in Berlin, 60 to the Egyptian Museum in Cairo, 20 to Oxford, and the remainder to other museums or to private individuals. There are two in the Metropolitan Museum in New York.[50]

They were all official communications from the monarchs of Babylonia, Mitanni, and other Asiatic countries, and from the provincial governors in Phoenicia, Syria and Palestine. The earlier ones were addressed to Amenhotep III and the later ones, which constituted the majority, were sent to Akhenaton. On moving the capital from Thebes Akhenaton had brought the letters received before that time and deposited them in the official archives of his new city of Akhet-Aten on the plains of Amarna. The majority of them came later and were also filed away in the same archives.

These letters were written with great courtesy, such as would be expected in the East. They deal with political conditions, social affairs, the exchange of gifts and slaves, inquiries regarding the king's health and welfare, and other things too numerous to mention. One long letter, written to Amenhotep III, deals with a very delicate matter pertaining to a princess of Babylon who had been given in marriage to the king but who had not been seen or recognized by anyone from Babylon. The "Merry Emperor" replied, saying that the Babylonian king Kadashman-Bal sent ambassadors who never frequented the king's court and were moreover of adverse bias. In concluding he said, "Send a *kamiru* who knows thy sister."

Another letter was from the land of Ube, which according to some authorities corresponds to the Hobah of the Bible, the city to which Abraham pursued the conquerors of Sodom. From this place, if indeed it be that place, Itadama writes:

To the king my lord . . . Behold now Namyauza hath delivered us to the Habiri all the king's cities, in the land of Kadesh and in Ube. But I will march forth and if thy gods and thy sun go before me I will restore these places from the Habiri to the king that I may show myself subject to him.[51]

Nearly 300 of these letters were written by the governors of various cities or districts in Palestine, Phoenicia, and southern Syria. About 150 were from Palestine proper.

The general tenor of most of these letters was that the Habiru were overrunning the land, and that financial and military aid against the Habiru were imperative if the king of Egypt hoped to maintain control of Palestine.[52]

Of particular interest was a series of seven letters from Abdi-Heba, governor of Urusalem (Jerusalem), who pleaded for help to prevent the loss of that country. In part they read:

To the King, my lord, say. Thus saith Abdi-Heba thy servant. At the feet of the King, my lord, seven times and seven times I prostrate myself . . . The whole land of the King has revolted. There is not one governor that is loyal to the King, all have rebelled. May the King harken unto Abdi-Heba and send troops, for if no troops come this year, the whole territory of my lord the King will be lost. The Habiru are capturing the fortresses of the King. May the King care for his land. The Habiru are taking the cities of the King . . . If there are no archers this year, then let the King send a deputy that he may take me to himself together with my brothers and we die with the King, our lord.[53]

No aid was ever sent in response to the appeals. Akhenaton was much too busy building a new capital and endeavoring to reform the faith of his people.[54]

From the Biblical point of view, the Tell el-Amarna tablets have proven exceedingly important in the field of research, so important that many regard them as constituting the most important discovery ever made in Egypt. The very fact that most of these tablets were written in Babylonian cuneiform, even though they came from various countries, indicates that the Babylonian cuneiform was the one general system of writing readily understood by almost all the people of Bible Lands during that particular period, and perhaps long before and after. Thus Biblical characters could converse rather freely with the various peoples as they moved from country to country, just as the Bible represented them as doing.

Then, too, there was the name "Habiru" or "Apiru" figuring prominently in the letters, and it soon came to be regarded by many reputable scholars that etymologically and philologically Habiru and Hebrew were the same. Both the Habiru and the Hebrews are represented as coming from the general direction of Seir or Edom; the name of Joshua as a leader appears in both the Bible and the letters; both accounts represent the native princes as allying themselves with the invaders; and both accounts involve many of the same place names. These and other facts have caused Caiger to say: "Moreover, the circumstances of the Habiru invasion are precisely, on the face of it, those of the Hebrew invasion, as regards the date, the locality, the results, and the actual place-names concerned." H. R. Hall sums it up by saying, "We may definitely say that in the Tell el-Amarna Letters we have Joshua's conquest seen from the Egyptian point of view." [55]

According to the Biblical account, the Hebrew departure from Egypt must have taken place about 1446 B.C., just after the long despotic reign of Thutmose III (the Oppressor) and during the beginning of the reign of his son Amenhotep II (1447-1425 B.C.). Allowing forty years for Israel's wandering in the wilderness, their entry into Canaan would correspond with the invasion of the land by the Habiru described so vividly in the letters received by Amenhotep III and Akhenaton. Israel would, therefore, have entered Canaan about 1406 B.C. and made their conquest of the land during the following forty years.

KING TUT'S TOMB

The glamor that accompanied the discovery of the tombs of various pharaohs in the Valley of the Tombs of the Kings and on the plain of western Thebes stimulated in many archaeologists a desire to locate the tomb of King Tut-ankh-amen. That widespread desire was deepened in 1907 when T. M. Davis was searching in the Valley of the Tombs of the Kings and found caches of large, inscribed and sealed pottery jars containing magnificent canopic vases and other royal funerary objects that apparently had been brought to Thebes on the abandonment of the capital at Ahket-Aten and hidden away in this valley by Tut-ankh-amen. Nearby, hidden under a stone, Davis found a beautifully engraved cup inscribed with the name Tut-ankh-amen, and in a nearby pit-tomb he found some fragments of gold foil which bore the names of both the king and his queen Ankhesenpa-aton.[56]

A third find was a cache of large, sealed pottery jars containing a number of plain and decorated pottery vases, in which, in turn, were a number of head shawls and other pieces of linen, one of which was inscribed with the date of the sixth year of the reign of Tut-ankh-amen, along with the Royal Necropolis Seal. The excavators felt confident that these finds represented a "gathering up of oddments" after the funeral ceremonies were over, or else "a hasty collection of scattered fragments after the tomb had been plundered."

Davis felt so confident that King Tut's tomb was nearby that he continued to search until 1914, when he was obliged to give up the search because his concession came to an end.[57]

When Lord Carnarvon and Howard Carter fell heir to the concession, they felt they had considerable grounds for believing that the tomb of Tut was situated in this particular part of the valley. They therefore excavated in place after place in this area for six years and removed several thousand tons of debris, but without success. Their long and fruitless efforts caused them to wonder if they should try elsewhere. After consultation, they decided to try for another short campaign of two months. Accordingly, they set the workmen to digging a triangular area near the tomb of Rameses VI. After moving considerable rubble they came upon ancient ruins in the form of workmen's huts built over masses of flint boulders. Removing these, they located a step cut into the rock, then a stairway of sixteen steps leading down to a sealed doorway. With a good deal of emotion, Carter examined the seal impression on the door and found it to be a Royal Necropolis Seal of the jackal and nine captives.

Believing he had found the entrance to the tomb for which they had long searched, Carter halted work and wired the news of his discovery to Lord Carnarvon, who at the time was in London. Within two weeks Lord Carnarvon and his daughter Lady Evelyn Herbert, arrived to watch the excavations. In the meantime, Carter employed Callender the Egyptologist to aid them.

Returning to the spot on November 24, Carter ordered his men to clear the stairway again. Then with Lord Carnarvon and others, he descended the sixteen steps and carefully inspected the sealed doorway, only to make the breath-taking discovery that among others the seal of Pharaoh Tut-ankh-amen was on the door.

Now they knew that somewhere beyond the door lay the long-sought-for tomb, with perhaps the pharaoh's secret treasure store intact. Yet they were made uneasy to find apparent evidences that there had been at least two successive openings and reclosings of the tomb. On closer investigation it was decided that this resealing could not have taken place later than the reign of Harmhab, or from ten to fifteen years after Tut's burial.[58]

After photographing the door and its seals, they removed the plaster covering and opened the door, only to find themselves in a debris cluttered passageway some thirty feet long. When this was cleared they stood before a second doorway, on which they also found the impressions of the royal seal of Tut-ankh-amen and of the Royal Necropolis Seal. Feeling that the decisive moment had arrived, Carter with trembling hands made a tiny breach in the upper left hand corner of the door and inserted an iron testing rod. On finding an emptiness on the other side, he lit candles as a precaution against possible poisonous gases. Then after enlarging the hole he stuck a candle in and peered around.

Lord Carnarvon, Lady Evelyn Herbert and Callender stood anxiously waiting to hear the verdict. At first nothing could be seen, the hot air escaping from the chamber causing the candle flame to flicker, but as Carter's eyes grew accustomed to the darkness details of the room emerged slowly from the mist; strange animals, statues, and gold—everywhere the glint of gold. For the moment—an eternity probably to the others standing by—Carter was struck dumb with amazement. Then Lord Carnarvon could keep his silence no longer and asked, "Can you see anything?" "Yes, wonderful things," was the answer, and the gap was then opened wider for further investigation with an electric torch. "Surely never before in the whole history of excavation had such an amazing sight been seen as the light of our torch revealed to us," wrote Carter afterwards when reporting on the sight revealed to the company as each in turn stepped up to the peephole.[59]

Careful notes were made of the seal impressions on the door, all blocking was removed, the door was opened and the excavators cautiously entered a fine room twenty-six feet long and ten feet wide. By the aid of electric torches they were able to examine more carefully the extent of their discovery. As they looked about them it seemed as if an entire museum was there in that one room.

At their feet, near the doorway, was a beautiful semi-translucent alabaster wishing cup with lotus-flower handles supporting the kneeling figures which symbolized eternity. On the right the excavators saw three golden couches made in the image of animals.[60] Next on the right, on either side of a fine doorway, stood two life-size and life-like figures in black, facing each other like sentinels, "gold kilted, gold sandalled, armed with mace and staff." They were fashioned after the likeness of the king himself, and on their foreheads were the sacred cobras. They stood there, "mutely telling of their long watch."

To the left were four overturned chariots, glistening with gold and inlay; behind the chariots was a portrait of the king. All about the excavators, on the floor and stacked high in the room, were chests, trunks, inlaid caskets, a heap of curiously shaped boxes, beds, stools, tables, beautiful alabaster vases, decorated walking sticks, weapons, inlaid coffers, and innumerable cases of food, clothing, and provisions for the king's sustenance in the spirit world.

The most remarkable object was the throne, which was made of wood and overlaid with gold. Its legs were shaped like a lion's, and its back was embellished by serpents with upraised heads. On the face of its back panel the king and queen were portrayed on a background of gold. Their royal robes were of silver, inlaid with faience, colored glass, and precious gems. The king wore a rich and elaborate crown adorned with feathers, sacred cobras, and sun disks. The lovely young queen wore the customary high crown and held a small vase in her left hand. With her right hand she touched the broad collar of her husband with a drop of perfume from the vase. Above the royal couple there shone the Aton, with the bright rays ending in life-giving hands. This marked the throne as a relic of the earlier days of Tut-ankh-amen's reign when his court was at Tell el-Amarna.[61]

Bewildered by the number of unusually valuable objects, it was some time before Carter and Carnarvon "realized with a start that neither sarcophagus nor mummy was to be seen in this museum of treasures." [62] Then it became apparent to them that this was just the antechamber and that the main room was beyond a sealed doorway between the two sentinels at the northern end of the room.

In the meantime a fourth sealed doorway was discovered. Behind it Carter and Carnarvon found another room (later called "the annex"), smaller than the first, but so packed with chairs, beds, coffers, and vases, it was impossible to enter. In the antechamber there had been some sort of an attempt to tidy up after the plunderer's visit, but in the annex everything was in confusion, showing the haste in which the contents had been ransacked.[63]

Standing in the midst of an infinite variety of treasures of such historic and esthetic value, and feeling confident there were others of rarer value within the yet unopened tomb room, Carter came to the full realization of his deep need of further expert assistance in photographing, recording, crating, and preserving the fabulous yet fragile finds. Therefore, after resealing the entire complex and setting a heavy guard, including Callender to keep constant watch, he and Lord Carnarvon returned to Cairo to contact suitable specialists to assist them.

Eventually, Harry Burton was secured as photographer, Hall and Hauser as draftsmen, Arthur C. Mace and Lucas for laboratory work, Alan Gardiner to handle the inscriptions, and Professor James H. Breasted to determine the historical significance of the seal impressions on the doors. Recording quarters were provided, and a laboratory was established for on-the-spot analysis.[64]

Carter returned to the Valley of the Tombs of the Kings with his enlarged staff and a better lighting system, and reopened the tomb on December 16th. On the 18th Burton took his first photographs in the antechamber, and on the 27th the first object was brought out of the tomb. It was only the beginning.[65]

Artistic objects of historical interest so crowded the anteroom, and pieces of fine furniture, curious looking boxes, artistically painted chests and inlaid coffers were piled so high that movement was difficult. Yet there could be no haste, for in these containers were thousands of things of beauty in themselves and of enormous archaeological value. Many of the curious boxes and fine chests were filled with fine linens and silks and innumerable changes of every kind of rich clothing known to the royalty of that day. One elaborately decorated robe had on it nearly fifty thousand beads, and the entire surface of the sandals worn by the sentinels at the doorway was covered with gold decorations. Yet each article and object, both large and small, had in its turn to be photographed, recorded, and treated or restored in a manner appropriate for its preservation. Carter spent three weeks of painstaking effort inspecting, reconditioning and caring for the many objects found in a beautiful gesso and painted wooden casket, the outside adornment of which he said "far surpassed anything of the kind that Egypt had produced." [66]

There were many chests of gems and jewels, fine bronze work, plaques of pearl, and gold, gold, gold almost everywhere. There were exquisitely carved vases and centerpieces of alabaster, such as a graceful boat adorned with ibex heads at prow and stern, and made to appear as though it were floating in a pool. And there was an alabaster lamp of unique design, on which rested a chalice engraved with Egyptian hieroglyphics conveying the wish for "millions of years of life" for King Tut-ankh-amen.[67]

Many of the articles had to be sprayed with certain preservatives or treated with suitable chemicals and allowed to set before they could be touched. Also required was much restoration, not only legitimate but absolutely essential to a proper appreciation and study of the objects and materials. The woodwork on the chariots, for example, was in good condition and needed little in the way of repairs, except for the gesso and gold covering the surface and the restoration of a few fallen pieces of inlay. The leather of the horse trappings was quite another matter because the leather had almost entirely perished, "leaving nothing but the gold ornamentation with which it was covered. New harness had to be made to which the original gold could be affixed." [68] Thus, no effort was spared in caring for the three great animal-sided couches, the four large chariots, the golden throne, and hundreds of other objects so that no harm or damage could come to some costly or rare article of Egyptian art and workmanship.

On May the 13th thirty-four heavy packing-crates of objects were loaded on small flatcars and taken, by way of a portable railroad, five and a half miles to a waiting steamboat on the Nile. Seven days later they were in Cairo where they were appropriately displayed in the museum. Meanwhile, news of the discovery had sped around the world, and "King Tut" had become the fashion. Visitors converged on Egypt, and the tomb area was so thronged that at times the work of the excavators was seriously hindered.

By February 16th, just three months after the excavators had first entered the tomb, the clearance of the anteroom had advanced sufficiently to enable them to proceed with plans to enter the sealed door between the two sentinels. Invitations were sent out, a low platform was moved up before the door, and final preparations were completed for the "official opening."

Then, on the morning of February 18, 1923, the Queen and Crown Prince of the Belgians, Lord and Lady Allenby, and sixteen other distinguished archaeologists and Egyptian officials took their places on closely arranged chairs in the anteroom, and amid a dead silence that gripped the watchers, Carter mounted the platform and, cautiously avoiding the seal impressions, began to pick out the uppermost layer of masonry that filled the doorway.

Excitement ran high as Carter made a small opening. Mace and Callender went to his assistance. After about ten minutes of further work, a subdued murmur arose as Carter took a flashlight and poked it through the hole.[69] He could see nothing but a shining wall, and although he shifted his light he could see only the continuation of a wall that shone with a soft lustrous brilliance such as he had never seen before.

With the assistance of Mace and Callender, Carter removed one stone after another from the masonry doorway. As more of the door was removed the men, with the spectators, were thrilled with the realization that they now actually faced the sepulchral chamber, and that the shining wall was the near surface of an immense golden shrine built to cover and protect the king's sarcophagus.

Everyone waited with bated breath while Carter took an electric lamp and let himself down through the hole. Lord Carnarvon and Lucas followed Carter into the sepulchral chamber and were "stricken mute by the splendor of the sight." [70]

The enormous shrine measured seventeen by eleven by nine feet high and almost filled the room. It was completely covered with gold, and here and there on its sides were brilliant blue enameled tiles on which were written magic symbols intended to protect the dead. On the walls of the burial chamber were scenes from the life of the king, the last of which was of his funeral procession. The narrow corridor between the shrine and the chamber wall was so cluttered with fine funerary gifts for the king as to cause the archaeologists to proceed with caution. Among these were the oars of the funeral bark for the king's use on his journey to the other world.

At the east end of the shrine were doors, closed and secured by bronze bolts but not sealed. With trembling hands, Carter drew back the bolts and the doors swung back as if oiled the day before. The opened doors revealed a second shrine, óver which was draped a linen pall with gold rosettes. Between the gold covered walls of the two shrines lay a collection of jewels and amulets, including a number of beautiful scarabs in red, blue and green glaze. The doors to the second shrine were both bolted and sealed. The sight of the sealed door brought "audible sighs of relief" from all three men, for they now knew that no tomb robber had been beyond this point, and that they would find the mummy in its casket exactly as it had been laid away 3300 years before.

Closing the shrine door "as silently as possible," they went to the other end of the burial chamber and found an open door leading into an annex, which appeared to have been a kind of "treasure room." On guard near the entrance of this room was an ebony and gold figure of the god Anubis, the jackal god, crouched on top of his shrine. Behind Anubis the floor of the chamber was covered with boxes, shrines, model boats, another chariot and one special tier of ivory and wooden coffers, studded with gold and inlaid with faience. The treasure-trove of the store chamber was a large shrine-shaped chest. It stood facing the doorway on the farther side of the room, and was mounted on a wooden sled. It was surmounted by a cornice of sacred cobras, inlaid with gold and enamel, and guarded at each of its four corners by Isis, Nephthys, Neith, and Selket. Their outstretched arms enveloped the shrine in an attitude of protective care, and in their faces was such grace and naturalness, such "compassion and pleading" that Carter suggests that he "felt it almost sacrilege" to break their solitude of thirty-three centuries. "I'm not ashamed to confess" said he "that it brought a lump to my throat."

It took time and a great deal of care to dismount the guardian goddesses and dismantle the outside protective canopy of wood. Then came the startling revelation! In the center of the big wooden sled stood a smaller sled, the top of which was draped with a beautiful linen pall, placed there nearly 3300 years ago. When the pall was lifted a chest of translucent alabaster appeared. It was nearly cubical in shape, and had sides of gold over which were hieroglyphics filled in artistically with black paint. At its corners in carved relief were the same four guardian goddesses. When the lid was raised there appeared four delicately carved alabaster likenesses of Tut-ankh-amen's head, all wearing on the brow the pharaonic insignia of the vulture and the sacred cobra—emblems of Upper and Lower Egypt. These heads turned out to be the tops of four receptacles, each of which held a most beautiful inlaid gold coffin—exact replicas in miniature of the great golden coffin in which King Tut's mummy was later found—but containing the viscera of the king. This canopic shrine not only represented the highest attainment of the art of the Egyptian goldsmith and jeweler, but was a ready reminder of the beautiful and ornate Ark of the Covenant made a bit more than a century before at Mt. Sinai by Moses and the Hebrews.[71]

After finding the canopic shrine, the explorers reluctantly came to the conclusion that it was impossible to carry the work further that season. The heat in the narrow valley was becoming intense. To expose the rich and delicate fabrics of the tomb to the risks of the hot season was considered to be inadvisable, and despite the eagerness of the explorers and of the public to reach the heart of the mysteries of the tomb, it was decided to close the operations and to resume them in the autumn of 1923. Accordingly, the door was carefully barricaded, the workmen who had excavated the entrance so short a time before filled it up again, and Tut-ankh-amen was left to sleep for a little longer in the tomb where he had lain for 3300 years.[72]

Before the excavators could resume operations, Lord Carnarvon died. It was with a heavy sense of loss that Carter and his associates returned in the autumn and resumed their work by removing the remains of the masonry wall between the antechamber and the tomb room.

In all, there were four shrines, one within the other, each "similar in design and even more brilliant in workmanship" than the last. The four shrines were in eighty sections, each of which had to be carefully removed to the antechamber. The labor took more than eighty days, in addition to the time consumed in moving the shrines to the museum. Removal of the linen pall that covered the second shrine proved a delicate task, for its tissue was much decayed. It was put on a roller, treated at the laboratory, and then was relined.

It was "an indescribable moment" when Carter unsealed and drew back the bolts of the last doors, revealing "an immense yellow quartzite sarcophagus, intact, just as the pious hands had left it." It was covered over with religious inscriptions and pictures, and was topped with a beautiful rose granite lid. In bas-relief at the four corners of the sarcophagus stood the four goddesses, Isis, Nephthys, Neith, and Selket, who spread protecting arms and wings "as if to ward off" any intruder attempting to disturb the sleeping king within.

For a time the excavators stood in awe before this eloquent sight. They then took its measurements: nine feet long, four feet ten inches wide, and four feet ten inches high. Pulleys were arranged and the huge rose granite lid, weighing over a ton and a quarter, rose from its bed. When the linen shrouds were removed there was revealed the beautiful sight of a golden effigy of magnificent workmanship of the young king, filling the whole interior of the sarcophagus. The form itself was rendered in low bas-relief, the head and hands in the round. The arms were crossed on the breast, and the hands held the flail and scepter (rod and staff); both adorned with lapis lazuli.

Around the symbols on the forehead was a tiny wreath of flowers, the last farewell offering of the widowed young queen to her husband. This sight so deeply moved Carter and his associates that he afterward wrote:

Among all that regal splendor, that royal magnificence—everywhere the glint of gold—there was nothing so beautiful as those few withered flowers, still retaining their tinge of color. They told us what a short period three thousand three hundred years really was—but Yesterday and the Morrow. In fact that little touch of nature made that ancient and our modern civilization kin.

This beautiful outermost coffin enclosed a second, also mummiform and of equal beauty with the first. Within the second was the third and last, of solid gold and adorned with jewels. The highly decorated lid was fastened to the lower part by eight gold tenons held in place by gold pins. The proportions of this magnificent form-fitting coffin casket are so correct, the design that mingles sacred symbols with unfolding wings so suitable, the coloring of burnished gold and sparkling gems so enchanting, and the craftsmanship so perfect, that it has long remained Egypt's most exquisite piece of work, and the most marvelous thing of its kind known to the world today. It is of solid gold and weighs 1800 pounds. Its intrinsic worth is more than $1,000,000 according to the present market value of gold.

When the final lid was raised by its handles, the mummy of the king lay disclosed. Over the face was a mask of beaten gold, another gold portrait of their ruler, while about the body was disposed layer after layer of beautiful objects. Beneath the mask was a lovely diadem and about the neck a heap of amulets and necklaces. On the chest were breastplates of gold, along the right thigh was the Vulture of Upper Egypt, along the left thigh the Cobra of Lower Egypt, emblems detached from the crown. Over the legs were four collarettes, over the feet were gold sandals, over the toes and fingers gold stalls, about the arms bracelets of gold and silver inlaid with precious stones. Altogether 143 objects were dispersed about the body in 101 separate groups.[73]

The discovery of the tomb of King Tut-ankh-amen and what it revealed is without doubt one of the most fascinating stories in the history of archaeology. Never before had such a find been made. Never had fancy conjured up such magnificence. Its worth would easily run into many millions of dollars, yet Carter and every other archaeologist knew that as an emblem of a lost civilization the tomb of Tut-ankh-amen was priceless.

The knowledge it brought to light has helped to fill the almost empty gap there once was in Egyptian history. It has told us much of the splendor and the enormous wealth of those ancient people. It has confirmed many things found in the Egyptians' Book of the Dead. And it has shown us what kind of burial the people of ancient times, and especially their religious leaders could give a king who returned the people and the nation to their "old time religion," in this case, to the worship of Amon and their pantheon of lesser deities. The discovery throws no special light upon either the sojourn of the Israelites in Egypt or on their departure, but it and the Tell el-Amarna tablets do give considerable evidence as to the time of the Exodus.

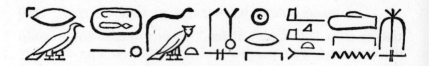

CHAPTER XVII

Archaeological Discoveries in Syria

THE PHOENICIANS WERE descendants of Canaan who settled on the shore near Tyre and Sidon about 2700 B.C. Their name "Phoenicia" or "Purple Land" was given them by the Greeks, who knew them from the purple dye they extracted from the murex shells so plentiful along their coast.

The Phoenicians themselves were artisans, manufacturers, traders, transporters, and colonizers. But primarily they were mariners who courageously sailed the seas and traded their grain, glass, dye, cloth, paper, wine, oil, and wood for lead, tin, iron, copper, ivory, silver and gold. They were invaluable to David and Solomon in their building and shipping activities. Also they were "bearers of civilization," for they imparted knowledge of the sciences and of the art of writing. Their principal cities were Byblos (Gebal), Tyre, Sidon, Serepta, Beirut, Ugarit (Ras Shamra), and Baalbek, but most of their monuments have been destroyed or have crumbled to dust through the centuries. As outstanding archaeological discoveries, we cite the Dog River Inscriptions and the discoveries at Byblos, Ras Shamra, and Baalbek.

THE DOG RIVER INSCRIPTIONS

A few miles north of Beirut the Dog River passes through a picturesque mountain defile and empties into the Bay of St. George. Along the coastline and across the river runs a historic road that has existed from earliest times. South of the river and 100 feet above this road are rugged cliffs upon whose faces have been carved a series of wonderfully fascinating inscriptions, memorials of the conquerors of antiquity who passed this way and, in passing, stopped to leave the record of at least some of their achievements.

More than a dozen inscriptions are cut in individual panels six to seven feet in height by three feet in breadth, and are hewn to a depth of five or six inches in the mountain wall. The passing centuries have exacted their due until most of the records are weathered beyond recognition, yet in the not-too-distant past they all were quite legible, and a few are yet useful in supplying information for a more complete picture of ancient history.

These inscriptions are in cuneiform, hieroglyphics, Greek, Latin, one in French and one in English. They tell of the Roman legions, of Greek conquests, and of the crusading knights, but the majority commemorate the exploits of valiant Assyrian and Egyptian monarchs.

Some of these paneled inscriptions are illustrated. Rameses II (1301-1234 B.C.), for example, is shown offering sacrifices to Amon-Ra in commemoration of his Hittite and Syrian conquests.

Singularly enough, beside the five panels of Rameses is that of the Assyrian King Esarhaddon (680-669 B.C.), who 600 years later returned from a successful invasion of Egypt and recorded his exploits, showing himself in cap and curly beard standing in majesty while Tarhakah of Egypt and Baal of Tyre kneel in chains to kiss the hem of his royal robe. Other well-known Assyrian kings who have inscribed tablets above the Dog River are Tiglath Pileser, Ashurnasirpal, Shalmaneser, and Sennacherib.[1]

Here also the Crusader, the Saracen, the Turks, the French and the British have inscribed tablets telling of their military achievements. "Here, side by side, graven upon this towering rock cliff," says Heusser, "some of these have looked out over the same restless sea for almost three millenniums, mid springtime and harvest, dawn and sunset, storm and cloud." [2] So graphic and so famous are these rock-carved tablets that the place has long been styled "The Pass of the Conquerors," a veritable "International Hall of Fame"—military fame of course, yet archaeologically significant.

BYBLOS (GEBAL)

A few miles north of Beirut lies the ancient seaport of Gebal, the intellectual and religious center of the ancient Phoenician world and the chief center for the papyrus or paper industry. Under the Greeks it was known as Byblos; today it is known as Jebeil. From its Greek name and from its renown for the manufacturing of writing material we derived our word "Bible."

In the Old Testament Gebal was distinguished by its artisans, who assisted Solomon in the building of the Temple at Jerusalem (I Kings 5:18), and by its shipbuilders, who added greatly to the glory of Tyre (Ezekiel 27:9). At various intervals since 1860 the French have excavated here. First under Ernest Renan, then under Pierre Montet, and in more recent decades under Maurice Dunand. Many buildings, tombs, inscriptions, artifacts and coins have been found.

In 1923 Montet uncovered the sarcophagus of Ahiram, King of Gebal. It had been prepared by his son and dated sometime about 1250 B.C. On its side is shown a carved likeness of Ahiram sitting on a winged-sphinx throne before a table of offerings. Inscribed on the lid of the sarcophagus are the words:

> Itobaal, son of Ahiram, King of Gebal,
> has made this sarcophagus for Ahiram
> his father as a resting place for eternity.[3]

The inscription is written in the Phoenician alphabet, and ranks as one of the earlier known examples of the Phoenician script.[4]

Montet also found a lengthy inscription telling of the long journey and experience of one Wen-Amon, who was sent by the priests of Thebes and Rameses XII (c. 1115 B.C.) on a journey from Tanis to Dor, Tyre, Sidon, Byblos, and to Cyprus, and then back to Egypt. His chief mission was to purchase cedar of Lebanon for building a celestial boat for the Egyptian god Amon-Ra. In considerable detail he narrates his experiences, and is exceedingly graphic in telling of being robbed at Dor and unmercifully delayed at Byblos. When the Canaanite prince at Byblos objected to delivering the lumber until he received gifts and a larger sum of money, Wen-Amon replied,

"There is no ship on the waters that does not belong to Amon. The sea is his, and the Lebanon is his, of which you say: 'It is mine!' " [5] Eventually a commission was sent to Egypt and returned with four jars of gold, five jars of silver, twenty pieces of Egyptian linen, 500 rolls of finished papyrus, 500 cowhides, 500 ropes and a personal gift for the prince. On receiving these, the prince ordered the lumber cut and Wen-Amon's ship loaded.

The last of the narrative is broken away, yet the tenor of the story would indicate that Wen-Amon returned safely with his cargo to Egypt.

In 1930 Dunand discovered an inscription on stone in a new form of hieroglyphic script. "Subsequently he found a number of inscriptions on copper in the same writing. The total number of characters identified is over eighty . . . the language is Semitic and the date not later than 2200 B.C." However, a fuller interpretation of these writings on copper has not been made available.[6]

RAS SHAMRA

On the northern coast of Syria forty miles southwest of Antioch, opposite the island of Cyprus, there was a thriving seaport city known as Ugarit, or Ras Shamra. As a mighty commercial and religious center it served as a junction between the Mediterranean and the Euphrates and between the civilizations of the Nile valley and of Asia Minor—a veritable juncture of great thoroughfares from various centers of culture.

The city was founded in the Early Bronze period, was mentioned in Egyptian inscriptions, in the Tell el-Amarna letters, and in Hittite documents. In the fifteenth and fourteenth centuries B.C. Ugarit enjoyed unusual prosperity, but was damaged by an earthquake about 1350 B.C. Afterward it prospered under Hittite and Egyptian influence until about 1200 B.C. it was invaded from the north and from the sea and left in ruins. In modern times it appeared as a mound three-fifths of a mile in diameter and sixty-five feet in height.

The attention of the scholarly world was attracted to this rather lovely spot by means of a chance discovery in the spring of 1928. While a Syrian was cultivating his field, his plow struck what proved to be one of the stone slabs of the convex roof of a fine vaulted tomb. On removing the slabs, he found many valuables, including some objects of gold. When he sold these to an antique dealer the police questioned him and reported the matter to the department of antiquities, which sent representatives to the site and recovered some beautiful Cypro-Mycenaean pottery of the thirteenth century B.C.[7]

In the following year excavations were begun by Claude F. A. Schaeffer and another French archaeologist, G. Chenet, and continued for three months every year from 1929 through 1939.

In a cemetery near the seaport some tombs of the kings of the city were uncovered. Many wonderful things were found at depths of from two to six feet, including second millennium B.C. pottery, small goblets imported from Cyprus, magnificent vases similar to those found in Cretan palaces, large storage jars like those used during the time of Christ, a complete table service 3400 years old, a whole set of weights ranging from an Egyptian *mina* (437 grams) down to small fractions of it; a well-preserved bronze figure of the Egyptian hawk god Horus, a bronze figure of a seated god, a splendidly preserved figure of the Phoenician war and weather god Reshef, and a golden statue of the Phoenician goddess Astarte.[8]

Several royal tombs were also discovered, but many of them had been robbed. Some things of value, however, had been left, such as a beautiful vase of translucent alabaster, an exquisitely carved ivory jewel box lid, a cylinder seal of a deceased king, and a stele of Baal, one of the few known representations of this local god.[9]

At the foot of a cellar stairway, a pile of seventy-four well-preserved weapons and tools was found. These included "four large bronze swords nearly three feet long, eleven lances of various shapes, twenty-seven flat axes, fourteen large hoes, two pretty daggers with inlaid handles, four sickles, nine chisels and drills, and a graceful tripod with little bells shaped like pomegranates suspended from it." [10] Had these pieces not been coated with patina, a fine green rust that gathers on ancient copper when exposed to earth or air, they could easily have been mistaken for tools only recently come from the forger.

The most important find, however, was the temple library containing hundreds of clay tablets dating from the fifteenth and early fourteenth centuries B.C. written in a cuneiform script, the earliest known alphabet using wedge-shaped signs. This library was housed in a building located between two of the city's great temples, the one dedicated to Baal and the other to Dagon, and was evidently used for instruction as well as for filing information. This was evidenced by the quantity of tablets that the excavators took to be practice "sheets" from the copybooks of the schoolboys of the day. There were dictionaries of some of the eight languages in which the tablets were written, including ancient Hebrew written in the cuneiform alphabetical script, the Babylonian language in the conventional cuneiform script, the Sumerian language, Egyptian hieroglyphics, Hittite scripts, and three unknown languages, one of which appears to have come from Cyprus or Crete. There was a register of ships that used the harbor. There were medical and veterinary treatises, legal texts, wills, letters and seals. The majority of these tablets were religious and the gods frequently mentioned were those our Bible often mentions as being common to the Canaanites. Baal was represented as the high god over all the pantheon of gods. And, strange to say, some tablets contained ceremonial rituals or liturgies that are quite similar to those in the Bible, such as: the trespass offering (Leviticus 5:15), the peace offering (Leviticus 22:21), the tribute offering (Deuteronomy 6:10), the wave offering (Exodus 29:24), first-fruits (Exodus 23:19), burnt offering (Leviticus 4:12), whole burnt offering (Leviticus 6:15), offering for "expiation of the soul" (Leviticus 4:2), and the new moon offering (I Chronicles 23:11).[11] One offering to one of their pagan deities was a kid boiled in milk, which was quite the reverse of Israel's law (Exodus 23:19).

The Phoenicians have long been given credit for inventing the alphabet, but here was evidence that the kings of Ras Shamra had used a genuine alphabetical script for many years before the time of the Phoenicians, another indication that writing was well-known from very ancient times. Some of these tablets written in archaic Hebrew and said to have been in existence at the time of Joshua, contain the Divine Names and mention the sacrifices instituted by Moses. But this is not all. There are references that tell of the tabernacle and its furnishing—things introduced by Moses in the wilderness—such expressions as the courtyard of the Tent, the Holy Place of the

Holy Places, the Table of Gold in the Sanctuary, guests of the gods, the priest, Ark of the Covenant, certain offerings on the hearth or ashpit, the sacred number seven, "Rephaim" for the dead, and Leviathan.[12]

BAALBEK

In the middle of the fertile Bekaa plain, between the Lebanon and Anti-Lebanon mountain ranges, are spread the gigantic ruins of Baalbek, which the Greeks and the Romans called "Heliopolis," the "city of the sun."

Its beginnings go so far back as to be lost in the mist of legends of former ancient temples "sacred to the worship of Baal, the controller of human destiny." One tradition persists that Baalbek was "Baalath," where King Solomon built one of his store and chariot cities and the magnificent "house of the forest of Lebanon" (I Kings 7:2-5). However, we do know that in Solomon's day it was a place of beauty and a very busy city of commerce on the trade route between Tyre and Tadmor (Palmyra).

During the early centuries of our Christian era Baalbek was exceedingly prosperous, even famous. Its buildings as we now know them were begun by the Roman Emperor Antoninus Pius (A.D. 138-161) and continued by Septimius Severus and other rulers down to Caracalla (A.D. 211-217). Being a center of sun worship, it acquired renown as a seat of an oracle, and was visited by leading rulers and prominent people from far and near.

Under Constantine Baalbek's temples became Christian churches, but when the Arabs captured the city in the seventh century they converted the entire temple area into a strong fortress that played an important role in the wars of the Middle Ages. It was sacked, pillaged or almost destroyed a number of times, but usually revived after each of its reverses. However, in 1664 and again in 1795 it was violently shaken by earthquakes, from which it never recovered.[13]

First known in Europe through two English architects, Wood and Dawkings, who visited it in 1751, Baalbek has since been visited, marveled at and described by so many travelers that it has easily become one of the most famous ruins in the world. Only with the Temple of Amon at Thebes, the ruins at

Palmyra, and the Parthenon at Athens can these ruined buildings be compared. Baalbek has survived because it was built compactly, yet on a colossal scale seldom approximated. Excavations were carried on by the Germans and the French. In extent the ruins are only about 950 feet in length by some 650 feet in breadth. Yet there is, in this mixture of Roman and Byzantine work, a "mingled vastness and delicacy," that gives the observer "an emotion of deep serenity," and when once seen clings to one's memory always.[14]

The remains of various buildings compose these ruins, yet those in clear outline are: The Forecourt, the Great Court, the Temple of the Sun (Jupiter-Baal), and the Temple of Bacchus.

The Forecourt is reached by ascending a 150-foot wide ruined stairway, entering the acropolis through a 200-foot wide colonnaded portico, and then through one of three very large doors. The shaped court is a hexagonal 212 feet in diameter. In its six angles were six irregular rooms, the smaller of which were probably used by the temple priests as wardrobes for their vestments and the larger as dressing rooms.

The Great Court is a vast enclosure 385 by 400 feet and in a way corresponds to the hypostyle halls or courts of the Egyptian temples. However, it is less crowded, and is light and airy and open to the sun, as is the great court in Akhenaton's temple at Amarna. Here, the court is bordered by delicately chiseled arches and graceful rose and acanthus cornices. Under the cornices are exedras (permanent masonry seats), four of which are semicircular and eight of which are oblong. All have open fronts with two columns of red granite supporting the semicircular ones and four the oblong ones. Most of these columns have disappeared, though several of their bases remain. The partition walls of the rectangular exedras have two rows of superimposed niches, in which were placed statues with two small columns on each side.[15]

As its center and focal point of interest the Great Court has an altar at which sacrifices were made to the gods. Today the pavement is littered with beautifully sculptured cornices, pedestals of statues, broken columns and inscriptions in Greek and Latin—remnants of some of the things which were once there.[16]

The Temple of the Sun (Jupiter-Baal) is reached over a ruined flight of stairs extending up from the west end of the Great Court. The temple was the principal structure of the entire acropolis. All the aforementioned courts with all their sculptures and furnishings were only intended as an annex to this temple dedicated to the sun god Jupiter-Baal.[17]

This "marvel of architectural beauty" was erected on a massive substructure or platform twenty-six feet higher than the surrounding buildings, and fifty feet above the level of the town. The temple itself was 310 feet long and 175 feet wide. It was formerly enclosed by fifty-four Corinthian columns, ten in front, ten in back, and seventeen on each side. Of these fifty-four, only six remain standing. These columns with their bases and capitals measure sixty-six feet in height and seven feet four inches in diameter. There they are, standing so graceful, so erect, "like masts dominating the wreckage around them, the last mute witnesses of past glories." They are easily classed as "the most photographed columns in the world," and may they long remain to show the work of the Roman masters in stone.

A portion of the north wall of this temple is now exposed to view. It consists of thirteen courses of drafted stones, each course nearly four feet high. Outside these temple walls and twenty-nine feet from them runs an enclosing wall, which in its north side contains nine stones, each about thirty feet long. These, however, are small compared with the gigantic blocks in the west wall, which are among the largest stones ever used in a building. One of these is about sixty-four feet, another over sixty-three feet and a third sixty-two feet in length. Each is about thirteen feet high and ten feet thick, and weighs nearly 1000 tons. Many have looked upon these stones and admired the engineering skill that succeeded in placing them into position.

At the quarry about three quarters of a mile away there lies a still larger stone which, for some reason, was never completely separated from a portion of the rock beneath it. This stone is seventy-one feet long, fourteen feet high, and thirteen feet wide. Its weight is estimated at about 1300 tons. To move such a stone would challenge the science of our present day, and it is thought that the reason for it being yet in the quarry is that it constituted too great a feat for even the old Roman engineers of that day.[18]

The Temple of Bacchus lies to the south of the Temple of the Sun and is built on the same level. It is commonly spoken of as the "Smaller Temple," yet it is 225 by 110 feet, which is larger than the Parthenon, and is surpassed in the beauty of its architecture by no similar edifice outside of Athens. It was originally surrounded by forty-two columns, each fifty-two and a half feet high. Many of these have been overthrown by earthquakes, but nine of the original fifteen columns forming the peristyle of the north wall still stand as they were placed there more than seventeen centuries ago.

The richness and beauty of its architectural splendors made the shrine of Bacchus at Baalbek one of the most beautiful of its kind in the world. They befit the god to whom the temple was dedicated. Of these, Leary says:

There are flowers and fruits and leaves, vines and grapes and garlands, men and women, gods and goddesses, satyrs and nymphs, and the youthful god himself, surrounded by laughing bacchantes. Most elaborate of all is the carving around the lofty central portal, which is probably more exquisite in detail than anything else of its kind in existence. The door-posts are forty feet high, yet they are chiseled with such a delicacy that they seem almost as light as a filigree of Damascus silverwork. Upon the under side of the lintel a great eagle holds a staff in its claws, while from its beak droop long garlands of flowers, the ends of which are held by genii.[19]

Of the ruins in general, Morton says:

These ruins are among the few left in the country which give an idea of the massive splendour of paganism. Every student of the Bible ought to see them. Their strength even in decay is astonishing. Many of the columns are of Egyptian granite, and it is said that it took three years to transport them from the Nile to Lebanon. Some of the stones are more massive even than the Herodian stones in the Wailing Wall. The pomp and pride of paganism just before the conversion of the Roman Empire has no more revealing memorial than these magnificent courts and buildings, forming a great city of temples dedicated to the Baal of Syria, the Helios of Greece and the Jupiter of Rome.

One tries to image the army of priests who ministered in this colossal sanctuary, the numbers of consecrated women, the sickening blood rites, the strange crowds from the east and the west who would meet there to propitiate their several deities; and one finds it almost impossible to reconcile the dark, primeval theology with the magnificence of its setting.

My memory of Baalbec is that of fruit blossom, and of a little Arab goat-herd who sat on the base of a column under an almond tree, playing a flute. While he played the white petals fell like snow on the grass around him.[20]

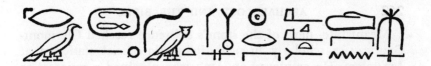

CHAPTER XVIII

Archaeological Discoveries in Trans-Jordan

THE LANDS "beyond the Jordan" have long interested travelers, research workers, and archaeologists. The deep-cut gorges, limitless plains, ruined cities, large dolmens, lonely menhirs, and ancient roads with their Roman milestones and scattered Greek inscriptions, have rightly challenged many to discover the intriguing stories behind all these remains of ancient civilizations.

Famous names such as those of Howard Crosby Butler, Rudolf Brunnow, Gottlieb Schumacher, Charles M. Doughty, Gertrude Bell, Alfred Musil, T. E. Lawrence, C. R. Conder, Selah Merrill, Fritz Frank, Albrecht Alt, John Garstang, George Horsfield, and Nelson Glueck are associated with surveys, researches, and excavations in this fascinating land. We mention but a few of the more outstanding discoveries.

THE MOABITE STONE

In 1868 a German missionary, Rev. F. A. Klein, was spending a short time at Dibon on the north shore of the river Arnon, fifteen miles east of the Dead Sea. A friendly sheikh directed his attention to an oval stone protruding from the surrounding soil. On its face was an inscription in ancient Hebrew characters, leading Klein to believe it was of historical value. He copied a few words from the monument and sent them to Berlin, and then began negotiations for its purchase from the Arabs of Dibon. Sensing the monetary value of the stone, and having had more than a year's experience bargaining with Arabs, Klein offered $400 on behalf of the Berlin Museum.

Meanwhile, news of the stone's existence reached Clermont-Ganneau, a scholarly French diplomatic official stationed at Jerusalem. He employed an Arab who obtained a squeeze, or paper-pulp impression of the inscription. A brief study of the inscription convinced him of the stone's unique worth, and he offered the extravagant sum of $1500 on behalf of the French government. The excited Arabs concluded the stone might bring considerably more if they could hold out a sufficient length of time while governments bid against each other for the prize.

Realizing the possible value of the stone and the opportunity for financial advancement, the Turkish governor of Shechem intervened and demanded that the stone be turned over to him. But the Arabs would not be done out of their treasure by a Turkish official. On the theory that if the stone were broken into many pieces they could sell it piece by piece and obtain more money for it, they heated it to a high temperature, and poured on cold water, breaking it into numerous pieces. Then, in keeping with Arab custom they distributed these fragments among the chief families of their tribe.

Clermont-Ganneau, through his Arab assistant, set about the difficult task of purchasing the fragments from the heads of the various Arab families. In each case he offered a very high price, and although he had considerable difficulty he eventually succeeded in obtaining almost every piece of the monument. Then, with the "squeeze" to guide him, he reassembled the stone piece by piece. Neatly mounted, it was placed in the Louvre in Paris. A replica of the stone is in the British Museum.

The Moabite Stone is made of black basalt and resembles a nineteenth century A.D. grave monument. It is three feet ten inches high, two feet in breadth and fourteen inches thick. On its face are thirty-four lines of alphabetical script that in dialect, style, and content resembles and supplements the account in II Kings 3 of Mesha, king of Moab, who revolted against Ahab. The stone was erected about 850 B.C. at Dibon by Mesha to celebrate his victory. The inscription reads in part:

I am Mesha, son of Chemosh . . . King of Moab, the Dibonite . . . My father ruled over Moab thirty years, and I ruled after my father. And I made this high place to Chemosh because of the deliverance of Mesha, because he saved me from all the Kings and caused me to see my desire upon all who hated me. Omri, King of Israel, oppressed Moab many days because Chemosh was angry with his land. And his son succeeded him, and he also said I will oppress Moab. In my days he spake according to this word, but I saw my desire upon him and upon his house, and Israel perished with an everlasting loss. Now Omri had possessed all the land of Medeba and dwelt in it in his days and half the days of his son . . . but Chemosh restored it in my day. . . .[1]

THE MEDEBA MAP

Early discoveries in the Holy Land were often found by chance. One of the most interesting of such finds was the mosaic map of Medeba—one of the oldest pictorial maps in the world. In 1896 the Greek Patriarch of Jerusalem ordered the rebuilding of the ancient Greek church at Medeba, a few miles east of Nebo, where Moses viewed the Promised Land. On December the 13th while the ruins of the old buildings were being cleared away and the foundations of the new were being laid, an extensive mosaic pavement, the floor of the ancient Byzantine church, was discovered.

On further investigation it proved to be a very large sixth century A.D. mosaic map, which originally covered an area about forty by sixty feet and represented the region from Egypt to Constantinople. Early church authorities had prepared it to show where Christian churches were located in this area. Unhappily, much of the mosaic was destroyed before its priceless value was realized. The remaining fragments, however, portrayed much of Judea in a rather primitive yet realistic manner. The place names were in Greek letters, the sea was in deep green, the plains in light brown, and the mountains in dark brown. The Dead Sea, the Jordan, and Jericho and Jerusalem were well preserved.

Jerusalem was oval shaped with one main colonnaded street running north-south through the center of the city to the plaza before the city's principal gate. Within the plaza and directly within the way of the street stands an impressive column, a fact which seems to explain why to this day the Arabs refer to the Damascus Gate as the "Gate of the Column." The city is shown with walls and an interior well filled with impressive buildings, of which the Church of the Holy Sepulchre is the most prominent. The map dates from about A.D. 500 or a bit later, and its discovery stimulated further researches in Judea and especially in the city of Jerusalem.

DIBON

East of the Dead Sea, on the road from Amman to Kerak, lies the mound-site of the ancient city of Dibon, referred to previously in connection with the Moabite Stone.

The fairly small mound of Dibon spread over two adjacent knolls, and here and there revealed remnants of walls and towers. It was not too imposing, yet the representatives of the American Schools of Oriental Research considered it well worth excavating as representative of the hitherto unexcavated sites of this area. Accordingly a number of short campaigns have been undertaken in which the directors and various members of the American Schools have participated with profit.

In one of the excavations the northern entrance to the city was uncovered, revealing three successive roadways that had been in use for approximately 3500 years. The entrance itself consisted of huge corner towers. Nearby were large grain storage bins in which were found considerable quantities of charred grain believed to date back to about 850 B.C. "The presence of grain in great quantities and the evidence of careful preparation for its cultivation, storage, and baking into bread attest its importance in the agricultural life of ancient Dibon." [2]

In adjacent rooms, thought to be a Moabite temple or palace-temple combination, stood fertility figurines and a rather remarkable incense stand. Here also were found stamped and incised jar handles, the first Moabite ostracon discovered in this area, and some of the finest and thinnest pottery yet discovered in the ancient world.

KING SOLOMON'S MINES AND SMELTERS

Ezion-geber, the twentieth halting place of the Israelites on their journey to the Promised Land (Numbers 33:35), and later the naval port of King Solomon, was located at the head of the Gulf of Akabah, a long, deep arm of the Red Sea. It was here that Solomon built his fleet for trading in southern countries and the countries of the East.

And king Solomon made a navy of ships in Ezion-geber, which is beside Eloth, on the shore of the Red sea, in the land of Edom. And Hiram sent in the navy his servants, shipmen, that had knowledge of the sea, with the servants of Solomon. And they came to Ophir, and fetched from thence gold, four hundred and twenty talents, and brought it to King Solomon.[3]

And the navy also of Hiram, that brought gold from Ophir, brought in from Ophir great plenty of almug trees, and precious stones.[4]

While Israel was yet in the process of entering the Promised Land, Moses had said to them:

For the Lord thy God bringeth thee into a good land . . . a land whose stones are iron, and out of whose hills thou mayest dig brass.[5]

The Scriptural narratives inform us that Moses formed a burnished copper serpent while yet in the wilderness, and that Solomon used copper on a lavish scale in his temple in Jerusalem and imported skilled coppersmiths to do some of the most important work.

And the pots, and the shovels, and the basons: and all these vessels, which Hiram made to king Solomon for the house of the Lord, were of bright brass. In the plain of Jordan did the king cast them. . . . And Solomon left all the vessels unweighed, because they were exceeding many: neither was the weight of the brass found out.[6]

Some scholars supposed that the accounts could not be true, others took it for granted that they were true, but no one did any investigating until 1936 when Nelson Glueck of the American Schools of Oriental Research set out down the Wadi Arabah —the Jordan rift valley between the Dead Sea and the Gulf of Akaba.

At numerous places throughout the Wadi Arabah, he and his associates found ancient mining and smelting sites, ruins of miners' huts, workers' encampments, small furnaces, and great heaps of slag, resulting from the initial roasting process. Some of the mining sites were found because of their names. One of the largest sites the Arabs called Khirbet en-Nahas which meant the "Copper Ruin." The slag and ore specimens on analysis showed up to 58.7 per cent iron and 10.3 per cent copper. Apparently the copper had been "mined, crushed and 'roasted' on the spot," then the raw materials were taken elsewhere to an industrial refinery to be turned into finished products. Numerous fragments of pottery found among the ruins indicated that the mines had been worked during the time of Solomon (1011-971 B.C.), down to the sixth century B.C.[7]

Following the clues furnished by these discoveries and "taking carefully into account the pertinent Biblical materials," Glueck proceeded down the Arabah until he reached the head of the Gulf of Akaba on the north shore. There, "halfway between the eastern and western sides" of the Gulf, he discovered an ancient mound the Arabs called Tell el-Kheleifeh. Glueck writes:

Striking the camel on the neck to make him kneel, I dismounted and threw the halter to one of the Arab guides to lead the beast to a near-by well. Then I hastily examined the site. After even a cursory examination of the pottery fragments found on top of the mound, I was able to date them in the period extending from the tenth to the sixth centuries B.C. This was the age of David and Solomon; of Elijah, Isaiah, and Jeremiah— of the House of David from its founding until its two Great Exiles and the return of the Jews to Jerusalem.[8]

Feeling there could be no question as to the importance of the site, Glueck announced "This is where we are going to dig." The results obtained during the three seasons (1938-40) of excavation that were to follow justified his decision.

During the first season the excavators discovered the ruins of four cities, one superimposed on the other. The uppermost of these was but a small trading settlement of the fifth century B.C. that apparently existed "on the trade for spices and incense from Arabia, in exchange for which were delivered the corn and oil and wine of Palestine" and certain products from Greece and other countries to the north.[9]

On the northwest corner of the lowest level which was identified as the Ezion-geber of King Solomon, the excavators uncovered a large smelting and refining plant for the reduction of copper and iron ores mined in the Arabah. It covered an acre and a half, and was constructed of sun-dried bricks "which had been made as hard as kiln-baked bricks by some terrific heat." [10]

During the second season a much more extensive system of

iron and copper refineries was found than had previously been expected. Indeed practically the entire town of the Ezion-geber of this tenth-century level was "a phenomenal factory site, of a nature unparalleled in the history of the ancient Orient. Ezion-geber was the Pittsburgh of ancient Palestine, and its most important port." [11]

The skill and technical ability evident in the location and construction of this important port and industrial city was indeed most illuminating. Lacking mechanical blowers, the builders had located their elaborate complex of industrial plants directly in the path of the prevailing northwest winds, which swept down the great rift valley between the mountains of Edom on the east and the hills of Palestine on the west. They had placed their furnaces toward the prevailing winds, pierced the walls of the furnace rooms with two rows of flues, and then built a complicated system of air channels connected to double rows of flue holes in the outer walls. In this manner, the almost continuous winds blowing down the Arabah furnished an ample supply of forced draft for the furnaces, eliminating the need for bellows. "The portion of the brick walls between the two rows of flues had been turned green by the sulphurous gases." [12]

Thus almost three thousand years ago, Solomon and his technicians employed what is essentially the principle used in modern times in the Bessemer blast furnaces. The excavator pronounced the smelter and refinery "the most elaborate antique structure of its kind ever discovered." He added:

There was, so far as I know, only one man who possessed the strength, wealth, and wisdom capable of initiating and carrying out the construction of such a highly complex and specialized site as this Ezion-geber. He was King Solomon. He alone in his day in Palestine had the ability and the vision and the power to build a great factory town and sea-port such a comparatively long distance from his capital city of Jerusalem. With the building of a new Ezion-geber, Solomon was able to have smelted and refined and worked into semi-finished and finished products the ore extracted from his great copper and iron mines in the Arabah. He was then able to export them directly by sea and by land in exchange for the spices and ivory and gold and precious woods of Arabia and Africa and India. The wise ruler of Israel was a copper king, a shipping magnate, a merchant prince, and a great builder." [13]

Many small yet significant objects were found on the site, among which were Aramaic and Greek pottery, an Egyptian cat amulet, crude figurines, fishhooks, arrow heads, rope, nails, fragments of safety pins, and many unbroken pots, one of which was full of resin. The greatest find of all, however, was made in the eighth-century level, when a native workman found a royal signet ring with the words "Belonging to Jotham" engraved on it. This was the official seal of King Jotham (749-734 B.C.) and had been used by the governor of the city who ruled in his name. This find confirmed the fact that Ezion-geber still belonged to Judah in the days of King Jotham. Glueck wrote:

When the Jotham ring came up it did not look like much but the workman knew that he would get something for it. When he looked at me, I nodded affirmatively. "How much do you think it is worth, Abbas," I asked him. Hesitantly, he looked at me, and said, "Perhaps two or three piasters?" A piaster is worth about a nickel. I gave him not three, but fifty. He looked at the money, then at me, and said, "But I don't want to take all your money from you." [14]

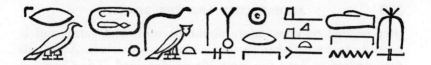

CHAPTER XIX

Archaeological Discoveries in Palestine

THE WORTH OF Assyria, Babylonia, Persia, Egypt, Syria, and even Jordan were of small account compared to the contribution made by Palestine to the moral, spiritual, and intellectual progress of mankind. The very nature and essence of many of these great and eternal values, however, were such that archaeologists could hardly hope to recover them by either topographical or excavational methods. And too, almost all researchers knew from the voluminous records that the avarice and cupidity of the rulers of surrounding countries had caused the repeated plunder of Palestine's wealth and destruction of its buildings.

Yet the Jewish, Christian, and Mohammedan world held what was considered a justifiable hope that sufficient cities and sites might be authoritatively identified, ruined buildings discovered, and inscriptions translated to aid definitely in corroborating, supplementing, and understanding the Bible and other ancient literatures. At least many desired to know what might be found. The work along scientific lines was begun in 1838 by Edward Robinson, and carried on by a host of good men and women from many lands and countries.

JERUSALEM

The site of supreme interest to everyone was Jerusalem, "the City of the Great King." The very thoughts of the place always brought "the overtones of great memories." There never had been any question about its identification with the general site it occupied. But the people wanted to have the lay of the land compared to the narratives said to have taken place there;

they wanted to know more about its walls and gates, and if possible to know what lay buried under its debris. Above all they desired to have the Holy Places identified. The Christian and Jewish world would and did give a good deal to have this work carried on. But there were many almost insurmountable difficulties athwart the path of the researchers.

The first consideration was the fact that the city had been besieged, captured, and destroyed in whole or in part more than forty times. Early tests showed the level on which New Testament characters walked to be on an average of thirty-five feet below the present ground level, and the level on which Old Testament characters walked to be another thirty feet deeper. And all, or almost all areas of Old Jerusalem were cumbered by modern buildings, or cemeteries, so that the major part of the city was inaccessible for digging. Yet researchers made direct diggings where possible, and tunneled under where permissible. Much has accrued from their labors, and much has come to light through chance discoveries.

Robinson's Arch

While carrying on researches in Jerusalem in 1838, Robinson discovered curved stones forming the spring of a huge arch forty feet north of the southwestern corner of the Temple area. The remnant of this forty-two foot wide arch, which came to be known as "Robinson's Arch," projected from the Temple area wall near the ground level and was made up of three courses of very large ancient stones, one of which measured nineteen feet and another twenty-six feet long. Robinson identified it as one of a series of arches supporting a bridge which in Herod's time spanned the Tyropoeon valley and connected the Temple area on Mount Moriah with the Western hill across the valley.

Some years later at the same place Charles Warren discovered the base of a pier supporting the western side of the arch. It rested on a pavement more than thirty feet below the surface of the ground, and with it were found other masonry courses of the same arch. Below this pavement, at a depth of another twenty-three feet, an ancient sewer aqueduct was unearthed, twelve feet deep and four feet wide, running parallel to but below the Tyropoeon valley. Above this aqueduct, and sticking fast in its vaulted roof, were two arch stones of an older bridge.

In reference to his discovery, Warren says:

If we are to suppose that the roughly-faced stones at the southwest angle were never exposed to view, we must presume, also, that the two apparent voussoirs (arch stones) lying on the aqueduct under Robinson's Arch, belonged to a bridge which crossed the Tyropoeon valley previous to the building of the southwest angle of the Sanctuary. This, says Dr. Thomson, would seem to imply that there was a bridge lower and more ancient than Robinson's Arch; and if the latter was constructed by Herod, the former could not have been of a later date than that of the restored Temple of Nehemiah, or even the Temple of Solomon itself.[1]

It is quite probable that these remains represent the bridge over the Tyropoeon valley on which, according to Josephus, Titus stood and pled with the Jews.[2]

Wilson's Arch

While making surveys in Jerusalem Sir Charles Wilson discovered another arch springing from the same wall some 560 feet north of Robinson's arch. This is a subterranean structure located under the present "Gate of the Chain." The arch, known as "Wilson's Arch," is in some respects similar to Robinson's although it is more complete, having twenty-five courses of stone, twelve on each side of the keystone. The work is so perfect as to evoke the admiration and wonder of all who view it. Some regard it as the most impressive specimen of Roman architecture about Jerusalem. At the time of its discovery, Wilson supposed it to be the only arch in this area, but Warren's excavations have since confirmed it as only one of a series of arches forming the base for a bridge across the Tyropoeon valley between the Temple area and Herod's palace on the Western hill, the present "Citadel," commonly known as "David's Tower." According to Josephus, the outer court of the Temple was entered on the west by four gates, the two principal ones being at the points indicated by Robinson's arch and Wilson's arch.

TOMBS OF THE KINGS

In 1850 Felicien de Saulcy, a Frenchman, made a trip to Palestine to rid himself of the grief caused by the death of his wife. While in Jerusalem he made a visit to the so-called Tombs of the Kings. Although the tombs were probably from the Herodian period, yet de Saulcy accepted as authentic a certain local tradition that they were the tombs of pre-exilic kings of Judah. Furthermore, he boldly asserted that fragments of a richly decorated sarcophagus lid he had found, belonged to the coffin of King David.

His reports were received with considerable skepticism, so he determined to explore the site more carefully and prove that he was right. Consequently in 1863 he received a permit of excavation from the Turkish government and continued his work.[3]

De Saulcy found a number of sarcophagi, which he removed to France and placed in the Louvre. One of these was inscribed twice, in different forms of the Semitic alphabet, to "Queen Sadan" or "Queen of Adiabene." This and other information led scholars to identify this tomb-complex as the mausoleum of Queen Helena of Adiabene in Mesopotamia, and her descendants. She and her son Izates were converted to Judaism during the first century A.D., and moved to Jerusalem where Queen Helena was very liberal in dispensing relief to the Jews during a famine—presumably the one foretold by Agabus (Acts 11:28). Izates had twenty-four sons; therefore an extensive family tomb was required.

This series of sepulchres is about one-half mile north of Jerusalem, and is regarded as the finest of the known tombs in or near the Holy City. On entering the gate, one descends a broad stairway leading into a small court. To the left a large doorway leads through a twelve-foot thick rock partition into an immense court eighty-seven by eighty feet, the floor of which is twenty-six feet below the surface of the ground. To the west of this are three stone steps and the beautifully ornamented entrance to the vestibule, which is thirty-nine feet wide. The doorway to the tomb is a large rolling stone similar to the one that sealed the tomb of Christ, about which "they said among themselves, Who shall roll us away the stone from the door of the sepulchre?" (Mark 16:3).[4]

The first room inside is about eighteen feet square, and from it passages lead off to other undecorated rock-hewn rooms. Except for the first, all the rooms contain funerary ledges or shelf-tombs sufficient to accommodate about thirty-two bodies, when buried in regular style, but twice that number when crowded.

SOLOMON'S QUARRIES

In 1852 Joseph Barclay was walking along the roadway parallel to the north wall of Jerusalem when his dog disappeared in a cave-like opening under the wall some 300 feet north of the Damascus gate. Upon removing the sand, dirt, and debris he found that the passageway led into a large cave of stratified limestone. Deeper in the cavern a precipice was found marking the boundary of the main cave, which could be reached only by descending rude steps cut from the native rock. At this point Barclay ignited a magnesium light and was deeply impressed by the many ramifications of the subterranean quarries, which were seen to run in three directions. The rocky pillars supporting the roof resembled the massive columns of a Norman cathedral whose naves and aisles ended in darkness.[5]

The quarry extends southward under the city for nearly 700 feet. At some places the roof is quite low; in others it is so high that the light of candles is swallowed up in darkness. Here and there are rocks that have fallen from the roof, and occasionally one encounters dangerous pitfalls from which stones have been taken. The markings in the rocks along the side and end walls show the very shapes of large building stones removed by cutting a series of parallel grooves with tempered copper tools, and by driving wooden wedges into the grooves. When water-soaked the wedges swelled and split away the large block. It was then an easy matter when one stone was removed for all the rest in the same tier to be taken out. All through the quarries are small shelves on which the ancients placed earthen lamps that gave light to the laborers.

The stone from this quarry is soft and white and beautiful— the best in the vicinity. From the nearness of the quarry, the generous piles of dressing chips, and the quality of the stone, it is quite easy to believe that the stones were shaped and dressed here, then taken on sleds to the nearby temple area where the temple was erected without the sound of hammer or ax, "nor was any tool of iron heard in the house, while it was in building" (I Kings 6:7). Experts say that enough limestone has been taken from these quarries to build Jerusalem and the Temple of Solomon several times.[6]

JERUSALEM'S ANCIENT WALLS

The present walls surrounding much of ancient Jerusalem are two and a half miles around and enclose 210 acres of land. They are from four to twelve feet thick and rise to an average height of forty feet. At the southeast corner of the Temple area they are eighty feet high. These walls, however, are little more than 400 years old, having been built by Suleiman the Magnificent during 1537-42. Only here and there were they constructed upon the foundations of the ancient walls.

Interest in identifying and tracing the ancient walls has been exceedingly wide-spread, and the actual excavational work has, for the most part, been carried out by Warren, Wilson, Frederick J. Bliss, R. A. S. Macalister, J. Garrow Duncan, C. L. Sukenik and L. A. Mayer.

In 1865 Warren was commissioned by the Palestine Exploration Fund to be the director of an archaeological campaign in Jerusalem. But he was so restricted by local official curbs that he could do little more than sink shafts near the walls, then tunnel back and examine the stones in the walls. Yet, he and Charles Wilson and other members of his staff did a heroic job for which they deserve much credit.

Seven shafts were sunk in the Tyropoeon valley near Robinson's and Wilson's arches, and the Wailing Wall. On tunneling back to the old wall at a depth of around ninety feet, the excavators found the ancient wall to be made up mostly of very large and "beautifully worked" stones "fitted together in the most marvelous manner, the joints being hardly discernible." [7] These stones had carefully wrought marginal draftings from four to six inches wide, identifying the wall as having been constructed by Herod the Great. In the course of these excavations, the excavators found quantities of pottery, many lamps, and a second pavement twenty-two feet below the present ground level. Below this pavement they discovered the stone signet of "Haggai, the son of Shebaniah." The latter find was rather significant, because the prophet had made such direct allusion to the signet.

Three shafts were sunk at varying distances from the southeast corner of the temple area, one 90 feet, another 100 feet, and the third 125 feet. At various intervals horizontal galleries were tunneled to the walls and careful inspections were made. The masonry was laid in courses of varying heights with a precision and fineness of joint surpassed only by the early Egyptian work on the pyramids. Near the southeast corner of the temple area, more than ninety feet below the present ground level, Warren made his most sensational discovery. It was a large stone three feet eight inches tall by fourteen feet long that weighed approximately 100 tons. It had a finely dressed face and had been quarried and set in place as "the chief corner stone." Some, in their enthusiasm, have called it the chief cornerstone of Solomon's temple. But this it could not well have been because it was the chief cornerstone of the great city wall enclosing the sacred temple area. Nevertheless it was exceedingly significant, for it was in all probability laid by King Solomon.

In the same area several stones were found that had red painted characters on them. Also fragments of pottery were found inscribed with the likeness of the sun and its beams. Because the characters and inscription were almost certainly Phoenician, here was confirmation that Hiram had sent some of his skilled stonemasons to Jerusalem at the request of Solomon to aid in the construction of the temple.[8]

In his efforts to trace the walls Warren sank many shafts on Mt. Ophel, which lies just south of the Temple hill. Here he discovered and laid bare the remains of David's wall for 400 feet. In places the old Jebusite foundations were visible under David's masonry.

Probably the most interesting of all Warren's finds was the discovery of the ancient Jebusite watershaft that now bears his name. Warren found that

. . . The early inhabitants of Jerusalem had made a rock-cut passage, similar to the one at Gezer, to enable them to secure water from the spring without going outside the city walls. From the cave in which the Gihon spring empties, a horizontal tunnel was driven back into the hill, some thirty-six feet west and twenty-five feet north. This led the spring waters back into an old cave, which thus served as a reservoir. Running up from this was a vertical shaft, perhaps forty feet high, at the top of which was a platform on which the women could stand to lower and lift their water vessels. From this a sloping passage ran on up, to open within the city walls.[9]

Joab and his men passed through this ancient aqueduct and somehow managed to scale the vertical shaft, thus gaining entrance into the fortress, which for so many years had defied the Israelites (II Samuel 5:7-9, I Chronicles 11:6).

During 1893-97 Bliss, under the Palestine Exploration Fund, traced and uncovered the old wall from the scarp at the southwest corner in the Protestant cemetery, along the southern brow of the Western hill, eastward to and including the Pool of Siloam. Bliss, assisted by A. C. Dickie, uncovered walls, gates, drains, aqueducts, paved streets, houses, and the Church of Eudocia, which once stood over much of the Pool of Siloam. His excavation made it clear that as early as Solomon's time the city wall had included both the southern hill known as Mt. Ophel, and the Western hill, sometimes erroneously called "Zion Hill."

During the winter of 1913-14, Raymond Weill excavated at the southern end of Mt. Ophel in the hope of discovering the tomb of King David. No definite traces of David's tomb were found, but Weill did uncover the ruins of a large tower twenty-four feet in diameter with walls four feet thick that extended down the eastern slope toward the Valley of the Kedron—over against the village of Silwan (Siloam). His suggestion was that this was the tower to which Jesus referred as having fallen and suddenly destroyed so many people (Luke 13:4).

In 1922 John Garstang, director of antiquities of Palestine, made a public appeal to archaeologists of all nations to unite their efforts in research that the problems of Jerusalem's history might be solved. A year later, the government of Palestine offered Mt. Ophel "as a site for international investigation." [10] The only response came from England, where the Palestine Exploration Fund, aided by the London *Daily Telegram,* raised funds and sent Macalister and Duncan, who carried on archaeological researches on Mt. Ophel, "The City of David," from October 1923 through the summer of 1925.

Macalister and Duncan uncovered a strong "Early Hebrew" and Jebusite wall in which was a fine gate and at a corner of which was a breach that had been repaired and replaced with a strong tower of a different type of masonry. The repaired breach they identified with that which David is recorded to have temporarily built up (II Samuel 5:9), and the strong tower of a different type as the "Millo," or "filling," which David had first built and which Solomon is said to have rebuilt (I Kings 11:27), making it into an exceedingly strong bastion. Some thirty feet to the east of this and running parallel to it, there is a splendid wall of a later period, thought to be the wall Hezekiah built. It has been suggested that these are the two walls mentioned in II Kings 25:4 in connection with the siege of the city by Nebuchadnezzar. This way "between the walls" can now be seen for about 150 feet. The location and setting fits well into the narrative, although final proof of its being the exact place cannot yet be offered.[11]

Traces of the "Third Wall" mentioned by Josephus was noticed by Robinson when he was in Jerusalem in 1838, and by others before him and many since, including Selah Merrill, United States consul, and L. B. Paton, director of the American Schools of Oriental Research, in 1903-04.[12] But so many of its stones had been carried away for other construction that quite a few people had come to wonder whether these men had seen actual wall remnants. Then in 1925, when repairs were being made on the Nablus road, directly west of the American School of Oriental Research, a very large building block "of distinctly Herodian type" was revealed. The Department of Antiquities cleared the stones, surrounded them by a rail and left them exposed.[13]

Challenged by this ancient wall section, Sukenik and Mayer of the Hebrew University at Jerusalem obtained a permit and excavated the wall at several points along the line indicated by the position of the stones. In 1926 Professor Romain, of the American Schools of Oriental Research, discovered that road repairs had partially uncovered great stones forming portions of a tower and gate in front of the school property. He notified Sukenik and together they excavated the area, which extended about twenty-six feet onto school property.

In 1940 more evidence of the road showed up at the northeast corner of the school property when Sukenik and Mayer excavated and uncovered foundations of a great tower that were forty-three feet wide and extended back under the tennis court. Other portions of the wall were found on the school property in 1942, and still another section in 1959.[14] Other portions of the wall and the foundations of a large tower were located a considerable distance east of the school grounds. Then apparently the wall turned south until it connected with the present wall near the southeast corner of the Old City. The remains of this wall fit the description given by Josephus of the "third wall," which was built by Herod Agrippa I.[15]

The Second Wall, built by Herod the Great about the time he built the Temple, has proven far more difficult to locate. Some authorities have supposed it was located in the present north wall of Jerusalem. And ruins of a gate structure built of Herodian stones have been found at the foot of the tower of Damascus gate. These stones are apparently situated just as they were originally laid, which would seem to identify this gate and wall with Herod the Great. If this is correct, it would have been the north wall enclosing the city when Christ was crucified, which would mean that the present site of the Church of the Holy Sepulchre would be incorrect, because the crucifixion took place "outside" the city. However, there are other indications that the present north wall may have been built by Hadrian some 100 years after Jesus' crucifixion.

Archaeological findings up to the present leave sufficient uncertainty to justify Albright in suggesting the impossibility of "proving" either the Church of the Holy Sepulchre or Gordon's Calvary and the Garden Tomb as the sites of Christ's crucifixion and burial.

THE SILOAM INSCRIPTION

During the summer of 1880 a number of boys were wading in the Pool of Siloam at Jerusalem. One of the boys waded about nineteen feet into the conduit, or rock-cut channel leading to the pool, slipped and fell into the water. As he scrambled to his feet he saw some peculiar marks cut in the east rock wall just above the water level. He told the other boys that he had seen something that looked like writing, and together they informed their teacher, Conrad Shick. He and Sayce visited the spot, and Sayce sat for hours in mud and water deciphering and copying portions of the inscription by candlelight.

The inscription, which lay partly in water, was made entirely accessible by cleaning the bottom and lowering the water level in the conduit. Then, Shick and Carl E. Guthe applied acids to the lettering and removed the lime deposits that had accumulated through more than twenty-five centuries of intermittent overflowing of spring water. They made several squeeze copies of the inscription, and Guthe succeeded in preparing a plaster cast.

With an eye to business, an unscrupulous person secretly cut the inscription out of the wall of the tunnel—breaking it in the process—and took it to his home in Jerusalem where apparently he hoped to make models of it, and sell them. However, the Turkish government succeeded in recovering the inscription and placed it in the Imperial Ottoman Museum in Constantinople.

The Siloam inscription consists of six lines written in ancient Hebrew—practically the same characters and alphabet as those of the Moabite Stone. The inscription reads as follows:

Now this is the story of the boring through; while the excavators were still lifting up their picks, each toward his fellow, and while there were yet three cubits to excavate, there was heard the voice of one calling to another, for there was a crevice in the rock, on the right hand. And on the day they completed the boring through, the stone-cutters struck pick against pick, one against the other; and the waters flowed from the spring to the pool, a distance of 1000 cubits. And a hundred cubits was the height of the rock above the heads of the stone-cutters.[16]

This inscription stands alone, with no name or date attached. Yet it needs none, as all authorities agree. It was written about 702 B.C. when Hezekiah, king of Judah, "made a pool, and a conduit, and brought water into the city" (II Kings 20:20). In greater detail the chronicler tells us how Sennacherib entered Judah and encamped against its "fenced cities," and how Hezekiah, on seeing his purpose to "fight against Jerusalem," called together "his princes and his mighty men" and said "Why should the King of Assyria come and find much water?" (II Chronicles 32:4). Together they repaired the old wall, constructed an outer wall, stopped the upper watercourse of Gihon (an intermittent spring well now known as "The Virgin's Fountain") in the valley of the Kedron, cut a conduit under Mt. Ophel, and brought water "straight down" into the

Pool of Siloam, which had been built within the western section of the city.

The diggers began at both ends and worked toward each other, a distance of 1777 feet. With only minor miscalculations, they dug the tunnel an average height of six feet through solid rock and came together, "pick to pick"—a notable engineering feat that corroborates and supplements the Biblical narrative. The inscription gives unmistakable evidence of a Hebrew alphabetical script in which Isaiah and other prophets wrote much of the world's most eloquent literature.

An English archaeological expedition under Montague Parker came to Palestine in 1909 and carried on researches in Jerusalem for two years. They began their work with the Siloam tunnel, which had been silted up until it appeared to have an average depth of about three feet. Parker's group cleared it of all its silt, and with Pere Vincent's aid made careful surveys, showing its real depth to be from five to six feet. They also explored more fully the caves about Gihon and the entire system of tunnels related to the spring, so that the uses of the system in directing the water into the city and as passageways were better understood.

After tunneling in various directions on Mt. Ophel, Parker's group endeavored to dig an underground passage to the Temple area. Finding this too difficult, they bribed the chief guard at the Temple, the chief sheikh, and other officials, and began to excavate at the Temple site under the Dome of the Rock, where the three Hebrew temples had once stood. After eight o'clock each evening the keys of the sacred building were in Parker's hands, and he and his men worked until near daylight, then returned the keys to the keeper and took their departure to sleep away the daylight hours and return in the evening. All night long, night after night, they probed the caverns and underground passageways seeking the Ark of the Covenant and the treasures that had been concealed by the temple priests of the Jews when the Babylonians captured Jerusalem. What they found possibly no one will ever know because they soon grew careless, leaving a pile of damp earth and debris in the Temple area after the break of day. A disgruntled workman spread the news and within a matter of minutes the Moslems of Jerusalem gathered by the thousands, threatening a general massacre of Christians. Parker and his men fled to their private yacht at Jaffa and escaped, and the bribed officials were arrested and imprisoned.[17]

INSCRIPTION OF THEODOTUS

While searching in the Kedron valley in the spring of 1914, Weill discovered some architectural fragments in an old cistern. Among these was an inscription dating before A.D. 70. It records the building of a synagogue by Theodotus, whose ancestors for three generations had been rulers of the same synagogue. It reads:

Theodotus, son of Vettenos, priest and ruler of the synagogue, son of a ruler of the synagogue, grandson of a ruler of the synagogue, built the synagogue for the reading of the law and for the teaching of the commandments; furthermore, the hospice and the chambers, and the water installation for lodging of needy strangers. The foundation stone thereof had been laid by his fathers, and the elders, and Simonides.[18]

Some have supposed this to be the "synagogue of the freedmen" mentioned in Acts 6:9, but there seems to be little or no proof of such an assumption. However, this does seem to be the earliest synagogue known in Palestine by its inscription.

"NO STRANGER IS TO ENTER"

In 1871 Clermont-Ganneau recovered an inscription that had been built into the wall of an enclosure at Jerusalem. The inscribed limestone block was twenty-three inches high, thirty-four inches long and fifteen inches thick. The inscription was from Herod's temple and was written in Greek letters over one and a half inches high; it read:

No stranger is to enter within the balustrade around the Temple and enclosure. Whoever is caught will be responsible to himself for his death, which will follow.[19]

Josephus tells us that beyond the Court of the Gentiles was an inner court, set apart by a low stone wall, beyond which none but Jews might pass. His description follows:

Proceeding . . . toward the second court of the Temple, one found it surrounded by a stone balustrade three cubits high, and of exquisite workmanship; in this at regular intervals stood slabs giving warning, some in Greek, others in Latin characters, of the law of purification, to wit, that no foreigner was permitted to enter the holy place, for so the second enclosure of the Temple was called.[20]

The inscription verifies Josephus' account and makes it easier to understand the passage in Acts 21:28,29 in which Paul, after his "purification," was accused of having taken Trophimus beyond this barrier, thus formally violating the Temple regulation.[21]

GRAVESTONE OF KING UZZIAH

In 1931 Sukenik was rummaging through the old collections of the Russian Archaeological Museum on the Mount of Olives when he discovered a beautifully carved slab of stone fourteen inches wide that bore a first century Jewish inscription. There, carved in the Aramaic used during the time of Christ, were the words: "Hither Were Brought the Bones of Uzziah King of Judah Do Not Open."

Immediately there was considerable discussion among scholars as to the date of the slab, for it was common knowledge that Uzziah reigned from about 786 to 735 B.C. After doing "that which was right in the sight of the Lord" and waging successful campaigns that brought national prosperity, Uzziah became proud with power and popularity. His reign ended in a conflict with the priests when he tried to usurp a priestly function and burn incense in the temple of Jehovah. When Azariah, accompanied by eighty other priests, rebuked him, Uzziah became angry and resisted them. Immediately he was smitten by God with leprosy and fled from the temple to suffer for fourteen years from the loathsome disease in a pest house (II Chronicles 26:1-21). During this time his son Jotham was co-regent with him. He died in 735 B.C. and was buried "In the field of the burial which belonged to the kings."

However, the inscription on the slab dates from six to seven hundred years after his death; this, and the text of the inscription itself led to the conclusion that for some unknown reason the grave of Uzziah was cleared and the remaining bones were gathered up and given a new burial place and gravestone. The reburial could have been made necessary by the construction work of Agrippa II in Jerusalem.

The slab confirms the Biblical account of King Uzziah, shows the reverence held for the graves of great men centuries after they had passed away, and is the longest Aramaic inscription we have from the time of Christ.[22]

ABSALOM'S PILLAR

Across the Kedron valley, east of the temple area, are three splendid monuments known as "Absalom's Pillar," the "Tomb of St. James," and the "Pyramid of Zacharias."

Absalom's pillar is a peculiarly attractive monument. Its base as far up as the cornice is a mass of solid rock twenty feet square and twenty-one feet high, carved from the living rock and completely detached from the cliff that surrounds it on three sides. Above the cornice is a circular structure, bound about by rope molding and crowned by an incurving funnel-shaped spiral peak of finely worked stone. The entire monument is forty-seven feet high.

Excavation has uncovered the entrance to the rising steps by which the interior of the memorial is reached. Within is an eight-foot square room with shelf graves on two sides.

Its Ionic pillars, Doric frieze and its general architectural style would class it as Hellenistic or Graeco-Roman, but these may be later embellishments. It is barely possible that the original structure was the pillar that "Absalom in his lifetime had taken and reared up for himself . . . in the King's dale" (II Samuel 18:18). Orthodox Jews who pass this way are known to have cast stones at it in memory of Absalom's rebellion against David.

THE POOL OF BETHESDA

The Pool of Bethesda has been identified with several different places, but excavators have now located it under the site of an early Christian church 100 feet west of the Church of St. Anne. The church was supported by five arches in commemoration of the five porches.

The pool, which is thirty feet deep, fifty-five feet long and twelve and a half feet wide, is reached by descending a flight of twenty-four steps through the vaults under the church floor.

The walls were formerly adorned with frescoes; one still traceable is a picture of an angel troubling the waters, evidence that it is the pool which by early Christian tradition was regarded as the scene of the miracle recorded in John 5:2-9.[23]

JERICHO

The mound that represents the Old Testament site of Jericho is now known as Tell es-Sultan. It stands in the Jordan valley, a mile and a half northwest of modern Jericho, beside the spring known as Elisha's fountain (II Kings 2:19-22). Because the mound is located at the crossroad of two very important highways and dominates the pass through eastern Judea up to Jerusalem, it has long been a strategic center second to few places in Palestine.

Warren probed the mound during the winter of 1868, but failed to find enough to interest him in continuing. Ernst Sellin and Carl Watzinger conducted scientific excavations at Jericho during 1907-09 and discovered enough to arouse widespread interest. While director of antiquities of Palestine from 1920 to 1926, Garstang became interested in the mound. Then in 1929, while a professor at the University of Liverpool, he returned at the head of a British expedition that excavated at Jericho in seven campaigns every winter or spring until 1936.

The results of Garstang's excavations have proven of the highest value, not only to the student of the Bible but also to the historian. "The story of its exvacation," writes McCown, "has been as full of dramatic surprises as the familiar Biblical account of its capture by Joshua." [24]

The excavations revealed a mound of about eight acres in extent, on which a series of successive towns had been built. The more ancient of these settlements seemed to date back to the late Stone Age because of the presence of stone implements, such as arrowheads, sickle blades, scrapers, borers, gravers, blades, and other domestic tools. Later cities, the earliest of which dates from about 3000 B.C., were more clearly outlined and were, in fact, more like real cities. There were five in number, and they have been assigned alphabetical names as follows: "City A," existed between 3000 B.C. and 2600 B.C., and showed Babylonian influence; "City B," founded about 2500 B.C., existed in the days of Abraham, and fell sometime after 1800

B.C.; "City C," founded between 1750 and 1700 B.C., suffered a violent destruction sometime between 1600 to 1550 B.C.; and "City D," the Old Testament city of Jericho destroyed by Joshua about 1400 B.C.

In "City C" the excavators found the richest culture of all. Among other things discovered was an imposing royal palace with grain storerooms, and a scarab signet with the name of "Nub, King of the North," whom the excavators took to be a Hyksos king who lived here at times, or at least whose authority extended over this area.[26] "City D" proved to be of primary importance to Bible students and historians, as well as to archaeologists, who had often discussed the correct date of Israel's exodus from Egypt and subsequent entry into Palestine. Scholars had differed by two centuries or more in their date for this event.[27] Of all places, it was at Jericho, the Canaanite city whose destruction had been accomplished by the Israelites under Joshua, where the question could be studied more thoroughly. There seemed no doubt this fourth city ("City D") was indeed that very city, and the excavators proceeded with eager caution.

"City D" was fortified by two thirty-foot high walls that ran nearly parallel, circling the summit of the mound. They were made of sun-dried brick, which were uniformly about four inches thick but varied in length from one to two feet. The inner wall varied from eleven to twelve feet in thickness, and was constructed on the foundation of an earlier wall. The outer wall was about six feet thick and stood on the edge of the mound. The space between them varied from twelve to fifteen feet and at frequent intervals was traversed by brick walls buttressing the enclosing walls. On top of the walls were houses, possibly built there to help relieve the congestion of the growing city. The outer wall seems to have been built later, but both walls had been in use for over a century.

Garstang found that this city had ended by violent destruction, accompanied by fire. The outer wall had fallen outward down the slope. The inner wall was found preserved only where it abutted upon the citadel or tower; elsewhere, together with the buildings upon it, it had been pulled outward and lay in "the space between the walls." Traces of intense fire appeared everywhere, including "reddened masses of brick, cracked stones, charred timbers," pockets of charcoal and gray ashes as much as two feet thick. Houses alongside the wall were found burned to the ground, their roofs fallen upon domestic pottery within. The remains of foodstuffs, including an abundance of wheat, barley, lentils, and dates, indicated that the city had been destroyed soon after a harvest. Everything gave the appearance of sudden destruction. Bread was ready for baking—some even in the oven—when destruction came and took the people away.

On the outskirts of the old city mound Garstang discovered a cemetery where he opened hundreds of graves that yielded quantities of pottery vessels, considerable jewelry, and about 170 scarabs. The pottery belonged to the Late Bronze Age (1500 to 1200 B.C.), and the Egyptian scarabs could be dated with accuracy because they mentioned the various pharaohs by name, and represented each of them from Thutmose II (1508-1504 B.C.). One scarab bore the names of Queen Hat-shep-sut and Thutmose III; another, that of Amenhotep II, who was depicted as an archer—which corresponds very well with his tomb records in Egypt. Then the series of dated scarabs all come to an end with the two royal seals of Amenhotep III who reigned 1413 to 1376 B.C. There was nothing else in the tombs to suggest a later date.[28]

On returning to the city mound, Garstang carefully compared the pottery fragments with those discovered in the tombs and found them to be of the same style. After examining approximately 100,000 fragments of pottery, 1500 unbroken vessels, as well as eighty scarabs, the fallen walls and other evidence, Garstang had no hesitancy in dating the fall of the city at about 1400 B.C., and identifying it as the Canaanite city of Jericho, which fell before the incoming Israelites led by Joshua. The burnt and charred remains evident everywhere were to him a confirmation of the Biblical account that the Israelites "burnt the city with fire, and all that was therein" (Joshua 6:24), and the fallen walls were a confirmation of how the Israelites entered "every man straight before him" (Joshua 6:20).

Desiring to exercise the greatest care possible, and in the spirit of a true scientist, Garstang called in three of Palestine's top ranking archaeologists and pottery experts: Pere Vincent,

Clarence S. Fisher, and Alan Rowe. When these authorities had carefully and independently examined the pottery, the charred ruins, and the fallen walls they signed statements with Garstang confirming the date of 1400 B.C., with the possible alternative of any date not later than 1377 B.C.[29]

Garstang states the case for a date about 1400 B.C., "or shortly thereafter," as follows:

(1) Scarabs of Amenhotep III (1412-1375) and pottery attributable to his reign are abundant. (2) No later scarabs, either ordinary or royal (with one exception to be mentioned below), were found. (3) Typical Late Bronze Age II pottery is extremely rare on the site and is apparently confined to a single building described below. Except for a fragment found on the site of this building, Late Mycenean pottery, which began to be imported about 1400 B.C. and was in full tide under Ikhnaton (1375-60) is wanting. (4) Only two tombs (4 and 13) had any deposits which can be dated later. A very careful search in all the region for a mile around the necropolis during one whole season succeeded in discovering only one more tomb and it belonged to the Middle Bronze Age. (5) There is no mention of Jericho in the Amarna tablets. (6) The mention of Israel in the Merenptah stele (1231 B.C.), far from indicating the date of the Exodus, proves that the Hebrews had long been settled in Palestine.[30]

Soon after the discovery Albright wrote: "Dr. Garstang's latest discoveries at Jericho have apparently established the fact that Jericho fell into the hands of the Hebrews about 1400 B.C. The writer's most recent stratigraphical and typological studies of the pottery of Ai (et-Tell) point to the same general period for its abandonment." [31]

Some few years later, McCown wrote: "There can be no doubt that it was the fourth city which the invading Israelites captured and devoted to destruction." [32] Frederick Kenyon wrote:

It will not be denied that, if the conclusions of the excavator are to be accepted (and Professor Garstang's statement of the evidence and his deductions from it have been confirmed by other experts), there is here a very remarkable correspondence with the Old Testament narrative.

One important consequence for Old Testament chronology will be noticed. If a date about 1400 B.C. is accepted for the fall of Jericho it carries with it the earlier of the two dates suggested for the Exodus.

The Israelites would have left Egypt about 1440, not in the reign of Merenptah, the successor of Rameses II. The Tell el-Amarna letters will then reflect the state of Palestine and Syria at the time of the invasion of Joshua, and the Habiru mentioned in them can hardly be other than the Hebrews. Further, the Ras Shamra tablets belong to the same period, and tell us much of the religious beliefs and practices of the inhabitants of Canaan among whom the Hebrews came.[33]

All this reckoning checked well with the chronology as given in the Bible, which says:

And it came to pass in the four hundred and eightieth year after the children of Israel were come out of the land of Egypt, in the fourth year of Solomon's reign over Israel . . . that he began to build the house of the Lord. (I Kings 6:1)

Solomon's reign, according to the general reckoning in the scholarly world, came about 970 to 930 B.C. The fourth year of his reign would come, if this general reckoning be nearly correct, at the approximate date of 966 B.C. When 480 years are added, it would give 1446 B.C. as the date for the Israelite departure from Egypt. Then allowing forty years for their wandering in the wilderness, we would arrive at the date of 1406 B.C., which would be sufficiently close to qualify for Garstang's date of "around 1400 B.C."

These finds and the interpretation given them were not satisfactory to some, however, for they could find no place in the scheme of things as they saw them for Joshua taking Jericho in 1400 B.C. For almost two decades thereafter there was constant opposition to Garstang's conclusions. Pressure was brought to bear to have Jericho re-examined.

This desire was gratified in the beginning of 1952 when a joint expedition of the British School of Archaeology and the American School of Oriental Research in Jerusalem began to re-excavate Jericho under the direction of Kathleen Kenyon. The work was diligently pursued for a number of campaigns, and the excavators dug deeper and "found a great deal more evidence for the earliest occupation of the site, including a stone city-wall erected before the invention of pottery, the earliest city fortification known." [34]

The evidence was "far too scanty," however, to ascertain anything regarding the Late Bronze occupation. The ruins and debris had been excavated so many times and in so many ways, and so much had been taken by former excavators and by natives, and so much destroyed by weathering, that virtually nothing discernible remained on the summit of the mound "from the period between 1500 to 1200 B.C." [35]

From year to year Old Testament Jericho has been in the process of becoming more and more difficult to understand. It now seems quite possible that further study of its Late Bronze ruins will best be made, not from the mound but from the records and remains of Garstang's finds, which are preserved in the Archaeological Museum at Jerusalem.

NEW TESTAMENT JERICHO

On January 10, 1950, the American Schools of Oriental Research and Pittsburgh-Xenia Theological Seminary, under the direction of James L. Kelso, began excavational work at the site of New Testament Jericho, which lies on the north and south banks of Wadi Kelt, almost a mile south of Old Testament Jericho. On January 26 the United Nations became a third partner in the expedition by guaranteeing the wages of up to 150 Arab refugee laborers a day.

In the campaigns that followed, Kelso and his associates uncovered the scanty remains of a great unified building complex they identified as the winter capital of Herod the Great and of his son and successor Herod Archelaus. There were the ruins of the civic center, together with its citadel, palace, courts, hippodrome, swimming pool, fountains, gardens, villas and other splendid buildings, much of which had been constructed of typically Herodian masonry with the smooth marginal draft on all four sides. The villas thinned out toward the east, and a little beyond them is modern Jericho, which Kelso thought might be on the site of the poorer sections of New Testament Jericho.

Here lay Graeco-Roman Jericho that Antony gave as a present to Cleopatra, which Herod the Great rebuilt and embellished, but which, as Josephus says and as certain charred remains indicate, was burnt by Simon immediately after the king's death, and then sumptuously rebuilt by Herod Archelaus.

The ruins of the place reminded the excavators of a miniature Rome or Pompeii, built by master builders imported from Rome.[36]

It was this city that Jesus "was come nigh unto" when "a certain blind man sat by the way side begging" and on hearing that it was Jesus of Nazareth that passed by, he put up the persistent plea, "Jesus, thou son of David, have mercy on me." Jesus gave him back his sight, and he "followed him, glorifying God" (Luke 18:35-43). It was here, in this city, that He met Zacchaeus, the wealthy tax-collector who repented of his wrong-doings and took Jesus to dine with him in one of the rich villas, the remains of which were found by Kelso.

SAMARIA

When Jeroboam I founded the northern kingdom in the tenth century B.C., he reigned at Shechem, but later moved his capital to Tirzah. Here, under the brief reigns of Elah and Zimri, national instability reached its height, and the thoroughly sickened people by an overwhelming majority made Omri their king (I Kings 16:16). When the new monarch had reigned here six years, he negotiated a deal with Shemer for a charming and beautiful hill site, which he named Samaria after Shemer. Here on this well-rounded hill, 300 feet above the surrounding valleys, he constructed his royal palace. Ahab, his son and successor, married beautiful, worldly Jezebel, and constructed a finer palace, and "reared up an altar for Baal in the house of Baal, which he had built in Samaria. And Ahab made a grove" (I Kings 16:31-32).

Persistent attempts were made by the Syrians to capture the city, but they were unsuccessful because God thwarted their plans through Elisha. Ahab reached his tragic end while fighting Benhadad in Bashan, and Jehu came to Samaria and had Ahab's seventy sons beheaded. But no new and better ways were found by the people who were so frequently denounced by the prophets. Shalmaneser I laid siege to the city in 725 B.C., and Sargon II took it in 722 B.C. Colonists from Assyria were settled here, but by 331 B.C. Alexander the Great came and took over the city. John Hyrcanus destroyed it in 120 B.C., but Pompey rebuilt the place in part. Then, when it was assigned to Herod the Great, he named it Sebaste in honor of

Augustus and built a royal palace to which he brought Mariamne, his new and beautiful Jewish bride. Here he later had her put to death, then walked the palace halls pleading in vain for her return.

At the beginning of the present century, the site of Samaria was an oblong mound crowning a hill that sloped gently upward to a height of 300 feet. Being unoccupied by any town or village, the exceedingly important historical site lent itself to research in the form of excavation. Only column-lined avenues were indicated above the ruins.

It was in 1908 that Harvard University undertook the excavation of this important site. Jacob Schiff generously donated $60,000 to the enterprise, and the University employed G. D. Lyon, George Reisner, and Clarence S. Fisher. This three-man archaeological team of almost unexcelled experience, carried on its work during 1908-10.

The first expedition began on the western brow of the mound and soon discovered massive walls, as much as ten feet thick, along the south cliff and on the west. In this wall was the western gate with its massive foundations and commodious entrance, which brings to mind the words of the doubting "lord" of Samaria who could not visualize the prophet's words of plenty, "Behold, if the Lord would make windows in heaven, might this thing be?" (II Kings 7:2). Yet it did come, and the official was trampled to death by the pressure of the crowds as they rushed to the gate on their way to get food in the deserted Syrian camps west of the city.

The second expedition from 1931 onward was organized on the initiative of Kirsopp Lake of Harvard and was placed under the directorship of J. W. Crowfoot, director of the British School of Archaeology in Jerusalem. The Hebrew University of Jerusalem and the Palestine Exploration Fund assisted.

The two expeditions unrolled a magnificent panorama that stretched from the time of Omri (875 B.C.) to the Byzantine period and even to the Crusader period—over 2000 years all told.

The excavators located the foundations of Omri's palace and the larger foundations and ruins of the palace of Ahab on the very summit of the hill of Samaria. Just inside the north wall of the palace area they found several thousand fragments of ivory, many of which had been ruined by fire. Some thirty or forty of the ivories were recovered in an excellent state of preservation. On some were portrayed the lotus, lions, sphinxes, and the gods Isis and Horus, indicating the strong influence of Egypt on the Israel of this time.

The collection of ivories included carved pieces of great variety and design both in size and decoration. Some were in the "round," some were plaques in low relief, and others were silhouettes or "pierced work." Some pieces were cut to receive color inlay, other pieces were overlaid with gold, or inlaid with lapis lazuli. These, the excavators thought, were originally mortised into the throne, into beds, couches, tables, cabinets, and perhaps also in the paneling of the walls and ceiling of the palace. All these discoveries gave substance to the account in the first Book of Kings (22:39) which lists the ivory house as one of the great achievements of Ahab—that is, the house he built for himself and his fastidious queen. They also confirmed the preaching of the prophet Amos, who said:

Woe to them that are at ease in Zion, and trust in the mountain of Samaria . . . That lie upon beds of ivory, and stretch themselves upon their couches. . . ." (Amos 6:1,4)

The houses of ivory shall perish, and the great houses shall have an end, saith the Lord." (Amos 3:15)

Of the ivories discovered, the majority are now in the collections of the Museum of Antiquities at Jerusalem, and the balance have been divided between the Palestine Exploration Fund Museum in London and the Fogg Museum of Art at Harvard.

At the north end of Ahab's palace courtyard the excavators located a cemented water pool, which they thought might have been the "pool of Samaria" in which Ahab's blood-stained chariot was washed (I Kings 22:38). In one of the palace storehouses they recovered the famous "Ostraca of Samaria," which consisted of several hundred potsherds inscribed in ink. Sixty-three of them contained fairly legible writing in ancient Hebrew.[37] They are notations concerning payments of taxes in oil and wine sent in by individuals to the storerooms of the royal palace. Ostracon No. 2 tells that in the tenth year of the king, there was sent to Gaddiyo, the royal steward (tax-collector), from the town of Ahaz, two jars to be credited to Abibaal, two to be credited to Ahaz, one to Sheba, and one to Meribaal.[38] Numerous other stewards had good Biblical names such as Nimshi, Ahinoam, and Gomer.

It is significant that these ostraca, dating from the ninth to the seventeenth year of Jeroboam II (782-742 B.C.), contain many names formed with "Baal," showing the great impact Baal worship, introduced by Jezebel, had upon the land of Israel. It may be noted in this relation that the seals and inscriptions of this period from Judah seem never to contain any Baal names.[39]

GEZER

Gezer, known today as Tell Gezer, was one of the oldest and best located cities of Palestine. Lying as it does on the edge of the fertile plain of Sharon, yet adjacent to the Shephelah on the southeast and southwest, Gezer is in the very midst of a land of plenty, its lofty elevation providing a clear view of the surrounding area. Its hillsides, sloping away in every direction, afford fields of pasture land and vast areas admirably suited to the seasonal need for threshing floors.

Gezer played an important role in both Egyptian and Palestinian history. On the occasion of Solomon's marriage to an Egyptian princess, it was given to her by her royal father as a present. It was rebuilt and fortified by Solomon (I Kings 9:16,17).

The excavation of Gezer was undertaken by the Palestine Exploration Fund under the supervision of R. A. S. Macalister, professor of Celtic archaeology in Dublin. Work was begun there in June, 1902. It continued, interrupted by winter weather and an outbreak of cholera, until August, 1905. It was renewed in the spring of 1907 and carried on until early in 1909. During this time hundreds of tombs and caves were thoroughly explored, more than half of the mound was excavated to virgin soil, and some seven or eight cities of various successive periods were found, superimposed one above the other.

Macalister found that the city had been occupied at first by a non-Semitic people, many of whom lived in caves, whose implements were of stone, and whose bones indicated were about five feet six inches tall. Some of these caves were natural, others had been cut out of the soft limestone rock. Some even had carefully carved stairways. One cave appears to have been used as a temple. In it were found a quantity of pig bones, which the excavator took to be sacrificial remains. Some walls in the larger rooms were adorned with pictures, several of them of cattle. One cow seemed to have knobs on her horns to keep her from goring. Another drawing represented a stag being killed with a bow and arrow.

These early men burned their dead, and one of the caves in the eastern end of the hill was used as their crematory. Steps in the rock led down to its entrance. The cave itself was thirty-one feet long, twenty-four feet six inches wide, and varied from two to five feet in height. Near one end, a hole had been cut in the higher portion of the ceiling to act as a flue. Below this, the fires that burned their dead had been kindled; cinders and charred bones of these far-off men were found as grim tokens of their funeral rites.

The occupation level immediately above was of a relatively modern city, the highly-civilized inhabitants of which occupied it to the end of the Hebrew monarchy. Around this city were two remarkably well built walls, about sixteen feet thick with narrow towers at intervals of ninety feet.[40] Scattered on the ground outside the principal gate large numbers of bronze arrowheads were found, evidence of a battle once waged for possession of the city. Inside were well built homes, together with indications that the people worked and traded much as they do today.

Among the many finds in the tombs at Gezer was an earthenware bowl containing some decayed matter in which a few mutton bones were mingled. A bronze knife lay in the bowl for cutting the meat, and a second bowl was inverted over the contents as though the meal was being kept warm until the person for whom it was intended should have need of it.

The excavators found an ancient "high place," with a row of eight rude stone pillars, the tallest of which was ten feet nine inches in height, and the shortest five feet five inches. Some of these were polished smooth by the kisses of the devotees. The discovery of this "high place" with its row of pillars, together with its pottery plaques of Astarte with rude exaggerations of sexual organs, gave vivid realism to Jehovah's strict command, "And ye shall overthrow their altars, and break their pillars, and burn their groves with fire; and ye shall hew down the graven images of their gods, and destroy the names of them out of that place" (Deuteronomy 12:3).

In a later stratum Macalister found a building he thought might have been a temple. One room, or assembly hall, was too wide to be spanned by a single roof beam. But two lengths of timbers had been joined together, their ends supported by a wooden column resting on a flat stone base. To slip the pillar from the footstones would bring the house down. This the excavator pointed out was what Samson did with the building at Gaza when he brought down the house and killed the many Philistine "lords."

Within the very heart of the city there is a great tunnel about 200 feet long, with a vertical depth of 94 feet. Here along this descending stair-cased tunnel, were smoke-stained niches wherein had set olive oil lamps to give light. At the bottom of the tunnel was a living spring that furnished a never-failing supply of water for the people both in time of peace and in time of siege. This tunnel was constructed about 2000 B.C. and abandoned about 1400 B.C.[41]

In the fourth Semitic level Macalister found a small limestone plaque four and a half inches long and two and three-fourths inches wide, which proved to be a school boy's exercise whereon he had made up a calendar giving the order of the chief agricultural operations through the year. It read:

> His two months are olive harvest;
> His two months are grain planting;
> His two months are late planting;
> His month is hoeing up flax;
> His month is barley harvest;
> His month is harvest in festivity;
> His two months are vine-tending;
> His month is summer fruit.[42]

"The use of the pronoun in 'his month' and 'his two months,'" says Wright, "is a Hebrew idiom which refers to the time during which a man works at some specific thing."[43]

It is written in perfect classical Hebrew and is signed by "Abijah," a name common in the tenth century, and therefore should fit well into the period between Solomon's restoration of the city about 950 B.C. (I Kings 9:15,17) and the destruction of the town by Shishak about 918 B.C.

KIRJATH-SEPHER

In April 1924, while riding through southern Judah on a field trip, Albright and a group of students of the American Schools of Oriental Research examined Tell Beit Mirsim, thirteen miles southwest of Hebron. They were impressed with its size, its splendid situation, and with the fact that the revetment of its ancient walls was still exposed in part, and that portions of the main gateway, opening slightly south of east, were still visible. The possibility of this being the site of the long-lost Debir, or Kirjath-sepher of the Bible, struck Albright with considerable force. After examining other mounds in that area and finding no serious competitor, he published his opinion in the preliminary report of the field trip.[44]

M. G. Kyle, president of Pittsburgh-Xenia Theological Seminary, read the report and was so impressed that he offered to undertake a joint excavation sponsored by the Seminary and the American Schools of Oriental Research. Albright accepted and the first campaign was launched in the spring of 1926. The second campaign followed from April to June 1928, the third from June to August 1930, and the last in 1932. Kyle served as president and Albright as director of the excavation. In the various campaigns they were assisted from time to time by twelve younger men, many of whom later distinguished themselves as research scholars and excavators in Bible Lands.[45]

The excavators found two good springs near the mound. These they thought were probably "the upper" and "the nether" springs that Caleb gave his son-in-law Othniel, through the intercession of his daughter Achsah (Judges 1:12-15).

They found successive occupations by Egyptians, Hyksos, Philistines, and Israelites, from the latter part of the Early Bronze Age (3000-2000 B.C.) to the fall of Judah at the hands of Nebuchadnezzar in 586 B.C. In the five occupation levels— the sixth waits to be excavated—they uncovered gates, walls, cisterns, a tower, a huge reservoir, four dye plants, spindle whorls for looms, a broken limestone mould for casting bronze axheads and lance heads, weapons, sickles, several standard weights, three small lion figures, more than a score of Astarte figurines, a serpent goddess, a stone lion, a libation bowl, a stone censer and a stone offering table with three lions in relief around the rim.[46]

Then there were four jar handles bearing the seal impression "To the King of Hebron," two jar handles with the inscription, "Eliakim steward of Jehoiachin," and a steatite scarab seal of Amenhotep III with the inscription "Nib-mu'a-Re, good god, lord of the two lands, who rises in every foreign land." [47]

The name "Kirjath-sepher" literally means the "book-town" and the excavators, together with many whose interest followed the excavations, had sincerely hoped they might find an extensive library, as had been found in certain Assyrian, Babylonian, and Egyptian city-mounds, or perhaps a scriptorium. But no books, tablets, or scrolls were found. In fact only a few inscriptions were located in the "dig," the more important of these being the seal impressions, and those on the signet rings, the longest of which was on that of Amenhotep III. The excavation cannot be said to have proven conclusively that the mound was that of Debir or Kirjath-sepher, nor was it rich in discoveries. Its greater value lay in the fact that it aided in establishing cultural levels for correlation with other Judean towns and furnished experience for a number of very fine men who have since made valuable contributions in the field of archaeological research.

MEGIDDO

Ancient Megiddo, the guardian of the impressive and strategic pass of Megiddo, is an oval, flat-topped mound covering thirteen acres on its summit and thirty-five acres on its slopes, and rises eighty-eight feet above the adjacent Plain of Armageddon. One of the most important city-mounds of the Near East, it long challenged man's investigations but received no archaeological attention until in 1903 when G. Schumacher of the German Oriental Institute cut a cross-section trench sixty-five feet wide and thirty-seven feet deep directly through the mound. Although the methods he employed were poor, Schumacher found flints, bronzes, scarabs, and vast quantities of pottery. After about two years he was forced to give up his work due to lack of funds.

His most remarkable discovery was made at the very beginning of his labors when, apparently excavating in the home of the governor of the town, he unearthed a beautiful jasper seal with the name of the owner inscribed. It read, "Shema, a servant of Jeroboam." The seal belonged to the time of Jeroboam II, who reigned over the kingdom of Israel in the first half of the eighth century B.C.

For twenty years the mound of Megiddo lay temptingly idle. Then in 1925 James Henry Breasted enlisted the interest of John D. Rockefeller, Jr., who, through the Oriental Institute of Chicago, provided almost unlimited funds to organize an expedition to excavate the mound of Megiddo. The expedition was to be the model, the shining example for all other excavations to follow. Because money was no problem the expedition was organized on a twenty-five year plan. Excellent living quarters were provided for the staff, and the best and finest scientific equipment known to the field of archaeology was purchased for their use. Substantial and extensive working quarters were erected, including an excellent library, well-lighted rooms with adequate tables and other equipment for drawing and recording, and long ranges of shelves to store pottery and similar objects. There was a fine studio for photography and reconstruction, and a large, fully equipped darkroom. There was even a captive balloon for use in photography, and a small railway for facilitating the movement of the many thousands of tons of earth and rubble. The mound and the entire area about it were purchased outright, so that the expedition might excavate unhampered, when it pleased, and as long as it pleased.[48]

A splendid staff was employed and charged to conduct the excavations according to every rule that would insure correct historical results. With characteristic thoroughness, C. S. Fisher, Palestine's most efficient field archaeologist, directed the expedition and carried the work forward until the summer of 1927, when the work was taken over by P. L. O. Guy, who carried on until 1934, when Gordon Loud became director.

The plan followed by each of these directors was to uncover and thoroughly study each city level before proceeding to the lower or older occupation level.

Fisher's first responsibility was to locate a place for the tremendous mass of earth deposit to be removed from the mound. He decided to use

the slopes to the east, where there is considerable rock outcrop and not much depth of earth. But as there were tomb entrances already visible, this space had first to be investigated lest valuable materials be hidden beyond hope of recovery. Through all of the subsequent campaigns the gradual clearance of these tombs provided a constant stream of skeletons, pottery, and other objects which tell their stories of the people who have lived on the hill above. They provided also the first great volume of reports.[49]

The soil on the surface of the mound was so thin that annual plowings and the careless removal of stones for building purposes by the natives had seriously disturbed the topmost occupation level. Within a few inches of the surface there appeared a variety of small finds such as English pennies, Hellenistic lamps, and Iron Age pottery.

The first find of any importance came to light when the workmen were removing a dump heap left by the Schumacher expedition. The Egyptian foreman discovered fragments of a stele on which was inscribed in hieroglyphics the name of She-shonk—the Shishak of the Old Testament in whose honor it had been erected (I Kings 14:25,26). This initial discovery provided contemporary evidence that Megiddo had been held for some time after Shishak's raid, and it gave striking realism to the Biblical story of this pharaoh's raid on Palestine. "Imagine my emotions," said Breasted, "as I sat there on that mound and read the name of Shishak on this broken monument, and recalled with vivid recollection when as a boy in Sunday School I had read of this very Shishak of Egypt who had attacked Palestine and carried away booty."[50]

David seems to have made some improvements at Megiddo, for in the lowest portion of the fourth level there was found a fairly well built structure, portions of which had later been incorporated into another building. In the main, however, the fourth occupation level was considered by the excavators to be Solomon's Megiddo, which he maintained primarily for military and governmental purposes.[51]

This fourth level city reflected the wise planning of a brilliant king in that an exceedingly strong stone wall twelve feet thick encircled the city at the edge of the mound, the regularly planned streets were laid out at right angles, and the street drainage and house plumbing were connected with a drainage system set beneath the streets—all in all "the work, not of peasants, but of skilled craftsmen." [52]

On the north side, facing the Plain of Armageddon and the Nazareth hills, there ran an extra wall pierced by a great double gate, through which a chariot road approached by the rampway from the west.

An enemy who forced this gate found himself, not inside the city, but in a paved and walled gate compound enclosure with the great walls and bastions of the real city gate towering above him. This gate was also double and much more massive, with guard rooms on either side before one passed through the second passage into the city. The stone sockets on which the two wings of the gate turned were still in place.[53]

After clearing the gateway, the excavators removed the rubble along the paved street leading southeast until they came upon a most interesting structure, which after investigation proved to be a stable compound measuring 166 by 83 feet, containing five units, each capable of accommodating twenty-four horses. In each unit the animals were arranged in two rows of stalls twelve on each side, facing each other across a main passage wide enough to accommodate chariots. Between each animal and its neighbor was a great stone pillar that served both as a support for the roof and as a hitching post, as holes drilled in the corners of the stone pillars indicate. Between each pair of pillars was a stone trough or manger from which the horses had eaten grain and hay. The stalls were paved with cobblestones to keep the horses' hoofs from slipping. Enough stables were found in this and other nearby units to accommodate 450 to 500 horses. The arrangement was so complete that standing near one of these stables one can almost fancy he hears the horses eating hay and stamping at flies the while.[54]

In connection with these stables the excavators found centrally located drinking troughs, parade grounds, storage silos, and rooms for the grooms. All these discoveries and similar ones at Taanach and other cities gave essence to the accounts in Kings and Chronicles:

And Solomon had four thousand stalls for horses and chariots, and twelve thousand horsemen; whom he bestowed in the chariot cities, and with the king at Jerusalem. (II Chronicles 9:25)

And Solomon had horses brought out of Egypt . . . a chariot came up out of Egypt for six hundred shekels of silver, and an horse for an hundred and fifty . . . And they brought unto Solomon horses out of Egypt, and out of all lands. (I Kings 10:28,29, II Chronicles 9:28)

Inside the city an area was uncovered that had no walls, floors, or other evidence of human habitation, although buildings were all about it. On digging downward the workmen opened up and followed a shaft for seventy feet down to rock bottom. Then at an angle of forty-five degrees the shaft descended another thirty-five feet down a flight of steps, and then as a tunnel it continued on a fairly level course for 165 feet where it led to a perennial spring which gave forth a never-failing supply of fresh water. The shaft and tunnel had been dug by hand "with an amazing degree of accuracy," and by this avenue the women of the city could visit the spring and bring up water when they desired, even in time of war when the city was being beseiged.[55]

In Solomon's time the shaft and tunnel were cleared of debris, and were possibly used through King Josiah's time, but soon thereafter their use seems to have been permanently discontinued.

While excavating on the seventh city level the excavators uncovered the remains of a palace destroyed between 1200 and 1150 B.C. Here, "in what may well have been the treasure room" of this palace building, they discovered nearly 400 pieces of exquisitely carved ivory, mingled with pieces of gold jewelry and alabaster.

This vast and significant assortment of ivories included medallions, plaques, panels, game boards, and game pieces; beads, rings, spoons, and figurines. Some were incised, whereas others were carved in the round or decorated in relief. One of the ivory plaques graphically depicts, in incised designs, the celebration of the victory of a prince or king, presumably the Canaanite king of Megiddo. Another was an ivory pen case belonging to an Egyptian official who must have been an "ambassador at large," for it bore the title, "Royal Envoy to every Foreign Country." [56]

LACHISH

One of the most remarkable of all discoveries made during the last half century was the ancient city of Lachish, which guarded the pass leading up to Hebron and Jerusalem and was exceedingly important in both sacred and secular history.

The Biblical narrative states that the incoming Israelites under Joshua took Lachish on the second day of the siege "and smote it with the edge of the sword" (Joshua 10:32), then passed on without burning the city (Joshua 11:13); and that King Rehoboam, some four and a half centuries later, fortified Lachish, and placed in it a commanding officer, "and store of victuals, and oil and wine . . . and shields and spears," and made it "exceeding strong" (II Chronicles 11:9-12).

During his excavations at Nineveh in 1850 Layard found that of all the forty-six cities conquered by Sennacherib during his famous campaign to Syria and Palestine in 701 B.C., Lachish seems to have been the source of his greatest pride, for upon his return to Nineveh he had his artists and sculptors record the taking of the city on his palace walls in thirteen panels, which when taken together, made up one of the most extensive and elaborate battle panoramas ever executed.

These and other records heightened general interest, yet the true location of the site of ancient Lachish was long a problem to the scholarly world. As early as 1890 Petrie and Bliss excavated at Tell el-Hesy, supposing it to be the site of Lachish; but no evidence as to its identification was found. Eusebius in his *Onomasticon* had declared Lachish to be just seven miles from Beit Jibrin (ancient Eleutheropolis). Albright read this and pointed out that the mound of Tell ed-Duweir was in the seventh mile from Beit Jibrin and that in this and in other respects it qualified admirably well as the true site of ancient Lachish. Tell ed-Duweir was a fine mound, well-located on the high road from Gaza to Hebron and Jerusalem. In ancient times it was on the very route by which the tides of culture, commerce, and military might had approached Judea from the southwest.

In 1931 certain influential men in England decided that it would be well to excavate Tell ed-Duweir to trace the sources of various foreign contacts that had influenced Palestinian culture, and to ascertain if Tell ed-Duweir were the true site of Lachish.

Henry Wellcome, Charles Marston, Robert Mond, and H. D. Colt sponsored the excavation and secured J. L. Starkey to head the expedition. Starkey, who had been working in Egypt, organized a strong staff, procured elaborate equipment, and began excavation in 1932. With untiring efforts and admirable skill, he continued the work until January 10, 1938, when he was tragically murdered by Arab brigands. The excavation was then carried on by Charles H. Inge and G. Lankester Harding who had worked with Starkey for some years. Olga Tufnell also aided with the work, especially in arranging the materials for publication.

Excavations revealed that the history of the city extended back at least to Canaanite times in the twentieth century B.C., and that there were signs of the Hyksos invasion of about 1700 B.C. About this time and in typical Hyksos fashion, a large rectangular enclosure of beaten earth was built on top of the mound to provide further protection for themselves and for their horses and chariots. This enclosure was surrounded by a great fosse, or dry moat, which made the city easier to defend. There is evidence, however, that at a later date the attackers were able to tunnel through the earthen embankments and get inside the city for hand-to-hand conflict.[57]

Outside the city the excavators uncovered three large rock-tombs, which from their contents were judged to be the tombs of important people—perhaps the local governors. The first one had not been robbed, but the burials had been destroyed by fire. There were three separate rooms in this tomb complex, and in these rooms were 192 Egyptian scarabs, including those of Thutmose III, Amenhotep II, Thutmose IV and Amenhotep III.

The latest scarab in this tomb was that of Amenhotep III,

just as it had been in the burials at Jericho. Then there was a definite break, for in the other tombs there were no scarabs until King Ai (1339-1328 B.C.). This break in the succession of Egyptian royal seals immediately following Amenhotep III could well have had considerable significance in connection with the Israelite occupation under Joshua.[58]

Another important discovery that aided somewhat in fixing the date when the Lachish of the Late Bronze Age was destroyed by fire, was an ordinary bowl, broken into twenty-five pieces, on which was inscribed a notation supposed to have been made by an Egyptian tax collector. It was of wheat deliveries from local harvest made in the "year four" of a certain pharaoh. After studying the character of the script, specialists in Egyptian affairs dated the writing "about the time of Pharaoh Merenptah," which if correct, would place the date about 1231 B.C. when Merenptah, on his "Israeli Stele," claims to have "plundered Canaan . . . captured Ashkelon . . . taken Gezer . . . and devastated Israel." [59]

Advocates of the late date for the entry of Israel into Canaan, believe that this destruction might have been wrought by the incoming Israelites under Joshua. This could not well have been the case, however, because the broken bowl was "found in the *burned* debris" of Lachish, and the Biblical record seems to indicate that after taking Lachish Joshua did not burn it but rather used it temporarily as a military base against Horam, king of Gezer (Joshua 10:31-34), and then passed on to Eglon, leaving Lachish standing on its tell, as he did in the case of other cities in this and other areas (Joshua 11:13).

During the second season's work at Lachish there was found, also outside the walls, a water vessel two feet high that has since become famous as "the Tell ed-Duweir ewer." Across the shoulders of this wide-mouth water jug there were figures of a lion, a bird, gazelles, trees, and a line of writing in early Hebrew characters. Subsequently there was also found at Lachish the first five letters of the Hebrew alphabet engraved on the face of a stairway, and also a red bowl, on which there was a Hebrew inscription, written in white paint, which read "His righteousness is my hand [or support]." These three inscriptions, when taken together with other similar early Hebrew writings, constitute an important link with the Sinai script of 1500 B.C. (discovered by Petrie), and the Phoenician alphabet writing of 1350 to 1200 B.C. from which the Greek, the Latin, and our own alphabet descended.[60]

On the surface area inside the city the workmen uncovered a rectangular shaft eighty-four by seventy-four feet that descended vertically for eighty-five feet through the limestone rock. This shaft, which Starkey pronounced as "one of the greatest engineering feats achieved by the ancient craftsmen of Judah," was on a scale that surpassed anything previously discovered in Palestine. There was no stairway down into the chasm, as other water shafts of Palestine often possessed; nevertheless the excavators concluded that the work was connected with the water supply of the city, perhaps originally dug as a water shaft but when no living stream was found being then used for a cistern. The excavators supposed this must have been dug during the Israelite monarchy.[61]

As to the Lachish of 701 B.C., which Sennacherib of Assyria besieged, the excavators found on the summit of the mound remnants of brick walls nineteen and a half feet thick, together with towers and battlements. In the center of the city stood ruins of a large building thought to be the palace-fort of the commanding officer; nearby was a large paved court, "presumably for military assembly and for horses and chariots." [62] Southeast of the governor's mansion, next to the city wall, was another building with five very long rooms, thought to have been storerooms for grain, wine, and oil, collected as taxes and for military purposes.[63]

Not far from the city gate were many graves and a deep pit into which had been thrown the bodies of at least 1500 people. Because the date of this deposit was set at about 700 B.C. and some of the bodies had been burned, it was thought probable that the bodies were those of Sennacherib's soldiers who had lost their lives besieging the city and had been buried in this common grave-pit. A number of skulls from this pit indicated head injuries received in battle. Three of these skulls showed that surgeons had performed on them the operation known as trepanning, in which square holes were sawed in the skull to relieve concussion or to remove "buttons" or bone growths.

Two of the victims had died as a result of the operation, but one had survived, as was evidenced by the growth of new bone about the wound.[64]

The two invasions of Nebuchadnezzar are reflected in the ruins of Lachish. The first came in 598-597 B.C. while Jehoiakim was king of Israel and rebelled against Babylon. The second came just before 586 B.C. when Judah fell under weak and vacillating Zedekiah. In the charred ruins of Lachish there was found a seal impression inscribed "Gedaliah, who is over the house." There is every reason to believe this official to be the same Gedaliah whom Nebuchadnezzar appointed governor over the people, who remained in the land of Judah after the fall of Jerusalem and who was subsequently murdered (II Kings 25:22, Jeremiah 41:1-3). According to Wright:

The seal had been impressed on clay which had been affixed to a papyrus document long since destroyed by the weather. Inasmuch as it was found at Lachish, it probably had been used by Gedaliah before the city fell to Nebuchadnezzar. This would suggest that he was one of the last prime ministers of Judah, since the title "who is over the house" was borne by the chief official of the land next to the King. His father, Ahikam, was a high royal official who had saved the life of Jeremiah after the latter's Temple Sermon in 608 B.C. [Jeremiah 26:13-15]; and his grandfather, Shaphan, was the Scribe or Secretary of Josiah [II Kings 22:3,8-22].[65]

Buried in a burnt layer of charcoal and ashes, in the guard room adjoining the outer gate of the city, were eighteen ostraca or pieces of thin pottery, on which were inscribed messages that came to be known as "The Lachish Letters." They were written with carbon ink by a certain Hoshaiah (Nehemiah 12:32, Jeremiah 42:1,43:2), a subordinate military officer stationed at an outpost near Jerusalem, to Joash the commanding officer at Lachish. These short messages were written during the last years of Jeremiah (c. 588 B.C.) and reflect the troubled period through which the kingdom was passing during Zedekiah's reign just before the fall of Lachish and some two years before the fall of Jerusalem. They were evidently written within a period of a few days or weeks, as is indicated from the similarity of the fragments, five of which fit together as pieces of one vessel.

Letter I contains a list of nine proper names: Gemariah son

of Hissiliah, Jaazaniah son of Tobshillem, Hagab son of Jaazaniah, Mibtahiah son of Jeremiah and Mattaniah son of Neriah.[66] Five of these names are found in the Old Testament. Three appear only in the days of Jeremiah: Gemariah (Jeremiah 29:3, 36:10), Jaazaniah (Jeremiah 35:3), and Neriah (Jeremiah 36:4). Other names include Mattaniah and Jeremiah, which occur in other periods as well as at the time of Jeremiah. The "Jeremiah" in this list does not seem to be the prophet, who was unmarried.[67]

Letter III is the longest and best preserved of all. It reads:

Thy servant Hoshaiah sends to report to my lord Yoash [Joash]: May YHWH [Yahweh or Jehovah] cause my lord to hear tidings of peace. And now thy servant hath sent a letter to Happiqqeah, and in it thy servant referred to the letter which my lord hath sent to thy servant yesterday, for the heart of thy servant hath been ill since thou didst send it to thy servant. And when my lord sayeth, "Thou dost not know it—read my letter"—as YHWH liveth, verily no one hath undertaken to read me a letter from thee at any time, nor have I read any letter which might have come to me from thee, nor have I seen anything of it at all.

And it hath been reported to thy servant, saying "The Commander of the host, Coniah son of Elnathan, hath come down in order to go into Egypt; and unto Hodaviah son of Ahijah and his men hath he sent to obtain . . . from him."

As for the letter of Tobiah, servant of the King, which came to Shallum son of Jaddua through the prophet, saying, "Beware!" thy servant hath sent it to my lord.

This report of certain men going down to Egypt seems to reflect the intrigues of the pro-Egyptian party under Zedekiah. The reference here and elsewhere to "the prophet" has been taken by some to refer to the prophet Jeremiah. In Letter XVI the prophet's name was written out, but unfortunately only the latter part of the name remained legible so that it read ". . . iah the prophet." In this case it would be easy to imagine it might be our prophet, yet we cannot be certain.

In Letter IV Hoshaiah writes:

And let my lord know that we are watching for the signals of Lachish according to all the indications which my lord hath given, for we cannot see Azekah.

Jeremiah mentions "fire" signals (Jeremiah 6:1), and tells how the king of Babylon "fought against Jerusalem, and against all the cities of Judah that were left, against Lachish, and Azekah: for these defenced cities remained of the cities of Judah" (Jeremiah 34:7).

Letter VI refers to the words of the princes as "weakening our hands," all of which makes interesting reading when compared with Jeremiah 38:4:

Therefore the princes said unto the king, We beseech thee, let this man be put to death: for thus he weakeneth the hands of the men of war that remain in this city, and the hands of all the people. . . .

Letter IX is brief, but quite to the point:

May YHWH cause my Lord to hear tidings of peace! . . . let him send . . . fifteen. . . . Return word to thy servant through Shelemiah telling us what we shall do tomorrow.

These letters reflect the tense social and political situation of the times when Jeremiah prophesied and was placed in prison. They also furnish direct evidence concerning the tools and ink employed in writing the Hebrew alphabet script used by Baruch.

And they asked Baruch, saying, Tell us now, How didst thou write all these words at his mouth? Then Baruch answered them, He [Jeremiah] pronounced all these words unto me with his mouth, and I wrote them with ink in the book. (Jeremiah 36:17-18)

Professor Haupert of Moravian College and Theological Seminary says:

The real significance of the Lachish letters can hardly be exaggerated. No archaeological discovery to date has had a more direct bearing upon the Old Testament. The scribes who wrote the letters (for there was more than one) wrote with genuine artistry in classical Hebrew, and we have virtually a new section of Old Testament literature: a supplement to Jeremiah.[68]

In commenting on these letters, Albright says:

In these letters we find ourselves in exactly the age of Jeremiah with social and political conditions agreeing perfectly with the picture drawn in the book that bears his name. The Lachish letters take place worthily between the ostraca of Samaria and the Elephantine Papyri as epigraphic monuments of Biblical history.[69]

BETH-SHAN

Where the Valley of Jezreel opens into the Jordan Plain about fifteen miles south of the Sea of Galilee there is a large mound more than 200 feet high and 900 feet long that is called Tell el-Husn, or the "Mound of the Fortress." In ancient times this was the strategic city of Beth-Shan, which guarded the eastern approaches to the Valley of Jezreel and the Plain of Armageddon. It was usually ruled by either the Egyptians or the Philistines or was held by some other foreign power until King David consolidated and extended the Hebrew kingdom. Nearby, on Mt. Gilboa, was fought the fatal battle between Saul and the Philistines, after which the victorious Philistines came to Beth-Shan where they placed Saul's head in the temple of Dagon, his armor in the temple of Ashtaroth, and his body on the wall of the city (I Samuel 31:10).

Here one of the first major excavations after the First World War was undertaken by the University of Pennsylvania under the direction of C. S. Fisher (1921-23), Rowe (1925-28), and G. M. FitzGerald (1930-33). During eight seasons ten occupation levels were laid bare over a wide area, after which a narrow cut was made down to virgin soil, which was reached at the eighteenth occupation level seventy feet below the present surface of the mound. Thus, the history of the city was found to extend from Arab times (after A.D. 636) back through the Hyksos occupation of about 1800 B.C. to the founding of the city about 3000 B.C.

The first level revealed the scant ruins of a city built by the Arabs shortly after their conquest in 637. Below this were the ruins of a Byzantine city, including a Christian church adorned with beautiful columns and having mosaic floors on which were pictured eighty-two birds of many varieties.[70]

There were five separate strata of Egyptian civilization dating from 1500 to a bit later than 1200 B.C., the cultures of which were usually a combination of Egyptian and Canaanite, indicating that the Egyptians ruled while the Canaanites made up the majority of the population.[71]

The most striking of the finds in this age bracket was a

series of Egyptian-Canaanite temples dating from Thutmose III (1479-1447 B.C.) to Rameses III (1198-1167 B.C.). Among these temple ruins there was a series of rather remarkable steles. Two were of Seti I (1318-1301), the first of which dated in the first year of his reign and narrates in some detail how he sent "the first army of the Ra," named "Plentiful of Valor," to Beth-Shan to repulse a coalition of local people who threatened Egyptian rule. The other stele has on it a reference to repulsing the "Apiru" or "Habiru" (probably the Hebrews) who were seeking more room. Some have identified these with the tribe of Manasseh who "did not drive out the inhabitants of Beth-Shan and her towns" (Judges 1:27).[72]

Numerous scarabs of the Egyptian pharaohs from the Eighteenth to the Twentieth Dynasties and several other inscribed steles were uncovered at Beth-Shan. The monument that caused the greatest excitement, however, was a nine-foot high stele of Rameses II (1301-1234 B.C.) dated in his ninth year. Its inscription consisted of twenty-four lines and was rather worn, so that whereas parts of it could not be read with certainty yet it was considered "a masterpiece of poetic literature." In flowing language it pictured the king as "a lion among the goats," "an eagle among birds," who made his enemies "fly like feathers before the wind." [73] Among his vainglorious boastings, which we know from previous inscriptions to be typical of the man, he made mention of the city of Ramses in Egypt, which the Israelites were said to have built during their Egyptian bondage (Exodus 1:11).

Unfortunately someone advanced the idea that the stele recorded the city of Ramses as having been constructed by Asiatic slaves as laborers. The Press caught up the idea and heralded it far and wide, and many were led to believe that Rameses II was for certain "the pharaoh of the oppression," and that Merenptah, his son and successor, was of necessity "the pharaoh of the Exodus." Then archaeologists and linguists who read the inscriptions were obliged to disillusion the public by advising that while the city of Ramses was mentioned, there was no allusion to the building of the city, nor any reference of any kind to the employment of Hebrews or Asiatics. Rowe, the excavator, said plainly, "The text contains no mention whatever of any such building operations, nor of the Israelites." [74]

A variety of artifacts was found, among which were "nearly fifty Hittite cylinder seals, gold rosettes, variegated Egyptian glass vases, gold pendants, and many beads and amulets; a bronze Syrian dagger, a magnificent bronze Hittite ax, a mass of silver ingots; and a gold armlet three and one half inches in diameter." [75]

But the most artistic object found in the excavation was a large basalt slab on which in low relief were the representations of a fierce combat between a lion and a giant mastiff. In the upper register the lion and huge dog stand on their hind legs, facing each other with open mouths; in the lower panel the dog attacks the lion by fiercely biting deep in his hindquarters, while apparently the lion is roaring and trying to make his getaway. Some supposed the lion to represent the Assyrian god Nergal and the dog to be the guardian of the temple, but all that is known for certain is that it was an ornamental casing for the lower part of a brick wall.

Sometime after 1167 B.C. the Philistines gained the ascendancy and were the lords of the town until David "the giant killer" came to power. On the north side of the mound, at the Philistine level, there was uncovered a temple which from all indications was the temple of Ashtaroth (Astarte) in which Saul's armor was placed. On the extreme south side of the high mound there was a temple, eighty by sixty-two feet, with its axis running east and west. It contained a long central hall with three circular stone bases on either side. This, the excavators concluded, must have been the temple of Dagon where Saul's head was placed.

The period of the Philistines in Beth-Shan was of comparatively short duration. They held it for near a century and a half, after which the place was left desolate. McCown points out that archaeology is compelled to leave the history of Beth-Shan practically a blank for 700 years, from 1000 to 300 B.C., "just as the Bible and other written records do." [76] Albright says, "From the Bible, which states that Beth-Shan was still standing in Philistine hands at the death of Saul, and from the total absence of any remains on the mound which can be dated between the tenth and the fourth centuries B.C., it becomes practically certain that it was captured and destroyed by David, shortly after 1000 B.C." [77]

BETH-ZUR

Four miles north of Hebron lies a conical mound that represents all that is left of the ancient city of Beth-Zur, an important military post of Old Testament times.

During the summer of 1931 the American Schools of Oriental Research and the Presbyterian Theological Seminary of Chicago united in the excavation of Beth-Zur.

As general director of the expedition, O. R. Sellers handled the finances, including the paying of the workmen and the giving of "baksheesh" for objects found; Albright was archaeological director; Glueck sorted the pottery; Aage Schmidt was draftsman; Cyrus H. Gordon was recorder, while Charles Nims and Milton Patterson handled most of the photography and assisted in sorting the pottery. The campaign lasted two months, and, though the excavators laid no claim to completeness they found many objects, traced the history of the city and made lasting contributions to the science of archaeological research.[78]

It was found that Beth-Zur had been occupied during the Middle Bronze Age (2000-1500 B.C.) but came to a tragic end about 1580 B.C. when the Hyksos were expelled from Egypt and Palestine. It was rebuilt in the time of the Judges, but was destroyed by fire about 1000 B.C. Rehoboam fortified Beth-Zur about 930 B.C., but it suffered a serious decline about 600 B.C. A little later it prospered under the Greeks, played a major role in the Maccabean wars—one great fortress was built and destroyed three times during the time of Judas, Jonathan, and Simeon. The place then went into decline as John Hyrcanus extended the Judean border to include Idumea.[79] By Byzantine times the people had migrated to the southeast and carried the name of the city and many building stones with them across the valley to a small hill nearer the highway and across from the place now called "Philip's Fountain."

During the short campaign there were found strong masonry walls, a fortress, a market place, a storeroom for a wine shop, many ovens, a cellar, a water reservoir, and extensive bathrooms, all of the Hellenistic period. There were Egyptian scarabs of Rameses II and Thutmose III, a Hebrew seal impression "Of Ge'alyahu, the son of the King." There were many small objects such as inscribed and uninscribed weights, spindle whorls, buttons, beads, rings, needles, arrowheads, spear points, and 279 coins—one of the finest selections of ancient coins ever to be found in so short a campaign. Yet "there were no hoards, and on only two occasions were two coins found together." Six of these coins are of the Persian period, and tend to indicate that the Jews used the Attic drachma standard during the period of Nehemiah and Ezra, as stated in the Book of Chronicles.[80]

The literary materials concerning Beth-Zur, as found in the Bible, I Maccabees and Josephus, were given striking confirmation by these coins and the abundance of other archaeological evidence uncovered in the excavation.[81]

GIBEAH OF SAUL

Four miles north of Jerusalem on the east side of the highway lies a small but important mound perched on the summit of a rather lofty limestone hill. The Arabs call the place Tell el-Ful (Hill of Beans) but in history it is Gibeah of Saul, or "the hill of Saul."

Here was located Saul's royal palace and citadel, where Israel's first king ruled over part of Palestine, and where came young David to hold high friendship with prince Jonathan and to console the king by drawing from his harp sweet strains of harmony as only David could.

Albright, then director of the American Schools of Oriental Research, devoted two short campaigns to the excavation of Tell el-Ful, one in 1922-23, and one in 1933. He was considerably hampered by the owners of the tell, who at first asked £400 ($1800) rental. They settled for less; but with the hope of getting more money, they frequently interfered by lodging petty complaints and unfounded charges. The district magistrate cleared Albright of all these unreasonable charges, and the work went forward.

The excavations of Gibeah showed that the small fortress village had been founded about 1200 B.C. and had continued with varying fortunes and misfortunes until it was finally destroyed by Titus about A.D. 70 during his march on and destruction of Jerusalem. In A.D. 385 Jerome described the place as "destroyed to its very foundations." [82]

The earliest level occupied in Gibeah dated from the time of the Judges and was found to have been burned, as described in Judges 20:40. The most exciting and most telling object found by the excavators was Saul's strongly constructed, two-story palace fortress. According to the measurements of the corner tower the entire castle must have measured about 115 by 170 feet, or nearly 15,000 square feet for each of the two floors. Its foundations were massive, its outer walls were laid with hammer-dressed stones eight and ten feet thick, and its roof was of cypress and pine timbers. All the palace was not excavated, nor were all the rooms determined, but the rustic simplicity of design and furnishings of the entire structure deeply impressed all who saw them and led to the conclusion that "Saul remained essentially a wealthy peasant, even after his coronation." [83]

In the light of what was found, McCown aptly sums it up in the following:

The best room Saul had for an audience chamber, where David might have played his little harp, barely equaled the modest modern living room, four-teen by twenty-three feet. Some of his pottery was painted with simple horizontal bands, but none of the highly decorated Philistine pottery and no foreign importations were found. Cooking pots of standard size, nine or ten inches across, other ware that had been hand burnished, some of it over a red slip, thin, light saucers, polished juglets, and wellshaped decanters appear. Some of the ware was of fine clean paste, much of it decidedly coarse. There were the usual finds of spinning whorls, grinding querns, and rubbing stones, a game board and a counter to speak of both work and play. Two bronze arrowheads and numerous round slingstones told of the serious business of war. Wine, oil and grain jars showed that the basement rooms were stored with food. Such are the remains found in a Hebrew "royal palace" of three thousand years ago.[84]

SHILOH

Shiloh, now known as Seilun, gained its fame as the place where in the high hill country of Ephraim, Joshua and the Israelites set up the tabernacle and around it built a town for the Ark's protection soon after they entered Canaan. Here the high priests, including Eli, lived and taught and officiated, and here devout Hebrews made pilgrimages for prayer and sacrifice. Here Hannah prayed, and here the youthful Samuel "ministered before the Lord" and became the first of a long line of illustrious prophets. In confirmation of his prophecy, the Philistines defeated Israel about 1050 B.C., captured the Ark of the Covenant, and left the town to sink into insignificance. Finally, fire reduced it to the scene of desolation pictured by Jeremiah almost 500 years later.

But go ye now unto my place which was in Shiloh, where I set my name at the first, and see what I did to it for the wickedness of my people Israel. (Jeremiah 7:12)

In 1922 Aage Schmidt found its ruins lying on an oblong hill with deep valleys on three sides. He sank twenty trial shafts and satisfied himself as to the importance of the site.[85]

In 1926, 1929, and 1931 systematic excavations were carried on by Schmidt and Hans Kjaer under the auspices of a Danish committee. Later, when Kjaer died of an illness brought on by exposure and overwork, Glueck acted as adviser and aided by identifying the pottery.[86]

The excavators found remains dating from the thirteenth to the eleventh century B.C., but none from the period between 1050 and 300 B.C. This parallels the Bible record that Shiloh was destroyed by the Philistines after the battle of Ebenezer and the capture of the Ark (c. 1050 B.C.) just as suggested in I Samuel 4:10-11. On the northern end of the mound the excavators found a rock-hewn quadrangle 80 by 400 feet. Because this was of sufficient size to receive a building of the dimensions of the ancient tabernacle or temple, they felt confident they had located the site of the ancient sanctuary in which Samuel had slept and heard the voice of the Lord calling him.[87]

Later, however, the excavators ascertained that the building remains they had found belonged to the Byzantine period, and therefore concluded that the Christians must have constructed a church building on what had first been the site of the Hebrew sanctuary.

There is general agreement among Palestinian scholars that "all that has been found by the Danes at Shiloh agrees exactly with what is implied in the Old Testament." And, too, there is hope that future campaigns may eventually discover the site and foundation of the tabernacle or temple structure.[88]

MARESHA

About a mile south of Beit Jibrin lies the Moresheth-gath

of the Old Testament, the home of the prophet Micah and the lesser known Eliezer ben Dodavah who prophesied evil things against Jehoshaphat's ships at Tarshish (II Chronicles 20:37). The place is sometimes called Tell Sandahanna, which is simply Tell Santa-Anna, from the nearby ruins of the church of St. Anne.

Rehoboam fortified Maresha as one of the outposts of Jerusalem, and here the armies of Asa defeated the forces of Kushim under Zerah the Ethiopian (II Chronicles 14:12). In 163 B.C. Judas Maccabaeus plundered and burned the city, and in 110 B.C. John Hyrcanus took the place but permitted the inhabitants to remain on the condition that they adopt circumcision and submit to Jewish law; they seem to have done this because the city is referred to later as "a colony of Jews." During the reign of Pompey the city of Maresha was given its freedom, but it came to an end in 40 B.C. when it was destroyed by the Parthians.[89]

In 1898-1900 Bliss and Macalister excavated the six-acre circular mound, and found strong walls, gates and buildings of the Greek or Hellenistic period (333 to 63 B.C.). These were built over the less imposing ruins of the Hebrew town in which the prophet Micah had lived.

In 1902 J. P. Peters was searching in the low limestone cliffs just a few hundred feet northeast of Maresha when he discovered two profusely decorated tomb complexes which soon came to be known as the "Painted Tombs of Marissa." These private yet extensive burial tombs of Sidonian immigrants, who settled in Maresha about the third century B.C., were artistically decorated with birds, animals and architectural designs which are not only attractive as objects of art but throw considerable light on the architecture, religion, and cultural relations of the Phoenicians who lived in Palestine at that time.[90]

On two opposite piers in the vestibule of the main tombroom of the so-called "Tomb of the Musician" are two paintings of very large candelabra which apparently had been used as stands for burning incense. These candelabra, which were originally painted a golden yellow, with flaming red wicks, gradually faded in color when the tombs were opened and their likeness is now preserved only in photographs.[91]

MIZPEH

In the spring of 1926 Badè, with the assistance of some of the staff of the American School of Oriental Research in Jerusalem, began excavation of a large mound eight miles north of Jerusalem known as Tell en-Nasbeh, which the excavators supposed was the ancient city of Mizpeh.

Mizpeh is referred to as the place to which Israel came to make Saul king (I Samuel 10:17) and the city in which Gedaliah had his headquarters until he was slain by Ishmael and other insurgents.   And here, two days later, a large number of unsuspecting pilgrims were treacherously slain and their bodies thrown into a pit or cistern (Jeremiah 41:1-9).

The city walls were of massive proportions for such a small town, averaging some seventeen feet in thickness and in one place reaching the width of twenty-six feet. Towers with sloping stone revetments strengthened the wall at more or less regular intervals.[92]

In the occupation level of the Israelite era the walls of a square building were found which, it is believed, are the walls of the sanctuary in which Samuel ministered to the Lord and where he brought together the people on the memorable occasion when he asked them to put away the strange gods and observe a day of national repentance (I Samuel 7:5-6). On hearing of this great assembly, the Philistines concluded that the Israelites meant to rebel against them, so they made preparations for war. At first the Israelites panicked, but Samuel encouraged them to trust in the Lord. In answer to Samuel's prayers, the Lord thundered with a great thunder and routed the Philistines. Israel pursued them and won a great victory. To commemorate the great deliverance Samuel set up a stone and called it "Eben-ezer," saying, "Hitherto hath the Lord helped us." This battle is the only one with which the name of Samuel is associated in the Bible, but it was so decisive that the Philistines "came no more into the coast of Israel . . . all the days of Samuel" (I Samuel 7:13).

As the excavation progressed, several jar handles with the words "Mizpeh" stamped in old Hebrew came to light. Then came a thrill when Badè and his assistants uncovered an ancient seal on which was engraved the likeness of a fighting cock and the words "Belonging to Jaazaniah, officer of the King."

Badè and his associates hoped to find the gates of the city and searched diligently for them, but they were not found until the fourth season. Interestingly, they were found to face, not toward Jerusalem, but toward Shiloh, which was the place of the tabernacle and therefore the focal point of worship during the earlier days of Samuel and of all Israel. The gate was thirteen feet wide and consisted of two portals, separated on each side by a cell-like guard room.[93]

McCown sums up the importance of this excavation thus:

. . . The excavation of Tell en-Nasbeh has abundantly justified itself in the light it has thrown on the cultural history of the Judean kingdom. The great walls, the remarkable gate, the houses, jewelry, pottery, utensils of all kinds, wine and oil presses, dyeing plants, indeed a whole gamut of life in a provincial city passes before one's eyes in the expedition's discoveries. The tombs cover not only the period of the city's history, but, since in the necropolis burials had repeatedly been made from the neighboring Byzantine ruin called Khirbet esh-Shuweikeh, they carry the story on down into Christian times. . . . Tell en-Nasbeh shows how valuable a contribution archaeology can make to history.[94]

BETHEL

Bethel, which lies about twelve miles north of Jerusalem, has long been a center of great interest to Jews, Christians and Mohammedans. The literal meaning of Beth-el is "The house of God (El)," and being regarded as such, it is mentioned in the Bible more often than any other city except Jerusalem. Here Abraham built an altar, Jacob saw angels ascending and descending on a heavenly ladder, Jeroboam erected his golden calf, and Amos, the straight-shooting shepherd-prophet, conducted a dramatic preaching mission.

In the autumn of 1927, Harold Wiener furnished funds with which Albright employed workmen and sank a shaft through twenty feet of debris on the unoccupied portion of the mound of Bethel. A wall was found standing to the height of twelve feet, and the pottery index indicated the earliest occupation as beginning around 2000 B.C., and the latest as that of the Hellenistic occupation of the fourth century B.C.

A large scale excavation was not carried out at Bethel, however, until the summers of 1934 and 1935 when Albright and Kelso led joint expeditions of the American Schools of Oriental Research and Pittsburgh-Xenia Theological Seminary in a fairly complete uncovering of the unoccupied portion of the mound.

On the lowest occupation level of Bethel the excavators found a well built city of fine quality early masonry, stone pavements, and sewer drains. It had been occupied almost continually from 2000 to about 1300 B.C., when it was destroyed by a great fire that left a bed of ash and charcoal, the like of which has seldom been seen in a ruined city of Palestine. Some regarded this destruction as having been wrought by the incoming Israelites under Joshua. Others veer away from the idea that Joshua burned Bethel because the Scriptural account says "the house of Joseph" took Bethel by strategy and by the sword and apparently settled quietly in the town (Judges 1:22-25). They believe the burning came later in the midst of that unsettled and turbulent period when Israel "forsook the Lord, and served Baal and Ashtaroth," and "the anger of the Lord was so hot against Israel" that He "delivered them into the hands of the spoilers that spoiled them." The terrific fire could well have come as a part of that "spoiling" operation (Judges 2:10-15).

The Bethel rebuilt after the great conflagration was crude in its masonry, possessed poor pottery, had little iron, and made use of almost no decoration—quite in harmony with the languid, lax and careless spirit that characterized the age of the Judges. There was found only the seven wick lamp which spoke of the artistic and the beautiful. All else was inexact and puerile. Of the three phases of this period, the first two were destroyed by fire. The third phase came about the time the Philistines destroyed Shiloh, in harmony with the word of the young prophet Samuel.[95]

Bethel's next occupation coincided with the reigns of David and Solomon. The excavators found the period of transition from the Judges to the united monarchy one of striking contrasts "both in culture and economy." The crude masonry pieces "so characteristic of the period of the Judges were replaced by well squared piers of semi-dressed stone." Iron became plentiful, deep plowing doubled production, and the population increased until Bethel came to be a fairly prosperous city which enjoyed "uninterrupted occupation" through the life of the Northern Kingdom, and showed no signs of destruction until after Jerusalem was destroyed at the hands of the Babylonians in 586 B.C.

It was during the middle of this long period of prosperity that Jeroboam established the royal sanctuary of the golden calf, and the plain but powerful shepherd-prophet Amos came to Bethel thundering against wrongdoing and prophesying that "the God of hosts" that "maketh the morning darkness, and treadeth upon the high places of the earth" should "visit the altars of Bethel" and that the horns of the altar should be "cut off, and fall to the ground" and that Bethel should "come to nought" (Amos 3:13,14, 5:5).

This did happen, early in the sixth century at the hands of the Chaldeans, and happened so accurately that Kelso, in commenting on the prophecies of Amos and the other pre-exilic prophets, wrote, "Their records and the ruins of the city tell the same story." [96]

Although the city was again rebuilt and survived through Maccabean, Roman, and Byzantine times, only remnants of these occupations remain—gateways, walls, streets, pottery and coins. The coins that aroused the greater interest were those of the First Revolt, and one that was minted when Jesus Christ lived at Nazareth as a small boy seven years of age.

AI

In 1934 and 1935 Mme Judith Marquet-Krause and her associates, among whom was Samuel Yeivin, excavated the site believed to represent ancient Ai, the second city to be destroyed by the incoming Israelites under Joshua. The work was interrupted by her untimely death, and although French archaeologists expected to resume the work at an early date, unfortunately it has not been continued.

According to Mme Marquet-Krause's partial interpretation of the finds and that subsequently given by M. Dussaud, Ai was a flourishing town between about 3000 and 2200 B.C. when it was destroyed. It lay in ruins ever afterward, except for brief occupation by the Hebrews about 1000 B.C.

The early city had strong walls, well constructed stone houses, a small shrine, a palace on top of the hill, and a nearby cemetery. The remains of a sacrifice lay before an altar in the shrine, attractive pottery was found among the burials in the tombs, and a variety of interesting artifacts were located at various places in the ruins. Among the latter were numerous Egyptian objects, showing that at this early period there was considerable trade between Egypt and Palestine.[97]

The failure to locate noticeable remains of any occupation between 2200 and 1000 B.C. has been accepted in certain quarters as reflecting unfavorably on the historical narratives of the Conquest. This need not be, however, for the excavation of Ai is as yet incomplete. And when complete, if it shows no occupation at that time, even then no one would be justified in interpreting the discovery, or lack of discovery, as reflecting on the reliability of the Biblical narrative. A book, the narratives of which have been found substantially correct in ninety-nine cases out of a hundred, will in all probability also be found correct in the hundredth case—when all the facts are known.

It is almost impossible to overestimate the effect of more than 3000 years of denudation on such an exposed summit.[98] And especially so because Ai could well have been a kind of fortified outpost, constructed of wood, and manned at the time by the men of Bethel as well as the men of Ai (Joshua 8:17), the burning of which would have left only ashes and charcoal, which could well have blown away. Furthermore, no one knows that Mme Marquet-Krause excavated the site of the Ai of Joshua's time. The writer was twice a guest at this excavation, and knows that there was uncertainty on this point. It is barely possible that the denudation was so complete that excavators could have merely failed to detect the few scant traces that may have remained of Joshua's Ai. Or on the other hand, the Ai that Joshua burned could well have been located at some nearby site, as was the Ezion-Geber of Moses' time, and possibly the Anathoth of Jeremiah's day. The matter of Joshua's Ai "must be left for the present as undetermined, but as deserving" of more careful researches in the future.[99]

DOTHAN

Nine and a half miles north of the city of Samaria lies an ideal tell, the top of which covers ten acres and the sloping sides another fifteen acres. The place is now called Tell Dotha, and it is all that is left of ancient Dothan, the city near which Joseph found his brethren and whence he was sold into slavery. Also, it was the place mentioned in connection with Elisha's disclosure of the secret movements of the Syrian army (II Kings 6:12-13).

Five or more seasons of excavation have been carried out at the site of ancient Dothan by the Wheaton (Illinois) Archaeological Expedition under the direction of Joseph P. Free.

The first season, which began March 28, 1953, was fruitful in that on the second day of digging the excavators came upon a group of six Middle Bronze Age (2000-1500 B.C.) bowls and juglets, which along with much other evidence attested to the occupation of the city in the Patriarchal Period, as implied in the reference to Joseph going "after his brethren" and finding them in or near Dothan (Genesis 37:17).[100]

In the second season the excavators uncovered a great city wall surrounding the city during the Early Bronze Age (3000-2000 B.C.). This wall was eleven feet thick at the bottom, and was found standing up to a height of sixteen feet. How much higher the wall had been the excavators were unable to determine. The greatest day of Dothan was at this period, after which it settled down to a "more ordinary existence through the time of Elisha, and until the Assyrian destruction of North Israel during the eighth century B.C." [101]

HAZOR

Hazor, the great city and fortified camp of the Canaanites, was located four miles west of the southern end of the "Waters of Merom," now known as Lake Huleh. The burning of Hazor by Joshua, as told in the Biblical narrative, marked a decisive phase in Israel's conquest of northern Canaan. The statement is terse and decisive:

And Joshua at that time turned back, and took Hazor, and smote the king thereof with the sword; for Hazor beforetime was the head of all those kingdoms. . . . And all the cities of those kings, and all the kings of them, did Joshua take, and smote them with the edge of the sword. . . . But as for the cities that stood still in their strength [on their tells], Israel burned none of them, save Hazor only; that did Joshua burn. (Joshua 11:10, 12, 13)

The magnificent mound covered some 200 acres, and rose out grandly on a low lying hill above the plain of Huleh. Its position was one of immense strategic importance because it dominated the several branches of the ancient highway leading from Egypt to Syria and on to Babylonia and Assyria.

Garstang carried on preliminary examinations of the mound of Hazor (now called Tell el-Qedah) in 1928 and concluded that Hazor was destroyed about 1400 B.C., but his examinations were much too brief and too superficial to be considered conclusive.

In August 1955 the James A. de Rothschild Expedition, backed by ample capital and directed by Yigael Yadin, began excavations at Hazor, and has carried on work there year by year. At times there have been as many as 200 laborers directed by a staff of forty-five archaeologists, architects, photographers, draftsmen, and students of archaeology. The mound is large, and the work is as yet incomplete; yet Yadin and his splendid associates have carried on excavations in eight different areas and have made some interesting and important discoveries.

The site comprises two distinct areas. The first, the main part of the city, known as "the mound of the acropolis," was perched high on a twenty-five acre plateau to the south. The second area, lying immediately to the north of the acropolis, was a large rectangular plateau comprising some 175 acres. About this on the western side was a "beaten-earth" wall more than 300 feet wide and still standing to a height of nearly fifty feet. Below this was a gigantic moat. The other sides of the rectangle were also protected by a wall and a moat, identifying the whole area as a huge, well-fortified enclosure "large enough to accommodate in emergency thirty thousand men with a corresponding number of horses and chariots." [102] This the excavators later designated as "the camp area," although it was at times used for residences.

On the mound of the acropolis the excavators found ten city levels. There were a number of citadels and temples on top of each other. On the Solomonic level was a splendid gate, identical with the Solomonic gate found in Megiddo. "This fact," writes Yadin, "not only confirms quite clearly the Biblical narrative (I Kings 4:15) that Megiddo and Hazor were both rebuilt by Solomon, but even indicates that both gates were built by the same royal architect." [103]

In the second area the excavators found a well built city with houses and drainage systems. The floors of these houses were "littered with Mycenean pottery, as well as many other vessels and objects of local make, all dating back to the last phase of the Late Bronze Age, i.e., the 13th century B.C." [104]

At the most northern tip of the enclosure there was a Canaanite temple fifty-five by eighty feet. The plan "consisted of three chambers built in succession from south to north: a porch, a main hall and a holy of holies." [105] In the holy of holies the excavators found the most complete set of ritual furniture and implements yet found in Palestine. Among these were an incense altar made of basalt, a large basalt basin, two large earthenware pots for storing oil and wine, three basalt slab offering tables, a basalt bowl with carved decorations, and pottery vessels for offerings. Also, in the holy of holies was "a small basalt statue of a man sitting in a chair and holding a goblet in his right hand," four bronze figurines, a large group of cylinder seals, and an Egyptian scarab seal belonging to Amenhotep III (1413-1376 B.C.).[106]

The excavators found another temple containing a stand for incense vessels, an offering table, and a Canaanite altar that weighed five tons. There was also a burial cave in which they found some 500 pottery vessels, and a large tunnel that was part of a network of underground tunnels.

Yadin does not claim, yet, that he has found proof that the city was destroyed by Joshua, but he aptly remarks:

Holding the Bible in one hand and a spade in the other, seemed to be the most successful method of discovering the relics of that biblical city, and determining the dates. Thus, for example, the fact that Solomon rebuilt Hazor and Megiddo (I Kings 9:15) was not only strikingly confirmed in the year's dig, but also enabled us to outline in advance, on the surface, the plan of Solomon's city gate by simply copying that of the gate discovered in Megiddo some years back by an expedition of Chicago's Oriental Institute. When finally the gate at Hazor was revealed and actually turned out as expected, our laborers thought we were wizards indeed.[107]

. . . Hazor was indeed one of the greatest cities in Canaan, and with its estimated forty thousand population deserved rightly the definition given to it in the book of Joshua: "For Hazor beforetime was the head of all those kingdoms." [108]

GIBEON

Eight miles northwest of Jerusalem lies the high oval-shaped mound of ancient Gibeon, famed not only as the home of the Gibeonites, who tricked Joshua and the incoming Israelites into making a perpetual league, but also as the place of Solomon's meaningful dream. Many times the mound had been examined by specialists, and long had it awaited excavation. Then, in the summer of 1955 James B. Pritchard journeyed to the Holy Land "to stake out a place to excavate for buried ruins" and decided to excavate ancient Gibeon.[109]

After further investigating the mound, he returned to America to confer with his sponsors, the University Museum of the University of Pennsylvania and the Church Divinity School of the Pacific at Berkeley, California, and to locate and employ suitable staff members for the expedition. This accomplished, he and his six assistants returned to Palestine with a zest and an eager anticipation worthy of those who go out to discover new worlds—only the parts they hoped to discover were, as they supposed, quite old.

Pritchard and his staff members established housing quarters in the American School of Oriental Research at Jerusalem. After three weeks of bargaining with the eight landowners involved, a lease contract was signed and the work was begun late in the spring of 1956 after the crops had been harvested. On the third day the excavators found the remains of a massive wall, revealing that a city lay buried only six to eight feet beneath the topsoil of the garden land of the mound.

A short time later a workman discovered a small hole in the ground. Because he could not find the bottom of the hole with his hand, a nail was attached to a piece of string and lowered sixteen feet. The hole was enlarged, and a workman was let down into the cavern. This proved to be the upper end of a 170-foot tunnel extending from the town square down through the limestone rock to a spring at the base of the hill. The passageway was so arranged that in time of enemy attack the occupants of the town could seal off the spring by closing and barring a stone door. This cleverly devised civil defense measure provided not only a spring, but also an easily accessible reservoir for the storage of water. A winding stone staircase led to the storage basins and to the spring.

Another source of water uncovered during this excavation was thought to be the Biblical Pool of Gibeon, at which the strange contest between the men of Abner and the men of Joab took place.

And Abner the son of Ner, and the servants of Ishbosheth the son of Saul, went out from Mahanaim to Gibeon. And Joab the son of Zeruiah, and the servants of David, went out, and met together by the pool of Gibeon: and they sat down, the one on the one side of the pool, and the other on the other side of the pool. And Abner said to Joab, Let the young men now arise, and play before us. And Joab said, Let them arise. Then there arose and went over by number twelve of Benjamin, which pertained to Ishbosheth the son of Saul, and twelve of the servants of David. And they caught every one his fellow by the head, and thrust his sword in his fellow's side; so they fell down together: wherefore that place was called Helkathhazzurim, which is in Gibeon. And there was a very sore battle that day; and Abner was beaten, and the men of Israel, before the servants of David. (II Samuel 2:12-17)

This pool was a great basin surrounded by a thirty-five foot spiral staircase hewn from the solid rock. At a depth of thirty-three feet the large hole ended, but a spiral stairway, approximately five feet wide and protected by a guard rail cut from solid rock, continued downward in a corkscrew tunnel for another forty-nine feet. At the end of this was a large circular room, twenty-three feet across, used for collecting water "from the water-table deep beneath the hill on which ancient Gibeon stood. A total of seventy-nine steps provided the citizens of Gibeon with access to one of the city's major water supplies." [110] Fortunately, this pool had later been used as a dumping ground, from which many interesting objects were taken.

The big moment came on August 2, 1956, when a dark-skinned boy named Suleiman—Arabic for Solomon—handed me a broken handle from a pottery jar with some strange letters scratched into the clay.

"Is this any good?" he asked.

Was it any good! There, spelled in Biblical Hebrew, was the word "Gibeon."

. . . The find was more than luck. We had washed and examined more than 35,000 pottery fragments to find that word. Later we found more than twenty additional broken handles bearing the word "Gibeon." Some, in addition, bore the names of the vintners who filled the pottery wine flasks. We also recovered forty stoppers and a broken pottery funnel, no doubt used to fill the wine jugs. To collect these Hebraic inscriptions, we scrubbed more than a hundred thousand potsherds, out of which we saved only sixty as convincing evidence that the thriving city of Gibeon was a source of wine for export.

The inscribed handles were a complete surprise. In sixty-seven years of digging on a hundred sites in the Holy Land, only two inscribed handles had been found. Needless to say, there was much excitement in camp and in Jerusalem, where most of the archaeologists gathered at night. The high point of excitement for me came one night when I flashed the electric light on a small handle I had found that day. On it I saw letters spelling the name "Hananiah." Suddenly, I thought, *This must be from the Book of Jeremiah.* I opened the Bible and began reading. In Jeremiah 28:1, I reread the passage about the false prophet Hananiah, who was from Gibeon. I had completely forgotten it. I did not sleep at all that night.[111]

Pritchard's excavations have partially uncovered five cities, dating from about 2800 to 100 B.C., built on five occupation levels, and have shed light on the activities of the ancient Gibeonites who won their right to live by a subtle deception of Joshua and the men of Israel. Gibeon is one of the largest and most promising sites in Palestine, and further work there will be awaited with keen anticipation of many other interesting things to be brought to light—perhaps "the great high place" at which Solomon sacrificed.

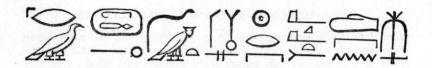

CHAPTER XX

The Dead Sea Scrolls

IN THE SPRING of 1947 a fifteen-year-old Bedouin shepherd and his friend were idly grazing their flocks on the limited herbage about Wadi Qumran, on the edge of the Judean wilderness just southwest of the north end of the Dead Sea, when an unwitting goat strayed off up the hillside, climbed a steep cliff and disappeared.[1]

The shepherd climbed the cliff in search of the goat and in the process came upon a cave entrance, into which he could only peer as he stood on tiptoe. In the dim light he could see, far in the cavern's interior, a number of large earthen jars on the cave floor. On throwing a stone he heard clanking sounds, and fled for fear of "jinn" spirits. The following day, the boys boldly climbed into the cave and began a search for the treasure they felt surely was hidden within the jars. However, they were disappointed to find that the jars contained only decaying rolls of leather inscribed with curious writing and wrapped in squares of coarse linen. There were at least eleven scrolls or portions, which when united later became seven fairly complete scrolls, together with many fragments—just how many will probably never be known. Only six of these were separate compositions. There were two versions of one of the compositions, making in all seven manuscripts or scrolls. Of these details, the Arabs knew little or nothing, yet they surmised that they had found "antikas" for which they might obtain money.

The shepherds carried the scrolls with them as they moved from place to place, and in time took them to an Arab sheikh in Bethlehem. He in turn introduced them to Khalil Eskander, a Syrian antiquities merchant, to whom they offered to sell the largest of the scrolls for the sum of twenty pounds.

The dealer turned them down, but thinking the manuscripts

328

were written in ancient Syriac, he passed the information on to his friend, George Isaiah, who contacted Metropolitan Athanasius Samuel of the St. Mark's Syrian Orthodox Monastery in Old Jerusalem.[2] The metropolitan was impressed with Isaiah's intimation that the scrolls were "wrapped up like mummies" and invited Isaiah and the Bedouins to bring the scrolls to the monastery. When the scrolls were brought the metropolitan broke off a bit and burned it, determining by the odor that it was leather or parchment. He supposed the language to be Hebrew, and therefore opened negotiations for purchasing the entire find. In July 1947, after more than two months of bargaining and many mishaps, five scrolls, the portion of one of the shepherds, were purchased by Metropolitan Samuel for the monastery.

Meanwhile, the other Bedouin had become discouraged, and he sought out another Bethlehem antiquities dealer, who contacted a fellow dealer in Jerusalem. Late in November 1947 the latter telephoned E. L. Sukenik, then professor of archaeology at the Hebrew University on Mount Scopus. Because of the hostilities preceding the Arab-Jewish war, contacts between Old and New Jerusalem were not only difficult but dangerous. Nevertheless, Sukenik and his friend arranged a secret meeting for November 25th in Old Jerusalem. There the Arab dealer told him of the discovery in the cave by the Dead Sea, and handed him a fragment of a scroll. Sukenik afterward said he could scarcely believe what his knowledge and senses told him was true—that he held in his hand a portion of two columns of a very old scroll written, not in Syriac, but in ancient Hebrew.

Sukenik's enthusiasm mounted, and four days later in the face of extreme danger he and the Jerusalem antiquities dealer made the perilous trip to Bethlehem, there to bargain for a sheaf of documents consisting of two complete scrolls, a scroll in three pieces, and a handful of fragments. Returning to Jerusalem with his prize, Sukenik learned the news that the United Nations had that day voted for the partitioning of Palestine.[3]

Many attempts were made by Metropolitan Samuel to find competent men to read and analyze his scrolls, but after learning for certain that they were written in Hebrew and not Syriac, he sought the aid of Stephan Hanna Stephan, a Syrian Arabist, and of Maurice Brown, a Jewish medical doctor, who in turn contacted Judah L. Magne, president of the Hebrew University. The metropolitan also talked with Pere A. S. Marmadji of the Ecole Biblique, who brought his guest, Pere J. P. M. van der Ploeg, an eminent biblical scholar from Holland. These men, each competent within his own field, failed to confirm the metropolitan's conviction that the scrolls were genuinely antique. At last, on February 18, 1948, he had the monk, Butros Sowmi, call the American School of Oriental Research, where in the absence of Millar Burrows he was invited by John C. Trever, acting director *pro tem,* to bring the scrolls there.

On February 19 the scrolls were taken to the American School in Jerusalem where Trever examined them. From one of the scrolls he copied out a portion of the Book of Isaiah, written in Hebrew characters—strange and apparently very old. On looking through a box of slides on "What Lies Back of our English Bible," Trever found samples of early Hebrew scripts, the oldest of which was a small fragment of a first century manuscript known as the Nash Papyrus, which contained the Shema (Deuteronomy 6:4-5) and the Ten Commandments. The Syrians then left, taking the scrolls with them.

The following morning Trever went to the monastery alone and finally persuaded the Syrians to return the scrolls for photographing the next day. While waiting for the scrolls to be returned, Trever and his colleague, William Brownlee, worked late into the night, looking up everything to be found in the library that might throw light on ancient Hebrew script. By midnight they felt quite certain that the script in the scrolls they were examining was as old as the oldest samples they had found, if not older. "Sleep," writes Trever, "came with great difficulty. The added evidence kept racing through my mind. It all seemed incredible. How could we be right?" [4]

On the return of the scrolls, Trever, with Brownlee's help, worked late in the afternoon copying and photographing, and fitting together detached pieces of two of the scrolls. The Syrian churchmen left two other scrolls at the school, after which they returned to the monastery.

Feeling reasonably certain of the value and antiquity of the find, Trever sought the opinion of Albright, then at Johns Hopkins University, to whom he sent prints of the photographs.

After examining the script, Albright responded by air mail with the following message:

My heartiest congratulations on the greatest manuscript discovery of modern times! There is no doubt in my mind that the script is more archaic than that of the Nash Papyrus—I should prefer a date around 100 b.c.— What an absolutely incredible find! And there can happily not be the slightest doubt in the world about the genuineness of the manuscript.[5]

The American School in Jerusalem was given permission to publish the texts of the scrolls belonging to the Syrians, and within a year after the first contact with the metropolitan interested scholars the world over had become fairly well informed concerning the general nature and contents of the manuscripts. Soon thereafter the Hebrew University, which because of the political situation had been prevented from previously doing so, published its first volume on the manuscripts. Thus the world became aware of the existence of other scrolls besides those in the possession of St. Mark's Monastery.

Most scholars, after acquaintance with them, generally accepted the authenticity of the scrolls, but it was felt that excavation of the cave in which they had been found was vital to their correct analysis and dating.[6] In August 1947 Metropolitan Samuel had sent Father Joseph (Yusef) to examine the site. He found broken portions of many jars and one jar in good condition, and many manuscript fragments with scraps of cloth in which the scrolls had been wrapped. He left, however, without removing anything from the cave.

In March 1948, the American Schools of Oriental Research made arrangements to visit and inspect the site, but were prevented by state of war. Later (November 1948) unauthorized and incompetent individuals dug in the cave, disturbing its contents and very possibly destroying forever vital evidence which would have aided greatly in the study of the manuscripts.

By February 1949 conditions had become sufficiently stabilized to permit the carrying out of orderly investigation. Captain Akkash el Zebn of the Arab Legion located the cave high up in the great limestone cliff, and G. Lankester Harding, director of antiquities of Jordan, and Pere Roland de Vaux of the Dominican Bible School of Jerusalem carefully excavated its floor area. They found some 800 scroll fragments belonging to about seventy-five different leather scrolls, a few fragments of papyrus scrolls, pieces of linen in which the scrolls had been wrapped, Roman lamps, portions of broken jars and potsherds belonging to about fifty jars and their covers. The pottery finds were at first thought to be of the Hellenistic Age (333-63 B.C.). Several of the leather scroll fragments proved to be parts of the original lot purchased from the Bedouins. Therefore the finds established the origin of the scrolls, and the style of writing confirmed earlier paleographical results, which dated the scrolls in the latter portion of the Hellenistic Age, with some belonging to the early Roman period.[7]

While excavating Cave I Harding and de Vaux had noticed below them a few hundred yards away to the southeast, a curious ruin or tell perched high on a grayish-white marl terrace. The natives called it Khirbet Qumran (the Qumran ruin). The excavators and others surmised that the people who once lived there might have had at least something to do with the scrolls in the caves. Little was done about the matter, however, until in 1951 when Harding and de Vaux returned under the auspices of the Jordan Department of Antiquities, the Archaeological Museum of Palestine, and the Ecole Biblique, and began serious excavational work at Khirbet Qumran.

After five seasons of work during 1951-1956, the excavators uncovered the ruins of an elaborate central building complex, the main floor of which comprised more than 15,000 square feet. It was a community center or monastery with a tower for defense, an extensive culinary department, a great assembly and dining hall, pantry, laundry, storerooms, spacious courts, and elaborate system of cisterns. Nearby were stables for horses, a community pottery, extensive pools for bathing or baptizing, and three cemeteries, one large and two which were smaller. But perhaps that which impressed the excavators most was a scriptorium or writing room forty-three by thirteen feet. In this there was a narrow masonry table sixteen and a half feet long, and two shorter tables, together with a long bench attached to the wall. In the debris of this room were three inkwells, two of terra cotta and the other of bronze. One of the inkwells actually contained the residue of dried ink, which had been made from lampblack and gum. Nearby was a double basin which was probably used for ritual washing before and after working with the sacred manuscripts.[8]

The excavational researches carried on at Khirbet Qumran made possible a reconstruction of the way of life of a monastic or a semi-monastic Jewish community living there from about 150 B.C. to A.D. 68. The scriptorium, pottery plant, style of writing, and way of life not only linked these people with the scrolls found in the nearby cave, but identified them as "the people of the scrolls" who "belonged to the Essene party." [9]

Pliny the Elder had indicated that in this very section of the country, and as far south as Ain Gedi, the Essenes had built themselves a little world of their own—a veritable "city in the wilderness." He, together with Philo and Josephus, writers of the first century A.D., had described the brotherhood of the Essenes as a sect of Jews numbering about 4000, who removed themselves "from the evils and wrongs which surge up in cities," and lived in colonies where they "devoted themselves to agriculture and other peaceful arts, and gave themselves to a contemplation of nature's verities." Their manner was very quiet, and their lives extremely simple and chaste. Although marriage was permitted it was not encouraged on the grounds that a single person could give himself more wholly to the things of the spirit. They prayed each morning with the rising of the sun, worked until the fifth hour, then bathed in cold water, clothed themselves in white garments, and ate a communal meal preceded and followed by grace. Then changing into their working clothes, they labored or plied their arts until the evening, and returned to supper in the same manner." [10] They then devoted themselves to prayer and a study of their national (Jewish) laws.

Candidates for membership had to go through a strenuous training for three years before full admission, after which their special doctrines were taught under vows of secrecy. These vows included a promise to preserve their special books, and not to reveal the names of angels.

Before Harding and de Vaux had completed their excavation at Khirbet Qumran, it was learned that the Bedouins of the Ta'amireh tribe had not only continued their searches in the Judean wilderness south of Qumran, but had brought in a considerable number of ancient manuscripts and fragments which they said they had found in caves. The prices they asked were rather high. On being questioned by de Vaux, the Bedouins openly spoke of hardships through which they had gone. To prove their point they eventually took de Vaux and Harding and their escort to caves in Wadi Murabba'at, twelve miles south of Qumran and three miles west of the Dead Sea. There, 200 feet above the floor of the wadi bed in the north face of a 600-foot deep gorge, they found four caves, two of which were carved deep into the cliff and contained "inscribed material and evidence of ancient occupations." [11]

The excavations that followed (January 21 to March 3, 1952) revealed that these caves carved 150 feet into the cliffside had been used by refugees and guerrilla bands long before David and his men camped in these or similar caverns while fleeing from Saul's hot anger 3000 years ago. Furthermore, in these caves the excavators found considerable written material, among which was a parchment tablet containing a list of names and numbers written in script of the seventh or eighth century B.C., a series of letters and contracts and a few Biblical fragments apparently left there by remnants of the army of Simon bar Cochba, the false Messiah who led the Jewish revolt against Rome in A.D. 132-135, and "a magnificent scroll" of the Minor Prophets copied during the second century A.D. "The preserved portion of the manuscripts extended from the middle of Joel to the beginning of Zechariah, including (in traditional order) Amos, Obadiah, Jonah, Micah, Nahum, Habakkuk, Zephaniah, and Haggai." [12]

Many of the Arabs of the Ta'amireh tribe were employed on the Wadi Murabba'at excavation, but scores of others began to search other caves in the cliffs west of the Dead Sea. When some of their number found "fragmentary remains" of manuscripts in a cave near Cave I—almost under the shadow of Khirbet Qumran—the archaeologists came to the realization that manuscripts might be found in any of the many caves of this area. They, therefore, organized an expedition into teams to explore all the caves of the cliffs and canyons for some five miles north and south of Khirbet Qumran. The whole area of the Judean wilderness above the western shore line of the Dead Sea became vibrant with life as literally hundreds of Arabs and archaeologists went in and out of caves until searches and soundings had been made in some 200 caves. From twenty-five of these the excavators recovered domestic pottery, the composition and form of which showed that it had been manufactured in the community pottery at Qumran. All evidence indicated intense and extensive occupation adjacent to the clefts and within the caves, all of which had "radiated out from the communal buildings at Qumran." In Cave III on March 14, 1952, the so-called "Copper Scrolls" were discovered.[13] Some few other finds resulted from this search, but soon the archaeologists returned to their main cave excavations and left the general search to the Arabs.

While working with the Arabs, the archaeologists had taught them to be careful with all discoveries, especially with manuscripts and fragments, and had set a price of about $2.80 per square centimeter of inscribed surface as the standard price to be paid for all manuscripts or fragments found and brought in to the proper authorities. This was so stimulating that an intense search was inaugurated by the Ta'amireh tribesmen.

These tribesmen directed their search toward locating and investigating caves in the marl terraces along the foothills below the cliffs. Immediately they met with success, and by late summer of 1952 it was discovered that they had teams working in shifts to hasten their exploitation of a cave carved in the terrace below and less than 200 yards from Khirbet Qumran. On hurrying to the spot, the director of antiquities found that the Arabs had excavated a few feet below the floor of the cave and had discovered the massive remains of hundreds of manuscripts—a veritable scroll library. Just how many hundreds of manuscripts and scroll fragments had been taken out may never be known, but on digging in the untouched levels of the cave Harding and de Vaux and their coworkers succeeded in recovering fragments and portions of more than one hundred different manuscripts. Subsequently some 400 manuscripts have been identified as coming from this cave. Among these were fourteen manuscripts of Deuteronomy, twelve of Isaiah, ten of the Psalms, and twelve of the Minor Prophets. Then there were such apocryphal and pseudepigraphical works as Tobit, Jubilees, Psalms of Joshua, pseudo-Jeremianic works, Testaments of Levi and Naphtali, Testaments of the Twelve Patriarchs, Enoch, and an apocryphal Daniel. There were commentaries on the Psalms, Hosea, Isaiah, and Nahum; and there was a document on astronomical observations, an "Exposition on the Book of Moses," and a calendrical work relating to the Zodiac.[14]

The archaeologists located Cave V north of Cave IV, and under the direction of the Arabs Caves VI, VII, VIII, IX, X, and XI were discovered in the vicinity. Manuscripts had been deposited in all of these caves. In Cave XI there was a magnificent scroll of the Book of the Psalms, a copy of Leviticus in ancient Hebrew script, a fragmentary copy of the "Description of the New Jerusalem," and a lost Targum of Job.

The unemployed Ta'amireh tribesmen organized themselves into teams and went in search of yet more caves and scrolls. They were eminently successful. The new finds, and those scrolls and fragments held out from Cave IV and other illegal digs, came in such large numbers that the department of antiquities, the Palestine Museum, and other institutions soon exhausted their financial resources for the purchase of antiquities. Still the precious scrolls kept coming. Private individuals and organizations came forward with funds with which the director of antiquities continued purchasing but on condition that the scrolls so purchased remained in the Palestine Archaeological Museum for editing, after which they were to be distributed to their respective owners. Among those who purchased lots on this basis were McGill University, Manchester University, Heidelberg University, the Vatican Library, and McCormick Theological Seminary of Chicago.[15] The terms of purchase were later changed, and this source of funds was cut off.

Among the hundreds of scrolls and the tens of thousands of fragments, there are to be found complete manuscripts or fragments of all the books of the Old Testament except the Book of Esther. Added to these are the many scrolls and fragments of scrolls of the Apocrypha, the Pseudepigrapha, and those which had to do with the social and religious well-being of the Essenes.

Among the more important scrolls originally found in Cave I by the young Bedouins, and those found in subsequent searches and excavations, we point up certain ones for the sake of becoming somewhat familiar with the nature of the scrolls and their contents.

The Book of Isaiah was well represented in the Qumran find. There were at least fourteen scrolls of the book in the original find and in Cave IV. The scroll of Isaiah found in Cave I, commonly known as St. Mark's Isaiah Scroll, was twenty-four feet long, ten inches high, and contained the entire Book of Isaiah. Only a few words are lost where the edge of the column had been broken at six points. It was written in an early form of the "square letter," which according to Albright places it in the second century B.C.—before 100 B.C.[16]

The scribe who copied the manuscript did not set his letters upon the lines, but suspended them beneath. He had noted and corrected his errors but had omitted portions, which were supplied by another hand. The text differs considerably in spelling and sentence structure, but agrees in almost every respect with the standard version of our Bible derived from the Masoretic or traditional Hebrew text. "There is nothing that can be called a major addition or omission," says Burrows, "nor is there any important dislocation or disarrangement of the text." Most differences "would not be evident in a translation." Chapter 40 follows immediately after Chapter 39 without the slightest break, showing that it was regarded as one composition.[17]

The Manual of Discipline, sometimes called the Rule of the Community, included two leather copies and one of papyrus. Trever and Cross dated the first two "in the first quarter of the first century B.C.," and they suggest the papyrus copy as being "earlier still." However, each of the copies of the manual seem to have been made, not at the founding of the Qumran community, but at a later time "when its practices had been systematically worked out." [18] The copy of the manual purchased by St. Mark's Monastery was written upon five sheets of coarse cream-colored leather, which were sewn together, and formed a scroll six feet in length and nine and a half inches in height. There were eleven columns of the text in the scroll, but the first part of the book was missing.

The manual contains detailed regulations relating to the requirements and ceremonies governing admission to membership in the sect, the social obligations and devotional duties of the members, the manner of dealing with differences between brethren, as well as statements defining the authority of the priesthood. The manual makes it plain that the members of the Qumran community considered themselves the true Israel. Therefore to themselves exclusively they applied the choice terms of the Old Testament describing the people of God, such as "the congregation of the Lord" (Numbers 27:17), and "the congregation of the Mighty" (Psalm 82:1). Going further, the Essenes ascribed to themselves the honor of being "the men who had entered into the New Covenant" as mentioned in Jeremiah 31:31-33.

At the very outset the manual states the object and order of the community as being:

To seek God . . . ; to do what is good and upright before him as he commanded through Moses and through all his servants the prophets; to love all that he has chosen and hate all that he has rejected; to be far from all evil and cleave to all good works; to do truth and righteousness and justice in the land; to walk no longer in the stubbornness of a guilty heart and eyes of fornication, doing all evil; to bring all those who have offered themselves to do God's statutes into a covenant of steadfast love; to be united in the counsel of God and to walk before him perfectly with regard to all the things that have been revealed for the appointed times of their testimonies; to love all the sons of light, each according to his lot in the counsel of God, and to hate all the sons of darkness, each according to his guilt in vengeance of God.[19]

Some regard the above as the latter part of the oath of initiation, others suppose it to be merely the description of what is to be given on such an occasion. At any rate there follows the obligations devolving upon those who enter the order:

And all who have offered themselves for his truth shall bring all their knowledge and strength and wealth into the community of God, to purify their knowledge in the truth of God's statutes, and to distribute their strength according to the perfection of his ways and all their property according to his righteous counsel; not to transgress in any one of all the words of God in their periods; not to advance their times or postpone any of their appointed festivals; not to turn aside from his true statutes, going to the right or to the left.

And all who come into the order of the community shall pass over into the covenant before God, to do according to all that he has commanded, and not to turn away from following him because of any dread or terror or trial or fright in the dominion of Belial. And when they pass into the covenant, the priests and the Levites shall bless the God of salvation and all his works of truth; and all those who are passing into the covenant shall say after them, "Amen! Amen!"

The ritual of initiation continues as the priests recount the blessings which follow obedience to the laws, and the Levites recount the iniquities of the wayward. Then the initiates who are entering the covenant make confession after them, saying:

We have committed iniquity, we have transgressed, we have sinned, we have done evil, we and our fathers before us, in walking contrary to the statutes of truth; but righteous is God, and true is his judgment on us and on our fathers; and the mercy of his steadfast love he has bestowed upon us from everlasting to everlasting.[20]

The priests then invoke a blessing on all who have entered the covenant and cast their lot with God:

May he bless you with all good and keep you from all evil; may he enlighten your heart with insight into the things of life, and grace you with knowledge of things eternal; may he lift up his loving countenance toward you to grant you peace everlasting.[21]

Once each year the entire community is to be reviewed in due order, one after another, in respect to the state of their spiritual welfare—first, the priests, then the Levites, and then the laity "one after another, in their thousands, hundreds, fifties and tens." The object of this covenant renewal ceremony was that every man in Israel might be made aware of his status in the community of God in the sense of "the ideal, eternal society." Any who did not undergo or pass the test were to be excluded from the community.[22]

The manual describes at some length the Two Ways, of good and evil, of light and darkness, which God sets before every man. It also gives prominence to the Two Spirits in Man—the Spirit of Truth and the Spirit of Wickedness or Perversity. Cross writes:

The Spirit of Wickedness, is none other than Belial, the "Prince of Darkness," Satan. The Spirit of Truth is otherwise called the holy spirit (not identical with the Holy Spirit, though often hard to distinguish) the "Prince of Lights," the "Angel of Truth." All men have their "lot" in one of these spirits, and thus are children of light or darkness. These two powers are locked in a titanic warfare, a struggle which mounts to a climax in the last times. The war is waged, not only between the opposing arrays of spirits and their human hosts, but also within the heart of each "son of light." For the people of the scrolls the end of the war is in sight. God is about to destroy forever the rule of the Spirit of Perversion, and bring an end to all darkness and wickedness.[23]

The remaining portion of the manual is taken up with a treatise on the rules governing the conduct of individuals, and the specific punishment for violations of the rules of the community.

Anyone who interrupts his neighbor in a public session is to be punished for ten days.

Anyone who lies down and goes to sleep at a public session is to be punished for thirty days.

Anyone who leaves a public session gratuitously and without reason for as many as three times during one sitting is to be punished for ten days. If he be ordered to stay and he still leave, he is to be punished for thirty days.

. . . . . .

If a man slander his neighbor, he shall be regarded as outside the communal state of purity for one year, and he shall also be punished. But if he slander the entire group, he is to be expelled and never to return.

If a man complain against the whole basis of the community, he is to be expelled irrevocably.

If he complain against his neighbor without legitimate cause, he is to be punished for six months.[24]

The Manual of Discipline closes with a splendid psalm in praise to God, two verses of which run as follows:

With the coming of day and night
I will enter the covenant of God;
and with the outgoing of evening and morning
I will speak his decrees;
and while they exist I will set my limit
so that I may not turn back.

When I begin to put forth my hands and my feet,
I will bless his name;
when I begin to go out or come in,
when I sit down or stand up,
and as I lie on my couch, I will sing aloud to him;
I will bless him with an offering of the utterance of my lips
more than the oblation spread out by men.
Before I raise my hand to satisfy myself
with the delights of what the world produces,
in the dominion of fear and terror,

in the place of distress with desolation,
I will bless him, giving special thanks.
On his might I will meditate,
and on his steadfast love I will lean all the day;
for I know that in his hand is the judgment of every living man,
and all his works are truth.
When distress is let loose I will praise him,
and when I am delivered I will sing praise also.[25]

The Habakkuk Commentary is written on two sheets of brown leather, which were sewn together and made up a scroll about five feet long and less than six inches high. It must have been somewhat longer originally, because the beginning column is missing or lost. It has carefully ruled lines and margins, and contains some of the most beautifully preserved writing of all the manuscripts, although it has suffered damage by worms and lacks a few lines of the text at the bottom of each column.

It consists of a very important Hebrew text of the Book of Habakkuk, of which only the first two chapters are supplied with a commentary. Some have thought it very strange that the comments do not continue for the third and last chapter, but Cross calls attention to the fact that "only rarely" do the Qumran commentators continue through "the whole of a short prophetic book." [26]

In the comments it is made plain that there are two spirits in the world, the "spirit of truth and the spirit of error." Many times and in many ways it is emphasized that all will be well with all who respect, honor and obey the "teacher of righteousness," and that eventually the "wicked priest" shall be destroyed because he "acted wickedly against God's elect." In commenting on Habakkuk 1:13, it says, "into the hand of his elect God will deliver the judgment of all the nations." [27]

The Copper Scrolls found in Cave III were a particularly fascinating find. The two copper rolls, badly corroded and brittle, were inscribed with Hebrew letters. For four years scholars waited anxiously to learn their contents, but the brittle condition of the copper made the task of unrolling the scrolls seem impossible. The riddle was solved by the ingenuity of H. Wright Baker, of the Manchester College of Technology, Manchester, England, who after careful planning fixed the rolls on spindles, filled them with plaster of Paris on the inside, and covered them with baked celluloid cement on the outside. He then used a rotary saw of the type used to split pen points to cut the rolls into strips, working so carefully that none of the manuscripts was lost in the process.

It was found that originally the two rolls formed a single document about eight feet long and ten inches high, and apparently was written after the middle of the first century A.D. —possibly only a short time before the Jewish revolt in A.D. 68.

Its contents proved to be a detailed account of the hiding places of about sixty caches of treasures, amounting in all to more than 200 tons of silver and gold, along with considerable incense. The places where they were said to be hidden are scattered over Palestine in general, but "chiefly in Judea and more particularly in Jerusalem, in the Temple precincts and in the necropolis of the Kedron Valley." These treasures were said to have been hidden in such places as cisterns, pools and tombs, but the directions given were so indefinite, and the amounts mentioned so fabulous that reputable scholars regard the information given in the Copper Scrolls as interesting, but entirely unreliable.[28]

The seventh of the manuscripts from Cave I was nine feet long by twelve inches high, and was in such poor condition that it was left to be studied last. On the basis of a few scraps that had been broken off, Trever had at first believed it to be the Book of Lamech. But after careful examination by Yadin and Nahman Avigad of the Hebrew University, it was identified as an apocryphal work related to the Book of Genesis. It was a collection of stories about Lamech, Enoch, Noah, and Abraham, and was written in much the same style as the book of Jubilees and other apocryphal literature. Avigad and Yadin continued with the deciphering of this scroll, and it has now had preliminary publication under the title, *A Genesis Apocryphon.*[29]

The Thanksgiving Psalms, when found at Qumran, were in the form of three badly mutilated leaves of leather. Originally they had been sewn together, and made up a scroll about six feet in length and thirteen inches in height. This was the hymn book of the community, or at least one of their hymnals. The hymns contained such doctrines as election by grace, repentance, forgiveness, and the new birth. With zest and deep emotion, the faithful must have sung these songs as by faith

they envisioned themselves standing in "the eternal congregation of God," holding "direct converse with Him," and sending
up a melody of praise to the Most High.[30]

The hymns were apparently composed by leaders of the community, and as such represented the most original literary
creations among the Dead Sea manuscripts. Yadin "doubts
that any language other than the original Hebrew can convey
the depth of emotion and the spiritual beauty of these verses." [31]

Fragments of the Damascus Document, sometimes called the
Zadokite Fragments, were found in the caves. These fragments,
together with a more or less complete document from the Cairo
Genizah, are a prolonged discussion of certain unspiritual religious leaders, apparently at Jerusalem, who "built a wall and
daubed it with whitewash," leading Israel astray. This brought
on the people severe divine judgments when they "turned aside
from the paths of righteousness, removed the landmark which
the forefathers had fixed . . . sought smooth things, chose
illusions, looked for breaches, chose the fair neck, justified the
wicked and banded together against the life of the righteous." [32]

In reaction to these abnormalities in religion, a group that
styled itself the "repentant of Israel" went forth from the land
of Judah and founded a colony near Damascus, and referred
to itself as the "remnant" that had "entered the New Covenant."

The group was governed by a "superintendent of the camp"
who was to show the members of the group the same compassion
a father shows his children, and was to instruct the many in
the "works of God and make them understand his wondrous
mighty acts." The members were to give to the superintendent
"the wages of two days for every month at least" to make up a
fund from which the judges might contribute to the support
of orphans, the poor, the needy, the aged, persons captured by
foreign peoples, unprotected girls, unmarriageable virgins, and
general communal officials.[33]

Each individual was to be registered by name, one after another; first, the priests; second, the Levites; third, the laymen;
fourth, the proselytes. It is in this order that they are to be
seated at public sessions, and in this order their opinions are
to be invited on all matters.

There were many rules, regulations, and obligations for those
who took the covenant.

They were not to substitute baptism for repentance of their sins, and in the process of their repentance they were to "confess and make restitution, that he may not bear sin and die." [34]

They were:

    not to rob the poor of God's people;
    not to make widows their prey or murder the fatherless;
    they were to distinguish between clean and unclean and to recognize holy from profane;
    to love each man his neighbor as himself;
    to seek each man the welfare of his fellow;
    to cheat not his own kin;
    to bring no charge against his neighbor except by due process, and not to nurse grudges from day to day;
    to keep away from all unclean things, in accordance with what has been prescribed in each case and with the distinctions which God Himself has drawn for them. [35]

And, with regard to the Sabbath, they were to observe and keep it holy, according to the following rules:

Let not a man do work on the sixth day from the time when the sun's disk is its full width away from the gate . . . On the Sabbath day let not man utter anything foolish or trifling . . . Let him not speak of matters of work and labor to be done on the morrow. Let not a man walk in his field to do the work of his business on the Sabbath. Let him not walk out of his city more than a thousand cubits. Let not a man eat on the Sabbath day anything but what is prepared . . . Let a man not commission a Gentile to contract business for him on the Sabbath day; Let not a man put on garments that are filthy . . . Let not a man go hungry of his own accord on the Sabbath. Let not a man walk after an animal to pasture it outside of his city more than two thousand cubits . . . Let not a man profane the Sabbath for the sake of wealth or gain. [36]

All these, and other stated rules and obligations they were to keep, and were to "walk in these ways . . . until arises the Messiah of Aaron and Israel."

Among the discoveries of Cave I, purchased by Sukenik for the Hebrew University, was the scroll he styled "The War Between the Children of Light and the Children of Darkness," but which most scholars merely call The War Scroll. It contains nineteen columns of writing and is nine and a half feet long and six and a quarter inches high. The scroll is well preserved except for the worn lower edge.

It is a kind of military manual giving directions for the conduct of a holy war between the Children of Light and foes foreseen as attempting to oppress the people of God in the last age, before the establishment of the Messianic kingdom. To the Qumran community this battle was always imminent.[37]

The manuscript yielded most valuable information as to details of organization, battle tactics, colors, signals, and armaments of war to be used by the Children of Light. They believed that victory was assured before the war began. In going into battle the "sons of Light" were to carry banners inscribed "The Truth of God," "The Glory of God," and "The Justice of God." On returning from the victorious war their banners were to read "The Deliverance of God," "The Victory of God," and "The Peace of God." The priests were to pray before and after battle. The scroll is full of "soldierly weapons," and the covenanters are ready to fight the final war of God. The victory in this final war is likened to the victory God gave Israel in the conquest of Palestine, yet Isaiah 40 is used as a type, which leaves us with the feeling that perhaps the battle is more spiritual than material.[38]

One of the strange ironies of history is that the Romans did come and either destroy or disperse the Essenes—leaving only their sacred scrolls behind. We can only hope they triumphed spiritually which, after all, is the greatest triumph. Perhaps it was for this that the Qumran community really aimed.

The discovery of the Dead Sea Scrolls was and is, for several reasons, one of the most significant events of this present eventful century.

The survival of the scrolls was considered impossible. Papyrus and leather scrolls would survive in Egypt, it was supposed, but not in Palestine where the moisture content was higher. Wise was the choice of the Essenes to wrap the precious scrolls in linen, secure them in earthen jars, and bury them in the caves and caverns in the dry and arid regions west of the Dead Sea. These "people of the scrolls" knew well the words of Jeremiah contained in the very books they buried:

Take these evidences of the purchase, both which is sealed, and this evidence which is open; and put them in an earthen vessel that they may continue many days. (Jeremiah 32:14)

That the scrolls were found at all, and especially at the time they were, is singularly significant. Origen, an Alexandrian Greek church father of the third century A.D., said that in his translations he had made use of certain manuscripts which he found together with other Hebrew and Greek books "in a jar near Jericho in the reign of Antoninus, the son of Severus." [39] Modern scholars supposed jars and caves as unsuitable for Biblical manuscripts, and therefore discounted his statement until the recent discovery of the scrolls.

The discovery is significant in that it brings us 1000 years nearer the original source of our Old Testament in its original language. Heretofore our oldest Hebrew manuscript of the Bible dated back only to the ninth century A.D. The Isaiah manuscript found in Cave I dates from the end of the second century before Christ, while other manuscripts of this and other finds are even older. Together, they now rate as the oldest existing manuscripts of the Bible.

The scrolls are significant in that they make an invaluable contribution to textual studies of certain portions of our Bible, and to the knowledge of Hebrew paleography. Previous to their discovery, there were only a few fragments of Hebrew writing that with certainty belonged to the centuries just before or just after the beginning of our Christian era. These consisted very largely of graffiti (short inscriptions scratched on ossuaries), tomb inscriptions, and such short compositions in Hebrew as the Nash Papyrus. Now with the large and ever-increasing fund of manuscripts and fragments, there will be sufficient materials to keep Hebrew scholars busy for decades.

The scrolls and the excavation at the Qumran community throw a bright and steady stream of light on the domestic, social, and religious lives of a relatively small yet most important sect of the Jewish people. These people were so deeply imbued with a spiritual ideal that they lived in anticipation of the Kingdom of God, and verily believed that God would use them "to prepare the way" for the coming of the "Anointed One" who would bring about a new order. The scrolls and the Qumran community show the Jewish spirit of Messianic expectancy at one of its very highest levels.

The scrolls are significant in that they give added understanding of certain persons and events in the New Testament.

One has to engage in only a brief mental stroll among the "people of the scrolls" to come to an awareness of an atmosphere of moral and spiritual worth from which John the Baptist could well have emerged. Yet the atmosphere and the scrolls themselves do but highlight the uniqueness and timelessness of John and his rugged ministry. It is now more than probable that great numbers of the Essenes were converted under the ministry of John the Baptist. And in speaking of Jesus and the first Isaiah scroll found, Parrot says:

Doubtless it was just such a roll that was handed in the synagogue of Nazareth to Jesus, for Him to unroll and read (Luke 4:16-17). We are brought nearer to every gesture of Jesus of Nazareth, for on the back of the parchment can still be seen the marks left by the fingers of the readers. This manuscript, hidden shortly before the Jewish War, some forty years after the death of Jesus, thus furnishes us with what is surely the most striking and intimate illustration of one of the acts of the Son of Man, witnessing also to the accomplishment of the prophecy He had just read to His unbelieving countrymen, written in just such a hand as this parchment has preserved for us to read, some two thousand years later.[40]

The Dead Sea Scrolls now rate as "one of the world's greatest historical treasures." And rightly so, for they, together with hundreds of other archaeological discoveries, throw added light on and bring an increased interest in and authority to the Bible—the greatest, the most reasonable, and the most delightful document in the world.

NOTES

(Complete references will be found in the Bibliography)

CHAPTER I

1. The form and content of this introductory chapter are the outgrowth of more than thirty years of reading, study, and research in great libraries, and of on-the-spot observations and experiences in topographical and archaeological field work in the many countries of the Middle East, which we know as "Bible Lands."

CHAPTER III

1. Robinson and Smith were the first known men of modern times to crawl through the Siloam tunnel, which they did with great difficulty, at times sliding on their stomachs through the water.

CHAPTER IV

1. In the "Boss of Tarkondemos," de Sayce thought he had found a key to the writing of the Hittites such as were the Rosetta Stone and the Behistun Inscription. "This 'Boss' consisted of a round silver plate, in form like half an orange, which must have covered the knob of a staff or dagger. This had been described by Dr. A. D. Mordtmann in the Journal of the German Oriental Society in 1872. The original was then in the possession of Alexander Jovanoff, a numismatist of Constantinople, who had obtained it at Smyrna. The 'boss' bore in its center a figure of the peculiar Hittite form, flanked on both sides by writing in the Hittite characters, while around the whole was an inscription in the cuneiform writing of Assyria. From this Sayce tentatively determined the values of a number of Hittite signs. The results were, however, attended with considerable uncertainty, since the Assyrian characters were capable of being read in more than one way. Using the key thus obtained, Sayce enlarged his list of supposed sign-values and in 1884 and 1885 published as known the values of thirty-two Hittite signs." Quoted from Barton, *Archaeology and the Bible,* p. 87.

CHAPTER V

1. For further suggestions regarding the manner in which Biblical cities were buried see Magoffin's, *The Lure and Lore of Archaeology,* p. 6;

Gordon, *The Living Past*, pp. 64-70; and Chiera, *They Wrote On Clay*, pp. 30-39.

2. Ezekiel 3:15.

CHAPTER VI

1. For further reading on the technique for uncovering a buried city see C. S. Fisher, *The Excavation of Armageddon*, in *Oriental Institute of Chicago*, No. 4, 1929; Breasted, *The Oriental Institute*, 1933, Vol. XII of the University of Chicago Survey, p. 240; Needler, *Palestine, Ancient and Modern*; Reisner, "Methods of Excavation," *Harvard Excavations at Samaria*, Vol. I, 1924; Gordon, *The Living Past*, pp. 60, 61; and *How To Observe In Archaeology*, British Museum, 1929.

CHAPTER VII

1. For Badè's staff as organized for the Tell en-Nasbeh expedition, see *A Manual of Excavation in the Near East*, pp. 51, 52.

2. Magoffin, *The Lure and Lore of Archaeology*, p. 89.

CHAPTER VIII

1. Badè, *A Manual of Excavation in the Near East*, p. 21.

2. *Ibid.*, p. 22.

3. See McCown, *The Ladder of Progress in Palestine*, pp. 9-14; and Guthe, "The Archaeological Detective."

CHAPTER IX

1. Wright says: "The new Carbon 14 method of dating ancient remains has not turned out to be as free from error as had been hoped. While some extremely important results have been obtained . . . , certain runs have produced obviously wrong results, probably for a number of reasons. At the moment, one can depend upon the results without question only when several runs have been made which give virtually identical results and when the date seems correct from other methods of computation." *The Biblical Archaeologist*, (May, 1955), p. 46.

2. See Van Beek, "A Radiocarbon Date For Early South Arabia," *Bulletin* of the American Schools of Oriental Research; and Price, "Dating the Fossils," *Signs of the Times*.

3. Albright, *From the Stone Age to Christianity*, p. 105.

4. See Kelso, "The Significance of Pottery in Dating," *The Biblical Archaeologist*; Maisler, "Archaeology and the State of Israel," *The Biblical Archaeologist*.

5. These principal types of masonry were worked out in Palestine under Albright's directions.

6. Barton, *Archaeology and the Bible*, pp. 208-9.

CHAPTER X

1. Robinson, Edward. *Bible Encyclopedia,* (H. W. Snow and Company, Toledo, Ohio, 1881), p. 829.

2. While excavating in Egypt, Petrie uncovered the ruins of an old seal engraver's workshop. In it were hundreds of scarabs, finished and unfinished. There were hundreds of clay moulds for casting, and lumps of various pigments for coloring the scarabs, as well as other appliances of the trade. The scarab maker's business came somehow to an untimely end about 570 B.C., and the engraver had gone, leaving all his stock of trade behind.

3. Burrows, *What Mean These Stones?* p. 192.

4. *New Standard Bible Dictionary,* 3rd rev. ed., pp. 847-48.

5. See Wright's short but splendid treatise on this subject in his *Biblical Archaeology,* p. 159.

6. Genesis 38:18, Job 38:14, Song of Solomon 8:6.

7. Jeremiah 22:24, Haggai 2:23.

8. Genesis 41:37-44.

9. Daniel 6:16-18.

10. Esther 3:12-13, 8:7-11.

11. I Kings 21:8.

12. Luke 15:22.

13. Matthew 27:63-66.

14. II Timothy 2:19.

15. II Corinthians 1:22; Ephesians 1:13, 4:30; Revelation 7:2-8.

16. James 2:2-4.

17. Miller, *Encyclopedia of Bible Life,* pp. 135-136.

18. Woolley, *Ur of the Chaldees,* pp. 36-41.

19. Albright, *The Biblical Archaeologist,* (Dec. 1942), p. 50, *The Archaeology of Palestine and the Bible,* p. 125; Free, *Archaeology and Bible History,* p. 221.

20. *The International Standard Bible Encyclopedia,* Vol. II, p. 1223.

21. Wright, *Biblical Archaeology,* p. 160.

22. See "Seals of our Nation, States and Territories," *National Geographic,* (July 1946), pp. 1-5.

CHAPTER XI

1. Price, *The Monuments and the Old Testament,* pp. 31-33; Hilprecht, *Explorations in Bible Lands During the Nineteenth Century,* pp. 75, 76. (References throughout this book to *The Monuments and the Old Testament* are to the revised edition of 1925, which has now been replaced by the 1958 edition indicated on the copyright page and in the bibliography.)

2. Price, *op. cit.,* p. 32.

3. Ceram, *Gods, Graves and Scholars,* p. 214.

4. Hilprecht, *op. cit.,* p. 79.

5. *Ibid.,* p. 78; Ceram, op. *cit.,* p. 215; Lloyd, *Foundations in the Dust,* p. 107.

6. Hilprecht, *op. cit.*, pp. 85-86.
7. *Ibid.*, p. 79.
8. Lloyd, *op. cit.*, p. 131.
9. Hilprecht, *op. cit.*, pp. 82, 83.
10. Isaiah 20:1.
11. Barton, *Archaeology and the Bible*, p. 465.
12. Robinson, *The Bearing of Archaeology on the Old Testament*, p. 96.
13. Price, *op. cit.*, p. 58. Sargon built and abandoned so many palaces that to this day there is a tradition in Iraq (Assyria and Babylon) that a new king shall abandon the palace of his predecessors and build himself another. The halls, courts and bedrooms of the old palace remain as they were without any one to occupy them.
14. *Ibid.*, p. 58.
15. Lloyd, *op. cit.*, p. 157. This proved the wisdom of making on-the-spot drawings of all important discoveries. Ever afterward this method has been followed on excavations.
16. During the University of Chicago excavations in 1929 at Khorsabad, Chiera discovered another large winged bull, and had it shipped to the Oriental Institute Museum of the University of Chicago. It weighed 40 tons and was 16 feet long and 16 feet high.
Hilprecht, *op. cit.*, pp. 88-90.
17. Layard, *Nineveh and Its Remains*, Vol. I, p. 2.
18. *Ibid.*, p. 6.
19. Quoted by Lloyd, *op. cit.*, p. 98.
20. Hilprecht, *op. cit.*, p. 93.
21. Lloyd, *op. cit.*, p. 112.
22. Kenyon, *The Bible and Archaeology*, p. 38.
23. See Barton, *Archaeology and The Bible*, p. 463; Pritchard, *The Ancient Near East Texts*, pp. 193, 194.
24. Pritchard, *ibid.*, pp. 191, 192.
25. Zephaniah 2:13, 14.
26. *The Babylonian Story of the Deluge and the Epic of Gilgamish*, pp. 1, 2 (from the British Museum).
27. Layard, *Nineveh and Babylon*, Vol. I, p. 589.
28. Luckenbill, *Ancient Records of Assyria and Babylonia*, Vol. II, p. 178.
29. Rawlinson, *The Seven Great Monarchies of the Ancient World*, p. 462.
30. Barton, *op. cit.*, p. 471.
31. Lloyd, *op. cit.*, p. 140.
32. II Chronicles 32:21, Isaiah 37:36.
33. II Kings 19:36-37.
34. See Luckenbill, *op. cit.*; Kenyon, *op. cit.*, pp. 147, 148; Price, *op. cit.*, pp. 328-330.
35. Assyrian bas-reliefs represent Esarhaddon bringing in captives after this fashion.
36. II Chronicles 33:11-13.
37. Finegan, *Light From the Ancient Past*, p. 181.
38. Lloyd, *op. cit.*, p. 165.

39. *Ibid.,* p. 166.

40. Kenyon, *op. cit.,* pp. 42-45; and *The Babylonian Story of the Deluge and the Epic of Gilgamish,* pp. 30-40.

41. Kenyon, *op. cit.,* p. 127.

42. *Ibid.,* p. 128.

43. Chiera, *They Wrote On Clay,* pp. 176-178.

44. Genesis 15:4.

45. For a most excellent handling of the customs revealed in these tablets see Gordon, *The Living Past,* pp. 156-178.

46. See Speiser, "Closing the Gap at Tepe Gawra," *Asia;* Speiser, "The Historical Significance of Tepe Gawra," Annual Report Smithsonian Institution.

47. Gordon, *op. cit.,* p. 65.

48. See Speiser in *Bulletin* of the American Schools of Oriental Research, No. 43, p. 20.

49. Lloyd, *op. cit.,* p. 169.

50. *Ibid.,* p. 170.

51. Hilprecht, *op. cit.,* pp. 207-208.

52. See George E. Mendenhall, "Mari," *The Biblical Archaeologist,* (Feb. 1948).

53. *Loc. cit.*

54. Parrot, *Discovering Buried Worlds,* pp. 31, 32.

55. *Ibid.,* p. 22.

56. *The Biblical Archaeologist,* (Feb. 1948).

57. Albright, *From the Stone Age to Christianity,* p. 111.

58. Parrot, *op. cit.,* p. 33.

59. *Ibid.,* p. 23.

60. As the goddess of love and war, and as the personification of the productive principle in nature, Ishtar was worshiped in various countries, under various names: Ishtar, Ashtaroth, Astarte, Anit, and Venus. Esteem for her increased until she was known as the "Queen of Heaven," against whom the faithful Hebrew prophets uttered their denunciations. See *The Biblical Archaeologist,* (Feb. 1948), and I Kings 11:33.

61. Albright, *op. cit.,* p. 323.

62. *The Biblical Archaeologist,* (Feb. 1948), p. 16.

63. Albright gave these words in a lecture in Pasadena College in the autumn of 1952.

CHAPTER XII

1. Daniel 4:30.

2. Isaiah 13:19.

3. Jeremiah 51:37.

4. Daniel 5:26-28.

5. Sears, *Pictorial Bible Biography,* p. 483.

6. Barton, *Archaeology and the Bible,* p. 483; Pritchard, *The Ancient Near East Texts,* p. 207.

7. Isaiah 45:1-3.

8. Kenyon, *The Bible and Archaeology*, p. 126.

9. Ceram, *Gods, Graves and Scholars*, pp. 290-292.

10. Smith, "Chaldean Accounts of Genesis" quoted by Caiger, *Bible and Spade*, p. 29.

11. See Hammerton, *Wonders of the Past*, p. 608.

12. Albright, *The Biblical Archaeologist*, (Dec. 1942), pp. 49-55.

13. Isaiah 21:9, Jeremiah 51:42.

14. Hammerton, *op. cit.*, p. 413.

15. Kenyon, *op. cit.*, p. 142; Finegan, *Light from the Ancient Past*, pp. 24-25.

16. Hammerton, *op. cit.*, p. 429.

17. Field Museum Leaflet #28 quoted by Marston, *New Bible Evidence*, p. 54.

18. Kenyon, *op. cit.*, pp. 112-113.

19. Hilprecht, *Explorations in Bible Lands During the Nineteenth Century*, p. 254; Lloyd, *Foundations in the Dust*, pp. 184-185.

20. Baikie, *The Glamour of the Near East Excavations*, pp. 241-242.

21. Kenyon, *op. cit.*, p. 114.

22. Finegan, *op. cit.*, pp. 26-27; Kenyon, *op. cit.*, pp. 116-117.

23. Hilprecht, *op. cit.*, pp. 409-415.

24. Lloyd, *op. cit.*, p. 147.

25. Hilprecht, *op. cit.*, pp. 141-155; Finegan, *op. cit.*, p. 20.

26. Lloyd, *op. cit.*, p. 148.

27. Adams, *Ancient Records and the Bible*, p. 67; Barton, *op. cit.*, p. 62.

28. Kenyon, *op. cit.*, p. 144; Chiera, *They Wrote on Clay*, pp. 154-155.

29. *The International Standard Bible Encyclopedia*, Vol. I, p. 271.

30. Langdon quoted by Marston, *New Bible Evidence*, pp. 261-263.

31. Hilprecht, *op. cit.*, p. 152.

32. Baikie, *op. cit.*, pp. 243-45.

33. This date may be lowered considerably according to the later reckonings. See Albright, *From the Stone Age to Christianity*, pp. 98-99.

34. Baikie, *op. cit.*, 247-249.

35. Price, *The Monuments and the Old Testament*, p. 366; Habershon, *The Bible and the British Museum*, p. 76; Barton, *op. cit.*, p. 480; Caiger, *op. cit.*, p. 177.

36. Finegan, *op. cit.*, p. 190.

37. Baikie, *op. cit.*, p. 244.

38. Woolley, C. Leonard, *Excavations at Ur*, pp. 187-192.

39. Marston, *The Bible Comes Alive*, p. 45.

40. Woolley, *op. cit.*, p. 125.

41. *Ibid.*, pp. 126, 127, 131.

42. For a thorough treatise on the royal cemeteries of Ur see Woolley, *Excavations at Ur*, pp. 52-90.

43. *Ibid.*, pp. 57-59.

44. *Ibid.*, p. 65.

45. *Ibid.*, pp. 65, 66.

46. *Ibid.,* p. 167.

47. *Ibid.,* pp. 67-69.

48. *Ibid.,* pp. 70-72.

49. *Ibid.,* pp. 74-75. In the largest of these stone tombs was found the so-called "Standard of Ur," which was an inlaid panel of mosaic work illustrating war on one side and peace on the other.

50. Woolley, *Ur of the Chaldees,* pp. 20-23.

51. Woolley, *Excavations at Ur,* pp. 33, 34. Flood deposits have been found at various other places in the Mesopotamian valley, and traditions of a great flood—"the Flood"—have been found with almost all the primitive peoples of the earth.

52. See Parrot, *The Flood and Noah's Ark,* p. 51; *Annals of Archaeology and Anthropology,* XX, p. 134.

53. See Parrot's table of flood deposits, *The Flood and Noah's Ark,* p. 52.

54. Burrows, *What Mean These Stones?* p. 70.

55. See Albright, *Bulletin* of the American Schools of Oriental Research (April 1957), p. 35.

56. In the May (1960) *Scientific American,* Professor Rhodes W. Fairbridge, of Columbia University, identifies the Great Flood of Genesis and pagan legend with "the greatest and fastest rise yet discovered in the geological record," which "reached its crest about 6000 years ago" (4000 B.C.). "The flood of the sea was joined by the floodwaters brought down from the highlands by rivers." In commenting on this view to the author, Dr. Albright writes, "Unfortunately he [Fairbridge] connects this period of incursions of the sea and tremendous river floods with the much later flood deposits in the valley of the Tigris and Euphrates. Aside from this, Fairbridge may be correct—though I should then be puzzled by the spread of the Flood Story over most of the world long after the settlement had been completed." For lengthy discussions of the Flood see Bright, "Has Archaeology Found Evidence of the Flood," *The Biblical Archaeologist,* Vol. V, 1942, pp. 55-62; Parrot, *The Flood and Noah's Ark,* pp. 45-53; Albright, *From the Stone Age to Christianity* (1957 edition), p. 9.

57. Compare Ezra 7:1-5 and I Chronicles 6:3-14 where it omits six names, and Matthew 1:8 where the three names of Ahaziah, Joash, and Amaziah are missing when compared with the accounts in Kings. Also see Wright, *Scientific Confirmation of the Old Testament,* pp. 189-197.

CHAPTER XIII

1. II Chronicles 36:22, Ezra 1:1-11.

2. Ezra 2:64-70.

3. See Habershon, *The Bible and the British Museum,* pp. 71, 81.

4. *Collier's Encyclopedia,* Vol. 9, p. 493.

5. Ali-Sami, *Pasargadae,* pp. 46-66; Ghirshman, *Iran,* p. 135.

6. Ghirshman, *Iran,* p. 135.

7. Ali-Sami, *op. cit.*

8. *Collier's Encyclopedia,* Vol. 15, pp. 567-8.

9. Ali-Sami, *op. cit.*, pp. 34, 91, 100.

10. *Ibid.*, p. 104.

11. Huxley, *From An Antique Land*, p. 220.

12. Ali-Sami, *op. cit.*, pp. 71, 72.

13. Albright, *The Biblical Archaeologist*, Vol 9 (Feb. 1946), p. 8.

14. Finegan, *Light From the Ancient Past*, p. 202.

15. Huxley, *op. cit.*, p. 221.

16. *Lands and People*, Vol. 7, p. 231; Ali-Sami, *op. cit.*, p. 15.

17. Finegan, *op. cit.*, pp. 199, 203-204.

18. Price, *The Monuments and the Old Testament*, p. 400.

19. *Ibid.*, pp. 402-3.

20. Daniel 8:2.

21. Esther 8:10; Albright, *op. cit.*, pp. 10-12.

22. Nehemiah 2:1-8.

23. Ghirshman, *op. cit.*, p. 216.

24. Halley's *Bible Handbook*, p. 110.

25. Price, *op. cit.*, p. 403.

26. Urquhart, *The New Bible Guide*, Vol. 6, pp. 354-56.

27. Esther 1:6.

28. Unger, *Archaeology and the Old Testament*, p. 309.

29. *The International Standard Bible Encyclopedia*, Vol. 2, pp. 108-9.

30. Albright, *From the Stone Age to Christianity*, p. 98.

31. *Ibid.*, pp. 98, 259; Carlton, *Buried Empires*, p. 34.

32. Albright, *From the Stone Age to Christianity*, p. 259.

33. Pritchard, *Archaeology and the Old Testament*, p. 211.

34. Barton, *Archaeology and the Bible*, pp. 378-407.

35. Pritchard, *op. cit.*, p. 211.

36. *Ibid.*, p. 211.

37. See Robinson, *The Bearing of Archaeology on the Old Testament*, pp. 87-89; Kenyon, *The Bible and Archaeology*, pp. 122-125.

38. Carlton, *op. cit.*, pp. 247-249.

CHAPTER XIV

1. Albright, *From the Stone Age to Christianity*, pp. 114, 115.

2. The Bible states that Solomon began building the Temple at Jerusalem in the *fourth year* of his reign and the 480th year after the Exodus (I Kings 6:1). Solomon began his reign about 971 or 970 B.C.; therefore the Exodus of the children of Israel must have taken place about 1447 or 1446 B.C. However, some scholars endeavor to have the Israelites leave Egypt at a later date—about 1290 B.C. or even 1220 B.C. Such a late date is hardly in harmony with Biblical chronology. For discussions of the subject see Unger, *Archaeology and the Old Testament*, pp. 140-152; Finegan, *Light From the Ancient Past*, pp. 104-108.

3. Hayes in *Everyday Life In Ancient Times*, p. 167.

4. Dunning, *Today on the Nile*, p. 27; Ceram, *Gods, Graves and Scholars*, p. 143; Hammerton, *Wonders of the Past*, Vol. I, p. 41.

5. Edwards, *The Pyramids of Egypt*, p. 34.

6. Wilson, R., *The Living Pageant of the Nile,* pp. 190-192.

7. There are many versions of this myth.

8. White, *Ancient Egypt,* p. 45.

CHAPTER XV

1. Hilprecht, *Explorations in Bible Lands During the Nineteenth Century,* pp. 634-635; Ceram, *Gods, Graves and Scholars,* pp. 129-132.

2. Wilson, C., *Picturesque Palestine,* p. 416.

3. Manning, *The Land of the Pharaohs,* pp. 76, 77.

4. Hayes in *Everyday Life in Ancient Times,* pp. 83, 99.

5. Ceram, *op. cit.,* p. 133.

6. Albright, *From the Stone Age to Christianity,* p. 115.

7. Moret, *In the Time of the Pharaohs,* p. 176.

8. Murray, *The Splendor That Was Egypt,* p. 254.

9. Petrie, *The Pyramids and Temples of Gizeh,* p. 74.

10. Many writers have held that only the Pharaohs could hope for eternal life, but further researches show that the people also expected an existence beyond the tomb. That hope was anchored in Osiris and the other gods they served, but more particularly in their king, who himself had become a god who ruled together with Osiris.

11. Petrie, *op. cit.,* pp. 80-90; Edwards, *The Pyramids of Egypt,* pp. 85-88.

12. Edwards, *op. cit.,* p. 86.

13. *Ibid.,* p. 80.

14. *Ibid.,* p. 88.

15. *Ibid.,* p. 92.

16. *Ibid.,* p. 94.

17. *Ibid.,* p. 95.

18. Hammerton, *Wonders of the Past,* p. 547.

19. Albright, *op. cit.,* p. 115.

20. Hammerton, *op. cit.,* p. 548.

21. Manning, *op. cit.,* pp. 59-60.

22. *Ibid.,* p. 60.

23. Edwards, *op. cit.,* p. 120.

24. Maspero, *History of Egypt,* pp. 194-195.

25. Edwards, *op. cit.,* pp. 122-128.

26. Leary, *From the Pyramids to Paul,* pp. 27-30.

27. Albright, *op. cit.,* p. 170; Edwards, *op. cit.,* pp. 30-38; Leary, *op. cit.,* pp. 27, 31, 38.

28. Leary, *op. cit.,* p. 34.

29. Murray, *op. cit.,* p. 295; Steindorff & Seele, *When Egypt Ruled the East,* pp. 122-123.

30. Edwards, *op. cit.,* p. 107.

31. *Ibid.,* pp. 106, 107.

32. Hammerton, *op. cit.,* p. 155; Edwards, *op. cit.,* p. 105; Moret, *op. cit.,* p. 171. Subsequent clearing of the sand, which perpetually drifts about the Sphinx, was done by the Ptolemies and the Romans, by Cap-

tain Caviglia in 1818; by Maspero in 1886 and lastly by the department of antiquities of Egypt in 1926. In 1837 Col. Howard Vyse made borings to the depth of more than twenty-seven feet in the back of the Sphinx and found only solid rock. On the southeast side of the Sphinx stands a temple building of polished granite, the Valley Building of the Pyramid complex of King Chephren. It is 140 feet square and 40 feet high. Here all preparations were made and all ceremonies performed previous to the King's burial. From this sacred edifice a long passage leads to a small room built of alabaster, a second passage leads to six long storage magazines, and a third leads to a fine causeway 15 feet wide and over a quarter of a mile long, which connects up with Chephren's Mortuary Temple at the Second Pyramid.

33. Ceram, *op. cit.*, p. 82.

34. Powell, *Against the Tide*, pp. 132-133.

CHAPTER XVI

1. Wilson, R., *The Living Pageant of the Nile*, p. 159.

2. Nahum 3:8.

3. *IX Iliad*, The Speech of Achilles.

4. White, *Ancient Egypt*, p. 80.

5. Hayes in *Everyday Life in Ancient Times*, pp. 164-165.

6. White, *op. cit.*, pp. 78, 79.

7. Wilson, R., *op. cit.*, p. 72.

8. *Ibid.*, p. 75.

9. Dunning, *Today on the Nile*, p. 69.

10. Finegan, *Light From the Ancient Past*, p. 113; Robinson, *The Bearing of Archaeology on the Old Testament*, pp. 64-66.

11. Dunning, *op. cit.*, p. 75.

12. Jarvis, *From Pharaoh to Farruk*, pp. 12, 13.

13. *The Legacy of Egypt*, p. 377.

14. Baikie, *The Life of the Ancient East*, p. 111.

15. Baikie, *The Glamour of the Near East Excavations*, p. 135.

16. Baikie, *A Century of Excavations in the Land of the Pharaohs*, p. 108.

17. Baikie, *The Life of the Ancient East*, pp. 128, 129.

18. *Loc. cit.*

19. Baikie, *The Life of the Ancient East*, pp. 165-167. The Biblical account states that Pharaoh's "horses, his chariots, and his horsemen" were drowned in the Red Sea, but it is not definitely stated that Pharaoh himself was drowned. See Exodus 14:23-27.

20. Wilson, R., *op. cit.*, p. 128.

21. Powers, *Egypt*, p. 245.

22. Murray, *The Splendor That Was Egypt*, p. 58; Powers, *op. cit.*, pp. 263-266.

23. Murray, *op. cit.*, pp. 139, 140.

24. Petrie, *Six Temples at Thebes*, pp. 13, 14; Petrie, *Seventy Years in Archaeology*, pp. 171, 172.

25. This is a free version gleaned from Petrie, Barton, and others.

26. Wilson, J., *The Burden of Egypt*, p. 204.

27. Bell, *The Spell of Egypt*, p. 217.

28. Steindorff & Seele, *When Egypt Ruled the East*, p. 261.

29. Murray, *op. cit.*, p. 176.

30. *The Biblical Archaeologist*, (Sept. 1944) p. 47.

31. Finegan, *op. cit.*, p. 106; Unger, *Archaeology and the Old Testament*, p. 44.

32. Wilson, R., *op. cit.*, p. 66.

33. Jarvis, *op. cit.*, p. 8.

34. Wilson, J., *op. cit.*, p. 67.

35. Jarvis, *loc. cit.*

36. Wilson, J., *op. cit.*, p. 66. Punt is now identified as that part of the African Somaliland lying along the Gulf of Aden at the southern extremity of the Red Sea.

37. Wilson, J., *op. cit.*, p. 69.

38. *Ibid.*, p. 70.

39. Ceram, C. W., *Gods, Graves and Scholars*, pp. 164-167.

40. *Ibid.*, pp. 168-196; Masters, *The Romance of Excavations*, pp. 100-105; Baikie, *The Glamour of the Near East Excavations*, pp. 143, 144.

41. Masters, *op. cit.*, pp. 99, 100; Baikie, *The Life of the Ancient East*, p. 130.

42. Baikie, *The Glamour of the Near East Excavations*, p. 144.

43. Wilson, J., *op. cit.*, p. 203.

44. Powers, *Egypt*, p. 158.

45. Queen Tiy remained in the palace at Thebes, but often visited her royal son at Akhet-Aten (Amarna).

46. Jarvis, *op. cit.*, p. 205; Breasted, *A History of Ancient Egypt*, pp. 365, 366.

47. White, *op. cit.*, pp. 80, 81; Wilson, J., *op. cit.*, p. 217.

48. Steindorff and Seele, *op. cit.*, pp. 214, 215; Wilson, J., *op. cit.*, p. 211.

49. Breasted, *op. cit.*, pp. 55, 56.

50. The clay tablets varied in size from $2 \times 2\frac{1}{2}$ inches to $3\frac{1}{2} \times 9$ inches. The royal writings were beautifully done, others were not so well done, but are legible.

51. Robinson, *op. cit.*, p. 58.

52. *Ibid.*, pp. 58, 59.

53. *Ibid.*, p. 58; Pritchard, *The Ancient Near East Texts*, pp. 262-274; Finegan, *op. cit.*, pp. 98-100.

54. Robinson, *op. cit.*, p. 58.

55. Hall, *Ancient History of the Near East*, p. 409.

56. *Bulletin* of the Metropolitan Museum of Art, New York, 1922-23, p. 6.

57. *Ibid.*, p. 7.

58. Carter, *The Tomb of King Tutankhamen*, Vol. I, p. 138.

59. Ceram, *op. cit.*, p. 184.

60. Carter, *op. cit.*, p. 112.
61. Steindorff and Seele, *op. cit.*, pp. 133-135; Baikie, *The Life of the Ancient East,* p. 157.
62. Ceram, *op. cit.*, pp. 184, 185.
63. Carter, *op. cit.*, p. 114.
64. *Bulletin* of the Metropolitan Museum of Art, New York, 1922-1923, p. 8.
65. Ceram, *op. cit.*, p. 190.
66. *Bulletin* of the Metropolitan Museum of Art, New York, 1922-23, p. 9.
67. Steindorff and Seele, *op. cit.*, p. 235.
68. *Bulletin* of the Metropolitan Museum of Art, New York, 1922-23, p. 9.
69. Ceram, *op. cit.*, p. 192.
70. *Ibid.*, p. 193.
71. Although the viscera of no one was in the sacred Ark of the Covenant, yet on its top lid were two angelic beings with outstretched wings, and within were the two tables of the law.
72. Serious differences arose with the Egyptian government over the manner in which finds should be divided. The case was submitted to an international commission, which eventually arrived at a satisfactory adjustment.
73. Carter, *op. cit.*, pp. 183-188.

CHAPTER XVII

1. Wilson, C., *Picturesque Palestine,* Vol. II, p. 31.
2. Heusser, *The Land of the Prophets,* pp. 32-33.
3. Adams, *Ancient Records and the Bible,* p. 94.
4. Kenyon, *The Bible and Archaeology,* p. 166.
5. Pritchard, *The Ancient Near East Texts,* p. 20; Albright, *From the Stone Age to Christianity,* p. 164.
6. Kenyon, *op. cit.*, p. 167.
7. *The Biblical Archaeologist,* Vol. 8, No. 2, pp. 42-43.
8. *National Geographic,* Vol. LVIII, No. 4.
9. Hammerton, *Wonders of the Past,* Vol. 1, p. 187.
10. *National Geographic,* Vol. LVIII, No. 4, pp. 513-14.
11. Marston, *New Bible Evidence,* p. 189.
12. *Ibid.*, pp. 190-192. The question has often been asked, "How came these parallels in religious usage, ceremonies, and even terminology?" At the present only certain possibilities may be suggested, any of which is hazardous. However, there is a tradition which suggests that during the latter part of the fifteenth century there was a colony of people from the southern portion of the Wadi Arabah (the Rift valley between the Dead Sea and the Gulf of Akaba) who migrated to Phoenicia and settled at or near Ugarit, or Ras Shamra. If Moses received the Law and set up the tabernacle at Mount Sinai about 1446 B.C., as Biblical chronology

seems to indicate, then this group could have received these things through
Jethro, Moses' father-in-law, and transmitted them to the Phoenicians.
Or, it is possible that some from among the Israelites, or the Canaanites,
journeyed northward and conveyed information regarding Israel's taber-
nacle and ceremonies. For such an example see Judges 1:22-26. There
was but slight difference between the language used by Moses and the
Phoenicians, and perhaps less difference between his and that of the
Arabs called "Midianites," of whom Jethro was priest.

13. Leary, *Syria, The Land of Lebanon,* p. 191.
14. Curle, "Baalbek, Splendid In Its Ruins," *Wonders of the Past,*
Vol. I., p. 435.
15. Alouf, *History of Baalbek,* p. 113.
16. Leary, *op. cit.,* p. 195.
17. Alouf, *op. cit.,* p. 117.
18. Leary, *op. cit.,* pp. 198-200.
19. Leary, *ibid.,* p. 197.
20. Morton, *In the Steps of the Master,* pp. 300, 301.

CHAPTER XVIII

1. Price, *The Monuments and the Old Testament,* pp. 144-146.
2. Reed, "A Recent Analysis of Grain From Ancient Dibon in Moab,"
Bulletin of the American Schools of Oriental Research, No. 146 (April,
1957), p. 9.
3. I Kings 9:26-28.
4. I Kings 10:11.
5. Deuteronomy 8:7,9.
6. I Kings 7:45,46,47.
7. Glueck, "On The Trail of King Solomon's Mines," *National Geographic,* Feb. 1944.
8. *Ibid.,* p. 234. These excavations were under the auspices of the
American Schools of Oriental Research, with the generous support of the
American Philosophical Society, Western Theological Seminary, Pittsburgh, and Sir Charles Marston of England.
9. Glueck, *The Biblical Archaeologist,* Vol. II (Dec. 1939), p. 40.
10. Glueck, *National Geographic,* Feb. 1944, p. 242.
11. Glueck, *The Biblical Archaeologist,* Vol. II (Dec. 1939), p. 38.
12. Glueck, *National Geographic,* Feb. 1944, p. 242.
13. Glueck, *The Biblical Archaeologist,* Vol. II, No. 4 (Dec. 1939).
14. Glueck, *National Geographic,* Feb. 1944.

CHAPTER XIX

1. Stewart, *The Land of Israel,* p. 192; Thompson, *The Land and The
Book,* p. 515.
2. Josephus, *Wars* I, VII, 2. Barton seems to think it the bridge destroyed by Pompey when he captured Jerusalem in 63 B.C., and that it had

been used by the Maccabean rulers as an early access to the Temple from their palace. See Barton, *Archaeology and the Bible,* p. 259.

3. Macalister, *A Century of Excavation in Palestine,* pp. 26-28.

4. Matson, *American Colony Palestine Guide,* pp. 57-58.

5. King, *Recent Discoveries on the Temple Hill,* p. 14; Halley, *Pocket Bible Handbook,* p. 91.

6. Wallace, *Jerusalem, The Holy,* pp. 127-29.

7. Wilson & Warren, *The Recovery of Jerusalem,* p. 98.

8. *Ibid.,* pp. 107-108.

9. Finegan, *Light From the Ancient Past,* p. 149.

10. McCown, *The Ladder of Progress in Palestine,* p. 236; Kenyon, *The Bible and Archaeology,* p. 177.

11. Barton, *Archaeology and the Bible,* pp. 239-242.

12. Josephus, *Wars* V, IV, 2.

13. McCown, *op. cit.,* pp. 247-248.

14. For a careful discussion of this subject see *Bulletin* of the American Schools of Oriental Research No. 89 (Feb. 1943), pp. 18-21.

15. McCown, *op. cit.,* pp. 247-249.

16. Barton, *op. cit.,* p. 475; Finegan, *op. cit.,* p. 160; Pritchard, *The Ancient Near East Texts,* p. 212.

17. This episode was recounted to the writer on a day while in the Temple area. Also see McCown, *The Ladder of Progress in Palestine,* pp. 232-234.

18. Finegan, *op. cit.,* p. 228.

19. *Ibid.,* p. 246.

20. Josephus, *Wars* V, V, 2; cf. VI, II, 4; Ant. XV, VI, 5.

21. Parrot, *Discovering Buried Worlds,* p. 106.

22. Wright, *The Biblical Archaeologist* (May, 1938), pp. 8, 9. Much of this article is incorporated in this write-up of the gravestone of King Uzziah.

23. Matson, *op. cit.,* p. 128.

24. McCown, *op. cit.,* p. 69.

25. Garstang, *The Story of Jericho,* pp. 83-84.

26. *Ibid.,* p. 106.

27. Albright, *The Archaeology of Palestine and the Bible,* p. 55.

28. Robinson, *The Bearing of Archaeology on the Old Testament,* p. 176.

29. Marston, *The Bible Comes Alive,* pp. 89, 278, 279; Garstang, *op. cit.,* p. 61.

30. *Ibid.,* p. 129; McCown, *op. cit.,* pp. 79, 80.

31. Albright, *op. cit.,* p. 234. Later Albright modified his reckoning and with Dr. Wright dated the fall of Jericho a few decades later, probably 1375-1300 B.C. See *The Biblical Archaeologist,* Sept. 1940. Also, Pere Vincent changed to the late date of 1250 B.C.

32. McCown, *op. cit.,* p. 79. McCown did agree, however, with regard to the exact date.

33. Kenyon, *The Bible and Archaeology,* p. 189.

34. Wright, *Biblical Archaeology,* p. 79.

35. *Ibid.,* p. 79.

36. *Bulletin* of the American Schools of Oriental Research, Dec. 1950.

37. Jack, *Samaria in Ahab's Time,* p. 37.

38. *Ibid.,* pp. 79-98.

39. Albright, *Archaeology and the Religion of Israel,* p. 160.

40. Macalister, *op. cit.,* p. 223.

41. *The International Standard Bible Encyclopedia,* Vol. II, p. 1224.

42. Albright, "The Gezer Calendar," *Bulletin* of the American Schools of Oriental Research, (Dec. 1943), p. 22.

43. Wright, *op. cit.,* pp. 180-181; Albright, *Bulletin* of the American Schools of Oriental Research, (Dec. 1943), p. 78.

44. Albright, *The Archaeology of Palestine and the Bible,* p. 63.

45. Kelso, Sellers, Glueck, Aage Schmidt, Paul Cully, William Gad, Robert Montgomery, Cyrus Gordon, J. A. Huffman, A. Sacrisalo, Labid Sorial, Bulos el-Aradj, Revs. Lee and Webster and many distinguished visitors remained for short periods of time.

46. Robinson, *op. cit.,* p. 185; Albright, *The Archaeology of Palestine and the Bible,* pp. 70-77.

47. Albright, *The Archaeology of Palestine and the Bible,* p. 92.

48. Fortune favored the expedition in that the mound was owned by Mrs. Oliphant, who long years before had purchased it and held it for just such a purpose.

49. McCown, *op. cit.,* p. 175.

50. As related by Fisher in his *The Excavation of Armageddon,* p. 4.

51. *The Biblical Archaeologist,* Vol. 4, No. 1, p. 13.

52. Guy's work quoted by McCown, *op. cit.,* p. 182.

53. McCown, *op. cit.,* pp. 179-181.

54. Taken from Guy's report as quoted by Duncan, *Digging Up Biblical History,* Vol. I, p. 249; Wright, *op. cit.,* p. 132.

55. McCown, *op. cit.,* pp. 183-185.

56. *Ibid.,* pp. 185, 186; Pritchard, *Archaeology and the Old Testament,* pp. 34, 35.

57. Wright, *The Biblical Archaeologist,* (Dec. 1938), p. 23.

58. Marston, *op. cit.,* pp. 237-240.

59. While Lachish is not mentioned in Merenptah's list, yet he described himself as having devastated this very section of the country.

60. Kenyon, *op. cit.,* pp. 193, 194.

61. Marston, *op. cit.,* pp. 231-235.

62. Wright, *The Biblical Archaeologist,* (Dec. 1938), p. 27.

63. *Loc. cit.*

64. *Ibid.,* pp. 28-30; Wright, *Biblical Archaeology,* p. 168.

65. Wright, *Biblical Archaeology,* p. 178.

66. Marston, *op. cit.,* p. 201.

67. *Ibid.,* pp. 201-203; Free, *Archaeology and Bible History,* p. 223.

68. *The Biblical Archaeologist,* (Dec. 1938), p. 32.

69. Albright, *The Archaeology of Palestine and the Bible,* p. 43.

70. Barton, *op. cit.,* p. 133.

71. About 1167 B.C. the Philistines gained the ascendancy and were the lords of the town until King David reduced their power and eventually put them down altogether. See Kenyon, *op. cit.*, p. 199.

72. McCown, *op. cit.*, p. 165; Joshua 17:11-13.

73. Robinson, *op. cit.*, p. 48.

74. Rowe, *Beth-Shan*, p. 33; Barton, *op. cit.*, p. 134; McCown, *op. cit.*, p. 165.

75. *The International Standard Bible Encyclopedia*, Vol. I, p. 453.

76. McCown, *op. cit.*, p. 170.

77. Albright, *The Archaeology of Palestine and the Bible*, pp. 43, 44.

78. Sellers, *The Citadel of Beth-Zur*, pp. 5-6.

79. *Ibid.*, p. 71; McCown, *op. cit.*, p. 223.

80. Albright, *The Archaeology of Palestine and the Bible*, p. 227; Albright, *The Biblical Period*, pp. 54, 55.

81. McCown, *op. cit.*, p. 305.

82. *Ibid.*, p. 208.

83. Albright, *The Archaeology of Palestine and the Bible*, p. 48.

84. McCown, *op. cit.*, p. 209.

85. Barton, *op. cit.*, p. 134.

86. Albright, *The Archaeology of Palestine and the Bible*, p. 230.

87. *Ibid.*, pp. 57, 160-161; Albright, *Archaeology and the Religion of Israel*, pp. 103-104.

88. Wright, *Biblical Archaeology*, pp. 88, 120-122; Albright, *The Archaeology of Palestine and the Bible*, pp. 160-162; Albright, *From the Stone Age to Christianity*, p. 215.

89. Smith, *Historical Geography of the Holy Land*, pp. 228, 229.

90. McCown, *op. cit.*, p. 148.

91. Albright, *Archaeology and the Religion of Israel*, pp. 144-145.

92. Albright, *The Archaeology of Palestine and the Bible*, p. 49.

93. McCown, *op. cit.*, p. 211.

94. *Ibid.*, p. 214.

95. Kelso, "The Significance of Pottery in Dating," *Biblical Archaeologist*.

96. *Ibid.*, p. 41.

97. Albright, *From the Stone Age to Christianity*, p. 114.

98. Albright, *Bulletin* of the American Schools of Oriental Research, April, 1936, p. 26.

99. *Bulletin* of the American Schools of Oriental Research, (April 1936), pp. 18-26; Kenyon, *op. cit.*, p. 190.

100. See Free's extensive and well prepared reports of his and Mrs. Free's work at Dothan as given in *Bulletin* of the American Schools of Oriental Research, October, 1954; 1955; 1956; and May, 1956.

101. Wright, *The Biblical Archaeologist*, (Dec. 1, 1954), p. 104.

102. Yadin, *The Biblical Archaeologist*, (Feb. 1956), p. 4.

103. Yadin, *The Biblical Archaeologist*, (May 1958), p. 46.

104. Yadin, *The Biblical Archaeologist*, (Feb. 1956), p. 9.

105. *Ibid.*, p. 34.

106. *Loc. cit.*

107. Yadin, *The Biblical Archaeologist,* (May 1958), p. 30.
108. Yadin, *The Biblical Archaeologist,* (Feb. 1956), p. 11.
109. *The Biblical Archaeologist,* Vol. XIX, No. 4 (Dec. 1956), p. 41.
110. Pritchard, *op. cit.,* p. 90.
111. Pritchard, "We Found the Lost City," *The Saturday Evening Post.*

CHAPTER XX

1. The Arab lad who first found the scrolls was Mohammed Adh-Dhib (Mohammed the Wolf). There are other stories of just how he first located the scrolls.

2. By his own followers Athanasius Samuel is called "Metropolitan," which corresponds to the office of archbishop in certain other churches.

3. This story is graphically told in a splendid film entitled "The Dead Sea Scrolls."

4. Trever, *The Biblical Archaeologist,* Sept. 1948, pp. 50-52.

5. *Ibid.,* p. 55.

6. Dr. Solomon Zeitlin, professor of Rabbinic Literature at Dropsie College (Philadelphia), contended that the scrolls were of medieval origin, and that modern scholars were being treated to a gigantic hoax similar to the Piltdown hoax in the science of Anthropology. G. R. Driver of Oxford University and Toviah Wechsler of Jerusalem also opposed the early dating of the scrolls. See Burrows, *The Dead Sea Scrolls,* pp. 38-44.

7. Cross, *The Ancient Library of Qumran and Modern Biblical Studies,* pp. 7-8. The excavators also found a few pieces of Roman pottery from approximately the time of Origen (A.D. 200-215). These gave considerable support to Origen's report that in his translation of the Book of Psalms included in his *Hexapla,* he made use of three other Greek translations, including one manuscript which he found "in a jar near Jericho in the reign of Antoninus the son of Severus (A.D. 198-217)." This would indicate that Origen had found scrolls in a cave near Jericho—probably this very cave. See *The Biblical Archaeologist,* Dec. 1950, p. 97.

8. Cross, *op. cit.,* p. 49.

9. *Ibid.,* p. 40. The pottery, coins, and other artifactual evidence indicate a break in the occupation of the place from 31 to 1 B.C. The excavators supposed this to have been caused by an earthquake, the signs of which were evident at various places.

10. Josephus, *Wars* II, VIII, 5.

11. Cross, *op. cit.,* pp. 11-13.

12. *Ibid.,* p. 14.

13. *Ibid.,* pp. 15-16.

14. *Ibid.,* pp. 30-36.

15. *Ibid.,* pp. 27-28.

16. Albright, *The Biblical Archaeologist,* Sept. 1948, pp. 60-61.

17. Trever, *The Biblical Archaeologist,* Sept. 1948, p. 49.

18. Cross, *op. cit.,* p. 90.

19. Burrows, *The Dead Sea Scrolls,* p. 371.

20. *Ibid.,* p. 372.

21. Gaster, *The Dead Sea Scriptures*, p. 40.

22. *Ibid.*, p. 42.

23. Cross, *op. cit.*, pp. 156-157.

24. Gaster, *op. cit.*, pp. 53-54.

25. Burrows, *op. cit.*, pp. 385-386.

26. Cross, *op. cit.*, p. 124.

27. Burrows, *op. cit.*, p. 367.

28. Cross, *op. cit.*, pp. 16-18.

29. Trever, *Bulletin* of the American Schools of Oriental Research, October 1949, pp. 9-10.

30. Gaster, *op. cit.*, p. 13.

31. For quotes from hymns see Gaster, *op. cit.*, pp. 138, 154, 177-178; also Burrows, *op. cit.*, pp. 400-415.

32. Burrows, *op. cit.*, pp. 349-351; Gaster, *op. cit.*, p. 67.

33. Gaster, *op. cit.*, p. 83; Burrows, *op. cit.*, p. 363.

34. Burrows, *op. cit.*, p. 363.

35. Gaster, *op. cit.*, p. 69.

36. *Ibid.*, pp. 77-78.

37. Cross, *op. cit.*, p. 157; Pfeiffer, *The Dead Sea Scrolls*, p. 72.

38. Pfeiffer, *loc. cit.*

39. *The Biblical Archaeologist*, Dec. 1950, p. 97.

40. Parrot, *Discovering Buried Worlds*, p. 117.

BIBLIOGRAPHY

Adams, J. McKee. *Biblical Backgrounds,* Broadman Press, Nashville, 1934.
———. *Ancient Records and the Bible,* Broadman Press, Nashville, 1946.
Albright, W. F. *The Archaeology of Palestine and the Bible,* Fleming H. Revell Company, New York, 1933.
———. *From the Stone Age to Christianity,* Johns Hopkins Press, Baltimore, 1940.
———. *Archaeology and the Religion of Israel,* Johns Hopkins Press, Baltimore, 1942.
———. *The Biblical Archaeologist,* Dec., 1942.
———. *The Archaeology of Palestine,* Penguin Books (Pelican Series), Harmondsworth Middlesex, England, 1949.
Albright and others. *The Haverford Symposium on Archaeology and the Bible,* American Schools of Oriental Research, New Haven, 1938.
Ali-Sami, *Pasargadae,* Iran Government Publication.
Allis, Oswald T. *The Five Books of Moses,* The Presbyterian and Reformed Publishing Co., 2nd ed., Philadelphia, 1949.
Alouf, Michel M. *History of Baalbek,* American Press, Beirut, 13th ed., 1925.
Badè, W. F. *A Manual of Excavation in the Near East,* University of California Press, 1934.
Baikie, J. A. *A Century of Excavations in the Land of the Pharaohs,* Religious Tract Society, London.
———. *The Life of the Ancient East,* The Chautauqua Press, Chautauqua, New York, 1925.
———. *The Glamour of the Near East Excavations,* Seely Service Co., London, 1927.
Baly, Denis. *The Geography of the Bible,* Harper and Brothers, New York, 1957.
Banks, Edgar J. *The Bible and the Spade,* Association Press, New York, 1913.
Barton, George A. *Archaeology and the Bible,* American Sunday School Union, Philadelphia, 7th ed. revised, 1937.
Bell, Archie. *The Spell of Egypt,* Page Co., Boston, 1916.
Belloc, Hilaire. *The Battle Ground of Syria and Palestine,* J. B. Lippincott Company, Philadelphia, 1936.
Breasted, James H. *A History of Ancient Egypt,* Charles Scribner's Sons, New York, 1912.
Burrows, M. *What Mean These Stones?* American Schools of Oriental Research, New Haven, 1941.

366

Burrows, M. *The Dead Sea Scrolls,* The Viking Press, New York, 1955.

Burton, Harry. *The Tomb of Tut-Ankh-Amen,* Geo. H. Doran Co., New York, 1923.

Caiger, Stephen L. *Bible and Spade,* Oxford University Press, London, 1935.

Carlton. *Buried Empires.*

Carter, Howard. *The Tomb of King Tutankhamen,* Cassell & Co., Ltd., London, 3 vols., 1933.

Casson, Stanley. *Progress of Archaeology,* Whittlesey House, McGraw-Hill Book Company, Inc., New York, 1932.

Ceram, C. W. *Gods, Graves and Scholars,* Alfred A. Knopf, Inc., New York, 1932.

Chapman, Mark B. *Mounds, Monuments and Inscriptions,* Publishing House of M. E. Church, Nashville, 1901.

Chiera, Edward. *They Wrote On Clay,* University of Chicago Press, Chicago, 1938.

Clay, Albert. *Light on the Old Testament from Babel,* The Sunday School Times Co., Philadelphia, 1907.

Cobern, Camden M. *The New Archaeological Discoveries,* Funk & Wagnalls Co., New York, 1928.

Cross, Frank M. *The Ancient Library of Qumran and Modern Biblical Studies,* Doubleday & Co., Inc., Garden City, N.Y., 1958.

Cust, Lionel. *Jerusalem,* The Macmillan Co., New York, 1924.

Davies, A. Powell. *The Meaning of the Dead Sea Scrolls,* New American Library of World Literature, Inc., New York, 1956.

DeHass, Jacob. *Buried Cities Recovered,* Bradley Garretson Co., Philadelphia, 1887.

Duncan, J. Garrow. *Digging Up Biblical History,* The Macmillan Co., New York, 2 vols., 1931.

Dunning, H. W. *Today on the Nile,* Gay & Bird, London, 1907.

Edwards, I. E. S. *The Pyramids of Egypt,* Penguin Books, Harmondsworth, Middlesex, England, 1949.

Enniss, Peyton. *The Ancient Stones Cry Out,* Biblical Treasures, New York, 1939.

Finegan, Jack. *Light From the Ancient Past,* Princeton University Press, Princeton, N.J., 1946.

Free, Joseph P. *Archaeology and Bible History,* Wheaton: Van Kampen Press, 1950.

Fritsch, Charles T. *The Qumran Community,* The Macmillan Co., New York, 1956.

Gadd, C. J. *The Stones of Assyria,* Chatto & Windus, London, 1936.

Garstang, J., and J. B. E. Garstang. *The Story of Jericho,* Marshall, Morgan and Scott, London, 1948.

Gaster, Theodore H. *The Dead Sea Scriptures,* Doubleday & Co., Inc., Garden City, N.Y., 1956.

Ghirshman. *Iran,* Iran Government Publication.

Glueck, Nelson. *The Other Side of Jordan,* American Schools of Oriental Research, New Haven, 1940.

Glueck, Nelson. "On the Trail of King Solomon's Mines," *National Geographic*, Feb. 1944.

Gordon, Cyrus H. *The Living Past*, The John Day Co., Inc., New York, 1941.

Grosvenor, Gilbert, ed. *Everyday Life in Ancient Times*, National Geographic Society, Washington, D.C., 1951.

Guthe, Carl E. "The Archaeological Detective," Scientific Paper No. 194, New York State Museum.

Habershon, Ada R. *The Bible and the British Museum*, Gospel Publishing House, New York.

Hall, R. H. *Ancient History of the Near East*, Methuen & Co., Ltd., London, 1926.

Hammerton, J. A. *Wonders of the Past*, Wise & Co., New York, rev. ed., 2 vols., 1937.

Harris, Charles. *The Hebrew Heritage*, Abingdon Press, New York, 1935.

Heusser, A. H. *The Land of the Prophets*.

Hilprecht, H. V. *Explorations in Bible Lands During the Nineteenth Century*, A. J. Holman & Co., Philadelphia, 1903.

Hoskins, Franklin E. *From the Nile to Nebo*, The Sunday School Times Co., Philadelphia, 1912.

Huxley, Julian. *From An Antique Land*, Brown Publishers, Inc., New York.

Innes, T. Christie. *Thrilling Voices of the Past*, Pickering & Inglis, Ltd., London, 1937.

Jack, J. W. *The Date of the Exodus*, T & T Clark, Edinburgh, 1925.

———. *Samaria in Ahab's Time*, T & T Clark, Edinburgh, 1929.

———. "The Lachish Letters, Their Date and Import—An Examination of Professor Torczyner's View," Palestine Exploration Fund Quarterly Statement, London Fund's office, 1938.

Jarvis, H. Wood. *From Pharaoh to Farouk*, The Macmillan Co., New York, 1955.

Kelso, J. L., "The Significance of Pottery in Dating," *The Biblical Archaeologist*, (August 17, 1926).

Kenyon, Sir Frederick. *The Bible and Archaeology*, Harper and Brothers, New York, 1949.

———. *The Bible and Modern Scholarship*, Harper and Brothers, New York, 1949.

Kinns, Samuel. *Graven in the Rock*, Cassell & Co., Ltd., London, 2 vols., 1895.

Kraeling, Emil G. *Bible Lands*, Rand McNally & Co., Chicago, 1952.

Kyle, Melvin G. *The Deciding Voice of the Monuments*, Bibliotheca Sacra Co., Oberlin, Ohio, 1924.

Layard, A. H. *Nineveh and Its Remains*, London, 2 vols., 1849.

Leary, Lewis G. *Syria, The Land of Lebanon*, McBride, Nast & Co., New York, 1913.

———. *From the Pyramids to Paul*, Thomas Nelson & Sons, New York, 1935.

Lissner, Ivar. *The Living Past,* G. P. Putnam's Sons, New York, 1957.

Lloyd, S. *Foundations in the Dust,* Oxford University Press, London, 1947.

Luckenbill, D. D. *Ancient Records of Assyria and Babylonia,* University of Chicago Press, Chicago, 2 vols., 1927.

Luke, H. C., and J. Garstang. *The Traveller's Handbook for Palestine and Syria,* The American Colony Stores, Inc., Jerusalem, 1925.

Macalister, R. A. S. *A Century of Excavation in Palestine,* Fleming H. Revell Company, New York, 1934.

McCown, Chester C. *The Ladder of Progress in Palestine,* Harper and Brothers, New York, 1943.

Magoffin, Ralph. *The Lure and Lore of Archaeology,* The Williams & Wilkins Company, Baltimore, 1930.

Maisler. "Archaeology and the State of Israel," *The Biblical Archaeologist,* (Feb. 1952).

Manning, Samuel. *The Land of the Pharaohs,* Religious Tract Society, London, 1887.

Maspero, G. *Manual of Egyptian Archaeology,* G. P. Putnam's Sons, New York, 1902.

————. *History of Egypt,* Vol. XI, Grolier Society Publishers, London, 1923.

Masters, David. *The Romance of Excavations,* Dodd, Mead & Co., Inc., New York, 1923.

Matson, G. Olaf. *American Colony Palestine Guide,* Jerusalem: The American Colony Stores, Inc., 3d ed., 1930.

Miller, Madeleine, and J. Lane. *Encyclopedia of Bible Life,* Harper and Brothers, New York, 1944.

Moret, Alexander. *In the Time of the Pharaohs,* G. P. Putnam's Sons, New York, 1911.

————. *Kings and Gods of Egypt,* G. P. Putnam's Sons, New York, 1912.

Morton, H. V. *In the Steps of the Master,* Dodd, Mead & Co., Inc., New York, 1936.

Muir, James. *His Truth Endures,* National Publishing Co., Philadelphia, 1937.

————. *The Spade and the Scriptures,* Broadman Press, Nashville, 1940.

Murray, John. *Handbook For Travellers in Lower and Upper Egypt,* John Murray, London, 1891.

Murray, M. A. *The Splendor That Was Egypt,* Philosophical Library, Inc., New York, 1949.

Needler, Winifred. *Palestine, Ancient and Modern,* University of Toronto Press, Toronto, 1949.

Nevinson, Henry W. *In the Dark Backward,* Harcourt, Brace & Co., Inc., New York, 1934.

Newman, John P. *The Thrones and Palaces of Babylon and Nineveh,* Nelson and Phillips, New York, 1876.

Nicol, Thomas. *Recent Archaeology and The Bible,* William Blackwood & Sons, Ltd., Edinburgh, 1899.

Parrot, Andre. *Discovering Buried Worlds,* Philosophical Library Inc., New York, 1955.

Parrot, Andre. *The Flood and Noah's Ark,* Philosophical Library Inc., New York, 1955.

Petrie, Hilda. *Side Notes on the Bible,* Search Publishing Co., Ltd., London, 1933.

Petrie, W. Flinders. The *Pyramids and Temples of Gizeh,* Leadenhall Press, London, 1885.

———. *Six Temples at Thebes,* Bernard Quaritch, London, 1897.

———. *A History of Egypt, The 17th and 18th Dynasties,* Charles Scribner's Sons, New York, 1904.

———. *Seventy Years in Archaeology,* Henry Holt & Co., Inc., New York, 1932.

———. *Palestine and Egypt,* Society for Promoting Christian Knowledge, London, 1934.

Pfeiffer, Charles F. *The Dead Sea Scrolls,* Baker Book House, Grand Rapids, 1957.

Powers, H. H. *Egypt,* The Macmillan Co. (The University Travel Series), New York, 1924.

Price, Ira M., Ovid R. Sellers, and E. Leslie Carlson. *The Monuments and the Old Testament,* Judson Press, Philadelphia, rev. ed., 1958.

Pritchard, James B. *Archaeology and the Old Testament,* Princeton University Press, Princeton, N.J., 1958.

———. *The Ancient Near East Texts,* Princeton University Press, Princeton, N.J., 1958.

———. "We Found the Lost City," *The Saturday Evening Post,* Feb. 8, 1958.

Rawlinson, George. *The Seven Great Monarchies of the Ancient World,* John W. Lovell Co., New York, 2 vols., 1862.

Reed, W. L. "A Recent Analysis of Grain From Ancient Dibon in Moab," *Bulletin* of the American Schools of Oriental Research, No. 146 (April, 1957), p. 9.

Renouf, Le Page. *The Religion of Ancient Egypt,* Charles Scribner's Sons, New York, 1879.

Robinson, Charles. *The Pharaohs of the Bondage and the Exodus,* Century Co., New York, 1887.

Robinson, George L. *The Bearing of Archaeology on the Old Testament,* American Tract Society, New York, 1941.

Rowe, A. *Beth-Shan,* University of Pennsylvania Press, Philadelphia, 1930.

Sayce, A. H. *The Higher Criticism and the Verdict of the Monuments,* E. & J. B. Young, New York, 1894.

———. *Assyria, Its Princes, Priests and People,* Religious Tract Society, London, 1894.

Sears, Robert. *Pictorial Bible Biography,* Robert Sears, N.Y., 1846.

Sellers, Ovid R. *The Citadel of Beth-Zur,* Westminster Press, Philadelphia, 1933.

Smith, George A. *Historical Geography of the Holy Land,* Hodder & Stoughton, Ltd., London, 1931.

Sparrow, Gerald. *The Sphinx Awakes,* Robert Hale, Ltd., London, 1956.

Speiser, E. "The Historical Significance of Tepe Gawra," *Annual Report of Smithsonian Institution,* 1933.

———. "Closing the Gap at Tepe Gawra," *Asia,* Sept. 1938.

Steindorff & Seele, *When Egypt Ruled the East,* University of Chicago Press, Chicago, 1945.

Stewart, R. L. *The Land of Israel,* Fleming H. Revell Company, New York, 1899.

Thompson, W. M. *The Land and The Book,* Thomas Nelson & Sons, New York, 1910.

Torczyner, Harry. *Lachish I (Tell el Duweir) Lachish Letters,* Oxford University Press, New York, 1938.

Unger, Merrill F. *Archaeology and the Old Testament,* Zondervan Publishing Co., Grand Rapids, 1954.

Urquhart. *The New Biblical Guide,* W. P. Blessing, Chicago, 6 vols., n.d.

Van Beek, G. W. "A Radiocarbon Date For Early South Arabia," *Bulletin* of the American Schools of Oriental Research, October, 1956.

Wallace, E. S. *Jerusalem, The Holy,* Fleming H. Revell Company, New York, 1898.

White, J. E. *Ancient Egypt,* Thos. Y. Crowell Co., New York.

Williams, M. O. "At the Tomb of Tutankhamen," *National Geographic,* May, 1923.

Wilson, Charles. *Picturesque Palestine, Sinai and Egypt,* D. Appleton & Co., New York, 1883.

Wilson, Edmund. *The Dead Sea Scrolls,* Oxford University Press, New York, 1955.

Wilson, John. *The Burden of Egypt,* University of Chicago Press, Chicago, 1951.

Wilson, Robert. *The Living Pageant of the Nile,* The Bobbs-Merrill Co., Indianapolis, 1924.

Wiseman, D. J. *Illustrations From Biblical Archaeology,* Eerdmans Co., Grand Rapids, 1958.

Woolley, C. Leonard. *Abraham—Recent Discoveries and Hebrew Origins,* Charles Scribner's Sons, New York, 1936.

———. *Digging Up the Past,* Penguin Books, Harmondsworth, Middlesex, England, 1937.

———. *Ur of the Chaldees,* Penguin Books, Harmondsworth, Middlesex, England, 1940.

———. *Excavations at Ur,* Barnes & Noble, Inc., New York.

Wright, G. Ernest, *Biblical Archaeology,* Westminster Press, Philadelphia, 1957.

Wright, G. Frederick. *Scientific Confirmation of the Old Testament,* Bibliotheca Sacra Co., Oberlin, Ohio, 1906.

Yaggy, L. W. Haines. *Museum of Antiquity,* J. B. Furman & Co., Western Publishing House, Chicago, 1884.

Index

372

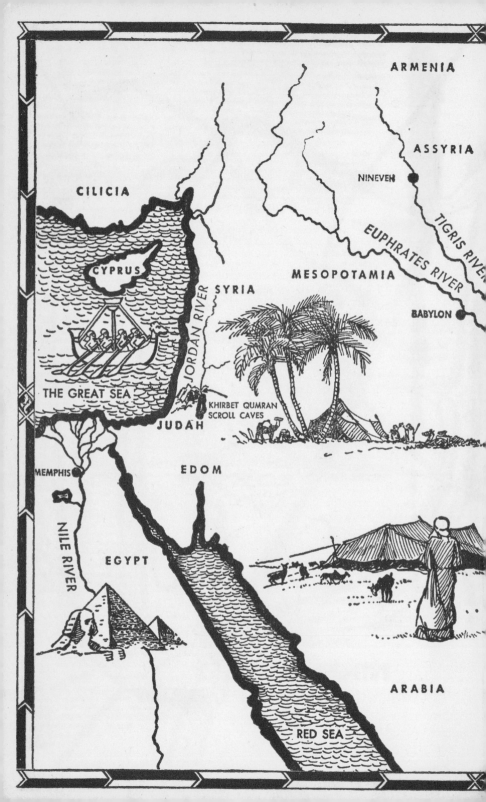